JOHNSON
AFTER
TWO
HUNDRED
YEARS

JOHNSON
AFTER
TWO
HUNDRED
YEARS

════════

Edited by

PAUL J. KORSHIN

upp

Philadelphia · 1986

UNIVERSITY OF PENNSYLVANIA PRESS

Designed by Adrianne Onderdonk Dudden
Copyright © 1986 by the University of Pennsylvania Press
All rights reserved

Library of Congress Cataloging-in-Publication Data

Main entry under title:

Johnson after two hundred years.

Includes index.
1. Johnson, Samuel, 1709-1784—Criticism and
interpretation—Addresses, essays, lectures.
I. Korshin, Paul J.
PR3534.J63   1986   828'.609   85-29445
ISBN 0-8122-8016-4 (alk. paper)

Printed in the United States of America

CONTENTS

Part Three
INTERPRETATIONS OF
JOHNSON'S WORKS

ABBREVIATIONS

Boswell, *Life*

Boswell's Life of Johnson, ed. George Birkbeck Hill, rev. L. F. Powell, 6 vols. (Oxford: Clarendon Press, 1934–64 [Vols. I–IV, 1934; Vols. V and VI, 2nd ed., 1964])

Johnson, *Letters*

The Letters of Samuel Johnson, ed. R. W. Chapman, 3 vols. (Oxford: Clarendon Press, 1952)

Johnson, *Works* (1787)

The Works of Samuel Johnson, LL. D., ed. Sir John Hawkins, 13 vols. (London: Stockdale, 1787)

Johnson, *Works* (1825)

The Works of Samuel Johnson, LL. D. (Oxford English Classics.) 11 vols. (Oxford: Talboys and Wheeler, 1825)

Johnson, *Works*

The Yale Edition of the Works of Samuel Johnson, in process [12 vols. to date] (New Haven: Yale Univ. Press, 1958–   )

Johnson, *Lives*

Lives of the English Poets, ed. George Birkbeck Hill, 3 vols. (Oxford: Clarendon Press, 1905)

PAUL J. KORSHIN

Preface · The Paradox of Johnsonian Studies

Two hundred years after Samuel Johnson's death, his reputation as a literary and cultural figure is greater than it has ever been in the present century. On 13 December 1984, the bicentennial of his death, Britain's leading national newspaper, *The Times*, devoted an entire editorial to the occasion. Entitled "An English Saint Remembered," it is quite a remarkable tribute:

> Samuel Johnson died in the evening of 13 December 1784, two centuries ago. He is a more suitable patron saint for the English than our Palestinian soldier-saint, George, or that other candidate for the role, Thomas à Becket. For one thing, Johnson spoke English. More than that, his work as a lexicographer and Hercules of English literature helped to make English the world language that it has become. The chief glory of the English is their language; and Johnson's *Dictionary*, the only one in any language compiled by a writer of genius, had a lot to do with its rise to glory.

The commemoration of a literary figure's greatness these days inevitably attracts the attention of the mass media and so, accordingly, the BBC mounted both radio and television programs celebrating Johnson's life, intellectual achievements, and conversation. But more traditional scholarly celebration is nearly always part of the notice that we accord a great writer and, in Johnson's case, the year 1984 was the occasion of about a dozen different learned conferences around the world devoted to his life and works. Scholarly admirers of his life and works contributed about one hundred learned papers on a great number of Johnsonian subjects in 1984, about half of them at one conference. This was perhaps the most appropriate of Johnsonian occasions, a week in July at Pembroke College, Oxford, Johnson's undergraduate home for the fifteen months in 1728–29 that he studied at Oxford. The essays in this volume (with one exception) derive from that conference.[1]

In 1884, the centenary of Johnson's death, *The Times* had dismissed the need for any formal commemoration of that occasion. Such celebrations were far less common in the late nineteenth century, in the nascence of the modern academic profession, than they are today. Several years ago Donald Greene noted this dismissal, adding, "When commemorations of the second centenary of Johnson's death take place, I predict that the attitude of *The Times* will be very different."[2] The attitude of *The Times* was indeed different but, somewhat paradoxically, its very difference owed something to the commemorative and other collections of essays that various scholars or groups of scholars have published over the last twenty-five years. Indeed, it is somewhat surprising that so much of Johnsonian scholarship during this last quarter century has appeared in this form rather than in traditional refereed journals, but it should be clear, I think, that the space that might be available in scholarly or literary journals for essays about Johnson is not and never has been adequate to contain the output of those interested in writing about him.[3] The first of the recent commemorative volumes, *New Light on Dr. Johnson*, consisted of essays published on the occasion of Johnson's 250th birthday, 18 September 1959; while its editor, the late F. W. Hilles, stressed the growing interest in his writings as opposed to his life and character, he had to concede that nearly half of the contents had been published previously in—for the most part—learned journals.[4] Later collections have been more thoroughly devoted to original essays and, at the same time, most of them have expanded upon the now fashionable paradox that Johnson, for all his fame as a man of letters, still owes more of his reputation to a book about him, Boswell's *Life*, than to an appreciation of his own writings. Even *The Times*'s 1984 leader writer (probably that newspaper's literary editor, Philip Howard) was familiar with this curiosity: "It is an irony that might have amused [Johnson] eventually, after a bear's growl or two, that his *Life* written by his young Scottish friend is far more widely read than any of [his] own more literary works."[5] Johnson, according to this paradox (only a journalistic writer would describe it as an "irony"), is misunderstood, neglected, "unknown" because certain popular descriptions that Boswell gives of him or certain memorable conversations that Boswell presents as being his have superseded his writings as the principal method by which succeeding generations have become acquainted with him.[6]

The seductive popularity of Boswell's biography is not something that scholars first discovered in the 1950s. In 1923, Percy Hazen Houston, the author of one of the first major twentieth-century critical studies of Johnson, conceded exactly the same thing—although in less paradoxical terms—that Johnsonians of the last thirty years have argued: "Indeed, the worthy Doctor, by the wonderful chance of having had men of genius as biographers, remains to-day one of the two or three outstanding figures in eighteenth-century letters, though most of us have scarcely turned the pages of his ponderous volumes."[7] Perhaps Houston's study (deriving from a Harvard dissertation of 1910) is, as Clifford and Greene describe it, "grounded in the old prejudices . . ."[8] But it is significant that Houston, his prejudices notwithstanding, both in his book and in his much earlier dissertation, cites Johnson almost exclusively from his works and almost never from the conversations in Boswell's *Life*.[9] The prejudice that Houston and the Johnsonians who came to maturity in late Victorian England had to overcome was simply that, as Macaulay had put it in his famous review of Croker's edition of Boswell's *Life*, "Johnson, as Mr. Burke observed, appears far greater in Boswell's books than in his own."[10] The popularity of Boswell's *Life of Johnson* is, without doubt, unrivaled by any other biography in literary history. Between the end of the eighteenth century and 1887, when George Birkbeck Hill's definitive edition appeared, there were approximately one hundred editions of the *Life*. In roughly the next half century, until L. F. Powell's revision of Hill in 1934, about one hundred more editions of the *Life* were published, some of them reprintings of Hill's 1887 text and notes, others entirely new preparations, usually much less ambitious than Hill's work. These editions vary in format from a single volume to four or even six volumes; some of them include many illustrations, themselves part of a nineteenth-century tradition that begins with Croker. There can be little doubt, then, that Boswell's biography helped to make Johnson known to generations of readers.

But which Johnson were these readers becoming acquainted with? According to the paradox of Johnsonian studies in this century, they were reading about a literary figure whom Boswell shapes according to his own biases and whom he presents through conversations and casual remarks that, in printed form, he had sometimes altered from his own notes in order to change their effect, even their meaning. I think that there is some truth to these views, although no one has yet studied every one of the Johnsonian conversations in the *Life* to analyze their accuracy. A closer look at Boswell's work, however, does not entirely support the notion that his generations of readers failed to meet the real Johnson in his pages or knew Johnson primarily from his conversations rather than from his own writings. The titlepage of Boswell's first edition states that the work comprehends "a series of his epistolary correspondence and conversations with many eminent persons and various original pieces of his composition, never before published." (Most later editions of the *Life* do not reproduce this title-page.) The order in which Boswell lists these three items—correspondence, conversations, compositions—is apparently significant. The *Life* includes 344 of Johnson's letters to Boswell and others; this correspondence forms a substantial portion of the work.[11] Johnson's conversations comprise just under one-fourth of the pages of the first edition (and, of course, about one-third of these conversations consist of remarks by other people, the "eminent persons" of Boswell's subtitle). But the correspondence actually takes up more space in the life than the famous conversations do. Moreover, while Boswell sometimes does not print the complete text of a letter (always scrupulously indicating any lacuna), Johnson's letters are his own writing, not the thoughts of someone else. The third item on Boswell's list—compositions—is equally interesting, for the *Life* includes a number of excerpts from Johnson's writings that were previously unpublished, consisting of some shorter pieces in their entirety, about a dozen legal arguments that Johnson composed for or dictated to Boswell, selections from Johnson's diaries, and a number of his prayers and meditations. Boswell also quoted liberally from Johnson's better known writings. The total portion of Boswell's *Life* that consists of Johnson's miscellaneous writing, then, is fairly substantial, about one-third of the work. Indeed, if we recognize that nearly ten percent of the first edition of the *Life* consists of Boswell's scholia and the printing of documents like Johnson's honorary degrees and his will, it would be fair to say that the largest single component of the biography is Johnson's own writings, the very things that generations of readers have been supposed not to read. When we consider how little of Johnson's life Boswell knew at first hand—his first meeting with Johnson occurs about one-fifth of the way into the text of his first edition—we may remark that the major narrator of Boswell's *Life of Johnson* is Johnson himself.

There can be no question that the conversations are a memorable, perhaps the most memorable, part of the *Life*, but even those, if we give them a closer look, turn out to be not exclusively conversations but in large part specimens of his conversation. That is, Boswell often recorded things that Johnson said rather than his interactions, in dialogue form, with himself and others; he might more accurately have described the result as "Johnson's sayings and *some* conversations with eminent persons." The *Life*, in fact, has a great deal more in common with the old Renaissance continental tradition of the *ana*-book, an anthology of the sayings of a famous man (like *Scaligerana*, *Poggiana*, and so on), than most of us recognize today. Johnson's contemporaries were aware of this tradition; one of them, Robert Southey, even described the Life as "the *Ana* of all *Anas*."[12] Once again, a close scrutiny of the actual conversations that Boswell prints reveals that there are only a few dozen of considerable length. So the Johnson that generations of readers of Boswell's *Life* became acquainted with was, to a surprising extent, Samuel Johnson himself, expressing his own thoughts in his own writings, especially in those most personal of all documents, his letters. The figure who Macaulay ignorantly thought appeared far greater in Boswell's biography than in his own writings was actually Johnson himself, anthologized, perhaps, in an unusual way, but Johnson all the same.

The scholarly paradox continues, however, for some Johnsonians may say that the snippets of Johnson's writings that Boswell prints, even though they form so large a portion of the *Life*, are not the same thing as his literary compositions taken at length, unanthologized and unabridged. Yet it may be possible that well-meaning Johnsonian scholars have been blinded by the exceptional popularity of Boswell's *Life* and have therefore failed to perceive that Johnson's own writings have never fallen into eclipse but have rather remained constantly available and in print for more than two centuries. During the century and a half when four or five generations of readers are supposed to have acquired their impressions of Johnson's greatness from Boswell, his works enjoyed a popularity that no other writer of eighteenth-century England could share (although individual books like *Robinson Crusoe* and *Gulliver's Travels*, and perhaps only these, have been more popular). In the nineteenth century, the period when, presumably, everyone met Johnson through Boswell's account of him, more than fifty editions of his collected works appeared, more than one-third of them sufficiently ambitious to comprise from eleven to sixteen volumes. But the two-volume edition, in double-columned royal octavo, was the most popular collection, especially in the United States, where at least twenty different printings of it appeared. By modern standards, this edition leaves much to be desired, but it does include most of the major works, including *The Rambler* and *Idler*, Johnson's contributions to *The Adventurer*, *Rasselas*, the so-called "Tales of the Imagination," *Irene*, almost all the poems, the shorter biographies, the *Lives of the Poets*, "Political Tracts," "Philological Tracts," a number of dedications, and the *Journey to the Western Isles of Scotland*. That so few copies of these books survive today suggests that they were simply read until they fell to pieces. *The Rambler*, as a separate work, had another three dozen or so nineteenth-century editions in addition to its appearance as part of the collected works. *Rasselas* was even more popular and was evidently in print almost constantly. As the *New Cambridge Bibliography of English Literature* notes laconically, "An English or American [edition of *Rasselas*] has appeared roughly every year since 1759."[13] It seems highly unlikely that so many publishers issued editions of Johnson's writings, whether individual pieces or collected works, without an expectation that an audience was available for them.

The paradox of Johnsonian studies, then, that Johnson is better known through Boswell's biography than from his own writings, may require revision and may not actually exist at all. I would point out, however, that in the half century from 1885 to 1935 there were few collected editions of Johnson's works, although individual items, especially *Rasselas* and the *Lives of the Poets*, continued to be in demand. Yet at the same time, with the growth of mass public education, the consequent demand for textbooks and anthologies of literature led to a number of Johnson's writings, especially essays, being published in what were essentially texts for secondary school and college students (Johnson, in fact, makes a better subject for the anthologizer than Boswell, since essays are easier to collect or excerpt than biography). And I would emphasize again that Boswell's *Life* includes such a large selection of Johnson's own writings that it is an anthology as well as a biography. Perhaps students of Johnson may be able to turn this paradox to good use instead of lamenting that the audience for eighteenth-century literature may be likely to know Johnson better from a biography than from his own works and apologizing for Johnson's strengths because Boswell's real or imagined prejudices present us with a flawed view of the man. What I want to suggest is that Johnson's reputation is quite unique among all figures in all literatures: he is the only major writer whom we know not only from his works but also through an attractive narrative account of his life. Aware as we are of Boswell's shortcomings, we should also recognize that—if we leave aside the portions of the *Life* that consist of Johnson's own writings, Boswell's scholia, and Boswell's commentary—the specimens of Johnson's conversation that Boswell presents have a very special value if we use them carefully.

Johnson's principal contemporary biographer may be occasionally flawed, but we all make selective use of his specimens of his subject's conversation. For example, let me consider for a moment Johnson's famous toast at Oxford, "'Here's to the next insurrection of the negroes in the West Indies.'" [14] This quotation, which is widely known, is an example of Boswell when he is open to the most doubt. The occasion of the remark is not Oxford but Boswell's September 1777 visit to the home of Johnson's friend Dr. John Taylor at Ashbourne, where he stayed with Taylor and Johnson, who was also visiting, for ten days (14–24 September). After supper on 23 September, Boswell records, Johnson dictated to him one of his legal arguments in favor of a former slave who was claiming his liberty in the Court of Session in Scotland. Boswell writes, "He had always been very zealous against slavery in every form, in which I with all deference thought he discovered 'a zeal without knowledge.' Upon one occasion, when in company with some very grave men at Oxford, his toast was, 'Here's to the next insurrection of the negroes in the West Indies.' His violent prejudice against our West Indian and American settlers appeared whenever there was an opportunity."[15] This toast, it is clear, was not part of Johnson's conversation at Ashbourne in September 1777; Johnson made it at Oxford, time, place, and company unstated. Boswell does not say that he heard Johnson make the toast, a good sign that he had not heard it but instead probably owed the story about it to someone else's recollection, that is, to hearsay. Neither the manuscript of the *Life of Johnson* nor Boswell's papers indicates any particular source for this statement. Yet, while the toast does not have the marks of Boswell's greatest reliability about it, the sentiments that it embodies appeal greatly to our twentieth-century notions about equality, racism, and so on. Here is Johnson, whose political views, according to the old stereotype, were strongly conservative, advocating rebellion against established authority (something that he strongly condemned, say, in the context of seventeenth-century England) because he believed that slavery was abhorrent and wicked. Even scholars who are the most critical of Boswell's accuracy and general usefulness have cited this toast with approbation.[16] In fact, what we learn from an analysis of the matrix where the toast appears is that Boswell does not share his friend's abhorrence of slavery. Indeed, he thinks that Johnson shows "'a zeal without knowledge'" in his dislike of the institution, and attributes Johnson's sentiments not to antislavery attitudes but to his dislike of British colonial settlers in the New World.

Many of the specimens of Johnson's conversation in the *Life* are, or should be, open to the same doubts. We cannot always be sure of Boswell's source or of the accuracy of his own transcription. Moreover, Boswell mentions at different times in the *Life* that Johnson could talk with ease on contradictory sides of the same question, so he undermines, perhaps unwittingly, the credibility of some of his own presentations.[17] Johnson seldom, if ever, presents contradictory statements about the same subject in his *published* writings, so here Boswell's *Life* enjoys a special strength in that it prints such a large selection of his letters and other works. Yet, despite the potential inaccuracy of Boswell's specimens of Johnson's talk, students of Johnson have long used—and continue to use—the *Life* selectively, as a source of Johnson's opinions on many topics. Perhaps the *Life* is not a completely *reliable* source of Johnson's opinions, but it presents a body of such views as exists for no other writer. This practice of selective quotation is a tacit affirmation of Houston's remark that some of Johnson's enduring reputation is due to "the wonderful chance of [his] having had men of genius as biographers" (from the context,

Houston shows that "men of genius" really refers to Boswell alone). Houston and his generation, unaware of the process of the making of the *Life of Johnson*, were willing to concede Boswell the status of genius because they recognized his work as a classic. They did not scrutinize his finished product closely. Boswell's nineteenth-century editors, from Malone through Hill, did not weigh the cumulative effect of the work they were annotating. Even Hill was under Boswell's spell, for he saw him as a genius and the *Life* as "the biography which of all others is the delight and boast of the English-speaking world."[18] That this great literary classic was only one-third Boswell's biographical narration and two-thirds Johnson's correspondence and writings, specimens of conversation, and scholia never occurred to Hill or Boswell's many other editors. No doubt the *Life* achieved classic status in part because it received so little critical analysis, because its audience loved it without realizing that it was an artfully prepared anthology, a collection of biography and Johnsoniana. Now that we are able to study the composition and construction of large portions of the *Life*, we can sustain doubts about some things that it contains but a fresh generation of scholars continues to quote selectively from it. There is good reason for this continued reliance on Boswell: we are convinced that, despite his faults, he was nevertheless a witness of Johnson's character and personality over a span of more than twenty years, and there are those who are satisfied that Boswell was internally consistent in the portrait of Johnson that he draws. This reliance is further evidence that the paradox of Johnsonian studies, however tenuous, continues to influence the way we think about Johnson.

Perhaps, as I said earlier, we should abandon the antiquated notion that Johnson is somehow "better known" from Boswell's *Life* than from his literary productions. The anthology form of the *Life* simply acquaints us with a different view of Johnson from that which his works yield, yet since such a large portion of it is pure literary Johnson anyway, the *Life* is also a stimulus to further reading of the works. No doubt some of the nineteenth-century demand for editions of Johnson's collected works and the constant request for new editions and reprintings of *Rasselas* result from Boswell. Who, reading the *Life of Johnson* for the first time, and knowing nothing else of its subject, would not want to read more of his writings than the *Life* already provides? While the *Life* must have been—and may still be—the only reading of Johnson's works that some people ever undertake, it would certainly be fair to say that Boswell has undoubtedly provided the stimulus for further knowledge of its subject. This quality—stimulating greater interest in an author—is one that all good biographies share, just as Richard Ellmann's life of Joyce and Martin Gilbert's still incomplete life of Winston Churchill must persuade many readers to study *Ulysses* or *The History of the English Speaking People*.

Instead of regarding Johnson as "unknown" or badly known, with Boswell, incredibly, as the scapegoat, it may be constructive to ask what Johnsonian scholarship has ascertained to date about Johnson and his works. So far as a bibliography is concerned, the existing study, published in 1916, revised in 1925, and somewhat augmented in 1939, is outdated, incomplete, and largely unscientific, a situation entirely consistent with the state of bibliographical studies for other major eighteenth-century authors.[19] The absence of reliable texts of Johnson's works can hardly advance studies of his life, writings, and thought, yet the modern edition of his works, thirty years after its start, has issued just twelve volumes and is at best only half finished. A biography based on extensive archival sources, similar to Irvin Ehrenpreis's definitive life of Swift (3 vols., 1962–84), that would replace Boswell and his eighteenth-century contemporaries, does not yet exist.[20] Our knowledge of the canon of Johnson's writings is still incomplete.[21] Studies of Johnson's intellectual development, reading, scholarship, and the numerous influences upon him—when we compare them with the state of knowledge about writers like Spenser and Milton—are obviously still in their infancy. Large portions of his career have received little attention: his literary apprenticeship is a good example. Some of his major works lack an authoritative interpretation: *The Rambler*, for example, Johnson's longest single work, has never been the subject of a book of any sort, to say nothing of a scholarly work. Although T. S. Eliot has proclaimed Johnson a major English poet, no scholar has ever written a book about his poetry (by contrast, Andrew Marvell, whose poetry Eliot also singled out for similar praise, is the subject of a scholarly industry that has produced dozens of critical studies). Scholars have barely studied some important genres of Johnson's writing, like his substantial correspondence, at all.[22] Johnson's linguistic writings, including his thousands of definitions for the *Dictionary*, have barely been studied, except to be treated as irrelevant curiosities or the source for witty quotations. We still manage conveniently to ignore his relationships with many of his contemporaries, particularly women. And there are other Johnsonian topics that have been the subject of a single book or at most two books, although we might well expect that, with any other major author, subjects like politics, literary criticism, and literary biography would receive fairly constant revision and reinterpretation. The true paradox of Johnsonian studies, I suspect, is that our fascination with his biography, his biographers, and the tensions among them has absorbed such a great proportion of scholarly energy. Johnson is not so much unknown as "too little and too lately known."

The following essays attempt to speak to our state of knowledge of Johnson. Several deal with aspects of his life and career, but the majority provide interpretations of his works, especially works that we

[xvii]

have tended to overlook, or of his intellectual growth and relationships. They demonstrate that the paradox of Johnsonian studies may be losing its force. A restudy of Johnson's life permits us to see that an accurate biography need not depend on Boswell's famous work; indeed, we can now accept that Boswell's *Life of Johnson* is actually an important interpretation rather than a primary source for Johnson's life. A careful reading of Johnson's lesser works, including items like book catalogues, travel literature, periodical essays, book reviews, and personal correspondence, shows us that these writings, as a group, are not minor at all but rather represent a coherent guide to his intellectual achievement and development. And a revaluation of Johnson's major writings—*The Rambler*, the *Dictionary*, his edition of Shakespeare, and the *Lives of the Poets*—has allowed students of the eighteenth century to see him in the context of his age's literary achievement, in the same way that studies of Elizabethan and Jacobean England have permitted us to see Shakespeare. The essays in this book, each in its own way, continue that revaluation of Johnson and steadily diminish the effect of the old paradox that has so long affected his reputation.

N O T E S

1. The exception is the essay of Bertram H. Davis, "Johnson's 1764 Visit to Percy," which the author read at a meeting in 1982.

2. Donald J. Greene, "Johnson, Stoicism, and the Good Life," in *The Unknown Samuel Johnson*, ed. John J. Burke, Jr. and Donald Kay (Madison: Univ. of Wisconsin Press, 1983), p. 17.

3. The first journal devoted principally to Johnson and his circle, *The Age of Johnson*, will begin to appear as an annual in 1986.

4. *New Light on Dr. Johnson*, ed. Frederick W. Hilles (New Haven: Yale Univ. Press, 1959), pp. ix–x, xi–xii.

5. "An English Saint Remembered," *The Times*, 13 December 1984, p. 15.

6. John J. Burke, Jr., comments, "If we are going to know Johnson better, we must read him, and that is a point Johnson scholars have been insisting upon for more than three decades, with some effect" (in *The Unknown Samuel Johnson*, ed. Burke and Kay, p. 7).

7. Percy H. Houston, *Doctor Johnson: A Study in Eighteenth Century Humanism* (Cambridge, Mass.: Harvard Univ. Press, 1923), p. 3.

8. See *Samuel Johnson: A Survey and Bibliography of Critical Studies* (Minneapolis: Univ. of Minnesota Press, 1970), p. 21.

9. Clifford and Greene, *Samuel Johnson: A Survey and Bibliography*, p. 21, see scholars' concentrating on Johnson's writings rather than his casual conversation as a trend beginning in the 1950s, perhaps first in W. J. Bate's *The Achievement of Samuel Johnson* (1755). In fact, there are signs of this phenomenon thirty years earlier, as early as Houston's book.

10. See Macaulay's 1831 review in *Johnson: The Critical Heritage*, ed. James T. Boulton (London: Routledge & Kegan Paul, 1971), p. 429. Macaulay misrepresents Burke's com-

ment; actually, he "affirmed that Boswell's 'Life' was a greater monument to Johnson's fame, than all his writings together," not at all the same thing that Macaulay says. See Boswell, *Life*, I, 10.

11. See *Letters*, I, v.

12. The *New English Dictionary* uses this quotation to illustrate the word *Ana*, s. v. B1. See also my "*Ana*-Books and Intellectual Biography in the Eighteenth Century," *Studies in Eighteenth-Century Culture*, 3 (1973), 191–204.

13. *New Cambridge Bibliography of English Literature*, II (1971), col. 1130.

14. *Life*, III, 201.

15. Ibid.

16. See, for example, Donald J. Greene, *The Politics of Samuel Johnson* (New Haven: Yale Univ. Press, 1960), p. 270.

17. For one instance of Johnson's ability to "talk upon any side of a question," see *Life*, I, 465.

18. *Life*, I, xli.

19. G. Thomas Tanselle, "The Descriptive Bibliography of Eighteenth-Century Books," in *Eighteenth-Century English Books considered by librarians and booksellers, bibliographers and collectors* (Chicago: Association of College and Research Libraries, 1976), pp. 22–33, authoritatively discusses the state of descriptive bibliography for the period, noting the lack of reliable studies for such major figures as Pope, Swift, and Johnson.

20. Robert Folkenflik's essay, "Johnson's Modern Lives," below, pp. 3–23, comments in detail on the state of Johnsonian biographical studies in the last forty years.

21. For the latest account of the state of work on Johnson's canon, see John L. Abbott's essay, "The Making of the Johnsonian Canon," below, pp. 127–39.

22. Isobel Grundy's essay, "The Techniques of Spontaneity: Johnson's Developing Epistolary Style," below, pp. 211–24, begins an assessment of the literary values of Johnson's correspondence.

Part One

JOHNSON'S LIFE

ROBERT FOLKENFLIK

1 · Johnson's Modern Lives

In the first seventy years of the twentieth century about fourteen biographies of Johnson (depending on how one counts) were published.[1] In the 1970s there were eight. Or, to put it another way, it took forty years to reach the total published in the last decade alone. How many biographies we count depends on what we choose. If we demand that the biography be of a certain length (say 30,000 words), F. E. Halliday's heavily illustrated *Doctor Johnson and His World* (1967), though one hundred and twenty-eight pages exclusive of end matter, will just make it. If we limit the consideration to biographies just of Johnson, Hesketh Pearson's *Johnson and Boswell: The Story of Their Lives* (1958) will go, as will his account of Johnson in *The Lives of the Wits* (1962). I omit dual and collective biographies, short biographies, and those that do not present a chronological account of Johnson's life. But if one were to include only those biographies that deal with Johnson in some way from birth to death, James L. Clifford's two volumes would have to be omitted.[2] Clifford's volumes, whether he intended to go on to a third or not, are certainly among the best we have. I will not consider any collective biographies or accounts of Johnson in the biographies of others (for example, J. A. Cochrane's *Dr. Johnson's Printer: The Life of William Strahan*).

The tone of the early years is fairly caught by S. C. Roberts's *The Story of Doctor Johnson: Being an Introduction to Boswell's Life*, though he is hardly the worst offender and went on to do respectable work. This book is intended for boys who will grow up to read Boswell.[3] Hugh Kingsmill's *Samuel Johnson* (1933) is the first in this century not to use the honorific title. Some nineteenth-century biographies, such as Leslie Stephen's (1878), did not bother with the title, though his was part of the English Men of Letters series. Incidentally, it is not right simply to lay this tendency at Boswell's door; the earliest biographies of Johnson more often than not use the doctorate in their titles, or, as Boswell did, refer to Samuel Johnson, LL. D, and to "Dr. Johnson" throughout.[4]

Christopher Hollis wrote the only biography of Johnson during the twenties. His *Dr. Johnson* (1928) is certainly as bad as can be found. One of the problems of biography is how to begin. The first crucial fact of biography is the birth of the subject. Hollis solves this problem by claiming that "If one would write about Johnson, it is necessary . . . to find something to say about him. It is not enough to tell the world that he was born at Lichfield, or that he gave oysters to his cat, or what he said about a woman preaching, for the world knows all these things already."[5] On the next page, however, we find him saying "I have told you that I would not tell you that Samuel Johnson was born at Lichfield. In telling you that I would not tell you, I told you once. Now I tell you again. Samuel Johnson was born at Lichfield in the year 1709." Not satisfied with a preteritio, Hollis gives us a taste of the bumptious garrulity to come. The first chapter of the book, in which this passage appears, is entitled "Johnson the Tory." This is the keynote, though the rest of the book uses topics reached chronologically as points of departure for Hollis's remarks. The first page asserts that "Macaulay's paradox remains a truth . . . [Johnson's writings are] fading; while those pecularities of manner and that careless table-talk . . . are likely to be remembered as long as the English language is spoken in any quarter of the globe.'"[6] Although I will save most of my general remarks for later, the primary rule of Johnsonian biography is that the worth of the biography varies inversely with the number of favorable references to Macaulay.

It is not accidental that Hugh Kingsmill is the first to avoid the honorary doctorate in the title. The superiority to Hollis's book in the previous decade is clearcut. Michael Holroyd claims in an introduction to Kingsmill's work that in *Samuel Johnson* (1933) "his intention . . . was to qualify, by implication, the unstinted praise given by Macaulay and Carlyle to Boswell's *Johnson*."[7] If so (and Macaulay's explicit praise is highly paradoxical, coming from a man who had so much ill to speak of both the biographer and his subject), it is most apparent in the chapter called "Boswell's *Life of Johnson*,"—which curiously precedes Kingsmill's chapter on the *Lives of the Poets*—though we can credit Holroyd's comment that Johnson was "his favorite figure in English literary history." Again, we are speaking of a "figure" rather than a writer. Witness the proportions of chapter V: "Eccentricities—Shakespeare—Mr. and Mrs. Thrale—Dr. Taylor." Yet this is not entirely fair to Kingsmill, who pays attention to the writings even though the chapter heads include only three works (which always share the billing). In his biography of Kingsmill Holroyd extravagantly praises this book ("the writing . . . is distinguished by great wisdom, much tenderness, and a deep knowledge and understanding of human nature"). Holroyd, who believes it Kingsmill's best biography, finds it faulty only in its extreme love of Johnson and sympathy for him.[8] In discussing the *Life of Savage*, Kingsmill says that "Johnson's sense of reality and sympathy are equally balanced," and at his best one can say as much for him as well.[9] Kingsmill had begun as an admirer of Strachey. Perhaps his genuine admiration for Johnson makes this literate book worthy of notice as the first adult biography of Johnson in the twentieth century. Although his comments on the writings tend to be slight, his response to Chesterfield's essays in *The World* is urbanely decisive and shows a good understanding of the Johnson–Chesterfield relationship: "Chesterfield was facetious in the last style likely to conciliate Johnson."[10]

In the next decade, Joseph Wood Krutch's *Samuel Johnson* (1944) was far more substantial than Kingsmill's relatively short book. It ran to 554 pages, exclusive of notes, whereas Kingsmill's book was 244 pages long in much larger type without notes. Krutch is forthright and energetic. His performance as biographer is very different from his psychoanalytic Poe of the twenties. Although uneven and now somewhat dated, it is the first serious modern biography of Johnson and was recognized as such by Edmund Wilson and F. R. Leavis. The writings of Johnson matter in this book. In his autobiography *More Lives than One*, Krutch says his intention was both to "write a full biography" incorporating new knowledge and to "revise as far as possible the popular notion of Johnson as hardly more than the convenient subject of Boswell's amusing portrait."[11] In this he succeeded, and his book is certainly far more accurate and fuller than Kingsmill's and the others up to his time.

The next important biographer of Johnson, one with unique virtues, is James L. Clifford, whose *Young Sam Johnson* (1955; published in England as *Young Samuel Johnson*) and whose more recent *Dictionary Johnson: Samuel Johnson's Middle Years* (1979), which Clifford liked to speak of as "Middle Sam," were written on a scale that would have made them part of the longest modern biography of Johnson had he covered the whole life. It was his original intention only to take Johnson to the point where he met Boswell (the second volume ends with the pension). Clifford died shortly after completing the manuscript in 1978.

Before considering these volumes, however, I will discuss a number of books published prior to Clifford's second volume. In looking even at the major biographies I will necessarily be rather like that pedant in Hierocles whom Johnson mentions: I will produce a few bricks and let the reader imagine the edifices of which they are part.

That the next decade should see the publication both of Charles

Norman's *Mr. Oddity* (1951) and James L. Clifford's *Young Sam Johnson* (1955) keeps us from making hasty generalizations about the course of Johnsonian biography. Norman, following the practice of Lytton Strachey with a vengeance, turns conversations or quotations into drama. The book even opens with a *dramatis personae*: "Hon. Topham Beauclerk, who resembled Charles II, . . . Edmund Burke, Esq., a friend of the Americans . . . Mrs. Samuel Johnson, an understanding woman . . . Mrs. Hester Thrale, Johnson's 'Mistress' . . . Lords, Ladies, Actresses, Doctors, Poets, Hacks, Adventurers and Ghosts, etc. etc." [12] The jocularity and the crude one-dimensionality of these "characters" prepare us for a performance unlike any other biography of Johnson.

If the mindreading implied by Norman's usual procedure is off-putting, there is an occasional effect of immediacy. Norman's emphasis on the bad relations between Johnson and his mother is a theme picked up (with a mention of his indebtedness) by James Clifford, who was never too high-toned to take help wherever he could find it. (Clifford's dramatic opening to *Young Sam Johnson* may well be the result of seeing the striking effect of Norman's opening *Mr. Oddity* with Johnson's interview with the king—it is characteristically presented as the "Prologue.") And Norman, unlike even the best biographers, quotes not just Johnson's letters to Hill Boothby, but Hill Boothby's back to him.

M. J. C. Hodgart's short *Samuel Johnson and his Times* (1962) has been virtually disowned by the author himself in a review of Wain's biography as the seduction of a virgin author by a publisher. While the notion of a short (this one is under 50,000 words) life-and-times biography is a generic contradiction in terms, this book has some virtues. A number of the quotations from Johnson's works and Hodgart's comments are fresh. From the start he puts forth ideas about Johnson that were not part of the common coin of Johnsonian biography: "He was first and foremost a poet, and his poetic imagination illuminates his prose and dazzles in his conversation, which is the most splendid ever recorded." [13] This is a good antidote for all those biographers who start by talking about Johnson's heavy prose. He also adjudicates well between the claims of Boswell and Mrs. Thrale on Johnson's friendship. Macaulay is quoted only to dispute rightly his picture of Johnson as a stay-at-home.

The next group of biographies I will discuss can also be considered among the category of the short life-and-times. All these are frankly meant for a popular audience and emphasize the illustrations.

F. E. Halliday's *Doctor Johnson and his World* (1968) seems intended as an introduction for the young. He prefaces the book with personal remarks:

> I first read Boswell's Life of Johnson as an undergraduate, more than forty years ago. Since then it has been my constant bedside and breakfast-table book. Boswell led me to the Memoirs of Mrs Thrale and Fanny Burney, and, of course, to the works of Johnson himself.[14]

Johnson's works come in almost as an afterthought. His Johnson inspires a latter-day peace of the Augustans, and Halliday expresses the hope that "this book, with its illustrations, will introduce many readers besides Benedict and Kate [the dedicatees] to a similar lifelong delight." The only improvement on Roberts's book of 1919 is that now girls as well as boys are taken as proper readers of Boswell's *Johnson*.

Peter Quennell's *Samuel Johnson: His Friends and Enemies* (1972) begins with a chapter called "Streatham Park" and introduces us to Johnson from the perspective of the Thrales.[15] This method refreshingly dodges the earlier biographical ploy that operates from Boswell's point of view. Quennell, who had previously written a biography of Pope and a group of sketches of Boswell, Gibbon, Sterne, and Wilkes under the title *Four Portraits*, sees this book as a "conversation-piece, in which my hero stands at the centre of the picture, surrounded by his friends and enemies against the background of his social period." His many years of service as a professional biographer with a special interest in eighteenth-century subjects (Queen Caroline, Casanova, Hogarth) do not prove to be an asset. The account of Johnson's life until he meets the Thrales is handled so briskly that the reality behind it suffers: "At Birmingham he encountered a middle-aged widow, Mrs Elizabeth Porter—she had three children, the eldest, her daughter, Lucy, being nearly grown up—and immediately fell deep in love" (p. 29). This bustle makes it sound as though Johnson met her after she was widowed and as though it was not just a "love-match," as he later insisted, but love at first sight. In some ways this book reads like a biography of Hester Thrale *manqué*. The chapter "'The Horrour of the Last'" is about the death of Henry Thrale and her subsequent life. We only learn of Johnson's death in the epilogue.

Quennell is most at home writing the pen portraits that his title suggests. The chapter "The World of Women," for example, troops through Mrs. Delany, Elizabeth Montagu, Elizabeth Vesey, Hester Chapone, Elizabeth Carter, Hannah More, Mary Wollstonecraft, Molly Aston, Mary Aston, Bet Flint, Margaret Rudd, Kitty Fisher, Lady Diana Beauclerk, and Fanny Burney. Since Johnson never met Mrs. Delany and he was not there on the one occasion Kitty Fisher left her card, the book might better be called, *Samuel Johnson: His Friends and Enemies and Others*. The inclusion of Mary Wollstonecraft, who met him late in life, is honorable. His influence on her early career is readily apparent in her works, and it deserves more recognition in her intellectual development. On the other hand, so good and important an early friend as Cornelius Ford goes unmentioned.

Margaret Lane's *Samuel Johnson and his World* (1975) is another short popular biography with numerous illustrations. It is modest, informed, and limited. (Inoffensive, as F. R. Leavis might put it.) Her color plate of the portrait of Tetty comes closer to making the appeal of Samuel Johnson's wife apparent than any other, though it is not quite true to the colors of the original at Four Oaks Farm. Another sumptuous color plate may cause even the most knowledgeable Johnsonians puzzlement: "Selina, Countess of Huntingdon, with two of her children, Elizabeth and Ferdinando." Two pages later, by way of an account of Hill Boothby's religious views, she quotes Miss Sainthill in *The Spiritual Quixote* and from there it is a short jump to the Methodism of the "redoubtable Selina, countess of Huntingdon, wife of the ninth Earl," a convert who proselytized the aristocracy in the Midlands.[16] Admittedly, this series allows the author to slip in all sorts of marginal information, but the short life-and-times is designed to abuse the notion of relevance. Perhaps the appearance of Selina, who receives as much attention as Hill Boothby, can best be accounted for when we notice that the author of this biography is the wife of the fifteenth Earl of Huntingdon. But on the whole her focus is on Johnson, and she has a sound conception of relevance.

Since this is the only biography of Johnson written by a woman, it is a shame that she misses the opportunity, as the other biographers except Norman also have, of quoting and commenting on Hill Boothby's letters to Johnson. Because it has become clear in this century that Johnson intended to remarry and Hill Boothby was probably the one he had decided upon, it would be good to get as close as we can to hearing her voice; the letters have been in print since 1805.[17] This biography is far better than Halliday's or Quennell's, and the proportions of text to illustrations is better. If the intention is to grace a coffee table, it should be the choice.

Coming before the biographies of Quennell and Lane, Christopher Hibbert's oddly named *The Personal History of Samuel Johnson* (1971), the work of a military historian and biographer, is soldier-like, accurate, and lucid, but it lacks a feel for the writings. The account of *The Life of Savage*, for instance, is limited to an enumeration of the qualities they shared that made Johnson sympathetic to his older friend. There is no sense of the satiric side of the biography or of the sort of balance that Johnson is attempting for all his sympathy. This one does not pretend to new material, but it follows the lead of the best scholarship and the biographies of Clifford and Krutch.

The same year also saw a biography that was psychoanalytic in orientation and written by a nonprofessional, George Irwin. Although there had been some earlier studies of Johnson that were psychoanalytic or psychiatric, the results were not very impressive. Even those that were not biographies proper were necessarily highly biographical.[18] The emphasis on Johnson's neuroses, however distasteful it seems to some critics, is important as part of his biography because it sees the compulsive tics and other neurotic behavior (too often treated as lovable eccentricities) as part of the whole personality and strongly related to the themes of the writings. It would be hard to deny that there was a good deal of psychopathology in Johnson's everyday life. The interest to the biographer of psychoanalysis is its promise to see the man as a coherent whole through raising to consciousness those things that are unconsciously expressive or unrecognized for what they actually are. The psychoanalytic consideration of Johnson in biography has been carried out most ably by Bate, whose employment of analytic concepts has been very tactful.

Irwin expanded his useful article, "Dr. Johnson's Troubled Mind" (1963), which dealt with Johnson's relation to his mother as the key to an understanding of Johnson's life, into a book: *Samuel Johnson: A Personality in Conflict* (1971). Hence this account highlights personal relationships: those of Johnson's parents, Johnson's childhood relationship to his mother and his later failure to visit her, his marriage to Tetty and his "transference relationship" to Mrs. Thrale, which concludes the book in 1781, a few years before Johnson's death and after the completion of *The Lives of the Poets*. Both Norman and Clifford had noted the important discrepancies between Johnson's attitude towards his mother and his behavior, but Irwin makes it the key to his interpretation of Johnson. The encouragement given him by Greene and Clifford in expanding the article probably accounts for the change in the title.

The psychological pathos of Irwin's book is often genuinely suggestive, but the tone fills the drama of Johnson's life with mawkishness. After quoting a letter sent to Tetty looking forward to her "tenderness and affection," Irwin says:

> Poor Johnson. It was not to be. That tenderness and affection he had known during their courtship and the first months of their marriage, tenderness and affection he had known for the first time in his life, had come to an end. He and his wife were to drift still further apart. The brief period of love he had known had gone forever, but the memory of it remained to be enhanced by time. If it was Johnson, the inveterate self-reproacher, punishing himself for his shortcomings as a husband, that grieved so excessively after the death of his wife, it was Sam Johnson, the unloved little boy, longing to feel again the security Tetty had once given him, that grieved so piteously.[19]

When his mother is dying and Johnson fails to visit her (the keystone that upholds this interpretation), Irwin claims:

> It was not the dear little old lady in the bookshop at Lichfield,
>
> > The gen'ral fav'rite as the gen'ral friend
>
> that he could not bring himself to face; it was the tyrant of his childhood of whom the child-within-him was still afraid.[20]

The original article works up the thesis to a more apocalyptic (or at least melodramatic) point:

> A few days after his mother's death Johnson wrote in his weekly column in the Idler: "The life which made my own life pleasant is at an end." . . . Poor Johnson, torn by inner conflicts, tortured by guilt and fear, had no idea what his real sentiments were. Had he written, "The life which made my own life Hell is at an end," he would have been much nearer the truth.[21]

Mrs. Thrale in this reading fills the role of the psychoanalyst for Johnson, whose love and hate "is, in psychotherapy, characteristic of the transference formed by the most severely disturbed patients. . . . the manner in which she was able, through not becoming emotionally involved herself, to accept his outbursts of rudeness and resentment is characteristic of the experienced analyst who remains free from counter-transference" (pp. 130–31). Irwin makes use of Freud, Jung (slightly), Ian Sutie, and Charles Ryecroft. His emphasis on self-fulfillment derives from Ryecroft. That the portrait is far from satisfactory has more to do with Irwin's limitations as a biographer than with any inherent shortcomings of psychoanalysis.

John Wain's *Samuel Johnson* (1974) is more ambitious than most. It runs to 240,000 words, just a little less than Bate's. Wain is both a poet, whose translation from the Latin of Johnson's poem with the unpromising title "In rivum a Mola Stoana Lichfieldiae Diffluentem" is extraordinarily good (had he done nothing more, Johnsonians should remember him with gratitude), and a skillful novelist.[22] We are not apt to forget that he is a novelist. The biography opens with Sarah Johnson's putative reactions to the noises in Lichfield as she gives birth to Sam, and throughout the book there are touches that remind us a novelist is in bondage. Early on he claims, "If one were writing an historical novel about Johnson instead of a biographical study, this would be a fine opportunity for some chiaroscuro" (p. 60). When an unexpected gift and the promise of more money makes Johnson's education at Oxford possible, Wain comments, "Then came one of those reversals of fortune that one would never dare to put into a novel. (Though, since it was a stroke of luck afterwards ironically reversed, it would go well enough into a novel by Thomas Hardy.)" (p. 40). This is a nice touch. Less happy is his account of Johnson's arrest: "The author of *The Rambler* in Prison! The author of the Dictionary compelled to listen to the argot of thieves and desperadoes! It would make a subject for the pen of Fielding. None other would be equal to it" (p. 205). The lack of any actual details or dialogue leads him to novelistic surmise.

The key to Wain's biography is nostalgia. He is aware of the parallels between his own life and Johnson's as one of the strengths of his biography:

> Perhaps more than most, I am in a position to see his life from the inside. I was born in the same district as Johnson—some thirty miles away—and in much the same social *milieu*. I went to the same university, and since then have lived the same life of Grub Street, chance employment, and the unremitting struggle to write enduring books against the background of an unstable existence. The literary and social situation that Johnson knew in its early days, I know in its twilight. (p. 14)

This is the fellow-feeling of someone born in a later, lesser age. And as we learn from his autobiography, *Sprightly Running* (1962), Wain shares other characteristics as well that he does not mention: poor eyesight for one. Although he uses the first-person pronoun more than the other biographers (with an awareness that he is of interest in his own right), his use of "we" is less marked by the sense that we are all like Johnson (something that is of great importance for Bate) and more by his sense of being one who shares particular experiences with Johnson. Johnson had been a hero for him from the time he was an undergraduate at Oxford. There is no question that this biography is deeply felt and long pondered.

Wain compares Oxford teaching of the twentieth century unfavorably with the notorious dons of the eighteenth, despite quoting some of the later acid comments of Gibbon:

> The temptation to spend one's time in drinking and social climbing must have been as great as the temptation for present-day dons to spend their time running up to London to appear on television or acting as consultants to industry. I am aware of no convincing reason why twentieth-century Oxford should feel moral or intellectual superiority over eighteenth-century Oxford, though there is admittedly a difference in efficiency. (p. 50)

That, I take it, is the sometime professor of poetry cocking a snook at his colleagues, but his nostalgic treatment of Johnson's milieu has other consequences that are less fortunate. Wain always has one eye on modern times: "Because his own early life in a family circle had been unhappy, he did not suggest that people should not have families or that children should be given numbers or brought up in state crèches" (p. 45). This is part of Wain's account of Johnson's concept of the relationship between the individual and society, but one could be forgiven for coming away with the notion that Johnson was against socialism. Again, he takes Josiah Wedgwood's having his incapacitating leg lopped off so that he could go about his business more easily as characteristic of England in the eighteenth century—"the toughness, the realism, the determination to be up and doing, whatever the price that had to be paid." Fair enough; the anecdote is a good one. But he continues, "Wedgwood knew that if he did not succeed in the pottery industry, he could not simply subside into comfortable obscurity as the tenth vice-president in some large faceless corporation, with his name on the door and a carpet on the floor" (p. 44). If Wedgwood knew that, he was far more prescient than his admirers have given him credit for being. Although Johnson may never have hit anyone with a book, Wain intends to hit numerous moderns with this one.

Wain's Johnson becomes a very special sort of other self for him, and I think that he conceives himself as very Johnsonian in writing this book. The book is for the modern equivalent of Johnson's common reader: "This book . . . is addressed to the intelligent general reader. The specialist in Johnson studies has in the last thirty years, been adequately catered for" (p. 13). True, Clifford's first volume only took Johnson down to 1749, but Joseph Wood Krutch does not deserve such a dismissal. Two of Wain's other heroes, Edmund Wilson and F. R. Leavis, had welcomed Krutch's book precisely because it was bringing a more adequate conception of Johnson to just such an audience, and Krutch in his foreword notes that "the very intensity of this specialization [on Johnson] (as well, of course, as the tremendous reputation of Boswell's *Life*) has tended to discourage any attempt in recent times to produce a large inclusive book which would serve to give the general reader a running account of Johnson's life, character, and work as they appear in the light of contemporary knowledge and contemporary judgment."[23] But his attitude to scholarship, despite (or because of) Wain's own years as an academic, verges at times on the dismissive. His note on sources proclaims that "There is no research in this book" and further indicates that "As far as possible I have avoided reading modern studies of Johnson" (p. 380). In the body of the book he says that the *Lives of the Poets* "is a work of memory, judgement, and love, not a work of research" (p. 345). Yet the amount of new material that Johnson turned up (as well as remembered) is substantial. When Wain says of Savage's "On Public Spirit" "I have not read this poem and have no intention of reading it" (p. 278) we can take this as an allusion to some Johnsonian passages, but in the twentieth century it sounds like truculent ignorance.

In fairness to Wain, I should note that in the preface to his second edition (1984) he indicates that by "research" he means manuscript and other primary research (the sort of thing that Clifford is best at), and he mentions how many silly mistakes he has corrected. Yet when his fifth chapter continues to be "Ah, Sir, I was Mad and Violent," we may wonder how serious his intentions are. Clifford corrected this to "rude and violent" in 1955; it also appears in Waingrow's collection.[24] Here was a chance for Wain to make use of Boswell's inability to read his own handwriting.

One of the strongest elements in Wain's attraction to Johnson is surely Johnson's attitude to cant. Wain gives a modern instance: "The kind of political trained parrot who refers to the slave states of Eastern Europe as 'people's democracies' is indulging in cant." (p. 247). This is cant, and we all recognize it as such, but Johnson is far more concerned with our own cant. The cant of the "free world" would be his main target, as can easily be shown by his ironic comments on the Seven Years War in *Thoughts on Falkland's Islands*:

> It is wonderful with what coolness and indifference the greater part of mankind see war commenced. . . . Some indeed must perish in the most successful field, but they die upon the bed of honour, "resign their lives amidst the joys of conquest, and, filled with England's glory, smile in death."

Johnson continues "The life of a modern soldier is ill represented by heroick fiction."[25] Wain has let his own anticommunism dictate his treatment of this topic. In fact, Wain's partial apology for Macpherson is a good example of what Johnson would have considered cant: "He was co-operating with the *Zeitgeist*" (p. 330). The precise parallel can be found in *Rasselas* when the Prince, having heard too much windy jargon, bows ironically and the philosopher "departed with the air of a man that had co-operated with the present system." One would have hoped that Wain, whose knowledge of Johnson's works is certainly intimate, could not use such a sentence with a straight face. My main point here, however, is that, as so often in this book, Wain's wish to make it directly relevant to the modern reader leads to some distortion of Johnson. I would not deal with Wain at such length if I thought his book were simply a bad one. His is the most vigorous of modern biographies of Johnson, and he emphasizes the writings while making intelligent use of Boswell. In a sense his performance is akin to some things Johnson himself might do if we could transport him to the twentieth century, and it is not hard to see why some of the most knowledgeable Johnson scholars are admirers of the book.

Of all the modern biographers, James Clifford most conceives of his task as a collaborative one in which modern scholarship is making known more than was ever known before about Samuel Johnson. Clifford's self-conception is overly modest, for he is certainly in the forefront of those who have increased our knowledge of Johnson. Typical of Clifford's tone is the following account of snippets from Johnson's lost letter to Richardson quoted in a Sotheby's catalogue:

The only "book" that Johnson was having printed at this time was the collected version of the *Rambler*, and this must be what Johnson was referring to. Could Johnson have been making so many changes in proof that he was causing trouble for Richardson's compositors? Had he sent as copy the original issues, with manuscript changes which were hard to read? Or could he have sent copy made up partly of original issues and the rest in his own handwriting? Or was he merely making Richardson's subordinates do the proofreading? Until the complete letter is found we cannot be sure.[26]

In instances where Clifford has the information he needs, his account is meticulous and readable; but he is the most future oriented of our biographers, and the quest from puzzles to portraits, to echo the title of his book on biography, is endless. As an example of Clifford going Clifford one better, a comparison of the chapter "A Harmless Drudge" in *Young Sam Johnson* with "Lexicographer at Work" in *Dictionary Johnson* (1979) would suffice. New information had been found, and Clifford took advantage of it to deepen his account of the making of the *Dictionary*.

The difference between *Dictionary Johnson* and *Mr. Oddity* (or still worse, *Ursa Major*) can be gauged from the titles themselves. Clifford's eye is firmly on the work, and for this he has good Johnsonian precedent. *Idler* 102 says that "the gradations of a hero's life are from battle to battle, and of an author's from book to book."[27] Clifford's chapters are apt to be called "Lexicographer at work," "*The Rambler*," "*The Dictionary*," "Speaking his Mind—*The Literary Magazine*," "*The Idler*," "*Rasselas*": these are not catchy titles, but they put the literary emphasis strongly forward. Only three chapters of Krutch's twelve are named for works. And in Clifford's "The End of Tetty," much of his chapter is devoted to a discussion of the effect on the *Rambler* essays of Tetty's approaching death. His intention, never fully satisfied (and in some sense unsatisfiable), is to give us the life of Johnson as accurately and as fully, given his awareness of biography as an art, as possible.

Clifford's biography is oriented toward the perfect biography yet to come. But as a theorist of biography, he is aware that "all biographies need not conform to a single set of standards, that quite legitimately there are different kinds of life writing, each with its own possibilities and rules."[28] In *From Puzzles to Portraits* (a title that shows his procedure in an intermediate stage) his chapter "Form—Types of Biography" identifies his early life of Mrs. Piozzi (1940) as "scholarly-historical" and *Young Sam* as "artistic-scholarly."[29]

The difference between Clifford and Bate can be seen through their handling of gaps in the chronological record: "Unfortunately for a biographer, the winter months of 1750 which followed are a blank period. There are no surviving letters, no journal entries, or publications. Yet we do know that he lived through unusual events which appear to have had no effect upon him whatsoever." After describing the earthquakes of February and March, he can only ask "What happened at 17 Gough Square?" and speculate intelligently on why Johnson never mentioned the events. Bate speaks of a period of six months in 1745:

> Wondering what he did at this time . . . people have for generations speculated about causes. Did he quarrel with Cave, and is that why no more writings appeared every month in the Magazine? Or had he perhaps—the thought, though insane, persists—joined the Jacobite rebellion of 1745 and hurried north to support the Stuart cause, or, staying in London, served as a sort of underground agent? There is a tendency in human nature whenever we are considering the lives of others, to expect them to proceed at a far brisker pace than we ourselves do, not because we are uncharitable but because our vicarious interest is better able to notice results than to share the actual process and daily crawl of other people's experience. In viewing others, however well-intentioned our empathy, our imaginations are naturally less fatigued and clogged with the distractions, uncertainties, and inner resistances that make up so much of daily life. Hence even the sympathetic biographer or critic, who may take ten years for a book, can become puzzled or suspicious if his subject seems to tarry for ten months between writings, and is ready to assume that only something very specific or concrete could have intervened. Especially if his subject had written rapidly before, it does not now seem "in character"—it is not at all like him—to stop suddenly in this way. What could have happened? Or perhaps he did not really stop. Perhaps there were works hidden away that can yet be discovered? [30]

Clifford's attitude may turn up new material, but Bate's has made a biographical asset of a liability. The missing period becomes the occasion for a thoughtful account of what it means to live a life as well as to write one.

Clifford's *Young Sam* is unusual among Johnson biographies in that it only covers a period in Johnson's life, and perhaps as much as anything this helps to give the book its almost optimistic character. It closes with a quick glimpse of what is to come in the most positive terms:

> In 1749, however, Johnson could hardly have guessed what was in store for him. He could have had no premonition of the brilliant social life at Streatham or in the London bluestocking assemblies. Only in his fondest dreams would he have imagined a personal meeting with the King, or an honorary doctor's degree from the university he had attended only thirteen months and left because his toes were sticking out from his shoes. But most astonishing of all would have been the knowledge that a Scottish boy of eight in far-off Edinburgh was preparing to assist him towards immortality. [31]

This is hardly to say that Clifford is unaware of the other side—the "life radically wretched" that Johnson spoke of in his letter to Mrs. Thrale. But it is suggestive that while the first chapter of *Young Sam Johnson* is "There's a Brave Boy," the equivalent one in Wain is "A Poor Diseased Infant." Wain strikes the balance neatly in his epigraph from *Alice in Wonderland*:

> —He taught Laughing and Grief, they used to say.
> —So he did, so he did.

Bate's biography focuses on the psychological and symbolic and gives us, insofar as the biographer hedged by his impossible art can, an interior life of Johnson. In *The Achievement of Samuel Johnson*, Bate's splendid biographical sketch, which composes the first chapter, is entitled "A Life of Allegory," and Keats's phrase well describes the full-length book of twenty-two years later. Many of the biographers of Johnson have noted Mrs. Thrale's comment on his favorite books, but Bate alone seems to see their large symbolic relevance:

> The three books of which he never tired, said Mrs. Thrale, were *Robinson Crusoe, Pilgrim's Progress*, and *Don Quixote*. He would have gone on reading them, he would never exhaust them, because here—as in no other works—his identification was almost complete. These three wanderers—one a castaway, one a pilgrim, and one on an impossible quest—were prototypes of what he felt to be his own life.[32]

When he discusses that seemingly odd title, *The Rambler*, he notes Arthur Murphy's suggestion that Johnson had in mind Savage's *The Wanderer* and adds:

> For years a part of himself had identified with those, like Savage, who lived on the fringes of society, just as another part of him identified with the wanderers in those three books of which he never tired. . . . Between a pilgrim, who travels with "settled direction" or aim, and the "straggler" he at bottom felt himself to be ("one who *rambles without* any settled direction")—the definitions are from the *Dictionary*—there was a middle position, a "rambler," which would not be claiming too much but which would also not preclude moving at times into purpose and direction" (p. 290).

He also remembers the importance of these books when he comes to discuss *Rasselas* and the role of pilgrimage in that fiction. Indeed, the second part of the biography, "In the Middle of the Way: The Moral Pilgrimage," draws its title from Dante but has behind it the weight of this identification. In his preface Bate characterizes Johnson as "a heroic, intensely honest, and articulate pilgrim in the strange adventure of human life" (p. xx). This pilgrim's progress clearly plays an allegorical role for us. It is to Bate's credit that the characterization is not merely honorific but becomes one of the deeply felt themes of the biography.

Wain has a chapter entitled "Mentors," which takes up Ford and Walmesley. He notices, as have many, most notably Clifford, that Ford's role in Johnson's life was important. But Bate goes beyond noticing the practical advice, the image of the uncloistered and worldly scholar, the nicknames, and sees how much Ford served as a model for Johnson. He notes shrewdly that Ford's marriage to a woman thirteen years older than him may have helped Johnson to see his marriage to Tetty as a possibility. Clifford comments on Johnson's brief Latin diary that "References to Ford stand out among the meager entries as memorable landmarks."[33] Bate notes "Before the age of twenty, there are only three brief entries. They are simple records of fact. The first is the date of his birth in 1709. The second entry is his visit with Cornelius Ford, sixteen years later. Coming as it does, in this sparse list of the major events of his life . . . it is like the record of a second birth. Such indeed it was" (pp. 54–55). The chapter is called "A Second Beginning: Cornelius Ford."

Bate's ability to interpret Johnson rests on this seeing of the symbolic meaning of things, which is also part of what makes him so good a reader of Johnson's writings. For example, Johnson took a large number of books to Oxford and then left them there when he returned. Of this episode Clifford says:

> He had brought to Oxford what would have been an extensive personal library for an undergraduate of those days—well over a hundred volumes. Though troublesome and expensive to transport, they represented one item which Michael could supply with ease.[34]

At the end of the Oxford period Clifford comments: "Obviously intending this as no final departure, he left his extensive library with Taylor for safe keeping. As Sam said goodbye to his friends, he could have had no intimation that it would be almost twenty-five years before he would again see his beloved college" (p. 128). The irony here is bittersweet.

Bate, whose work is informed by a pathos that is very different in thought and rhythm from the other biographies, treats this episode far differently. He discusses it in terms of Johnson's breakdown following his return from Oxford, in context of his living at his family's expense while they were growing poor:

> Significantly there seems to have been no pressure on him, during all this time, to get back the large number of books he had taken from the bookshop and had left at Oxford, where they were now lying unused. They had represented a very large investment for Michael, and the expense of shipping them back was nothing in comparison with their

value. We can only assume Michael did not dare to bring up the subject to his son, whose state of mind he was afraid to upset any further. That his son did not insist on returning the books, when the family need was so great, indicates how completely he was absorbed or lost in his own psychological struggle. (p. 127)

In passages like this Bate seems to be engaging in precisely that kind of act of the imagination described by Johnson in *Rambler* 60 which is necessary to feel as one's own emotions the events of the life of another. It is no surprise that this imagining of the meaning of events verges at times on identification, but what we should notice here is that it enables Bate to understand what those books might have meant to Samuel and to Michael Johnson. Finally, the strength of Bate's book comes from Bate's belief in biography as a form of knowledge critical as well as historical. Such a belief is readily apparent in his influential *The Burden of the Past and the English Poet*, which attempts to read literary history from the perspective of the individual poet's recognition of the burden placed upon him by past poetic achievement.[35]

Some generalizations and conclusions are in order. First, though some of the biographies of Johnson have scholarly virtues (Krutch, Clifford, Hibbert, Bate), it would be wrong to talk of a scholarly vs. a popular tradition. All of the major biographers of Johnson write for the intelligent general reader (to use Wain's formulation); significantly, no major biography of Johnson has been published by a university press. Clifford, both in the extent of his research and the proportioning of his books (especially *Dictionary Johnson*) in response to new material, can most clearly be called a scholarly biographer.

Most of the biographers of Johnson in this century had already written biographies of others. Kingsmill of Arnold and Frank Harris; Krutch of Poe; Vulliamy and Quennell of half a dozen eighteenth-century figures apiece; Lane of Edgar Wallace, Beatrice Potter, and the Brontës; Clifford of Mrs. Thrale; Hibbert of Mussolini, Garibaldi, and Dickens; Bate of Keats.

The worst biographies have nicknames for the title: *Ursa Major* and *Mr. Oddity* (this last is an impossible concoction—if the sobriquet had caught on he would have been known as Oddity Johnson—at least Norman did not make it Dr. Oddity). Clifford's *Dictionary Johnson* is just right for the middle years, for this is how he was known, and it was typical of the eighteenth-century to identify a man with his foremost literary achievement: Estimate Brown or even Corsica Boswell.

It would be wrong to see an evolutionary development of Johnsonian biography. While there is improvement from Kingsmill to Krutch to Clifford and Bate, we still have such retrograde books as Peter Quennell's *Samuel Johnson: His Friends and Enemies*—Quennell himself would seem to be among the latter—and such nugatory productions as F. E. Halliday's *Doctor Johnson and His World*.

The improvement of Johnsonian biography has a great deal to do with the continuing effort of scholarship to uncover the facts of his life and the greater critical sophistication with which his works are discussed. It has much to do with that double tradition of Johnson that Bertrand Bronson analyzed, and as the recognition of his importance as a writer, rather than just as a personality ("like a character in one of our older novels, and on the same level of objectivity and familiarity," as Bronson puts it), rises, so does the quality of the biographies.[36] The first three chapters of John Bailey's *Dr. Johnson and his Circle* (1913) in the Home University Library of Modern Knowledge are "Johnson as a National Institution," "The Genius of Boswell," and "The Lives of Johnson and Boswell." The image that the title gives of a conversation piece is typical of the Boswell-centered approach of both criticism and biography early in the century. That first chapter head, however, could serve as a starting point for a more conscious study of the meaning of Johnson. F. R. Leavis in praising Krutch attacks precisely this notion of Johnson:

> Mr. Krutch's book, I must confess, surprised me very agreeably. It is not only inoffensive; it is positively good. I had better add at once that I write in England and as an Englishman. In this country, to those seriously interested in literature, the cult of Johnson is an exasperation and a challenge. It is a branch of good-mixing, and its essential raison-d'être is anti-highbrow; it is to further the middlebrow's game of insinuating the values of good-mixing into realms where they have no place—except as a fifth column, doing their hostile work from within. Johnson, one finds oneself having again and again to insist, was not only the Great Clubman; he was a great writer and a great highbrow—or would have been, if the word, and the conditions that have produced it, had existed; that is, he assumed a serious interest in things of the mind, and, for all his appeal to "the common reader," was constantly engaged in the business of bringing home to his public and his associates, whose cult of him was a tribute to the force with which he did it, that there were standards in these things above the ordinary level of the ordinary man.[37]

Beneath the rhetoric of the forties and Leavis's own combination of intellectual elitism with antibourgeois and anti-upperclass social values, we can see the importance of the break with what Bailey called "Johnson as a National Institution," of which the idea of the Great Clubman is only a part. It also helps to explain why most of the best biographies of Johnson in the last forty years are by Americans— Krutch, Clifford, Bate. Americans are free of this particular notion, or if they share it, they do so only in an attenuated or more conscious form. This notion may also help to explain why F. E. Halliday, a scholar who wrote *The Cult of Shakespeare*, should turn up as a biographer of Johnson. Additionally, despite the crankiness of Leavis's critical discriminations, his distinction between the inoffensive and the good (with its implied third category of the offensively bad) is one useful way to lump the biographies of Johnson.

C. E. Vulliamy's *Ursa Major*, which he calls "A Study of Dr. Johnson and his Friends," is sometimes singled out as the worst of twentieth-century biographies. Clifford and Greene refer to its "vituperative, debunking sketch" among the volumes that contain short accounts of Johnson's life.[38] And indeed, apart from iconoclasm, it is difficult to see what would lead this Welsh Fabian (anticlerical and antimonarchic) turned military man to write about Johnson. Part of the answer is precisely that he is attacking most the Johnson who appears in Boswell's *Life*, the national institution:

> Nothing pleases the ordinary man so much as the setting-up, for his comfort, of someone in whose virtues, genius and integrity he can place unbounded reliance. The impulse is normally pre-adolescent, it is that of the hero-worshipper, yet we find it prolonged into adult life where it becomes the basis of cults, of "immortal memories" and of admiration societies innumerable.
>
> . . . If it were not for Boswell the ordinary man would never have heard of Johnson at all, and there would be no admiration society in Lichfield. As it is, Johnson has become one of the great national properties, like Robin Hood or Guy Fawkes or Nelson or Shakespeare. He is given the credit for things which he never said, or could have said; his image is crudely represented on trade-marks and advertisements (in one of which he is actually shown with a mug of beer) and he has become the central figure in cults or groups where his own writings are totally unknown.[39]

From such an analysis, which has something in common with those of Leavis, Edmund Wilson, and Donald Greene, a telling account of the writings could ensue, but what he has to say of Johnson's works and life is usually imperceptive.

One of the obvious battles being fought implicitly in biographies of Johnson is political. Vulliamy's attack is that of a man of the left (who has opted to some degree for bourgeois individualism and taken the King's shilling as well). Wain's is the book of a man who loathes Communism (a whole chapter of his autobiography is taken up with an open letter to the "Comrades" on his month-long trip to Russia). Johnson can become a counter for certain nationalistic and conservative ideas, though his own politics do not easily translate into contemporary terms. (In fact, one of the difficulties with Donald Greene's valuable Namierite account of Johnson's politics is that the constant analogies with politics of the 1950s—it appeared in 1960—have dated and they have their own problematic aspects as well.) Hollis writes as a Catholic Tory, whose allegiance is to de Maistre, Belloc, and Chesterton.[40] This is hardly to say that other biographies of Johnson do not contain a politics (often a nostalgic one), but only that these are the most obvious.

In his foreword Krutch says that "Two readers whose knowledge and judgment command the greatest respect have accused me of 'being hard on Boswell.'"[41] It may be that all of the better biographers of Johnson—Kingsmill, Krutch, Clifford, Wain, Bate—have been hard on Boswell in one way or another. This is accounted for in different ways by the various biographers—Krutch is struck by the contrast between Boswell and Johnson; Kingsmill, who later compiled an anthology called *Johnson without Boswell*, by Boswell's distortions; Clifford, by the early information that Boswell lacked. From the perspective of biography as an art, Boswell is the burden of the past (to use Bate's phrase) or in Harold Bloom's formulation, the strong predecessor whom the ambitious biographer must overcome. To write a life of Johnson is potentially the most ambitious undertaking for a biographer, since Boswell's *Johnson* is by consensus the greatest of English biographies. Of course, if the quality of the biography varies inversely with one's high opinion of Boswell, we can expect Donald Greene's biography in progress to be the best of all.[42]

Although those who merely follow Boswell may be expected to write limited books, a contempt for Boswell along the lines of Vulliamy's may also be productive of bad books. And to ignore Boswell entirely would be a mistake. A fighter can tie one hand behind his back, but heavyweight competitions are not won that way. Some of the worst biographies of this century, however, are admiring in their attitude towards the *Life of Johnson*, if not necessarily towards Boswell himself.

What we must recognize is that there is room in the future for not just one life of Johnson but many. We can still use a good portrait-length biography—longer than Bate's sketch in *The Achievement of Samuel Johnson* but not so long as Krutch, Wain, Bate, or Clifford—to fill the place occupied by the short life-and-times. The perfect biography is far from an ignoble intention, but there undoubtedly will be a number of good biographies of Johnson in the future, as there have been in the past.

NOTES

1. In addition to those I discuss here see H. M. Luckock, *A Popular Sketch of Dr. Johnson's Life and Works* (Lichfield: Mercury Press, 1902); John Dennis, *Dr. Johnson* (London: George Bell & Sons, 1905); Kenji Ishida, *Dr. Johnson and His Circle* (Tokyo: Kenkyushua, 1933) [in Japanese]; S[ydney] C[astle] Roberts, *Doctor Johnson* (London: Duckworth, 1935); Aleyn Lyell Reade, *Johnsonian Gleanings*, Vol. X, *Johnson's Early Life: The Final Narrative* (London: privately printed, 1946); Charles Marshall, *Doctor Johnson* (London: Thomas Nelson & Sons, 1947); Ivor Brown, *Dr. Johnson and His World* (London: Lutterworth Press, 1965).

2. I have omitted Volume X of Reade, *Johnsonian Gleanings* (11 vols. [privately

printed, 1909–52]) which summarizes his new understanding of the first forty years of Johnson's life and provides some of the new material used by writers in this century, on the grounds that Reade did not intend it as a full biography, although it is a narrative. All the serious biographers of Johnson have been indebted to this amateur whose work began with genealogy.

3. S. C. Roberts, *The Story of Doctor Johnson* (Cambridge: University Press, 1919), p. vi.

4. Before Boswell's *Tour*, biographies by Thomas Tyers, William Cooke, and William Shaw provide examples. A number of the eighteenth-century biographies are usefully collected by O M Brack, Jr. and Robert E. Kelley in *The Early Biographies of Samuel Johnson* (Iowa City: Univ. of Iowa Press, 1974).

5. Christopher Hollis, *Dr. Johnson* (London: Victor Gollancz, 1928), p. 7.

6. Hollis, *Dr. Johnson*, p. 5.

7. Kingsmill [Hugh Kingsmill Lunn], *Samuel Johnson* (London: Barker, 1933); Michael Holroyd, Introduction, *The Best of Hugh Kingsmill* (Harmondsworth: Penguin Books, 1973), p. 15.

8. Michael Holroyd, *Hugh Kingsmill* (London: The Unicorn Press, 1964); quoted from Viking Press edition (New York, 1934), pp. 142–43.

9. Kingsmill, *Samuel Johnson*, p. 43.

10. Kingsmill, *Samuel Johnson*, p. 55.

11. Joseph Wood Krutch, *More Lives than One* (New York: William Sloane Associates, 1962), pp. 284–85.

12. Charles Norman, *Mr. Oddity* (Drexel Hill, Pa.: Bell Publishing Co., 1951), p. xi.

13. M. J. C. Hodgart, *Samuel Johnson and his Times* (London: Batsford, 1962), p. 13.

14. F. E. Halliday, *Doctor Johnson and his World* (London: Thames & Hudson, 1968), p. 4.

15. Peter Quennell, *Samuel Johnson: his Friends and Enemies* (London: Weidenfeld and Nicolson, 1972). All references will be by page in the text.

16. Margaret Lane, *Samuel Johnson and his World* (London: Hamilton, 1975), p. 85.

17. *An Account of the Life of Dr. Samuel Johnson from his Birth to his Eleventh Year, Written by Himself. To which are added Original Letters to Dr. Samuel Johnson, by Miss Hill Boothby* (London: Richard Phillips, 1805). For speculation about Johnson's intention to remarry and the evidence on which it rests, see Donald and Mary Hyde, "Dr. Johnson's Second Wife" in *New Light on Dr. Johnson: Essays on the Occasion of his 250th Birthday*, ed. Frederick W. Hilles (New Haven: Yale Univ. Press, 1959), pp. 133–51. A diary entry (copied by Boswell) speaks explicitly of his "intention to seek a new wife" on 22 April 1753. The Hydes, in their canvass of candidates, speak of Hill Boothby as a "tantalizing possibility" (p. 145). Clifford is circumspect; Wain thinks it would have been a good marriage and Bate considers her "almost certainly the wife he had in mind" (W. Jackson Bate, *Samuel Johnson* [New York: Harcourt Brace Jovanovich, 1977], p. 320). On the basis of the letters between them I would agree with Bate.

18. The psychoanalytic or more generally psychological reading of Johnson needs separate treatment. Most such accounts are not biographies. They would include Walter B. C. Watkins's two chapters on Johnson that form the centerpiece of his *Perilous Balance* (Princeton: Princeton Univ. Press, 1939), a psychological portrait, but not Freudian; Robert Wieder, *Le Docteur Johnson, critique littéraire (1709–84): essai de biographie psychologique* (Paris: G. Legrand, 1944); Edward Hitschmann, "Samuel Johnson's Character: A Psychoanalytical Interpretation," *Psychoanalytical Review*, 32 (1945), 207–18; E. Verbeek, M.D., *The Measure and the Choice: A Pathographic Essay on Samuel Johnson* (Ghent: E. Story-Scientia, 1971).

19. George Irwin, *Samuel Johnson: A Personality in Conflict* (Auckland: Auckland Univ. Press, 1971), p. 90.

20. Irwin, *Samuel Johnson*, p. 108.

21. "Dr. Johnson's Troubled Mind," *Literature and Psychology*, 13 (1963); reprinted in

Samuel Johnson: A Collection of Critical Essays, ed. Donald J. Greene (Englewood Cliffs, N.J.: Prentice-Hall, 1965), p. 27.

22. John Wain, *Samuel Johnson* (London: Macmillan, 1974), p. 298. All references hereafter will be by page in the text.

23. Krutch, *Samuel Johnson* (New York: Henry Holt, 1944) p. vii.

24. James L. Clifford, *Young Sam Johnson* (New York: McGraw-Hill, 1955), p. 121 and n.; *The Correspondence and Other Papers of James Boswell Relating to the Making of the "Life of Johnson,"* ed. Marshall Waingrow (The Research Edition of the Private Papers of James Boswell, 2) (New York: McGraw-Hill, 1969), p. 57.

25. Johnson, *Works*, X, 370.

26. James L. Clifford, *Dictionary Johnson: Samuel Johnson's Middle Years* (New York: McGraw-Hill, 1979), p. 96.

27. Johnson, *Works*, II, 312.

28. *Biography as an Art: Selected Criticism 1560–1960*, ed. James L. Clifford (New York: Oxford Univ. Press, 1962), p. xvii.

29. James L. Clifford, *From Puzzles to Portraits: Problems of a Literary Biographer* (Chapel Hill, N.C.: Univ. of North Carolina Press, 1970), p. 85.

30. Clifford, *Dictionary Johnson*, pp. 71–72; Bate, *Samuel Johnson*, p. 233.

31. Clifford, *Young Sam*, pp. 323–24.

32. Bate, *Samuel Johnson*, p. 276. All references hereafter will be by page in the text.

33. Clifford, *Young Sam*, p. 86.

34. Clifford, *Young Sam*, p. 125.

35. Bate, *The Burden of the Past and the English Poet* (Cambridge, Mass.: Harvard Univ. Press, 1970).

36. "The Double Tradition of Dr. Johnson," in *Johnson Agonistes and Other Essays* (Berkeley and Los Angeles: Univ. of California Press, 1965), p. 157; originally published in *ELH*, 18 (1951), 90–106.

37. "Johnson and Augustanism," in *The Common Pursuit* (Harmondsworth: Penguin Books, 1962), p. 97; originally published as "Doctor Johnson," *Kenyon Review*, 8 (1946), 637–57.

38. James L. Clifford and Donald J. Greene, *Samuel Johnson: A Survey and Bibliography of Critical Studies* (Minneapolis: Univ. of Minnesota Press, 1970), p. 13. This book is of great value for anyone interested in the subject of biographies of Johnson.

39. C. E. Vulliamy, *Ursa Major: A Study of Dr. Johnson and His Friends* (London: Michael Joseph, 1946), pp. 315–16.

40. *Dr. Johnson* concludes with a comparison between Johnson and Louis-François Veuillot as kindred spirits. Veuillot has been characterized by Sir Paul Harvey and J. E. Heseltine as "probably the most militant and virulent Roman Catholic writer of the 19th century." This is an institutional English judgment—*The Oxford Companion to French Literature* (Oxford: Clarendon Press, 1959), p. 742—but it does show how lives of Johnson can give us the strangest of political bedfellows.

41. Krutch, *More Lives*, p. viii.

42. See Donald J. Greene, "Reflections on a Literary Anniversary" *Queen's Quarterly*, 70 (1963), 198–208, in which he fantasizes that Johnson and Boswell never met, and "'Tis a Pretty Book, Mr. Boswell, but—," *Georgia Review*, 32 (1978), 17–43, in which he expands on the opening allusion—"You must not call it a biography."

BERTRAM H. DAVIS

2 · *Johnson's 1764 Visit to Percy*

1

The parish register of St. Peter and St. Paul in the tiny Northampton-shire village of Easton Maudit contains a memorable entry for the year 1764: "Members, London Club visited here & attended Divine Service in Church. Johnson, Goldsmith, Sir J. Reynolds, Garrick, Shen-stone. also invited to the Mansion. Guests visited the Mansion & the Library."[1] Inevitably, the entry stirs the imagination. What a friendly act of Johnson and his London clubmates to endure the tumbling of a nine-hour journey in order to sample the rural Midland delights with the Vicar of Easton Maudit, Thomas Percy, who had not yet published his landmark *Reliques of Ancient English Poetry* and was still four years away from admission to their select group. But the entry gives one pause as well. Why was David Garrick, still nine years away from admission, among them? And why was Joshua Reynolds designated "Sir J." when he was not to be knighted until 1769? And how extraor-dinary that they should be accompanied on a 1764 visit by the poet William Shenstone, who had been dead since February of 1763 and had not even been elected to Johnson's club posthumously.

The entry, obviously, is without authority, even if not totally wrong. Its dark ink and latter-day calligraphy, in contrast to the antique pal-lor of the entries around it, point unmistakably to some of the reg-ister's later pages, kept in the same hand and intense black by the Reverend F. T. B. Westlake, D.D., Vicar of Easton Maudit from 1927 until his death in 1935. His own imagination stirred, Dr. Westlake un-dertook to commemorate an actual Johnson visit, which he knew to have been a remarkable event in the life of his little parish. No doubt it was he who attached the explanatory label, equally without authority, to the front pew at the south side of the church:

> Dr S. Johnson
> O. Goldsmith.
> D. Garrick.

worshipped here in this pew
with other members of
the Garrick Club, London.[2]

Dr. Westlake even illustrated his 1929 book, *Fame and Faith*, with a photograph of Johnson and Goldsmith enjoying afternoon tea in the vicarage garden—cutout figures, of course, superimposed on an authentic background.[3]

It is quite possible that Johnson drank tea in Thomas Percy's garden. Perhaps he sat in the front pew of the church, on the south side. But there is no evidence that Goldsmith joined him at tea, or that Garrick sat beside him at church, or that they, Sir Joshua Reynolds, and William Shenstone were ever Percy's guests in Easton Maudit. When Johnson arrived at the vicarage on the evening of 25 June 1764, he was accompanied, not by fellow club members, but by his blind friend Miss Anna Williams and his servant Francis Barber. Miss Williams stayed until 7 August, and Johnson and Francis Barber until 18 August, for a total of nearly eight weeks, during which no other members of Johnson's club are known to have been present.[4]

The visit by Johnson—already renowned for the *Rambler*, the *Dictionary*, *Rasselas*, and numerous other works—was clearly an historic occasion for both Easton Maudit and its thirty-five-year-old vicar, and it is surprising that Percy, who had a keen sense of history, did not himself commemorate it with appropriate devotion. His pocket diary contains entries for only 36 of Johnson's 55 days, all of them terse notes and some no more exciting than "Mr. Clark called" (19 July) or "At home all day" (28 July). In letters written during or shortly after the visit, Percy provided one or two vivid glimpses of Johnson's activities, but at no time does he seem to have attempted a comprehensive memorial. Under the circumstances, it is understandable that an enthusiast like Dr. Westlake would reach into his imagination for details that his predecessor had neglected to supply.

Percy's comparative silence, it should be said, did not reflect any want of enthusiasm of his own. A friend of Johnson's since 1756, he had long awaited a Johnson visit, but Johnson's procrastination had been more than a match for Percy's persistence. On 22 May 1761, Percy informed William Shenstone that Johnson had been resolving to visit Easton Maudit for two years, and he cautioned Shenstone against counting upon a proposed Johnson visit to Shropshire: "he is no more formed for long Journeys than a Tortoise."[5] On 12 September 1761, Johnson graciously declined what may have been Percy's first formal invitation:

as I cannot perhaps see another coronation so conveniently as this [of George III on 22 September], and I may see many young Percies, I beg your pardon for staying till this great ceremony is over after which I purpose to pass some time with you.[6]

But two more years elapsed without the promised visit, and on 3 September 1763, Johnson wrote again to assure Percy of his desire to see him in his own "fields and groves" and to announce his intention to bring Shakespeare "and strike a stroke at him with your kind help."[7] Seven months later—on 10 April 1764—Percy's Northamptonshire friend Edward Lye wrote Percy from London that Johnson, whom Lye had called upon, "inquired much after you, and doth not despair of seeing Easton."[8]

For Johnson, these were years of frequent depression, when his edition of Shakespeare, first proposed in 1756, languished until he aroused himself at the prodding of close friends and his own conscience. "A kind of strange oblivion has overspread me," he noted in his diary only eleven days after Lye's letter to Percy.[9] But the Shakespeare edition was nearing completion, and Johnson, apparently eager for a change of scene, was ready to yield to Percy's entreaties. In late May and early June, when Percy was in London overseeing press runs for the nearly finished *Reliques of Ancient English Poetry*, they settled upon a time for the visit: Johnson, Percy wrote to his Cambridge friend Richard Farmer on 19 June following his return to Easton Maudit, is "almost to the end of the last volume of Shakespeare but I expect him down here next week."[10] On the morning of 25 June Johnson, Miss Williams, and Francis Barber left London and, because the coach did not go through Easton Maudit, were probably met by Percy in Newport Pagnell and driven the nine miles to the vicarage.

Easton Maudit's sixteenth-century vicarage was a neat thatched cottage of three stories standing obliquely across the narrow highway from the Church of St. Peter and St. Paul. To the north lay the seat of Percy's patron, Henry Yelverton, Earl of Sussex—the "Mansion" of Dr. Westlake's parish register fantasy—a Jacobean manor house with "stately Groves" that sheltered the vicarage garden from the northern winds. The garden, as Percy viewed it, spread "conveniently" and "beautifully" about the cottage, its terraces bordered by a little meadow that sloped down to a brook, "regular, smooth & always limpid."[11] In the nearby woods, Percy wrote, hare and doe would sometimes stop to gaze at the visitor, and on one occasion a nightingale entertained him for over an hour with "such strains of Harmony, as . . . any of the softest Squeakers of the Opera never came up to."[12]

No doubt the vicarage was a comfortable place, with two good-sized parlors and the kitchen on the ground floor, several bedrooms upstairs, and two garrets which were probably servants' quarters. Percy's successor as vicar, Robert Nares, described two of the bedrooms as "really capital,"[13] but how the rooms were assigned in June 1764, is not apparent. The tradition persists among today's villagers that Johnson slept in the third-floor bedroom overlooking the back garden. If, as would seem likely, Johnson and Miss Williams occupied the two "capital" bedrooms, of which the third-floor room was one, the Percys had, of course, to withdraw into less than capital quarters where family privacy must have been at least as much a burden as a blessing. For by the summer of 1764, the "young Percies," if not yet many, had grown in number to include Anne Cleiveland Percy, aged four; Barbara Percy, aged three; and Henry Percy, aged one and a half. However comfortable, a cottage with three toddlers underfoot, a blind woman inevitably groping in unfamiliar surroundings, and two scholars bringing major works to publication—one of whom was given to unusual hours for rising and retiring—must have taxed even the "gentleness and joy" for which Percy's wife Anne was to be remembered by one of her admirers.[14]

2

For Johnson and Percy the Easton Maudit sojourn was both a work session and a holiday. The last volume of Johnson's edition of Shakespeare was in the press, and proof sheets of *Othello* arrived regularly for Johnson's inspection.[15] Percy had just finished transposing volumes one and three of the *Reliques* and was busy with a number of projects, including an edition of the *Spectator* and important odds and ends for the *Reliques*. Thus the nearly eight weeks were filled with fewer social activities than might have been expected. Edward Lye was the first and most frequent visitor. He came from his rectory a mile and a half away at Yardley Hastings to greet Percy's guests on the very evening of their arrival, and he returned two evenings later for tea and several times thereafter for tea or dinner. No doubt Lye, the editor of Junius's *Etymologicum Anglicanum* who was then at work compiling an Anglo-Saxon dictionary, was a made-to-order friend for Johnson. On the second day, Percy's only recorded visitor was the London printer Edmund Allen, a Northamptonshire native, who would later be Johnson's landlord when Johnson moved to his final residence in Bolt Court. Subsequent dinner guests included Mrs. Percy's brother, William Gutteridge, on 30 July and, on 1 August, Percy's friend Captain John Orlebar, a commissioner of excise from Hinwick, just across the county line in Bedfordshire.

More than three weeks of Johnson's stay were to elapse before Percy recorded any visits to Midland friends. On 18 July, he and Johnson dined at Ecton with Ambrose Isted, whose family was to be joined with Percy's in 1795 through the marriage of Samuel Isted and Barbara Percy.[16] On 21 July, Percy and Johnson visited Captain Orlebar at Hinwick, and on 23 July Percy and his wife introduced Johnson at the public day at Castle Ashby, the resplendent estate of the Earl of Northampton only a couple of miles from Easton Maudit. Miss Williams joined the other three for an "airing" by the neighboring village of Bozeat on 25 July, and two days later the same group visited Lord Halifax's estate at Horton, where they also had dinner. On 4 August, Percy and Johnson dined in Northampton with Richard Backwell, Member of Parliament for Northampton from 1755 to 1761 and the godfather of Anne Cleiveland Percy. Just a week after Miss Williams's 7 August departure, Percy's brother Anthony arrived from London and Mrs. Percy's sister and brother-in-law came from Bozeat to join the family at tea, and on the next day the three Percys and Johnson drove to Bozeat for a venison dinner.[17]

On the face of it, this summer activity would hardly qualify as exciting entertainment for Percy's distinguished guest.[18] If Johnson, as he declared to Boswell, found "the full tide of human existence" at Charing Cross, one wonders what he would have had to say for Easton Maudit, a village with scarcely a hundred people in it.[19] But Johnson was an adaptable guest, and meager as Percy's fare might seem, it was not without variety and substance. Richard Backwell could have fed Johnson's taste for politics, and the learned Edward Lye his linguistic interests. Percy's own interests were almost unlimited, and he was eager to explore them with his friends. Johnson, who loved coach travel, probably enjoyed rattling about the countryside in Percy's chaise, even if only for an airing by Bozeat. The great estates at Castle Ashby and Horton would have added zest to their rambles, and even the less imposing manors of Ambrose Isted at Ecton and Captain Orlebar at Hinwick were showpieces worth taking a curious and observant man to. At the vicarage itself, one of the terraces in the back garden has traditionally been known as "Johnson's Walk," and it seems likely that Johnson, who delighted in watering his tiny London garden, would have found pleasure in Percy's trim and green expanse. One wonders also whether he ventured into the nearby woods to be stared at by hare and doe, or to be serenaded by Percy's operatic nightingales.

Indispensable though it is, one misses in Percy's diary the bold strokes and varied colors that would have transformed its ink tracings into a vivid gallery of portraits, landscapes, and dramatic scenes. Percy simply had other thoughts. A working holiday for Percy and Johnson meant writing; for Percy, it also meant church, community, and household duties. "I have for these 3 months past hardly had time to breathe," he wrote to the Welsh scholar Evan Evans on 23 July, and perhaps that fact accounts for the paucity and brevity of his diary entries.[20] Indeed, the number of entries crossed out or moved from one day to another suggests that he sometimes waited so long to bring the diary up to date that his memory of specific events had grown dim.

During Johnson's first week, Percy had to devote time to haymaking on 27 June and to a turnpike meeting the next day. The diary does not reveal whether Johnson joined him in either activity, but as one who "well understood . . . the management of a farm,"[21] Johnson would presumably have welcomed the opportunity to observe Percy in his glebe lands, if not actually to assist with the haymaking process. Doubtless it is too much to hope that they enjoyed the hospitality shown to Percy in his bachelor years, when some of the village ladies came out to help him, and "when tir'd with ye Heat & Toil of the day," as Percy wrote his cousin William Cleiveland, "upon no other velvet Couch than a soft & fragrant Hay-Cock, . . . we sat down to drink Tea, and spent the afternoon in the most lively & chatty manner."[22]

The first literary activity noted in the diary is dated 29 June, when Percy was preparing the glossary to volume one (originally volume three) of the *Reliques*. He finished the glossary on 17 July and must have hurried it off to his London printer, for on 21 August, three days after Johnson's return to London, he sent the proof sheets to Sir David Dalrymple in Edinburgh with a plea for help in removing the "obscurities." Johnson, he wrote, "gives them up as inexplicable: and as he has a good deal of *Glossarizing* knowledge, it will be some honour to succeed, after he has given them over."[23]

Percy was also at work on an edition of Addison and Steele's *Spectator*, for on 25 May he had contracted with the publisher Jacob Tonson to have the first volume ready for the press within a month and the remaining seven by Christmas.[24] A 19 July diary entry, which he later inked over, perhaps because he was uncertain where it belonged, shows him correcting proof—"Finished 1 sheet of Spectator"—and entries for 6 and 11 August, similarly inked over, suggest that he was already well into the second volume. At the home of Henry and Hester Thrale on 3 April 1773, Johnson spoke approvingly of the still unpublished edition, and stated that "he had communicated all that he knew that could throw light upon 'The Spectator.'" The most likely occasion for Johnson to assist Percy was his 1764 holiday in Easton Maudit, and Percy did in fact record in one of his books an anecdote of Joseph Addison and the poet Edmund Smith which Johnson related to him on 21 July.[25]

Johnson also helped Percy with a minor project unmentioned in the diary, but doubtless undertaken during the first days of Johnson's visit. In December Percy had spent almost a week assisting his friend James Grainger to revise *The Sugar-Cane*, a poem that Grainger had written in the West Indies and brought back to England in manuscript late in 1763. The poem was published on 26 May 1764, and Percy, eager to serve the friend who had introduced him to Johnson in 1756, sought to enlist Johnson's aid in writing a review. This was not an easy task. A curious invocation in a manuscript version of the poem had aroused considerable mirth when it was read aloud to a gathering at the home of Joshua Reynolds early in 1764: "Now, Muse, let's sing of rats." "Percy had a mind to make a great thing of Grainger's rats," Johnson later said to Boswell. But worse than that was Grainger's implicit acceptance in the poem of the detested institution of slavery. In the end, Johnson consented—"in jest"—and, though he told Boswell that he only helped Percy, the review's critical sections are clearly in Johnson's style and have survived in a manuscript in Johnson's hand.[26] Perhaps Percy selected the illustrative quotations and prepared a first draft for Johnson's revision. The review, in any event, must have been sent to the *London Chronicle* toward the end of Johnson's first week at Easton Maudit, since the *Chronicle* published its first installment of the review in its issue of 3–5 July.

On 1 July, Johnson's first Sunday, Percy conducted services in the morning at Easton Maudit and, in the evening, at Wilby, a village about ten miles away where he had been rector since 1757. Johnson apparently did not accompany him to Wilby, but it is reasonable to assume that he attended the morning service with the rest of the Percy household, and perhaps had his first introduction to Percy's fellow villagers. He would also have witnessed the baptism of Beatrice Grant, daughter of parishioners Thomas and Juliana Grant. Percy selected for the occasion a sermon on charity that he had first preached at the little Shropshire church of Tasley in 1752, when he was just starting out as a curate, and its central theme should have had a special appeal for Johnson, who had expressed a somewhat similar view in the fourth essay for his *Idler*: "the transcendent Excellence of the Christian Religion," said Percy, "[is that it] makes cordial Charity and Love the great distinction & mark of its genuine Votaries."[27]

After the first of July, Percy's diary is blank for two weeks, although he noted near his 5 August entry that on 4 July he "drew a bill for six pounds at one month after date for Mrs Woolston on Brother." Percy's brother Anthony was then living in London, but both seem to have met in Bridgnorth, Shropshire, no later than 4 July to be with their father in what proved to be his last illness. In a letter written to his wife from Bridgnorth on 6 July, Percy asked her "to tell Mr Johnson that I went this day to inquire after the remains of Mr Higgs the old Clergyman I told him of."[28] Notations on two of Percy's manuscript sermons reveal that they were preached at Bridgnorth on 8 July 1764, one at St. Leonard's and the other at St. Mary's. And in one of his biographical manuscripts, Percy recorded that his father, Arthur Lowe Percy—twelve days short of turning sixty—died of dysentery and dropsy on 22 July, "a few days after he had with great devotion received the Eucharist at my own hands."[29]

Percy had returned to Easton Maudit by Sunday, 15 July, however, with the younger Anthony apparently remaining in Bridgnorth to look after their father. Perhaps the press of time was responsible for Percy's preaching at Easton Maudit that Sunday the same sermon he had preached at St. Mary's the Sunday before and, at Wilby, the same sermon he had preached at St. Leonard's. The St. Leonard's-Wilby sermon, which Johnson probably did not hear, was a further discourse on charity, based upon 1 Corinthians 14.[30] The St. Mary's-Easton Maudit sermon was a funeral oration on the vanity of human wishes, an obvious reflection of Percy's distress as he saw his father's life slipping from him, and delivered no doubt with a consciousness of Johnson's presence and of works in which Johnson himself had addressed the same theme.[31]

On the next day, Percy broke the silence of his diary by noting that he corrected a proof sheet of his *Key to the New Testament*, which was to be published in 1766. On 24 July, he began reading to Johnson his translation of Paul Henri Mallet's *Introduction à l'Histoire de Dannemarc*, to be published in 1770 as *Northern Antiquities*. Presumably Percy was unaware how Johnson felt about being read to. Boswell notes that, when Bennet Langton read Robert Dodsley's *Cleone* aloud to him, Johnson "turned his face to the back of his chair, and put himself into various attitudes, which marked his uneasiness"; and when Boswell offered to read some legal papers to him in 1772, Johnson stopped him with "No, Sir, I can read quicker than I can hear."[32] One can thus imagine Johnson's dismay on 26 July when Percy, with Johnson and Miss Williams as his audience, read again from Mallet and then picked up his recently published translation of *The Song of Solomon* and read aloud from that also.

On 29 July, Percy wrote to Richard Farmer that Johnson "goes away for 2 or 3 weeks, during which he is to leave his friend Mrs. Williams with us, and then he will return to spend some time with us again."[33] Percy gave no reason for Johnson's leaving. But on 27 July, Percy had received from his brother an account of their father's death, and with the family in mourning Johnson may have thought it a good time to leave it less encumbered and turn to a problem that had been in his thoughts before he left London for Easton Maudit. On 22 May, he had written to his old friend John Taylor to console him for a mind "harried" and a spirit "weakened," and he had suggested that he and Taylor might spend some part of the summer together at a private retreat.[34] At Easton Maudit, Johnson had already traveled about half the distance from London to Taylor's home in Derbyshire.

Whatever his reasons, Johnson changed his mind and remained at

Easton Maudit, where the assistance to Percy for which the visit is best remembered was still to be given. The dedication of the *Reliques* to the Countess of Northumberland required a tact and eloquence of which Johnson was a master, and in mid-August he took what Percy had apparently begun and turned it into the graceful dedication of the published work. His authorship, however, was not revealed until 1791, when Boswell, having been persuaded by Percy to cancel a page of the *Life of Johnson* alluding to it, neglected to delete the relevant index reference. Percy himself acknowledged Johnson's role in a letter to Dr. Robert Anderson dated 18 June 1800: "though not wholly written by him, [the dedication] owed its finest strokes to the superior pen of Dr Johnson."[35]

"When I have honestly confessed this," Percy continued, "I hope I shall be believed, when I declare, that I do not recollect that a single expression, sentiment, or observation of any kind besides, was suggested by him in the whole three volumes." There is no reason to dispute Percy's recollection, but it obscures a pervasive if inconspicuous Johnson role in *Reliques*. Johnson was the first to suggest publication of the folio manuscript of old ballads and romances that Percy had rescued from destruction at the home of Humphrey Pitt of Shifnal in Shropshire, where the maids were using it to light the parlor fire; and he had assisted Percy in securing a publisher for the *Reliques*, which had its beginnings in the manuscript. As a learned and judicious critic, he made his influence felt even if it was not turned upon specific problems of text and annotation. Percy's consultant in the development of the *Reliques* had, to be sure, been William Shenstone, on whose advice he depended very heavily. But after Shenstone's death in April 1763, Johnson—"my oracle," as Percy described him to Richard Farmer[36] in November 1764—must have assumed a new importance, and Percy's need for Johnson's advice and assistance probably helps to account for his repeated pressing until Johnson scheduled the Easton Maudit visit in June 1764.

The part of the *Reliques* for which Johnson was most likely to have provided specific assistance was the essay "On the Ancient Metrical Romances," with which Percy introduced his third volume. As early as 9 January 1758, Percy had written to Shenstone of Johnson's "great acquaintance with all our old English Romances etc of which kind of reading he is uncommonly fond."[37] At Easton Maudit, Johnson selected for his leisure reading Percy's folio copy of the old Spanish romance *Felixmarte of Hircania*, which he read from beginning to end,[38] and he also read Evan Evans's recently published *Some Specimens of the Poetry of the Antient Welsh Bards*.[39] In the summer of 1764, Percy's essay was still subject to revision—he did not correct proof of it until 1 November[40]—and it would have been natural for him to discuss the subject of romances with Johnson, and for Johnson to peruse what Percy had written about it. Perhaps Johnson suggested no emendations. But Percy was not given to imitating the Johnson style, and a few sentences that are conspicuous for the balance, antithesis, and precise detail in which Johnson delighted would seem to reflect Percy's awareness of Johnson's presence if not Johnson's actual correcting hand. "Thus began," goes one of them,

> stories of adventures with giants and dragons, and witches and enchanters, and all the monstrous extravagances of wild imagination, unguided by judgment, and uncorrected by art.

A few pages later, romances are said to be "far more spirited and entertaining than the tedious allegories of Gower, or the dull and prolix legends of Lydgate."[41]

In considering Percy's assistance to Johnson, one might go back to 1763 and Johnson's announced purpose to "strike a stroke" at Shakespeare with Percy's help. The statement was not mere flattery. An ardent student of the drama as well as of poetry, Percy had read close to two hundred early Restoration plays in preparing his "New Key" to the Duke of Buckingham's *Rehearsal*;[42] and he had prepared for the *Reliques* an entire section devoted to ballads that illustrate Shakespeare, as well as an introductory essay "On the Origin of the English Stage." Johnson, in fact, had expressed a desire to see Percy's essay.[43] The half dozen notes that Percy contributed to Johnson's edition, probably during the Easton Maudit visit, call for no special attention. But Percy brought to Johnson's work something of the comprehensive knowledge and interest that Johnson brought to Percy's, and it is reasonable to assume that the opportunity to have Percy join in a final stroke at Shakespeare was a motivation for Johnson's visit, just as having Johnson at hand for the final touches to the *Reliques* was a motivation for Percy's invitation.

Except for the writing of the dedication, Johnson's last days at Easton Maudit seem to have been no more eventful than the first. On 1 August, he prepared a note for Percy stating that the architect Sir William Chambers, author of *Designs of Chinese Buildings, Furniture, Dresses, etc.*, had confessed to him that his alleged conversations with a Chinese named Lepqua were apocryphal.[44] Barbara Percy's third birthday was on 3 August, but Percy gave no indication how it was celebrated. On Sunday, 5 August, he took Johnson to Wilby for the evening service,[45] and on 7 August he drove Miss Williams to Horton, where she caught the stagecoach, presumably for London. On the morning of 12 August, he preached another sermon on charity at Easton Maudit, and in the evening he escorted Johnson to church and a burial at nearby Piddington, where, Percy later recalled, Johnson rewarded a villager's kindness more handsomely than was expected.[46] On 16 August, Percy read some of Pope—*with* Johnson, not *to* him.

Before he left Easton Maudit, Johnson presented Percy with two gifts. One was his inkhorn, a bulbous, long-necked container six and a half inches tall and, Percy noted, "very convenient for . . . [Johnson], who often wrote standing."[47] The other was the *Nouvel Abregé Chronologique de l'histoire de France* (1747), which he had brought from London to read during the 25 June coach trip north.[48] On 18 August, Percy drove Johnson and Francis Barber to Newport Pagnell, and from there they took the berlin back to London.

3

Johnson wrote promptly after his return to thank the Percys for their hospitality.[49] Doubtless he was pleased to be back in London after such a long visit, and the Percys to have their home to themselves again. "A man who stays a week with another," Johnson once remarked to Boswell, "makes him a slave for a week,"[50] and Percy's impatience with the constraints of nearly eight weeks occasionally showed through. "Ever since I was in London," he wrote to Richard Farmer on 29 July, "I have been either hurried extremely, or have had the interruptions of company, or have been absent from home." But even the inconveniences of crowded quarters could not keep him from expressing the hope that Farmer might visit Easton Maudit before Johnson was gone: "If you will excuse the very indifferent accommodations you will be exposed to, in consequence of their filling my little house, so as to leave me never a room entirely vacant for an accidental friend, I wish you could give me your company while he is here."[51] Percy was obviously proud of his guest.

But what of Johnson's reaction to the visit? Perhaps the best answer to this question is to be found in the sheer length of his stay. The hapless Dick Shifter in Johnson's *Idler* 71 cut short his country idyll on the fifth day and retreated to his sanctuary in the Temple, though of course Dick had illusions about the country that Johnson was quite free of. Nor did he have such a host and hostess as Thomas and Anne Percy, who had done much to make Johnson's sojourn varied and comfortable. They had given him the opportunity to hasten his long awaited edition of Shakespeare to a conclusion. They had provided him with company and modest diversions, including an extended relief from the depression that made his life often such a torment. Percy could talk from a full mind: anecdotes flowed from him "like one of the brooks here," Boswell commented to Johnson approvingly during their tour in Scotland.[52] Doubtless Johnson had also found time to enjoy the Percy children, as he generally did in the families of his friends.[53] "After 165 years," wrote Dr. Westlake, "the shaft of the swing on which Dr. Percy's children flew high and low on the lawn remains to-day and is embedded deep in the heart of the great tree under which Dr. Johnson often took tea."[54] It is not easy to take issue with a man who can see into the heart of a great tree.

Joseph Cradock's wife was so fearful of Johnson that she wanted advance notice of an intended Johnson visit to Leicestershire so that she could leave town before he arrived. But Mrs. Percy assured her that Johnson was "by no means so formidable as he had been represented; for that he had once staid at Easton Maudit . . . and . . . was perfectly quiet and contented." To exemplify his "occasional politeness," she recalled that one morning, when her husband announced that he had arranged some books for Johnson's perusal after breakfast, "Johnson most courteously replied, 'No, Sir, I shall first attend upon Mrs. Percy to feed her ducks.'"[55]

If Cradock's assessment of Mrs. Percy was justified—that she was "without one jarring atom form'd"[56]—she must herself have been a major contributor to Johnson's peace and contentment at Easton Maudit. And with Percy away for a week or more attending a dying father, Johnson would have had an unusual opportunity to observe her, and perhaps to help her discharge some of her husband's household responsibilities in addition to her own. That he left Easton Maudit with much admiration for Mrs. Percy became very clear when he somewhat impoliticly compared her to her husband during a visit to Richard Farmer at Cambridge in February, 1765. "I can excuse . . . [Johnson's] *Dogmatisms* and *Prejudices*," Farmer wrote to Percy on 25 February;

> but he throws about rather too much of what some *Frenchman* calls the *Essence* of BUT: in plain *English*, he seems to have something to *except* in every man's Character. *Hurd* for instance comes off badly, and *Shenstone* still worse: he pitys *You* for your opinion of the latter. indeed what he takes from *you*, he gives to your better half—M[rs] Percy's judgment is, he assures me (where there has been an equall opportunity of information) much to be prefer'd to her husband's![57]

Percy replied, graciously, that he was glad that what Johnson took from him he gave to his wife, but he must have been stung by Johnson's invidious comment. "*I don't wonder,*" he informed Farmer, "*that I have greatly suffered in his opinion, for the respect I have expressed for my friend Shenstone: I know very well he can never forgive me for mentioning him and Shenstone in the same Page.*"[58]

Perhaps Johnson did resent being coupled with Shenstone in the Preface to the *Reliques,* when Percy explained his decision to edit the old ballads: "At length the importunity of his [Percy's] friends prevailed, and he could refuse nothing to such judges as the author of the RAMBLER, and the late Mr. SHENSTONE."[59] But Percy's analysis seems altogether too simple. His show of respect for Shenstone was not the sole barrier to a more favorable Johnson opinion of Percy's judgment. Their differences about Grainger's *Sugar-Cane* were another. Johnson, in fact, might never have joined in the review if he had not been a guest in Percy's house, and the somewhat severe strictures on *The Sugar-Cane* that he later prepared for the *Critical Review* seem almost to reflect a troubled conscience for the bland comments that he submitted to the *London Chronicle* for Percy's sake.[60] In nearly eight weeks, moreover, Johnson must have had countless opportunities to assess the relative judgments of his host and hostess in matters relating to their children, relations, servants, guests, visits abroad, and domestic arrangements, and the Percys would hardly have proved a unique family if an astute visitor had concluded in that time that the wife's judgment was often to be preferred to the husband's.

Johnson was not the only friend who intruded a "but" into his evaluation of Percy's character. Joseph Cradock, who looked upon Percy as "a steady friend," described him as "a most pleasing companion." But, he added, "there was a violence in his temper which could not always be controlled." Cradock also saw Percy—"when in good mood"—as "one of the most entertaining companions he had known."[61] Eight weeks were a long time for four adults and three young children to be crowded into a modest vicarage, and perhaps Percy's temper or changing moods required the occasional moderating influence of a wife who was all gentleness and joy, or were endured by a guest who seems to have remained uncharacteristically calm and contented throughout his visit. I "never found . . . [Johnson] more cheerful or conversible" than he was in 1764, Percy recalled some years later.[62] Johnson in *Rasselas* had the wise Imlac counsel the astronomer to "fly to business" and intelligent female companionship when his mind was troubled,[63] and plainly the Easton Maudit interlude supplied the often troubled Johnson with both. If Percy, with his inexhaustible resources of knowledge and anecdote, set the intellectual tone for his vicarage, Mrs. Percy, who knew well how to manage her household, would seem to have infused it with her own good spirit, and their combined talents seem to have provided Johnson with a summer retreat very much to his liking.

Johnson's doubts about Percy's judgment, it should be said, did not interrupt their friendship, even though in the long run they must have stood in the way of the friendship's maturing into the intimate relationship that Johnson shared with John Taylor, Sir Joshua Reynolds, Sir John Hawkins, James Boswell, and a few others. In November 1764, Percy was back in London to present the dedication copy of the

Reliques of Ancient English Poetry to Elizabeth Percy, Countess of North-umberland, and Johnson was the first person he dined with after his arrival and one of the last he called upon before he left. On the evening following the presentation on 22 November, Percy, Johnson, Goldsmith, and others gathered at Edmund Allen's for what was probably a celebration of the official launching of the *Reliques* in high places. With the blessing of Johnson's dedication, the *Reliques* was on its way. And Percy was on his way too, soon to be established in a noble family where the seeds of his social and clerical ambitions would find a rich soil. It is fortunate that Johnson did not postpone his visit to the Percys beyond 1764, for there were no more such summers at Easton Maudit. Thereafter Percy was a summer resident at Alnwick Castle in Northumberland, and bit by bit his scholarly activity gave way to the demands of a clerical life.

NOTES

1. The last name in the register is somewhat blurred, but Shenstone was clearly intended. For opportunities to visit the vicarage and to study the register, I am much indebted to the present vicarage owners, Mr. and Mrs. Eric Brook.

2. Johnson's club, founded in 1764, was known initially as simply "the Club" and later as the Literary Club. The Garrick Club was not established until 1831, 47 years after Johnson's death.

In his article "The Country Parson as Research Scholar: Thomas Percy, 1760–1770" (*Papers of the Bibliographical Society of America*, 53 [1959], pp. 219–39), Cleanth Brooks noted the discrepancies in the parish register relating to Reynolds and Garrick, but, probably because he was working from a photographic copy, was unable to decipher Shenstone's name or determine that the entry was not in Percy's hand.

3. Rev. F. T. B. Westlake, D.D., *Fame and Faith* (London: Skeffington, 1929), opp. p. 22. Inevitably errors carrying the authority of a parish register and a commemorative label have been repeated: "Among his [Percy's] visitors were Shenstone and Garrick, Goldsmith, and the great Doctor and his friend Miss Williams" (*The Victoria History of the County of Northampton* [London, 1937], IV, 12); "His [Percy's] house . . . was visited by Goldsmith . . . and by Garrick and Dr. Johnson, who are commemorated by a brass in the front pew of the church where they worshipped with other members of the Garrick Club" (*The Oxford Literary Guide to the British Isles* [Oxford: Clarendon Press, 1977], p. 94).

4. Unless otherwise noted, dates cited in this article are taken from Percy's diary, BL Add. MS. 32,336. That Francis Barber accompanied Johnson to Easton Maudit was stated by Percy in a letter to James Boswell dated 29 February 1788 (*The Correspondence and Other Papers of James Boswell Relating to the Making of the "Life of Johnson"*, ed. Marshall Waingrow [New York: McGraw-Hill, 1969], p. 268).

5. *The Percy Letters, VII: The Correspondence of Thomas Percy & William Shenstone*, ed. Cleanth Brooks (New Haven: Yale Univ. Press, 1977), p. 98.

6. *Letters* I, 135–36.

7. Ibid., I, 160–61.

8. BL Add. MS. 32,325, f. 212.

9. Johnson, *Works*, I, 77.

10. *The Percy Letters*, II: *The Correspondence of Thomas Percy & Richard Farmer*, ed. Cleanth Brooks (Baton Rouge: Louisiana State Univ. Press, 1946), p. 75.

11. Letter to William Cleiveland, 24 March 1757, BL Add. MS. 32,333, f. 13. An indispensable source of information about Easton Maudit is Sir Giles Isham's *Easton Mauduit and the Parish Church of St. Peter and St. Paul* (Northampton: Northamptonshire Record Society, 1961). "Mauduit" was the usual eighteenth-century spelling.

12. Letter to Thomas Apperley, 2 June [1756], Hyde Collection. Quoted by permission of Mrs. Donald F. Hyde.

13. Letter to the future Mrs. Nares, 23 June 1782, Old Vicarage, Easton Maudit. The letter has been printed in Anne Baker, "The Old Vicarage Easton Maudit: The Home of Mr. and Mrs. Eric Brook," *Northamptonshire & Bedfordshire Life* (January, 1978), p. 18. Detailed information on the parish, including the vicarage, is contained in a manuscript extract from the "Register of the Lord Bishop of Peterborough" in the Muniments Room at Christ Church, Oxford.

14. Joseph Cradock, *Literary and Miscellaneous Memoirs* (London, 1828), I, 239.

15. *The Percy Letters*, II, 76–77.

16. Another of Ambrose Isted's guests on 18 July was a Mr. Ekins, perhaps Jeffery Ekins, who, 18 years later, was to strike the bargain with Percy whereby Percy became Bishop of Dromore and Ekins assumed Percy's office as Dean of Carlisle.

17. Mrs. Percy's elder sister Mary married the Rev. Samuel Edwards, who officiated at the wedding of Thomas and Anne Percy on 24 April 1759. At this time he was curate of Bozeat, about a mile from Easton Maudit.

18. Percy's diary contains no reference to a visit to the Earl of Sussex's manor house, where Percy could have been expected to introduce Johnson both as a matter of courtesy and for its literary treasures. Since the omission could hardly have been an oversight, it is likely that the Earl was not in residence at Easton Maudit during Johnson's visit.

19. Boswell, *Life*, II, 337.

20. *The Percy Letters*, V: *The Correspondence of Thomas Percy & Evan Evans*, ed. Aneirin Lewis (Baton Rouge: Louisiana State Univ. Press, 1957), p. 95.

21. Sir John Hawkins, *The Life of Samuel Johnson, LL. D.* (London, 1787), p. 469.

22. Letter to William Cleiveland, 25 June 1757, BL Add. MS. 32,333, f. 16.

23. *The Percy Letters*, IV: *The Correspondence of Thomas Percy & David Dalrymple, Lord Hailes*, ed. A. F. Falconer (Baton Rouge: Louisiana State Univ. Press, 1954), p. 85. Dalrymple, a Scottish judge and writer, supplied a number of Scottish ballads for the *Reliques*.

24. *Illustrations of the Literary History of the Eighteenth Century*, VI, ed. John Bowyer Nichols (1831; rpt. New York: Kraus, 1966), p. 560.

25. Percy recorded the anecdote on the flyleaf of a copy of Smith's *Works* now among Percy's books at the Queen's University of Belfast (*The Library of Thomas Percy*, London, Sotheby, 23 June 1969, Lot 489). Johnson later used the anecdote in his life of Smith.

26. *Life*, II, 532–34; *Times Literary Supplement*, 13 August 1938, p. 531, and 16 February 1951, p. 108. The manuscript is in the Hyde Collection.

27. Bodley MS. Percy d. 3, f. 246.

28. D. M. Barratt, "The Diaries, Sermons, and Other Papers of Richard and John Higgs, 1677–1754," *Bodleian Library Record*, 4 (September, 1953), 273–77. John Higgs, curate of Quatford near Bridgnorth, had frequently substituted for Percy when Percy was curate of Astley Abbots and Tasley in Shropshire from 1751–56. Higgs died in 1763.

29. BL Add. MS. 32,326, f. 22. Percy's mother had died in 1760.

30. Bodley MS. Percy d. 3, ff. 259–72.

31. The sermon is in the collection of Mr. Kenneth Balfour.

It is not clear why Percy neither remained in Bridgnorth until his father's death nor returned to it after his death. He obviously felt strongly his obligation as host, but it is hard to believe that he would have placed it ahead of his obligation to a parent. Percy took his family ties seriously—indeed, with a religious conviction becoming his clerical office. His biographical account of his father, moreover, shows him to have been warmly attached to his father's memory. Under the circumstances, it seems likely that he returned to Easton Maudit from Bridgnorth believing that his father would be safe for the time being in his brother's care, and with the understanding that his brother would send for him if his father's condition required his presence. As it turned out, Anthony did not get word to him until 27 July, five days after their father's death.

32. *Life*, II, 156; IV, 20.

33. *The Percy Letters*, II, 77. Although Percy usually refers to Anna Williams as Miss during this period, he occasionally calls her Mrs., as in this letter. Johnson also called her Mrs. Williams in his letter to Percy announcing their forthcoming visit to Easton Maudit.

34. *Letters*, I, 167–68. Another possibility is that Johnson was proposing to visit Joshua Reynolds. He wrote to Reynolds from Easton Maudit in a letter of uncertain date (he misdated it 19 August, one day after he returned to London) to offer Reynolds his company if that would "exhilarate the languor of a slow recovery" from Reynolds's recent illness (*Letters*, I, 169).

35. Robert Anderson, *The Life of Samuel Johnson*, 3rd ed. (London, 1815), p. 309n. Percy's diary entry for 13 August is typically unrevealing: "Preparing dedication of old Ballads."

36. *The Percy Letters*, II, 79.

37. Ibid., VII, 10.

38. *Life*, I, 49.

39. *The Percy Letters*, V, 95–96.

40. Reading proof of the essay was one of Percy's last tasks before he presented the dedication copy to the Countess of Northumberland.

41. *Reliques of Ancient English Poetry* (London, 1765), III, iii and ix. The conclusion of another sentence on p. ix is similar in style: "antiquaries . . . have always fastidiously rejected the old poetical Romances, because founded on fictitious or popular subjects, while they have been careful to grub up every petty fragment of the most dull and insipid rhimist, whose merit it was to deform morality, or obscure true history."

42. Northamptonshire Record Office, Box X 1079 E (S) 1218. Percy's notes in the British Library's interleaved copy of Gerard Langbaine's *Account of the English Dramatick Poets* (1691) show that he had been reading Langbaine in the spring of 1764.

43. James Grainger, Letter to Percy, 6 April 1764, *Illustrations of the Literary History of the Eighteenth Century*, VII (London, 1848), 287.

44. The note is in Percy's copy of his 1762 work, *Miscellaneous Pieces Relating to the Chinese*, now in the Bodleian Library ("Johnson, Percy, and Sir William Chambers," *Bodleian Library Record*, 4 [December 1953], 291–92).

45. I have not found the manuscript of Percy's Wilby sermon.

46. Bodley MSS. Percy d. 3, ff. 280–95; d. 11, f. 8. This seems to be the incident that Boswell recorded following a meeting of the Club on 24 March 1775 (*Boswell: The Ominous Years 1774–1776*, ed. Charles Ryskamp and Frederick A. Pottle [New York: McGraw-Hill, 1966], p. 95). At the Club, Johnson and Percy argued at some length whether or not Johnson was generous—Percy insisting that he was—when he gave a man half a crown for a pint of wine. Boswell placed the man in Percy's parish, but perhaps Johnson and Percy were not explicit about the location.

47. The inkhorn and Percy's descriptive note are in the collection of Mr. Kenneth Balfour.

48. *The Library of Thomas Percy*, Lot 273.

49. *Letters*, I, 169 [20 August 1764].

50. *Life*, IV, 222.

51. *The Percy Letters*, II, 76–77. When Percy recorded Miss Williams's departure from Easton Maudit on 7 August, he appended a brief note to the diary entry: "NB. Mr. Johnson stays with us still." He later inked over the word "still," perhaps because it seemed to imply some irritation with Johnson's continued presence.

52. *Life*, V, 255.

53. Without citing any date, Percy noted that Johnson took time while he was at Easton Maudit to visit Captain Daniel Astle's daughter in Northampton (Bodley MS. d. 11, f. 8).

Croker, without specifying any time for the incident, stated that Johnson one day took Percy's little daughter on his knee and, when in answer to his question she confessed that she had not read *Pilgrim's Progress*, he set her down and took no further notice of her (*Life*, II, 238, n. 5). It seems unlikely that this incident occurred during Johnson's Easton Maudit visit, when Percy's elder daughter Anne was four and Barbara three—ages when an ignorance of *Pilgrim's Progress* would hardly have merited such a reaction, even from a more severe taskmaster than Johnson. Johnson would have had opportunities to see the Percy daughters in later years, when the Percy family frequently resided in London following Mrs. Percy's appointment as wet nurse to Prince Edward in 1767 and Percy's as chaplain in ordinary to George III in 1769. Although Anne might then have been a little old for Johnson to take on his knee, Barbara and their younger sister Elizabeth, who was born in 1765, would not.

54. Westlake, *Fame and Faith*, p. 22.

55. Cradock, *Literary and Miscellaneous Memoirs*, I, 240.

56. Cradock took his praise of Anne Percy from Nicholas Rowe's *Jane Shore*, II, i, 147–49.

57. *The Percy Letters*, II, 84–85.

58. Ibid., p. 87. "His mind was not very comprehensive, nor his curiosity active," Johnson wrote of Shenstone; "he had no value for those parts of knowledge which he had not himself cultivated" (*Lives*, III, 354).

59. *Reliques*, I, ix.

60. *Critical Review*, October 1764, pp. 270–77.

61. Cradock, *Literary and Miscellaneous Memoirs*, I, 238–39; IV, 292–93.

62. Anderson, *The Life of Samuel Johnson*, p. 300n.

63. Samuel Johnson, *The History of Rasselas, Prince of Abissinia*, ed. D. J. Enright (Harmondsworth: Penguin, 1976), p. 142.

FRANK BRADY

3 · *Johnson as a Public Figure*

Johnson fascinated his contemporaries. Late in life he remarked to Boswell, "I believe there is hardly a day in which there is not something about me in the newspapers," which was literally true.[1] But contemporaries saw him far differently from the way we do. For them, his reputation shifted over the years in reaction to his writings and behavior. For us, that reputation is fixed, and events in his life take on meaning from our sense of his career as a whole. Also, his contemporaries judged him in a context of values and attitudes that has become so distant in two hundred years that we are forced virtually to reconstruct it. The Johnson we see is a blurred, if overlapping, image of the Johnson they knew.

For contemporaries, Johnson's reputation pivoted on two crucial events. The first, his letter to Lord Chesterfield in 1755, crystallized that reputation; the second, his acceptance of a pension from George III in 1762, cast a persistent shadow over it. The letter to Chesterfield now seems a well-worn story: Johnson's assertion of independence and self-worth; the first sign of the withering away of the system of literary patronage; the proof that writers, other than dramatists, could make a living by their own exertions. This story, however, mixes truth and folklore. Johnson did assert his independence, but Pope had already shown by his translation of Homer that an author could support himself by his writings. In contrast, Johnson earned only the most precarious living until a pension from a royal, or Ministerial, patron made him comfortable.

What caught the public imagination at the time about the Johnson-Chesterfield encounter was that it illustrated a deep split in values. To simplify: since at least Elizabethan times, the English had been operating under two different value systems. According to the system dominant in 1750, society is always more important than the individual.

This concept finds its political ideal in Pope's "th'according music of a well-mixed State,"[2] but his metaphor can be generalized: society is like a grand choir which blends a multitude of weak, off-key voices into a whole of strength and sweetness. As an institution, society embodies a collective wisdom that corrects the eccentricities of its individual members: this was the position Swift had asserted in *A Tale of a Tub* at the century's beginning, and that Burke was still defending in his *Letters on a Regicide Peace* at its end.

The culture that values society over the individual will place great importance on appropriate social behavior—what the eighteenth century epitomized in the word "manners"—and its ideal in this period was the gentleman. The principle of subordination suggests that the king should exemplify this ideal, as the Prince Regent would when he rejoiced in being known as "the first gentleman of Europe," but if he fails to qualify, as was true of the first two Georges, then society will take its tone from some model of aristocratic breeding like Lord Chesterfield.

Already it will be apparent that the countersystem of values was that successively associated with the Puritans and Roundheads and Dissenters—and, in general, with the rising middle class. This system emphasizes the individual conscience, and its watchwords are religion and morality. Johnson, as his reputation grew in the 1750s, became recognized as the moral voice of the age. He could be a moralist in a narrow sense—"The woman's a whore, and there's an end on't"[3]—but in better moments he was a moralist in the broad sense that he defines in the *Life of Milton*: "We are perpetually moralists, but we are geometricians only by chance."[4] All our important decisions are ethical decisions; intellectual pursuits are peripheral rather than intrinsic to our lives. I like the way Bishop Percy phrased Johnson's moral concern: he "at once probed the human heart, where the sore was."[5]

Christianity was classless: at least it was held that subordination in this world would give way to equality in heaven. A gentleman, in contrast, belonged, or at least aspired to, a certain social class, as is illustrated by George III's compliment to Burke on his *Reflections on the Revolution in France*: "You have supported the cause of the Gentlemen."[6] In theory, the social standard represented by the gentleman and the moral standard represented by the Christian fit together. "Nothing is more certain," says Burke in the *Reflections*,

> than that our manners, our civilization, and all the good things which are connected with manners, and with civilization, have, in this European world of ours, depended for ages upon two principles; and were indeed the result of both combined; I mean the spirit of a gentleman, and the spirit of religion.[7]

But, in practice, the social and the moral often rubbed against each other; as the phrase, "a Christian and a gentleman," suggests, the two roles were not synonymous. A gentleman's most precious possession was his honor, an attribute difficult to define, though easy to recognize, involving a reciprocal relationship between social status and self-respect. When the signers of the Declaration of Independence mutually pledged their lives, their fortunes, and their "sacred Honor," what can be innocently construed today as a rhetorical flourish was deadly serious to them. A "manners" culture is apt to pay more attention to shame than guilt; to lose one's honor, for example, by being shamed in public could represent to a British gentleman what loss of caste would to a Brahmin: *Caleb Williams* traces the extreme example that illustrates the rule.

The century's worried preoccupation with dueling demonstrates how sharp the clash between social and moral could become. The church condemned dueling as a sin, and the state as a crime; a moment's reflection shows its stupidity; but every gentleman knew, like Hamlet, that he must "greatly . . . find quarrel in a straw / When honor's at the stake." As late as 1789, even the Duke of York felt compelled to fight a duel.[8]

Still, it may seem difficult to take Chesterfield seriously as an alternate model to Johnson. Yet contemporary writers often contrasted them, with Johnson's well-known remarks about Chesterfield set off against Chesterfield's supposed descriptions of Johnson as a "respectable Hottentot."[9] In 1787, fourteen years after Chesterfield's death and three after Johnson's, William Hayley, whose combination of mediocrity and popularity suggests that his views were representative, could publish a piece called *Two Dialogues: Containing a Comparative View of the Lives, Characters, and Writings of Philip, the Late Earl of Chesterfield, and Dr. Samuel Johnson*, in which their merits are assumed to be worthy of extended contrast.

For Chesterfield undoubtedly exemplified in polished form the most desirable external qualities of a gentleman: politeness, dignity, composure, ease and elegance of manner. Johnson, on the other hand, was constantly attacked for antisocial attitudes: sullenness, ferocity, censoriousness, and so forth. Even a generally favorable early biographer (Isaac Reed?) commented in the *Westminster Magazine* for September 1774:

> The Doctor has ever affected a singularity in his manners, and to contemn the social rules which are established in the intercourse of civil life. This habit he has indulged so far, as to subject himself to the charge of a morose, ill-natured pedant. Indeed, however partial we may be to the Doctor's abilities, we cannot help acknowledging there is but too

much justice in the remark. A confirmed haughtiness of temper, and a dogmatical manner of decision, acquired by long-established literary reputation, has so far possessed him, that his opinion often savours more of caprice than candour or judgment.[10]

Yet the situation was crisscrossed with ironies. Many unquestioning adherents to the code of manners would, at the same time, have placed far greater weight on their Christian faith. Johnson, on his part, constantly praised the social virtues, and Boswell stresses his concern with proper conduct. "In our Tour," Boswell says, "I observed that he was disgusted whenever he met with coarse manners." Elsewhere Boswell remarks,

> No man was a more attentive and nice observer of behaviour in those in whose company he happened to be, than Johnson; or, however strange it may seem to many, had a higher estimation of its refinements.[11]

When Johnson emerged, much impressed, from his famous interview with George III (that interview which Tom Tyers called "the greatest honour of his life"),[12] his mode of praising the King was to call him "the finest gentleman I have ever seen."[13]

Johnson held such a firm belief in his own good manners that, though generally impervious to criticism, he refused to acknowledge any resemblance between himself and Chesterfield's Hottentot, arguing in the face of general disbelief that it described Lord Lyttelton. Indeed, he commended Chesterfield's politeness to one acquaintance but added, "he did not think it worth his while to treat me like a Gentleman," quite possibly a sensitive point.[14] And Johnson was ready to display his manners whenever they occurred to him: every reader of the *Life* recalls the wonderful story of how Johnson, virtually in undress, bustled between Topham Beauclerk and the Comtesse de Boufflers to escort that distinguished lady to her coach, "eager to show himself," in Beauclerk's phrase, "a man of gallantry."[15]

Rasselas capped Johnson's reputation as a moralist. Anonymous, in *Lloyd's Evening Post* (2–4 May 1759), illustrates the general reaction, in "On Reading *Rasselas*, an Eastern Tale":

> He best, each avenue, which guards the heart,
> Takes by surprize, with ev'ry grace of art.
> . . . .
> What depth of sentiment, what height of thought,
> With what sublime, exalted morals fraught!
>
> (11. 5–6, 13–14)

Burke, commenting in the *Annual Register* that "perhaps no book ever inculcated a purer and sounder morality," further laments that while Johnson has

> done so much for the improvement of our taste and our morals, and employed a great part of his life in an astonishing work for the fixing the language of this nation . . . this nation, which admires his works, and profits by them, has done nothing for the author.[16]

But when a few years later a grateful nation—or a Ministry with its own motives—gave Johnson a pension, public reaction was often unfavorable. At first this might seem surprising: why should anyone have cared about Johnson's pension except to rejoice that an outstanding writer would no longer have to struggle with poverty? Who cared, for example, when Thomas Sheridan was given a pension except for Johnson himself, whose gratuitous rudeness about it transformed Sheridan from a friend into a lifelong enemy. But Sheridan's pension was granted for innocent elocutionary activities while Johnson's, his enemies guessed, was a political bribe.

On the face of it, Johnson's pension could be made to look suspect. There were the *Dictionary*'s definitions of "pension" and "pensioner," the widespread reputation as a Jacobite, and the well-known hatred of the House of Hanover. But more was involved. Pope, Johnson's predecessor as the most important literary figure of the century, had simultaneously insisted that he was an independent spirit and that envy must own he lived among the Great: he wanted credit for social standing as well as for moral superiority. Johnson also acknowledged the claims of rank and fortune: he told Boswell that if it were going to be known, one would gain more respect by dining with the first duke in England than with the first man for genius.[17] But Johnson's natural weapon was not the gentleman's sword; it was the folio with which he supposedly had knocked down the impertinent bookseller Thomas Osborne, or the oak stick with which he intended to defend himself if attacked by James Macpherson.[18] Even his physical grotesqueness seemed to disqualify him from any pretensions to social position. His adversaries mocked him as a literary Caliban.

Pensions and places seemed the natural prerogatives of the upper classes. For Johnson to accept a pension could be interpreted as a betrayal of his reputation for fierce integrity; it wiped out the significance of his letter to Chesterfield; it demonstrated Sir Robert Walpole's contention that every man—even Johnson—had his price. "Just for a handful of silver he left us," Browning was to write of Wordsworth after he had accepted a civil-service pension and the Laureateship in his old age.

This, to repeat, was the view expressed by Johnson's enemies. John Wilkes, in *The North Briton* no. 12 (12 August 1762), attacked on one front by associating Johnson with Murray of Broughton, a notorious traitor to the Jacobite cause. Charles Churchill attacked on another in his portrait of Pomposo:

> *Fame* around should tell
> How he a slave to int'rest fell;
> How, for *Integrity* renown'd,
> Which Booksellers have often found,
> He for *Subscribers* baits his hook,
> And takes their cash—but where's the Book?
>
> (*The Ghost*, III. 797–802)

The ironic reference to integrity depends for its effectiveness precisely on Johnson's high reputation for it. Churchill goes on:

> How to all Principles untrue,
> Nor fix'd to *old* Friends, nor to *New*,
> He damns the *Pension* which he takes,
> And loves the STUART he forsakes.
>
> (ll. 817–20)

Johnson, of course, could be conscious of rectitude. Had not Lord Bute assured him twice that his pension was granted not for anything he was to do, but for what he had done? Had he not pointedly reminded Bute in his letter of acknowledgment that

> you have conferred your favours on a man who has neither alliance nor interest, who has not merited them by services, nor courted them by officiousness. . . . I shall endeavour to give your Lordship the only recompense which generosity desires,—the gratification of finding that your benefits are not improperly bestowed.[19]

But whatever Bute said, did not the Ministry implicitly expect a *quid pro quo*? Charles Jenkinson, Bute's confidential agent and joint secretary to the Treasury under Bute's successor George Grenville, evidently did. In October 1763 Jenkinson gave Johnson some papers connected with the negotiations for the Peace of Paris, which he must have wanted Johnson to work up into a pamphlet defending the Peace. When Johnson did nothing for two years, Jenkinson asked for them back, informing Johnson with apparent irrelevance that since he was no longer secretary to the Treasury he had "no longer the payment of the Annual Stipend which you receive from the Crown."[20] Johnson, with unusual promptness, returned them the next day, declaring, "I once hoped to have made better use of them," but "much delighted," so he said, that they would be "employed for the same purpose by a Man so much more versed in publick affairs."[21]

Time passed, and with it a sequence of prime ministers: Grenville, Rockingham, Chatham, and Grafton. Since his edition of Shakespeare, which had appeared in 1765, Johnson had rested on his oars. Suddenly in January 1770 he published *The False Alarm*, the first of what was to be a series of four pamphlets. Though some biographers still assert that he was impelled to write one or more of these pamphlets by his intimacy with Henry Thrale,[22] no evidence connects any of them, except possibly *The Patriot*, with Thrale's election campaigns, while both external evidence and their contents do connect them to concerns of great importance, first to Grafton's and then North's Ministry.[23] According to William Gerard Hamilton, Johnson himself

> complained that his pension having been given to him as a Literary character he had been applied to by Administration to write political pamphlets and that he had received no reward or additional consideration for having written them, which seemed to imply that this was a command, and he was even so much irritated that he declared to a friend his resolution to resign his pension. His friend shewed him the impropriety of this [for, after all, what would Johnson have lived on?] and he afterwards expressed his gratitude and said he had received good advice.[24]

I am not suggesting that the Ministry threatened Johnson with the loss of his pension, though we must keep in mind that—as he himself was acutely aware—it was granted to him not for life but during the King's pleasure.[25] But it does seem likely that the Ministry put pressure on him, perhaps hinting that he might show his gratitude for money received. As late as 1782 he appears in a government summary of pensioners under "Writers Political" along with such people as Dr. John Shebbeare (with whom he was constantly and ignominiously paired—He-Bear and She-bear—by his enemies), rather than among those listed merely as "Literary."[26]

Nor is there much reason to believe that Johnson would have written these pamphlets of his own volition. After completing that long-promised edition of Shakespeare, Johnson apart from these pamphlets undertook only two sizable pieces: the *Journey to the Western Islands* and the *Lives of the Poets*, each written *con amore*. Though on the whole his views coincided with those of North and his Ministry, he grew to despise both.[27] Why then, as late as 1775, was he still defending what he had called, a year earlier, "a feeble ministry"?[28] Yet he was willing to claim reward. The following year he applied unsuccessfully for lodgings at Hampton Court from Lord Hertford, the Lord Chamberlain, speaking of himself as "a man who has had the honour of vindicating his Majesty's government."[29] And perhaps G. B. Hill was right in suggesting that North intended to pay him off cheaply with an Oxford D.C.L.[30]

Certain modern readers have felt able to praise Johnson's political pamphlets. John Wain, for example, asserts they contain "some of his most vigorous and exhilarating prose."[31] To me they seem far from his finest work. It is possible to agree with Paul Fussell that in these pamphlets Johnson "is behaving like a lawyer; he is finding, organizing, and articulating the most persuasive arguments on behalf of certain positions,"[32] without being much impressed by the results. They do illustrate Boswell's contention that Johnson "could reason close or wide, as he saw best for the moment," and Goldsmith's that when Johnson's "pistol misses fire, he knocks you down with the butt end of it."[33] But in *The False Alarm* and *Taxation No Tyranny* in particular, Johnson's arguments, whatever their legalistic merits, lack generosity of spirit. I once asked W. K. Wimsatt, perhaps the finest Johnsonian critic of this century, whether he would have liked to have met Johnson. (To make this story clear, those who never knew Wimsatt need to be told that he was 6'11" and formidable when roused in controversy.) "Oh, no," said Wimsatt. "Why not?" I said. "Because," replied Wimsatt, "he would have put me down." It is this side of his complicated character that Johnson exhibits in these pamphlets.

The Yale editor of Johnson's political writings speaks of these pamphlets as having exposed him to "an incredible amount of opposition invective."[34] Even apart from the fact that *Thoughts on Falkland's Islands* engendered few replies, the response to Johnson's other pamphlets is just what one would expect from any detailed knowledge of the political situation. Johnson's voice was respected, and the pamphlets are at least forceful; his opponents also perceived them as vulnerable to charges of sophistry and brutality, and they must have been delighted by the openings he gave them. Cooler heads inclined rather to deplore the loss of the moralist in the political battler. The Rev. Joseph Towers remarked that Johnson the pamphleteer "should not wholly lose sight of that liberality of sentiment, which should characterize the scholar; nor of that decency and politeness, which should adorn the gentleman."[35] Someone writing as "L" in the *Universal Magazine* for August 1784 comments in typical, if florid, fashion that by 1770 Johnson had

> attained to the most exalted height of reputation; and little discretion was requisite to maintain an enviable character of dignity, independence, and superiority. He thought proper, however, to descend from his splendid elevation (the object of literary reverence, if not of literary adoration) to become the partisan of administration, and to mingle with the mob of political pamphleteers; as if the Jupiter of ancient fable were to desert the heights of Olympus, leave his thunder and his eagle, and stoop to combat in the amphitheatre with contending gladiators.

Then, shifting to understatement, "L" continues:

As, in all these pamphlets, Dr. Johnson was professedly the champion
of Administration, this circumstance did not contribute to augment the
number of his admirers.[36]

In summarizing Johnson's disdainful reaction to the replies to *Taxation No Tyranny*, H. L. McGuffie states that his pamphlets so affected
his contemporary reputation that "between 1770 and 1784 even his
most friendly critics were constrained to apologize for him."[37]

It was not merely that they thought of biography in terms of panegyric that friends of Johnson like Fanny Burney and Hannah More
feared Boswell would display his defects; they feared further, I think,
that Boswell would fix for posterity those defects which had already
been too well publicized, especially those related to the manners–
morality distinction. Boswell's major predecessors, Sir John Hawkins
and Mrs. Hester Thrale-Piozzi, tend to reinforce the widespread impression that Johnson was a surly brute. Hawkins asserts that Johnson's

> dogmatical behavior, and his impatience of contradiction, became a part
> of his character, and deterred many persons of learning, who wished to
> enjoy the delight of his conversation, from seeking his acquaintance.

Though Hawkins then remarks that the remonstrances of Johnson's
friends (presumably including the author himself) "produced a
change in his temper and manners that rendered him at length a desirable companion in the most polite circles," he immediately undercuts any suggestion of improvement by adding, "His habits were
slovenly, and the neglect of his person and garb so great as to render
his appearance disgusting." Much later Hawkins returns to this topic,
in case any reader had missed the point: Johnson "appeared as insensible" to his appearance "as if he had been nurtured at the Cape of
Good Hope,"[38] a clear allusion to the Hottentot comparison.

According to Mrs. Thrale-Piozzi, "No praise was more welcome to
Dr. Johnson than that which said he had the notions or manners of a
gentleman," and he "always pretended extreme veneration" for "polished manners."[39] Yet her *Anecdotes* are notorious for their examples
of his rudeness to others. She defends their inclusion by comparing
her practice to Johnson's: he made many enemies "by telling biographical truths in his Lives of the later Poets," so

> what may I not apprehend, who, if I relate anecdotes of Mr. Johnson,
> am obliged to repeat expressions of severity, and sentences of contempt? Let me at least soften them a little by saying, that he did not hate
> the persons he treated with roughness, or despise them whom he drove
> from him by apparent scorn. He really loved and respected many
> whom he would not suffer to love him.

Following this with a remark Johnson made to Principal William Robertson, she comments, "I was shocked to think how he [Johnson] must have disgusted him." Johnson's talk, she says elsewhere, "had commonly the complexion of arrogance, his silence of superciliousness."[40]

Given such attitudes, it is hardly surprising that Boswell wished to vindicate Johnson "from the injurious misrepresentations" produced by Hawkins, and the "unfavourable and unjust impression" given by Mrs. Thrale-Piozzi; his *Life of Johnson*, he hoped, would "rescue his memory from obloquy."[41] But Boswell would not make his tiger into a cat; he had a complex truth to tell.

Boswell uses the issue of manners in the *Life* to bring out the difference between Johnson's image of himself and the way others saw him. When Johnson says, "I think myself a very polite man," Boswell comments in his journal (30 April 1778), "Curious this!" But in the *Life*, where he omits this comment, Boswell follows Johnson's self-description with an account of the only occasion in their relationship when Johnson was so rude to him that Boswell avoided his company for some time.[42]

This incident, too, is an example of how Boswell contrasts Johnson's theoretical belief in good manners to his practice, to that rudeness of which Boswell, like Mrs. Thrale-Piozzi, gives many instances. The difference between their portrayals of Johnson is that Boswell shades his much more carefully: he cites Dr. Burney on Johnson's "politeness and urbanity," calls up W. J. Mickle and Edmond Malone to attest to his usual kindness, and adds emphasis to Goldsmith's well-known judgment, "*He has nothing of the bear but his skin.*" Johnson himself construed his roughness as having moral effect, since it repressed "Obscenity and Impiety."[43]

Such patterning of example and comment forms part of a larger strategy. In the *Life*, Marshall Waingrow points out,

> Johnson's weaknesses . . . are methodically viewed under the aspect of his strengths: his indolence together with his energy, his excesses of appetite together with his abstemiousness, even his sexual irregularities together with the force of his conscience.[44]

Just before publishing the *Life of Johnson*, Boswell copyrighted separately two of its most eagerly awaited passages: *The Celebrated Letter from Samuel Johnson, LL.D., to Philip Dormer Stanhope, Earl of Chesterfield, Now First Published . . .*; and *A Conversation between His Most Sacred Majesty, George III, and Samuel Johnson, LL.D.* Copyright protected Boswell's literary property[45] but, even if inadvertently, it also directed interest to the turning points in the development of Johnson's reputation. The *Letter to Chesterfield* needed no more than to be reproduced; the *Conversation with George III* deflected attention from the royal pension to the King's eagerness to talk to his most famous literary subject. Johnson was at his best on each occasion. Demonstrating that the deference to rank required by society could be smoothly combined with a proper assertion of independence, Johnson exhibited in both instances with what precision he could balance the claims of manners and morals.

N O T E S

1. Boswell, *Life*, IV, 127. H. L. McGuffie corroborates Johnson's statement in *Samuel Johnson in the British Press, 1749–1784* (New York: Garland, 1976). According to McGuffie's figures for the same year (1781) as Johnson's statement, some 240 items (remarks and stories about Johnson, or extracts from and allusions to his writings) appeared in the British press; and there must have been more.

2. *Essay on Man*, III. 294.

3. *Life*, II, 247.

4. *Lives*, I, 100.

5. *Boswell in Extremes*, ed. C. McC. Weis and F. A. Pottle (New York: McGraw-Hill, 1970), p. 311.

6. *Correspondence of Edmund Burke*, vol. VI, ed. Alfred Cobban and R. A. Smith (Cambridge: Cambridge Univ. Press, 1967), p. 239.

7. *Reflections*, ed. C. C. O'Brien (Harmondsworth: Penguin Books, 1969), p. 173.

8. It was not coincidental that the most often quoted lines in Shakespeare during the first half of the eighteenth century were those from *Othello* beginning, "Good name in man and woman . . ./Is the immediate jewel of our souls" (see G. W. Stone and G. M. Kahrl, *David Garrick* [Carbondale: Southern Illinois Univ. Press, 1979], p. 560).

9. For examples, see items in McGuffie, *Johnson in the Press*, pp. 128, 135, 194; *Early Biographies of Samuel Johnson*, ed. O M Brack and R. E. Kelley (Iowa City: Univ. of Iowa Press, 1974), pp. 16–17, 69–70, 38–39, 101–102.

10. *Early Biographies*, p. 17. See the *St. James's Chronicle* (6 Sept. 1770), which defines Johnson's opposite as "Sir Charles Easy" (McGuffie, *Johnson in the Press*, p. 79).

11. *Life*, V, 307; III, 54.

12. *Early Biographies*, p. 73.

13. *Life*, II, 40.

14. *Life*, I, 267 and n. 2, 541. Johnson's judgment that Chesterfield's *Letters* "teach the morals of a whore, and the manners of a dancing master" (*Life*, I, 266) is much better remembered than his qualification about the book: "Take out the immorality, and it should be put into the hands of every young gentleman" (*Life*, III, 53).

15. *Life*, II, 405–406.

16. *Annual Register for 1759*, pp. 477, 479.

17. *Life*, I, 443.

18. *Life*, I, 154; II, 299–300. Sir John Hawkins makes much of the oak stick (2nd ed. [London, 1787], p. 491).

19. *Life*, I, 374, 376–77.

20. Donald J. Greene, *The Politics of Samuel Johnson* (New Haven: Yale Univ. Press, 1960), pp. 190–91. On the other hand, Lord Loughborough later told Boswell not even a "tacit understanding" that Johnson should write for the Administration was involved (*Life*, I, 373). And Jenkinson's remark would make immediate sense if Johnson was in the habit of applying to him to receive or expedite his pension.

21. *Letters*, I, 180.

22. For example, W. J. Bate, *Samuel Johnson* (New York: Harcourt, 1977), pp. 443–44; James L. Clifford, *Dictionary Johnson* (New York: McGraw-Hill, 1979), p. 275.

23. Boswell thought *The Patriot* was written to help Thrale in the General Election of 1774 (*Life*, II, 285–86), but *The Patriot* is first listed as this day published in the *London Chronicle*, 11–13 Oct. 1774, and most of the polling for Southwark, which took place on 10–13 October, finished on 12 October (*St. James's Chronicle*, 11–13 Oct. 1774). Johnson, in any case, speaks of it as having been called for by his "political friends" (*Life*, II, 288), a phrase which suggests the Ministry rather than Thrale. Also, the subject matter of *The Patriot* is far too general to have had much direct bearing on Thrale's campaign. The evidence connecting North's Ministry to *Thoughts on Falkland's Islands* and *Taxation No Tyranny* is too well known to need summary.

24. Marshall Waingrow, ed., *The Correspondence and Other Papers of James Boswell Relating to the Making of the "Life of Johnson"* (New York: McGraw-Hill, [1969]), p. 264. The "friend" referred to is Hamilton himself.

25. Waingrow, *Correspondence*, p. 264 and nn. 10, 12. George III, of course, was *not* pleased to augment Johnson's pension during the last few months of his life.

26. James L. Clifford, "Problems of Johnson's Middle Years—the 1762 Pension," in *Studies in the Eighteenth Century*, vol. III, ed. R. F. Brissenden and J. C. Eade (Canberra: Australian National Univ. Press, 1976), p. 19. Johnson, *Works*, X, xxv n. 2.

27. See Greene, *Politics*, p. 188.

28. *Life*, IV, 69 (Johnson to Warren Hastings, 30 March 1774).

29. *Letters*, II, 125 (Johnson to Hertford, 11 April 1776).

30. *Life*, II, 318 n. 1.

31. John Wain, *Samuel Johnson* (New York: Viking, 1974), p. 281.

32. Paul Fussell, *Samuel Johnson and the Life of Writing* (New York: Harcourt, 1971), p. 31.

33. *Life*, V, 17; II, 100.

34. *Works*, X, xxvi.

35. *A Letter to Dr. Samuel Johnson* (London, 1775), p. 1.

36. *Early Biographies*, pp. 40–41. For similar reactions, see items in McGuffie, pp. 70, 72, 84–85, 133, 159, 169.

37. "Dr. Johnson and the Little Dogs: the Reaction of the London Press to *Taxation No Tyranny*," in *Newsletters to Newspapers: Eighteenth-Century Journalism*, ed. D. H. Bond and W. R. McLeod (Morgantown: School of Journalism, West Virginia Univ., 1977), pp. 204–205.

38. Hawkins, pp. 164–65, 327. Hawkins does concede that Johnson was an admirer of those he considered well bred, like that "profligate worthless man," Tom Harvey (p. 407).

39. *Anecdotes of the Late Samuel Johnson*, in *Johnsonian Miscellanies*, ed. G. B. Hill (Oxford: Clarendon Press, 1897), I, 253–54, 319. Hill prints "he said" for "said he."

40. *Johnsonian Miscellanies*, I, 188–89, 347. A remark in her private journal underlines her attitude: "Although Mr Johnson would say the roughest, and most cruel Things he always wished for the Praise of good Breeding" (*Thraliana*, ed. K. C. Balderston [Oxford: Clarendon Press, 1942], I, 182).

41. *Life*, I, 28; IV, 347, 344.

42. *Boswell in Extremes*, p. 327; *Life*, III, 337.

43. *Life*, I, 286; IV, 250, 341; II, 66; IV, 295.

44. Waingrow, *Correspondence*, p. xlviii.

45. This is F. A. Pottle's explanation for separate copyright (*The Literary Career of James Boswell, Esq.* [Oxford: Clarendon Press, 1929], p. 138).

PAUL J. KORSHIN

4 · Johnson's Last Days: Some Facts and Problems

1

When Johnson returned to London from his last visit to Lichfield, on 16 November 1784, he had less than four weeks to live but, weak as he was with the progressive ailments that had troubled him for the last few years, he was about to enter upon a period of great activity. Always unwilling to face the fact of his own death, he would, in these last twenty-seven days of his life, see and converse with a large group of friends, discuss literary and scholarly projects as if he had another decade to contemplate them, write various letters and meditations, write and translate poetry, prepare two versions of his will, execute a number of final commissions, and sort through and destroy many of his personal papers. Such a range of activity would be most unusual for a man in perfect health; it is extraordinary in a man of seventy-five who was in failing health. Throughout this period, Johnson's inner circle of friends closely observed much of his activity, while an outer circle of acquaintances glimpsed him occasionally. Accounts in the London newspapers about his physical condition kept a still larger circle of watchers informed about his physical state. As his state of health gradually, perceptibly declined, that inner circle of watchers was transformed into his chroniclers. In the months and years after his death, on 13 December 1784, many of the members of that inner circle become Johnson's biographers, either producing memoirs about his life and last days, writing anecdotes about this brief period, or contributing what they remembered to other biographers outside this intimate group.

Johnson's last days, so intensely observed and so variously remembered, become the subject of many different pieces of evidence. This material is entirely textual—unless we except Reynolds's death mask—and the texts are numerous and conflicting. Some pieces of text overlap other pieces; some corroborate, some contradict; some pieces cast doubt on the veracity of one witness or another, others reveal witnesses that contemporary observers overlooked or neglected. All of these pieces of evidence require a collective scrutiny and analysis, for texts are often uncertain. As Derrida notes, "A text is not a text unless it hides from the first comer, from the first glance, the laws of its composition and the rules of its genre. A text remains, moreover, forever imperceptible. Its law and its rules are not, however, harbored in the inaccessibility of a secret; it is simply that they never can be booked, in the *present,* into anything that could rigorously be called a perception."[1] My purpose is not to analyze Derrida or to make a theoretical point about the Johnsonian texts. Derrida's comment, however, has a remarkably appropriate practical application to many, if not all, of the texts that surround and ultimately embody the story of Johnson's last days. They all seem to be part of the same genre—the memoir—but the *raison d'être* and methodology, the laws of composition, of each one are forever lost to us. We can never recover the intentions and purposes of Johnson's inner circle in writing their memoirs and anecdotes about his life, so that what they say, as well as what they suppress, may contain elements of a darkness that is "forever imperceptible."

Johnson's last days received greater attention from his friends—his memoirists—than any other part of his life. This situation is quite natural, for the end of a poet's life—its closure—like the conclusion of a literary work, always attracts greater emotion than its beginning or middle. Eighteenth-century observers were neither the first nor the last to attach special significance to an author's final weeks, days, or hours. Some of those who observed Johnson's last weeks were, like scholars today, capable of plain surmises or conclusions based on fragmentary evidence. How did they handle the facts, the hearsay, and the texts? What were their motives? How trustworthy are the results? A thorough revaluation of the available evidence may allow us to make some fresh considerations of the sources for Johnson's life and of literary biography in general.

There were two close, practically daily, observers of Johnson's last days, the translator, poet, and dramatist John Hoole and the attorney Sir John Hawkins, both friends of many years' standing. Others, like William Windham and Fanny Burney, kept diaries in which they recorded visits to Johnson's Bolt Court house and—at the end—to his bedside there. Still others did not write their own memoirs or diaries, but responded to requests from James Boswell for information— "anecdotes," as the eighteenth century called this kind of reminiscence—for his own life of Johnson. Both Hoole and Hawkins wrote formal, diary-like statements about Johnson's last month of life and later, of course, Boswell produced his own elaborate account, different from the first two in that he had not been an observer. Thus Boswell's text has none of the qualities of the eyewitness account, and very few of the diary or memoir; it is a biography, and hence more "literary" than earlier accounts. Since there are too many observers and commentators for me to examine every one in detail, I shall study only the accounts of John Hoole, Sir John Hawkins, and James Boswell, pausing to stress and scrutinize more closely certain problems that each one raises and drawing in corroboratory evidence from the wider circle of observers who have something significant to contribute.

2

John Hoole is the first memoirist whose work I want to study. Hoole did not visit Johnson immediately upon his return to London; his diary-like account begins on 20 November.[2] For the last twenty-three days of Johnson's life, Hoole paid a visit to Bolt Court every day, although he did not see Johnson every time he called. On eleven of those days, he wrote a brief entry of just a few lines, but the entries for the other twelve days are substantial, sometimes hundreds of words long. There is an immediacy about Hoole's longer entries, as if he had committed his recollections to paper very shortly after the events which they describe. Indeed, on the first day that he saw Johnson, Hoole tells us, "he again pressed me to think of all he had said, and made me promise to commit the whole to writing, which I faithfully assured him I would: he pressed my hand with much warmth, and repeated, 'Promise me you will do it': This I again assured him, on which we parted, and I promised to see him the next day."[3] The next day, "he asked me if I had done what he desired (meaning the noting down what passed the night before); and upon my saying that I had, he pressed my hand, and said earnestly, 'Thank you.'"[4]

I must emphasize here that Johnson was not asking Hoole to be the chronicler of his last moments. On 20 November, the day of their first conversation in Hoole's reminiscence, Johnson still hoped to recover from his illness, as he had earlier that year. Rather, he hoped to effect Hoole's religious conversion, to cause him to profit by his own example. In that 20 November entry, Johnson told Hoole that "he himself had lived in great negligence of religion and worship for forty years," and that he wanted him, too, to become an observing Christian (which Hoole definitely was not). The methodical keeping of a diary of one's spiritual experience was, as Johnson well knew, an important step toward spiritual regeneration; it is an exercise that the Methodists often insisted upon in their writings on conversion. Johnson even said to Hoole on that first day "that what a man writes in that manner dwells upon his mind."[5] Whether Johnson's example succeeded in converting Hoole I cannot say, but the evidence of his *Journal Narrative relative to Dr. Johnson's last Illness* is that the work is a record of what Hoole remembered about Johnson, not a record of the author's personal spiritual experience and religious rebirth.

If we could be certain that Hoole composed his *Journal* entry every night as soon as he returned home after seeing Johnson, as the first day's entry suggests he did, then his account would gain great status for its immediacy and for its pretensions to accuracy. My examination of Hoole's manuscript, however, does not conclusively prove that each day's entry is a discrete, separate entity. Rather, the variations in ink colors and quills suggest that Hoole filled a sheet or two at a time; there are almost no minute, day-by-day variations in ink and pen to imply that Hoole was writing his diary every night. Sometimes Hoole's text also tells us that he was probably writing some time after the events, as when, on 11 December, he quotes Johnson as saying: "'Then God bless you' (said he) 'you will find it better or easier (or words to that effect) every day.'"[6] The phrase "or words to that effect" is a rare lapse for Hoole, the only place in his narrative where he admits to having difficulty recalling what Johnson had said, and it may show that he did not compose each entry quite so immediately as he did the one for 20 November. I use the word *compose* deliberately, for there is more evidence available about his methods of composition, evidence that shows that Hoole was not writing a to-the-moment diary or memoir but a more formal work with, to use Derrida's phrase, "laws of . . . composition." This evidence consists of a series of letters that Hoole wrote between 30 November and 14 December 1784 to another member of the Johnson circle, William Bowles of Heale, near Salisbury, who was Sheriff of Wiltshire.[7] Johnson knew Bowles well, and had visited him at Heale for three weeks in August and September 1783.[8] There can be no question that Hoole wrote these letters just after or on the same day that he saw Johnson, for each one bears a postmark with the same date as that which he gives the letter. We can sense their immediacy in language, style, verb tenses, and in the keenness of detail that is sometimes lacking in the more formal *Journal Narrative*. For example, on 30 November, after bringing Bowles up to date on Johnson's health, Hoole writes; "Tomorrow there is to be a consultation, consisting of Dr. Heberden, Dr. Butter, Dr. Brocklesby & Mr. Cruickshanks the Surgeon. His legs are extremely filled—they cannot move the water and Dr. Johnson is very desirous to have them scarified in order to procure a discharge, but his physical friends seem to disapprove of the expedient as attended with great danger. However he means to press it again tomorrow."[9] Hoole's *Journal* is different and briefer: "With respect to his recovery he seemed to think it hopeless: There was to be a Consultation of Physicians next day: he wished to have his legs scarified to let out the water, but this his Medical friends opposed and he submitted though he said he was not satisfied." [10]

The differences between Hoole's two versions of the same events are quite characteristic of what we find in the comparison of his two accounts. The *Journal* uses the past tense where the letter uses the present, it makes a more definite judgment about Johnson's condition than the letter does, and it uses rather formal language ("Medical friends" for "physical friends") where the letter is colloquial. It would appear that Hoole is writing later than 30 November, long enough in the future for him to be able to add the comment about Johnson himself despairing of his recovery; from the letter to Bowles we get no sense that Johnson had lost hope, but rather that he hoped to try additional medical expedients to help him to recover. But the *Journal* entry for 30 November also contains some things that the letter of the same date does not, so evidently Hoole's memory returned to him when he wrote it, or perhaps he added things later of which he was less certain, although nothing in the available evidence points in this direction. There is a remote possibility that the letter to Bowles follows (is later than) the *Journal* entry and gives only a condensation of the longer record there.

No clue appears in the *Journal Narrative* about Hoole's method of composition, but from his letter to Bowles of 6 December we can gather some idea of how he went about it. He writes to Bowles, "You may depend upon it, my dear Sir, that I do not pass so much time without putting down many things that occur though I am sorry to say there are many others that escape my memory." [11] Apparently, then, Hoole made notes about some things that occurred during his visits to Johnson, but he does not say precisely *when* he took them, and he does concede that he forgot many things, even in the short interval between his seeing Johnson and his writing a letter about it the same or the next day. Some of the details that Hoole adds in his later *Journal Narrative* we know to be accurate, but just as often his corrections are mistaken. In his letter of 6 December, describing Johnson's taking the Sacrament for the last time on Sunday, 5 December, Hoole notes the presence of Bennet Langton, whereas in his Journal he does not mention that Langton was there (we can confirm his presence from Hawkins's account of that day). [12] Of course, that day's letter to Bowles may be later than the *Journal* entry for 5 December rather than earlier. If this is the case, then Hoole simply added one small fact that he had omitted earlier, Whichever the case, his method of composition suggests how uncertain is the memory of eyewitnesses.

Let me consider another example of how Hoole's accounts of the same events vary from one text to another. In his last letter to Bowles (14 December 1784), he writes as follows:

Yesterday morning I went between eleven and twelve and found him very composed in bed: he had (Frank said) a restless night but had dozed very quietly for about two hours, he continued to lie very still, to all appearances very easy: I staid with him till near three and several friends came in and looked at him, but he seemed to be asleep and spoke to nobody: the last time he spoke to any person was to a young woman named Miss Morris, who left the house when I came to him. Mrs. De Moulins told him that she only wished for his blessing and he said "God bless you!" He was persuaded to take a little milk while I was there. At three I left the house.[13]

Hoole contributes details that we cannot find elsewhere, including an important observation at the end of his letter about Joshua Reynolds's late-night visit to take a mold of Johnson's face for his death mask.

The last entry in the *Journal Narrative* is dated 13 December, but Hoole certainly wrote it no earlier than the 14th, for it mentions events of the following day. The relevant portion of it is as follows:

Went to Bolt Court at eleven o'clock met a young Lady coming from him which upon enquiry I found to be Miss Morris (a sister to Miss Morris formerly on the stage). Mrs. De Moulins told me that she had seen the Doctor, that by her desire he had been told that she came to ask his blessing and that he said, "God bless you!" I went up stairs into his chamber and found him lying very composed in a kind of dozing:—he spoke to nobody—Sir John Hawkins, Mr Langton, Mrs Gardiner, Rev Mr Strahan, Mrs Strahan, Doctors Brocklesby & Butter Mr Steevens & Mr Nichols the printer came there but no one chose to disturb him so as to speak to him. While Mrs Gardiner & I were there before the rest came he took a little warm milk in a cup when he said something upon its not being properly given into his hand and I believe this was the last time he spoke, but he seemed not to take the least notice of any present: he breathed very regular though short & appeared to be in a calm sleep or doze. I came away and left him in this state and never more saw him alive.[14]

The *Journal*, we may note, is better ordered as to the sequence of events on 13 December, although somewhat repetitious (it mentions Johnson's "doze" or "dozing" twice). Miss Morris's visit comes at the beginning rather than in the middle, and Hoole has managed to identify her as "a sister to Miss Morris formerly on the stage." But except for the list of visitors and the addition of Johnson's remark about the cup of milk, it is essentially the same account, simply more polished, more "literary" in a way that an epistolary text would not be. It gives every appearance that Hoole composed it after he wrote his letter to Bowles. What it omits is also interesting. The *Journal* entry is less precise about the time of Hoole's arrival and departure, Frank disappears (I shall have more to say about Frank Barber's disappearance later), and there is no mention of Reynolds's coming to take a cast of Johnson's face after his death.

Hoole, then, is an excellent witness to Johnson's last days, but his correspondence with William Bowles suggests that his *Journal Narrative* is not quite so artless a memoir as a reading of it alone might imply. Hoole's letters are epistolary in the best sense: they are quite unstructured, list facts without careful chronological arrangement, and often seem close to the events that he observed in such linguistic details as verb tense. The details that he cites in the *Journal Narrative* are not always identical with what he mentions in the letters, but the entries, especially the longer ones, are meditated, carefully arranged as to the details of time and place, and composed as if the work were meant to have a larger public. I have no intention of undermining Hoole's accuracy or questioning the reliability of his memory, but there are some interesting differences between the two bodies of evidence that he has left us. Since his memoir takes the form of a text, and his letters to Bowles another text, each with its own largely hidden methods and rules of composition, we cannot perceive exactly what the purpose of Hoole's *Journal* was. At the beginning, he undertook to write down his impressions of his visits to Johnson at his friend's request, probably as a spiritual record. Some of this record appears from time to time, perhaps most dramatically in Hoole's presentation of Johnson's thoughts on the typology of the Jews.[15] But as he maintained his *Journal*, Hoole transformed it into a more carefully planned narrative of Johnson's final days. Perhaps the secret of his text is that it is, after all, an account of Johnson's successful conversion, for Hoole is very frank about Johnson's religious doubts and just as candid about his belief that he had repented and his hope that he might be accepted at last.

3

Sir John Hawkins did not intend his *Life of Johnson* to be a mere memoir; what we know of his methods of composition shows that he made every possible attempt to be deliberate and to make scrupulous use of those personal papers of Johnson's that he possessed.[16] But, while Bertram Davis has analyzed Hawkins's *Life* in great detail, we still know very little about how Hawkins actually went about writing his text, how he did his research, wrote and revised his drafts, and the other intricate aspects of composition itself. We know less about the writing of this work than we know about Hoole's composition of his *Journal Narrative*. Many different scholars have praised or damned Hawkins for his real and imaginary strengths and weaknesses, but this kind of analysis is not my purpose here. I am interested only in what Hawkins tells us about Johnson's last days. This part of Hawkins's narrative begins with his telling us—in his usual somewhat verbose way—that Johnson "arrived in town on the sixteenth day of November," but there is no hint of immediacy until 27 November, when, for the first time, Hawkins records visiting Johnson at his house.[17] My guess is that Hawkins had not bothered to see Johnson at all during the first eleven days after his return from Lichfield, but from that point forward, Hawkins dropped by to see him at Bolt Court nearly every day. Most of these visits were disappointingly short or Hawkins chose to say almost nothing about them; for most of the days that Johnson continued to live, Hawkins presents just a few lines or sentences, little more than a brief paragraph. There are two exceptions. On 27 November, Hawkins gives a long account of the drafting of Johnson's will, which he supervised, and again, on 8 and 9 December, quite briefly, he mentions assisting Johnson to prepare a second version and a codicil and talks about Johnson's likely burial in Westminster Abbey. The other exception relates to the events of Sunday, 5 December, the day on which Johnson took communion for the last time.

As Hawkins presents his account of this day, we can see that it was a fascinating occasion, for Johnson was very weak, but strongly determined to go through with the ceremony, which exhausted him. Johnson had written a special prayer for the occasion, which he "uttered" with great eloquence and energy; sometime later in the day, he also wrote his last poem, a ten-line Latin translation of the Collect for the Communion Service (Hawkins does not mention this poem in the context of the communion, but he dated the poem "Dec. 5, 1784" in his 1787 edition of Johnson's *Works*). Hawkins had the manuscript of this prayer, for he prints it, without the deletion of the phrase "forgive and accept my late conversion" that Rev. George Strahan had omitted in his 1785 edition of Johnson's *Prayers and Meditations*. This circumstance gives rise to what Johnsonians would call the Late Conversion Problem, which I will discuss later. But at this point something happens which gives us a rare insight into Hawkins at work on his biography. There were two editions of his *Life of Johnson* in 1787, the first appearing in February as the first volume of his edition of Johnson's *Works*, the second as an independent volume in early June. Although, as Bertram Davis shows, there was much scorn and even ridicule of Hawkins's *Life* in the reviews from the moment the book appeared, and demand for a second edition would appear to have been uncertain, Hawkins undertook a thorough revision, according to his own standards, of the work. A collation of the two editions shows that Hawkins's revisions are all of minor points in the text, except for his adding an anecdote about Johnson's feelings toward Roman Catholics to the story of the execution of Dr. Dodd and another addition to the entry for 5 December 1784. This addition is quite long and highly important.

The addition begins with Hawkins saying, "While he was dressing and preparing for this solemnity [i.e., Holy Communion], an accident happened which went very near to disarrange his mind." That he should describe the following events as "an accident" is significant, as is the entire passage:

He had mislaid, and was very anxious to find a paper that contained private instructions to his executors; and myself, Mr. Strahan, Mr. Langton, Mr. Hoole, Frank, and I believe some others that were about him, went into his bed-chamber to seek it. In our search, I laid my hands on a parchment-covered book, into which I imagined it might have been slipped. Upon opening the book, I found it to be meditations and reflections, in Johnson's own hand-writing; and having been told a day or two before by Frank, that a person formerly intimately connected with his master, a joint proprietor of a newspaper, well known among the booksellers, and of whom Mrs. Williams once told me she had often cautioned him to beware; I say, having been told that this person had lately been very importunate to get access to him, indeed, to such a degree as that, when he was told the doctor was not to be seen, he would push his way up stairs; and having stronger reasons than I need here mention, to suspect that this man might find and make an ill use of the book, I put it, and a less of the same kind, into my pocket; at the same time telling those around me, and particularly Mr. Langton and Mr. Strahan, that I had got both, with my reasons for thus securing them. After the ceremony was over, Johnson took me aside, and told me that I had a book of his in my pocket; I answered that I had two, and that to prevent their falling into the hands of a person who had attempted to force his way into the house, I had done as I conceived a friendly act, but not without telling his friends of it, and also my reasons. He then asked me what ground I had for my suspicion of the man I mentioned: I told him his great importunity to get admittance; and further, that immediately after a visit which he made me, in the year 1775, I missed a paper of a public nature, and of great importance, and that a day or two after, and before it could be put to its intended use, I saw it in the news-papers.

At the mention of this circumstance, Johnson paused; but recovering himself, said, "You should not have laid hands on the book; for had I missed it, and not known you had it, I should have roared for my book, as Othello did for his handkerchief, and probably run mad."

I gave him time, till the next day, to compose himself, and then wrote him a letter, apologizing, and assigning at large the reasons for my conduct; and received a verbal answer by Mr. Langton, which, were I to repeat it, would render me suspected of inexcusable vanity; it concluded with the words, "If I was not satisfied with this, I must be a savage."[18]

This passage is one of the strangest revisions of the age, and the "transaction" it describes is one that surely qualifies as the literary theft of the eighteenth century. Hawkins calls it "an accident," as if he could not help himself, or as if the entire theft were not his fault, but that of the absent person—George Steevens is the man whom Hawkins is describing—against whom he claimed he was protecting Johnson.[19]

Hawkins did not invent this story, for others had heard of the theft. Hoole's narrative says nothing about it, but by early 1785 literary gossip began to make mention of what I shall call the Stolen Diary Problem.[20] The 1787 reviews of Hawkins's *Life* do not mention it, but somehow he must have decided, in the weeks after the publication of his first edition, that he had better address the matter, since it might possibly be better known than Hawkins's own motives. Now that we have this telling insight into Hawkins's thinking, we can examine his methods of composition in useful detail. We might well think that Hawkins, himself an attorney, in preparing a self-exculpatory statement to remove suspicion from himself, would have prepared his defense with a lawyer's attention to detail. But such is not the case. First of all, Hawkins describes as "an accident" something that was manifestly deliberate on his part. He recalls that a group of friends accompanied him in the search for Johnson's missing instructions. But when we compare his list of those present with John Hoole's list for the same day, we find that the extra cast of characters ("some others that were about him") sounds unrealistically large—five, possibly as many as seven people—for a search of Johnson's bedroom.[21] Hawkins casts suspicion on George Steevens based on the circumstantial evidence that Steevens had been trying to get in to visit Johnson, and that he suspected Steevens of having stolen a document from his house nine years earlier that later appeared in print. He blackens Steevens's character still further by citing the dead Anna Williams (she had died in 1783) as having told him that she had often warned Johnson about him, but without describing the context of such warnings. This circumstantial case seems not to have impressed Johnson, since, as Hawkins concedes, he said, "You should not have laid hands on the book." Furthermore, we know that Hawkins had no use for Frank Barber, Johnson's black servant, and it is to Frank to whom he attributes the story that Steevens had lately been importunate to visit Johnson.[22] Hoole, who was not possessed by Hawkins's feelings of guilt about this theft, quite routinely notes that "Mr. Steevens" visited Johnson the following Sunday, saying nothing about any efforts to restrain him, as if his visit were an ordinary event.[23] Hence we must wonder whether Hawkins attributed the suspicion of Steevens to the defenseless Frank Barber because he was the one member of Johnson's inner circle who could do little or nothing to defend himself. Hawkins writes that he took *two* parchment-covered notebooks and put them in his pocket, "securing them" while stealing them. Yet every time that Johnson mentions the object of the theft, which he does five times, he refers to it in the singular, not the plural: "a book," "the book," "my book." The discrepancy is Hawkins's, and it is most strange. Even stranger is the plain fact that nowhere does Hawkins say that he returned the diaries to Johnson. If Hawkins made this lengthy addition to his second edition to explain his actions, then we must wonder why he fails to mention returning the books—unless, of course, he is not trying to justify himself for returning them, he is justifying himself for *keeping* them. And keep them we know he did, for Hawkins would later tell Boswell, on 7 May 1785, "I have read his diary."[24] This admission is responsible for the famous Dark Hints controversy, for Hawkins then went on to mention Johnson's "strong amorous passions," yet without telling Boswell whether he had ever indulged them.[25]

Boswell alludes to Hawkins's long self-justification in a detailed footnote, saying, "But what [Hawkins] did was not approved of by Johnson; who, upon being acquainted of it by a friend, expressed great indignation, and warmly insisted on the book being delivered up."[26] He adds that Johnson's agitation over the incident "probably made him hasily burn those precious records which must be ever regretted." Boswell misinterprets Hawkins's own narrative or he had obtained further word about the stolen diary from someone else who was present for, as I have shown, Hawkins does not say that Johnson asked for the books back or that he actually did return them. There is, moreover, one more inconsistency. Hawkins explains that the next day, which was Monday, 6 December, he "wrote [Johnson] a letter, apologizing, and assigning at large the reasons for my conduct." Now, Hawkins's *Life* is in diary form at the very end. In the first edition, immediately after his account for 5 December, he goes on as follows: "6th. I again visited him," and continues with a paragraph about his visit. But, in the second edition, just after telling us that he wrote to Johnson on the *next* day to apologize, Hawkins inexplicably *changes* the date of his next visit from the 6th to the 7th.[27] This change tends to undermine the story about his delivering a letter of apology on the day following Sunday, 5 December. Boswell himself did not spot this inconsistency which, in fact, Bertram Davis was the first to notice, in 1960.[28] Boswell's nineteenth-century editors, beginning with Croker, were much less generous to Hawkins than he had been. Most of them reprint Hawkins's explanation in full, along with Boswell's rather gentle footnote, and add critical comments of their own. Percy Fitzgerald is representative: "This questionable transaction Sir John Hawkins passes by in his first edition; but the story got abroad, and he was obliged to explain it. The excuse he gave was, no doubt, a gross invention; and the charge against a third person, understood to be Mr. Steevens—a scandalous way of shielding himself. As Johnson had been busy destroying papers a day or two before, Hawkins's real motive was, no doubt, to secure the books for himself, though the fact that he called Langton's and Strahan's attention to what he was doing barely removes the act from the category of absolute theft."[29]

Whatever we call Hawkins's action, it is surely more important that his apologia is internally inconsistent, raising more questions than it answers, actually underscoring the author's unreliability because of the discrepancy in dates that makes the letter of apology less credible. To recall the words of Derrida, Hawkins's text must remain "forever imperceptible," although I am certain that there is some truth in this account.[30] Hawkins's narrative of Johnson's last days ends as impersonally as it began, as he tells us, "At eight in the evening [of 13 December], word was brought me by Mr. Sastres, to whom, in his last moments, he uttered these words 'Jam moriturus,' that, at a quarter past seven, he had, without a groan, or the least sign of pain or uneasiness, yielded his last breath."[31] Hawkins then proceeds somewhat to diminish the dramatic effect of his own narrative by discussing whether Johnson might have hastened his own death by lancing his own legs at eight o'clock on the morning of 13 December, but here, too, he is inconsistent, for he reports that Johnson's consequent loss of eight or ten ounces of blood caused him to fall into "that dozing which carried him off." How, then, Johnson, eleven hours later, and eight hours after John Hoole had recorded his last words, could awake and speak coherently to Francesco Sastres is another circumstance that defies explanation. We must leave Hawkins's *Life of Johnson* as we find it, an excellent source for uncorroborated information about Johnson, but somewhat questionable about the facts of his last days when there are other witnesses available.

4

The third account of Johnson's last days that I shall discuss is that of Boswell. It differs from those of Hoole and Hawkins, for Boswell was not a witness to any part of these final weeks. He first heard of Johnson's death on Friday, 17 December, in a long letter from one of Johnson's physicians, Richard Brocklesby.[32] The next day he received a letter from the bookseller Charles Dilly urging him to "announce my intention to publish the Life of D^r. Johnson," to which he responded on 23 December promising "that I intend to publish in the Spring my tour with D^r. Johnson, a good Prelude to my large Work his Life."[33] Boswell then commenced the literary activity that would culminate, just over six years later, in the publication of his *Life of Johnson*, a story that Marshall Waingrow has presented in his volume of the Yale Edition of the Private Papers of James Boswell.[34] The making of Boswell's *Life* is beyond my scope here; I am interested only in how he prepared his account of Johnson's last days. In this respect, I think it is important that Boswell could give no firsthand evidence himself. We could think of his position, then, as a shortcoming, for his account could have none of the immediacy that a witness's would have but, on the other hand, we can also regard his position as an advantage. Eyewitness testimony is notoriously unreliable: most of the theorizing about it has been the work of specialists in the law, and, from the eighteenth century to the present, there have been substantial doubts about its uses as well as substantial agreement, of course, that it does have a use, provided that we are aware of its inherent weaknesses.[35] Boswell, then, was in the same position as other contemporary biographers of Johnson who were unable to visit his bedside in that last month, but he was also privileged by having available reports from virtually everyone who was there, whether they came to him voluntarily or as the result of his soliciting them. He was privileged in another way. Boswell was a practicing barrister with considerable skill in sifting evidence, exploring and resolving conflicts in it. This fact does not mean that we can trust him unreservedly—after all, a barrister is always the advocate for one side of a story—but it does mean that Boswell would be likely to treat Johnson's last days with special attention.

Boswell, in his usual self-conscious way, approaches his account of Johnson's last days by striking a personal note. After an important section on Johnson's fear of death, his knowledge of his sinfulness, and Boswell's assurance to us of his penitence, he concedes that "this is the most difficult and dangerous part of my biographical work" and confesses his anxiety about it.[36] He then continues as follows: "It is not my intention to give a very minute detail of the particulars of Johnson's remaining days. . . . Yet it will be instructive, as well as gratifying to the curiosity of my readers, to record a few circumstances, on the authenticity of which they may perfectly rely, as I have been at the utmost pains to obtain an accurate account of his last illness, from the best authority."[37] The text that follows is in narrative form, not the day-by-day diary style that Hoole and Hawkins had employed, and it consists entirely of anecdotal material about the last days that Boswell had received from Johnson's physicians and friends. Hoole lent him the manuscript of his *Journal Narrative*, which Boswell acknowledges in his text (IV, 406), and of course he also had available Hawkins's *Life*. Boswell's distance from the events that he narrates diminishes his sense of Johnson's gradually declining health, which we gather so vividly from Hoole, but he gives us instead what I will call a series of declining plateaus. First, there is an account of the efforts of his four physicians and one surgeon (IV, 399–401); second, there is a discussion of his legacy to Frank and his will (IV, 401–403); third, there is a discussion of his disposition of his personal papers (IV, 401–406); fourth is a brief account of attendance upon him by his closest friends (IV, 406–407); fifth, Boswell gives some "particulars of his conversation within a few days of his death" from the recollections of John Nichols (IV, 407–10); sixth is a brief comment about Johnson's toleration for divines of communions other than the Anglican (IV, 410–11); seventh is a second collection of "characteristical" actions and comments toward and about his friends (IV, 411–16); and eighth, and last, is Boswell's account of Johnson's last prayer and his final moments (IV, 416–18). There is an aftermath as well, just as there was in Hawkins's *Life*. Hawkins, after mentioning Johnson's death, had added several pages about Johnson's attempt to mutilate his legs on the morning of his death. Boswell says nothing about this story, but instead introduces an account that Malone had given him, deriving from the man—William Windham's servant—who sat up with Johnson from Sunday night, 12 December, until ten o'clock on the morning of his death. The fact that Boswell avoids mentioning the self-mutilation but actually prints an account from the only witness to the event that overlooks it shows that he distrusted Hawkins, who is the only source for this story. The circumstance shows that Boswell did not use some evidence, but it also shows something else—he distrusted Hawkins so much, presumably because of the doubts about his veracity that his story of the theft of Johnson's diaries raised, that he would accept virtually nothing from his *Life* with respect to the last days unless he could obtain external corroboration for it.

Boswell's doubts and his method become clear when we examine his treatment of Johnson's last prayer, which brings me to the Late Conversion Problem.[38] Hawkins, who was present at the communion ceremony on Sunday, 5 December, says merely that Johnson "uttered the following most eloquent and energetic prayer."[39] This statement is not perfectly accurate for, as we know, Johnson had composed the prayer in advance and read it from his manuscript. The manuscript, which survives, is now in the Beinecke Library. Lest anyone think that Johnson recited the prayer from memory at the ceremony on 5 December, I should add that the testimony of the Rev. George Strahan, who conducted the communion service, indicates the contrary. Strahan's "Johnsoniana" contains the following brief comment: "The last time he received the Sacrament he pronounced the following prayer which he afterwards dictated to Mr. Strahan."[40] The copy which Strahan made from Johnson's dictation also survives; Strahan used it as the copy text for his 1785 edition of the *Prayers and Meditations* and, two years after his death (he died in 1824), his daughter deposited the manuscript of it, together with all of her father's copies of Johnson's prayers and meditations, most of them in Johnson's handwriting, at Pembroke College, Oxford.[41] Strahan's manuscript is in fact a close but not exact reproduction of the prayer; it contains two small verbal differences and many variations in capitalization and punctuation that are consistent with dictation.[42] When Strahan published this prayer the next year, he made three further deletions. Two of these are minor and appear to be accidental (Strahan was a dreadful copyist), but the third is his omission of the important phrase, "forgive and accept my late conversion," which Strahan actually lines out in the

Pembroke manuscript.[43] No doubt Strahan made this deletion, as Donald Greene has shown, because he misunderstood what Johnson meant by "conversion," and thought that the words might suggest an evangelical rebirth rather than a process long common to Anglicanism. The next version of the last prayer to appear is that in Hawkins's *Life*. Here we can see that Hawkins must have had Johnson's manuscript when he wrote, for he follows Johnson's text exactly, with only about a dozen variations in capitalization and punctuation. But, once again, Hawkins is not entirely trustworthy, for he printed another version of this prayer in Volume XI of his edition of Johnson's *Works*, with which the first edition of his *Life* appeared. This version of the prayer has two variations, quite minor, which show that Hawkins took them from Strahan's published text.[44] So, then, there are four versions of Johnson's last prayer—Johnson's autograph, Strahan's 1784 transcript of it, Strahan's 1785 printed version, and Hawkins's 1787 version in Johnson's *Works*, Volume XI (this version has the "late conversion" phrase, but adopts two additional variants from Strahan's 1785 printed version).

There is evidence of much corruption here, the result of careless copying, and several willful changes, including Strahan's deliberate deletion of one key phrase (Donald Greene calls Strahan's action "falsifying" and adds that Boswell is at fault for "perpetuating the falsification").[45] Boswell chose to print Johnson's last prayer from Strahan's emended 1785 printed version, reproducing exactly the three changes that I have mentioned. No doubt he was aware of the two different versions in Hawkins's *Life* and edition of Johnson's *Works*. But even if he did not notice the discrepancy between these two texts, he would already have had ample reason to distrust Hawkins's account of the last days. After all, he had noticed Hawkins's unconvincing attempt to explain his purloining of Johnson's diaries, and he must also have noticed that Hawkins introduces the text of the last prayer without any comment about how he had obtained it. I have said that Hawkins must have had Johnson's manuscript of the prayer; there seems to be no other way to account for his printing such an accurate text of it. Did that manuscript then pass to Boswell? We know that Hawkins assured Boswell, in April 1788, that he no longer had any of Johnson's books and manuscripts; in 1787 and 1788, through the intercession of Boswell, he had delivered all that he had to Frank Barber, Johnson's sole legatee, and John Nichols, the bookseller.[46] We also know that the manuscript of the last prayer was part of James Boswell's library, forming part of a lot of prayers that was knocked down to William Upcott for nine guineas in 1825.[47] However, the James Boswell whose library was sold in 1825 was Boswell's son, James Boswell the younger. Frank Barber clearly did receive the residue of Johnson's papers from Hawkins in 1787 and 1788, but he did not pass everything on to Boswell at once—or at all. Until his death in 1801, Barber continued to possess some of Johnson's manuscripts, and after his death his widow disposed of them. In this way, for example, a portion of Johnson's manuscript "Annals" reached the birthplace museum at Lichfield; perhaps Boswell's son obtained the manuscript of the last prayer in the same way.[48]

For Boswell to have had the manuscript of the last prayer in his possession when he was composing the *Life* and not to have used it is unlikely, for he was very proud of his ownership of Johnson's letters and documents, and almost invariably announces in the text of the *Life* whether the materials that he prints are in his possession. Yet the manuscript of the *Life of Johnson* shows that Boswell did not have the prayer available when he wrote his account of the last days, for he introduces the prayer in this way: "Almighty and most merciful Father I am now as to human eyes it seems &c," and then continues with a note to his compositor, "Take it in from 'Prayers & Meditations,' towards the end of the Book."[49] Strahan probably imagined that he had sound reasons for suppressing the "late conversion" passage, but Boswell, who had started his pages on the last days with a detailed account of Johnson's penitence (which is the very process of conversion) in the last months of his life, had no reason to wish to conceal the fact that Johnson had undergone a conversion by deliberately deleting these important words. Nor can I see any reason to invent any such reason based on Boswell's own religious doubts. My guess, then, is that Boswell, who seems always to have used those manuscripts of Johnson's that he possessed, did not have the manuscript of the last prayer when he wrote his account of the last days, early in 1791. I suggest, further, that his distrust of Hawkins's rendition of this period of Johnson's life caused him to avoid using the full text of the prayer that Hawkins had printed in 1787, for he could not trust the man's veracity. We can say, I think, that Boswell's *Life* continues the inaccuracy in the text of Johnson's last prayer that the Rev. George Strahan had introduced in 1785, but we cannot say conclusively that Boswell's error was deliberate.

Boswell's next problem was with Johnson's last moments and final words.[50] There was clearly no way that he could credit Hawkins's story that Johnson had suddenly awakened from his doze a few minutes before the end to say "Jam moriturus" to Francesco Sastres. Indeed, Sastres himself had told Boswell, in February 1786, his own version of the death: "This truly great man breathed his last Monday the 13th Decr. 1784, about half an hour after seven in the evening, whilest I was alone in the dining room waiting to see Franc in order to ask him how his master was."[51] Since Sastres, by his own admission to Boswell, had not been present, had not even been on the same floor of the house, when Johnson died, clearly Hawkins's telling us that Johnson said "Iam moriturus" to Sastres was inaccurate.[52] Boswell had seen

Hoole's manuscript *Journal Narrative*, with the account of Johnson saying "God bless you!" to Miss Morris and later mumbling something about the cup of milk not being properly put into his hand. He had also corresponded extensively with Hoole's friend William Bowles, so perhaps he had learned from Bowles how Hoole had described the last words in his letter of 14 December 1784. He would surely have noticed that Hoole's manuscript *Journal* added the story about the cup of milk, and he may have distrusted Hoole's memory for the reasons that I suggested earlier.

But Boswell also had another witness, one whom the other members of Johnson's inner circle virtually ignored. This was Johnson's black servant Francis Barber who, he knew, had spent more time at Johnson's bedside than any of his friends. Barber is practically invisible in the texts of Hoole and Hawkins; neither man mentions him more than three times in diary-like memoirs that cover several weeks. And, at one point, Hoole actually drops Frank from his *Journal*: while he tells Bowles, in his letter of 14 December, of Frank's presence, Frank disappears from the later text of his *Journal Narrative*. The invisibility of black servants is a phenomenon that students of black culture have often noted; in eighteenth- and nineteenth-century narratives by black slaves in the southern United States, we will come across white people speaking about blacks in their presence as if they were not in the room, that is, as if they were invisible.[53] Only one friend who visited Johnson in the last weeks noticed Barber in anything like his true role. This was Fanny Burney, who went to see Johnson on Sunday, 12 December, and who mentions Barber four times in less than one page, thus showing how constant was his attendance upon Johnson.[54] It is surely worth noting that the only observer of Johnson's last days to whom Barber was *not* invisible was also the only woman who kept an account, and who was, like him, subject to discrimination.

But Barber was not invisible to Boswell. Only three days after he answered Dilly agreeing to write a biography of Johnson, he wrote to his trusted agent in London, his brother Thomas David Boswell ("T. D.") about Johnson's death.[55] Boswell had used his younger brother since 1781, when T. D. returned to England from Spain, to handle his business affairs during his absence from London. From T. D.'s reply to his brother, dated 31 December 1784, we can see that Boswell had asked his brother to interview Barber at once about the circumstances of Johnson's last moments. Of 13 December, T. D. writes (giving the words of Barber): "The day following being that on which he died a Miss Morris daughter to a particular friend of his called and said to Francis she must beg to be permitted to see the Doctor, and earnestly requested he would give her his blessing. Francis went into the room accompanied by the young lady, and having delivered the message the Doctor turned himself in the bed and said 'God bless you my dear.'

These were the last words he spoke."[56] This letter, with a few minor changes, is the version of Johnson's last words that Boswell prints. The verisimilitude of this account is important: Barber remembered that Miss Morris was "daughter to a particular friend" of Johnson's (Hoole had described her as the sister of the actress Miss Morris); the request for a blessing is "earnest"; Barber goes into Johnson's bedroom with the young woman and delivers the message; and Johnson "turned himself in the bed" before speaking. Barber's story is obviously closer to reality than Hoole's report of these words, which came through Mrs. Desmoulins. Barber is precise about the incident, so his insistence that these were Johnson's last words may merit some credit. True, John Hoole prefaces his story about the cup of milk by saying, "While Mrs. Gardiner and I were there, *before the rest came*," but, as I have observed, Johnson's black servant was indeed invisible to Johnson's friends (with the exception of Fanny Burney).[57] Who, indeed, would have brought him and fed him the cup of milk other than his personal servant, Frank? So Boswell chose to trust the judgment and memory of the one witness whom other memoirists ignored, despite the fact that he was with Johnson, especially near the end, more than anyone else. In evidentiary terms, he had made a sound conservative choice by preferring to follow the account of the one witness against whose accuracy there was no existing scruple.[58]

5

I said at the beginning of this essay that, because of Boswell's position as a sifter of evidence rather than as an eyewitness to Johnson's last days, his final product is more "literary" than the memoirs of writers like John Hoole and Sir John Hawkins. His *Life of Johnson* is vastly more ambitious than any other contemporary treatment of Johnson and so, too, is his presentation of the last days. The memoirists who had firsthand evidence to present use the diary form, which tends to be relatively artless and straightforward, whereas Boswell constructed a narrative in which dates and times receive almost no attention until the very end. The rules of Boswell's genre, then, are simply different from those of Hoole and Hawkins. "Different" does not mean more or less accurate here; rather, it implies that Boswell composed his work in a special way and with a special purpose in mind. He achieves that purpose, which is to write the story of Johnson's life as if it were an epic, but that achievement does not make his work a fiction. As I have tried to show, he was highly scrupulous in dealing with evidence and, if he does not always make the correct evidentiary choice in terms of what we might conclude today, he nevertheless does tend to handle his information fairly but conservatively.

There is no particular need for me to vindicate or condemn Boswell's methods of composition—that I prefer to leave to the professional students of biography—but rather to stress that my interest has been to separate myths from realities in this brief but important period in Johnson's life. We will never be able to discover exactly what happened during his last days; the best that we can hope to do is to come close to the *archetype* of what happened. The archetype is a series of events—the ur-events—and it is not the same thing as reality, either. An archetype of this sort is nothing more than a reconstruction of a past that is largely inaccessible. The facts of Johnson's last days, although they are numerous, are far from being dense enough for us to arrive at the truth. But the recension of the available evidence that I have presented here reveals, despite Derrida's insistence that a text remains forever imperceptible, that the end of Johnson's life is still worth trying to interpret afresh. Some of the available accounts are very poor, others conceal or willfully distort, and still others try to shape Johnson into a creation for the ages. None of these literary efforts is without value, despite such weaknesses. Indeed, all of them, from the weakest to the best—those of Hoole, Hawkins, and Boswell—permit us to consider the literary and textual problems of an exciting and vital moment in literary history with a clinical gaze. Yet the accounts of these three major interpreters, whatever their strengths, also embody inconsistencies that should make us realize how uncertain an attainment is complete literary objectivity.

NOTES

1. Jacques Derrida, *Dissemination*, trans. Barbara Johnson (Chicago: Univ. of Chicago Press, 1981), p. 63 (italics in original).

2. Hoole's narrative first appeared in the *European Magazine*, 35 (Sept. 1799), 153–58; G. B. Hill reprinted it in *Johnsonian Miscellanies*, 2 vols. (Oxford: Clarendon Press, 1897), II, 145–60. A more correct edition, based on Hoole's manuscript, which Yale University acquired in 1968, is that of O M Brack, Jr. (Iowa City: Windhover Press, 1972). I shall quote Hoole from the still uncatalogued Yale MS throughout. This manuscript consists of six sheets: sheets 1, 2, and 6 are single folios; sheets 3, 4, and 5 are each folded in half to furnish four pages.

3. Entry for 20 November 1784; Yale MS f. 1^v.

4. Entry for 21 November 1784; Yale MS f. 2^r.

5. Yale MS f. 1^v. See Isabel Rivers, "'Strangers and Pilgrims': Sources and Patterns of Methodist Narrative," in *Augustan Worlds: New Essays in Eighteenth-Century Literature*, ed. J. C. Hilson et al. (Leicester: Leicester Univ. Press, 1978), pp. 194–95. Johnson also asked Francesco Sastres to "Write down what I have said" (Hoole, entry for 28 November 1784), but Sastres kept a far skimpier record than Hoole.

6. Entry for 11 December 1784; Yale MS f. 5, second recto. Brack, in the preface to his edition of Hoole's *Journal Narrative*, p. [7], agrees that Hoole did not keep his ac-

count consistently. See also his "John Hoole's Journal Narrative Relating to Johnson's Last Illness," *Yale Univ. Library Gazette*, 47 (1972–73), 107–108, for similar conclusions.

7. The letters are dated 30 November and 6 December 1784 (Bodleian MS Don. C. 52, ff. 94–97); and 11, 13, and 14 December 1784 (The Hyde Collection).

8. See *The Correspondence and Other Papers of James Boswell Relating to the Making of the "Life of Johnson,"* ed. Marshall Waingrow (New York: McGraw-Hill, 1969), p. 109 n. 3.

9. Bodleian MS Don. C. 52, ff. 94ᵛ–95ʳ.

10. Hoole, entry for 30 November 1784; Yale MS f. 4, first recto.

11. Bodleian MS Don. C. 52, f. 97ʳ.

12. Bodleian MS Don. C. 52, f. 96ʳ; cf. Hoole, entry for 5 December 1784 and Sir John Hawkins, *Life of Samuel Johnson, LL. D.*, 2nd ed. (London, 1787), p. 586.

13. Hoole to Bowles, 14 December 1784; quoted by permission of The Hyde Collection.

14. Hoole, entry for 13 December 1784; Yale MS f. 6ʳ⁻ᵛ.

15. Hoole, entry for 8 December 1784; Yale MS f. 5, first recto.

16. Bertram H. Davis, *Johnson before Boswell: A Study of Sir John Hawkins' "Life of Samuel Johnson"* (New Haven: Yale Univ. Press, 1960), passim, and *A Proof of Eminence: The Life of Sir John Hawkins* (Bloomington: Indiana Univ. Press, 1973), pp. 333–46, presents a detailed account of Hawkins's *Life*.

17. *Life*, 2nd ed., pp. 576, 580.

18. *Life*, 2nd ed., pp. 586–87. In a printed note to this passage, Hawkins states: "As I take no pleasure in the disgrace of others, I regret the necessity I am under of mentioning these particulars: my reason for it is, that the transaction which so disturbed him may possibly be better known than the motives that actuated me at that time." I do not know who the "others" are to whose disgrace Hawkins is so unwilling to contribute; doubtless he never thought for a moment that he was discussing his own disgrace.

19. On the identification of Steevens, see Davis, *A Proof of Eminence*, pp. 113, 258–59, 327.

20. See Davis, *Johnson before Boswell*, pp. 7, 10.

21. See Hoole, *Journal Narrative*, entry for 5 December 1784.

22. Hawkins shows his dislike for Barber in his criticism of Johnson for making Frank his sole heir; see his *Life*, 2nd ed., pp. 328, 586, 602.

23. Hoole, entry for 12 December; Yale MS f. 6ʳ. However, there is a hearsay account which A. L. Reade prints (*Johnsonian Gleanings*, 11 vols. [Privately printed, 1909–52], II, 39) that lends some substance to Hawkins's doubts about Steevens: "John Kemble told John Taylor [not Rev. John Taylor of Ashbourne, but the John Taylor (1757–1832) who was George III's oculist], on the authority of Malone, that

> when Mr. Steevens called, during the doctor's last illness, to inquire how he was, the black servant went and told the doctor that Mr. Steevens waited below. 'Where is he?' said the doctor. 'On the outside of the street-door,' was the answer. 'The best place for him,' was the reply."

That the story is thirdhand seriously compromises its accuracy.

24. *Private Papers of James Boswell*, ed. Geoffrey Scott and F. A. Pottle, 18 vols. (Privately printed, 1928–34), XVI, 84.

25. See Frederick A. Pottle, "The Dark Hints of Sir John Hawkins and Boswell," in *New Light on Dr. Johnson*, ed. Frederick W. Hilles (New Haven: Yale Univ. Press, 1959), pp. 153–62.

26. *Life of Johnson*, ed. G. B. Hill, rev. L. F. Powell, 6 vols. (Oxford: Clarendon Press, 1934–64), IV, 406.

27. *Life*, 2nd ed. p. 587.

28. Davis observes, "One exception to Hawkins' general honesty must be noted. In questions involving his own honor or reputation, he is not always reliable. . . . His account in the second edition [of his *Life*] . . . of his pocketing Johnson's diaries may be accurate, but it is rendered suspect because he changed a date in order to work in this defense of his own conduct" (Davis, *Johnson before Boswell*, p. 84 n. 66). Actually, Hawkins's changing the date does not accommodate his defense, it makes the entire story less credible.

29. *Life of Samuel Johnson, LL. D., together with a Journal of a Tour to the Hebrides*, ed. Percy Fitzgerald, 3 vols. (London, 1874), III, 168–69, note.

30. Boswell, after all, refers to Hawkins's apology in words different from those that Hawkins used (*Life*, IV, 406), so he must have obtained independent corroboration of it from another witness whom I cannot identify.

31. *Life*, 2nd ed., p. 590.

32. See Waingrow, p. 29, n. 1, and, for Brocklesby's letter, pp. 25–28.

33. "Register of Letters," 1 January 1783–20 October 1790, Boswell Papers, Yale University Library, M 255, pp. 230–32.

34. For an important appreciation of Waingrow's volume, see Donald Greene's review, "The Making of Boswell's Life of Dr. Johnson," *Studies in Burke and His Time*, 12 (1970–71), 1812–20.

35. For a recent study of the subject, see Elizabeth Loftus, *Eyewitness Testimony* (Cambridge, Mass.: Harvard Univ. Press, 1979), passim.

36. The section on Johnson's attitude toward death is in *Life*, IV, 394–98. See esp. IV, 398.

37. *Life*, IV, 398–99.

38. Donald J. Greene's famous essay, "Johnson's 'Late Conversion': A Reconsideration," in *Johnsonian Studies*, ed. Magdi Wahba (Cairo, 1962), pp. 61–92, studies the meaning of "conversion" in the context in which Johnson used it in his last prayer, but pays very brief attention to the physical transmission of the prayer (pp. 62–63).

39. *Life*, 2nd ed., p. 585.

40. Waingrow, p. 390.

41. Waingrow, p. 162, n. 15.

42. Where Johnson wrote "make this commemoration of him available," Strahan omitted "of him" and where he wrote "make the Death of thy son Jesus effectual to my redemption," Strahan wrote "Jesus Christ." See Johnson, *Diaries, Prayers, and Annals* (New Haven: Yale Univ. Press, 1958), pp. 417–18; cf. Strahan's manuscript, which I cite through the courtesy of the Hyde Collection, which has a copy of the original at Pembroke College.

43. Strahan's manuscript says, "Grant, O Lord, that my whole Hope and Confidence may be in his Merits & in thy Mercy," but the 1785 text says "and thy mercy." Strahan's manuscript says, "Support me by the Grace of thy Holy Spirit," while the 1785 text says, "Support me, by thy Holy Spirit." See *Prayers and Meditations* (London, 1785), pp. 222–23.

44. The two variations which Hawkins adopts are those that I cite in note 42, above. See Johnson, *Works*, 11 vols. (London, 1787), XI, 194.

45. "Johnson's 'Late Conversion,'" p. 63. Later (p. 92) Greene calls Strahan's deletion a "scandalous emendation."

46. See Waingrow, pp. 221–22, 274–75, 277–78, 280–81.

47. See *Bibliotheca Boswelliana* (London, 1825), p. 100 (lot 3166).

48. *Johnsonian Gleanings*, II, 56–57.

49. Manuscript of the *Life of Samuel Johnson*, f. 1033 (Boswell Papers, Yale University Library).

50. On the importance of "last words" in the eighteenth century, see O M Brack, Jr.,

"The Death of Samuel Johnson and the Ars Moriendi Tradition," *Cithera*, 19 (1980), 3–15.

51. Waingrow, p. 135.

52. Until now, nobody seems ever to have checked Hawkins's accuracy on the words "Jam moriturus," and no one seems to have noticed that neither Hawkins nor his stated source, Sastres, was with Johnson when he died. Lawrence Lipking, "The Death and Life of Samuel Johnson," *Wilson Quarterly*, 8, no. 5 (Winter 1984), 150, does not challenge Hawkins's account, and even *The Times*, in its leading article on the bicentennial of Johnson's death, assures us that "his last words were the stiff-lipped old Roman gladiatorial ones, *Iam moriturus*" ("An English Saint Remembered," 13 December 1984, p. 15). Perhaps Hawkins's version *is* correct, and Johnson really did use this Latin phrase; my point is that, in evidentiary terms, there is no corroboration for Hawkins's account and his only witness, Sastres, undermines Hawkins's statement in his testimony to Boswell.

53. The *locus classicus* for this phenomenon is Frederick Douglass's *Narrative of the Life of Frederick Douglass, an American Slave*, ed. Benjamin Quarles (Cambridge, Mass.: Belknap Press of Harvard Univ. Press, 1960), p. 58. I owe this reference to Professor Houston Baker.

54. See *Diary and Letters of Madame D'Arblay*, 7 vols. (London, 1842–46), II, 337.

55. "Register of Letters," Boswell Papers, M 255, p. 231. Frank Brady, *James Boswell: The Later Years, 1769–1795* (New York: McGraw-Hill, 1984), mentions how Boswell employed his younger brother on his business and other affairs in London during his absence in Edinburgh; see pp. 459, 481.

56. Boswell Papers, Thomas David Boswell to James Boswell, C 506 (31 December 1784).

57. As I have mentioned, a good example of this treatment is that of Hoole himself, who mentions Frank's presence in his letter of 14 December 1784 to William Bowles, but drops him from the entry for 13 December (to which the letter refers) in his *Journal Narrative*.

58. For further comment on the last words, see the exchange in the *Times Literary Supplement* on "Johnson's Last Words" between Donald Greene and Paul J. Korshin: 25 December 1981 (Greene); 29 January 1982 (Korshin); and 26 February 1982 (Greene). Boswell's introduction of Frank Barber's testimony on the final moments has gone entirely unremarked by all his subsequent editors, including Malone (eds. 3–6), all the nineteenth-century commentators, G. B. Hill, and L. F. Powell.

Part Two

JOHNSON'S INTELLECTUAL DEVELOPMENT

JAMES GRAY

5 · Arras/Hélas!
A Fresh Look at Samuel Johnson's French

1

One of the least discussed of Johnson's many talents is his extraordinary flair for languages. His skills in Latin and, to a lesser extent, in Greek and Hebrew, are quite well known, and the fact that he busied himself, in the aftermath of a stroke at the end of his life, with the translation of passages from the Low Dutch of Thomas à Kempis has often been noted.[1] But his readiness to translate from French and Italian and his creative propensities in those languages are matters that biographers and critics have tended to gloss over. While I will concentrate on Johnson's knowledge and use of French, it would be remiss for me to ignore his adroitness in other languages, and the remarkable ability he had to switch from one to the other, drawing on his phenomenal memory as well as his lexicographic acumen.[2]

That Johnson was well versed in French literature is noted by his early biographers and memoirists, and particularly by Murphy, Tyers, and Mrs. Piozzi. "Dr. Johnson was a great reader of French literature," wrote the last-named in her *Anecdotes*,

> and delighted exceedingly in Boileau's works. Molière I think he had hardly sufficient taste of; and he used to condemn me for preferring La Bruyère to the Duc de Rochefoucault, "who (he said) was the only *gentleman* writer who wrote like a professed author."

Mrs. Piozzi adds that Johnson was quite sharply critical of some of the French authors:

> The asperity of his harsh sentiments, each of them a sentence of condemnation, used to disgust me however; though it must be owned, that, among the necessaries of human life, a *rasp* is reckoned one as well as a *razor*.[3]

When she wrote these words, Mrs. Piozzi no doubt remembered that tour of France with Johnson, her husband, her daughter Queeney, and Giuseppe Baretti eleven years previously, when Johnson had composed amusing but disdainful distichs at every place where they had stayed. In her French Journal (1775) she recorded some of them:

A Calais   St. Omer   Arras   A Amiens
Trop de frais   Tout est cher   Hélas!   On n'a rien

Au Mouton (the sign of the Mouton d'Or at Neuf Chatel)
Rien de Bon.

These reflect his wry reactions to French life and customs, and his underlying distaste for much of the country and for many of its people and their ways of life.[4] His dogged unwillingness to speak French on that tour (though in a letter to Levet he said that he would try),[5] and his quick dismissal, in trenchant phrases, of several of the nation's leading authors, such as Rousseau and Voltaire, were typical, one supposes, of British xenophobia, and of an understandable antagonism towards the French during and after the Seven Years War of 1756 to 1763, as well as the continuing hostility that led, ultimately, to the Revolutionary War and the crushing defeat of Napoleon Bonaparte.

It is noteworthy, too, that some of Johnson's happiest moments on the tour were passed in inspecting libraries, such as the Benedictine Library at Rouen, where he conversed in fluent Latin with the Abbé Roffette, condemning the destruction of the Jesuit order and pronouncing "a long eulogium upon Milton with so much ardour, eloquence, and ingenuity, that the Abbé rose from his seat and embraced him."[6]

In his own Journal of the same tour, Johnson is often caustic. French cuisine appalled him. "Their meals are gross,"[7] he notes at one point. He was disgusted by the miserable treatment of the poor, and by the shocking disparity between the highest and lowest economic levels: "In France there is no middle rank."[8] Fontainebleu (which he insisted on calling Fountainblue) he found "a large mean town crouded with people," mainly beggars.[9] In the royal palace everything was "slovenly" except for the chief rooms. Versailles was another "mean town,"[10] and on the Sorbonne, for all its great library holdings, he commented, "Profit little."[11] At Chantilly, the estate of the Prince de Condé, he complained, "I walked till I was very weary, and next morning felt my feet battered and sore with pains in the toes." His technical note on the method used by the Prince to preserve his museum specimens, "Nothing was in spirit, all was dry," might well have applied to most of what he saw there.[12]

There were, to be sure, some bright moments, like the time when he met the French translator of *Rasselas*,[13] and the interlude at the

King's Theatre at Versailles, when Mrs. Thrale and he walked on the stage to survey the splendid auditorium. ". . . & now, says I to Dr. Johnson, what Play shall we act?—the Englishman in Paris? No indeed, says he,—we will act Harry the Fifth." [14]

It would be unfair to leave the impression that Johnson was just another disgruntled and dyspeptic traveller who found nothing but fault with the host country. Just as, on his Scottish and Welsh trips, he discovered natural and cultural phenomena of great interest and sublimity, so in France he commented favorably on such things as splendid architecture, well-kept houses, fine cathedrals, and magnificent scenery; but neither he nor Mrs. Thrale could be said to have fallen in love with the people. Had they been prepared, as other travellers, such as Garrick and Lord Chesterfield had been, to converse freely in French, their reactions would no doubt have been different. Mrs. Thrale did not mind chatting in an erratic way, but Johnson's pride and stubbornness made it impossible for him to be at ease in conversational French. [15]

2

His grasp of written French is quite another story. It is clear that, during the greater part of his professional career, Johnson was a successful practitioner of the art of translation. As we know, his first book, published in 1735, *A Voyage to Abyssinia*, was largely a translation, or, as he preferred to call it, an "epitome," of the French *Relation historique d'Abissinie* (1728), itself a translation from the Portuguese original of Father Jerónimo Lobo. In the 1730s and 1740s, moreover, he produced a number of pieces for the *Gentleman's Magazine*, including a sketch, based on Pierre-François Courayer's "Vie Abrégée de Fra-Paolo" from the French edition of Paul Sarpi's *Histoire de Concile de Trente* (1736) and "A Dissertation on the Amazons," from the Abbé de Guyon's *Histoire des Amazones anciennes et modernes* (1740). A more noteworthy example of his prowess as a translator was his annotated version (1739) of Jean Pierre de Crousaz's *Commentaire sur la Traduction en Vers de M. L'Abbé Du Resnel, de l'Essai de M. Pope sur l'Homme* (1738), accompanied by a literal interlinear rendering, into English, of Du Resnel's very faulty French translation of the *Essay on Man*. [16]

His interest in translations from French into English continued into the 1750s. We find him, for instance, on 3 February 1755, asking the novelist, Samuel Richardson, for information on the translated versions of *Clarissa*, which had been rendered into German (1748–51), French (1751), and Dutch (1752–55). [17] More significantly, he was invited in 1759 by his friend and protégée, Charlotte Lennox, to collaborate in a team translation of Père Pierre Brumoy's *Le Théâtre des Grecs*, a three-volume quarto work that still stands as an authoritative account of Greek theatre history. In this extensive undertaking, Johnson's assignment was to write the dedication and to translate the chapter on Greek comedy, as well as the conclusion to the whole work.[18]

The task was by no means an easy one, as Brumoy's French is vitiated by awkward and sometimes ungrammatical constructions. Elsewhere, I have shown that Johnson, following a philosophy of translation which he had enunciated in *Idler* 69 (11 August 1759), tried to strike a mean between the free and the literal in his rendering of the Brumoy text, but occasionally an unmistakably Johnsonian sonority rings through, as in this sentence on Aristophanes, in which Brumoy refers to the judgment of Plutarch,

> that his amours have more impudence than gaiety; and that he has not so much written for men of understanding, as for minds blackened with envy and corrupted with debauchery ("les amours moins egayés qu'effrontés; qu'enfin c'est moins pour des personnes sensées qu'il a écrit, que pour des hommes perdus d'envie de noirceurs et de débauches.")

The Johnsonian balancing of phrases here, and the substitution of "blackened" for "perdus," while still incorporating the notion of "noirceurs" and "débauches," produce a more telling emphasis than we find in the French original.[19]

It would be wrong, of course, to claim that even the Rambler could make a silk purse out of the sow's ear of Brumoy's clumsy and wandering prose. At best, as Abbott has suggested, we may admire Johnson for his skill and proficiency "in rendering the French of Brumoy into a supple and readable English."[20] At times he takes, to use Johnson's own expression, some "paraphrastic liberties" by changing Brumoy's word order, substituting elegant variations for pedestrian phrases, and replacing single words with Johnsonian "doublets" to achieve the kind of resonance to which Brumoy was so obviously a stranger.[21]

3

It would not be an exaggeration to say, then, that Johnson was a gifted translator, with that rare capacity for instantaneous rendition that we nowadays associate with United Nations interpreters, and for which we have the direct testimony of Edmund Hector, who took down the Lobo translation verbatim at Johnson's bedside in the 1730s, as well as the witness of Mrs. Piozzi in her *Anecdotes*.[22] When we turn to Johnson's own writings in French, however, a rather different picture emerges. While his translations are numerous, his extant compositions in French are disappointingly few: the verses quoted by Mrs. Piozzi, four letters, and eleven French phrases sprinkled through his correspondence, from 1755 to the time of his death in 1784.[23]

The paucity of French writings by Johnson may be accounted for in several ways. Unlike Lord Chesterfield, whose celebrated letters to his son and godson include a hundred and fifty in French,[24] Johnson lacked the Gallic connections and diplomatic training that would have stimulated him to write more frequently in the other language. Unlike Walpole, who was equally at ease in French and English, he had not had the benefit of regular tutorial lessons in his youth. Unlike Thomas Gray or Laurence Sterne or Tobias Smollett or Henry Fielding or even James Boswell (who wrote a crude but fluent French), he had never enjoyed the luxury of the Grand Tour. All the same, there is sufficient evidence to show that he had a good grasp of French grammar, for which I shall try to account later, and of what were then called "idiotisms" or idioms, and that he could, and often did, *think* in French.

The French phrases scattered through his letters are mostly commonplace. "A Dieu je vous commende," he wrote to Hill Boothby; "*Toujours* strawberries and cream," to Mrs. Thrale from John Taylor's farm in Ashbourne; the Vice-Chancellor of Oxford he describes as "un esprit foible"; the weather in August 1777, he categorizes, perhaps unidiomatically, as "à la merveille"; "I hope to be soon *sur le pavé*," he writes from his sickbed in 1782, using the phrase as an apparently mistaken equivalent for "on my feet," as he does again in referring to a Mrs. Sheward, a maidservant, whom he describes as "an old maid, . . . yet *sur le pavé*," which really means "homeless" or "out of work." On one occasion, he writes to Mrs. Thrale, "you felt yourself *gênée* by that debt," and asks, "Is there an English word for it?" Since *gênée* has the double meaning of "embarrassed" and "hard up," there is indeed no single English word for it.

The last use of a French phrase in Johnson's letters occurs on the occasion of his miraculous recovery from a stroke, when he announces his intention of going to the "feast" (an exhibition) at the Royal Academy: "I cannot," he writes, "publish my return to the world more effectually, for, as the Frenchman says, *tout le monde s'y trouvera*" (to Mrs. Thrale, 21 April 1784, Letter 955).

It should be noted that all but two of the letters in which French words or phrases occur were addressed to Mrs. Thrale, and it was to her, also, that two of the four extant letters in French were sent. The two others, composed on 31 March 1769, and probably 16 May 1771, were directed, respectively, to a very young lady called Louise Flint, and to the celebrated Comtesse de Boufflers—the one a playful letter of thanks to Miss Flint for translating into French Johnson's Strictures at the end of his edition of Shakespeare, and the other a brief letter of parting. Of the two to Mrs. Thrale, one was written at Oxford on 5

June 1775, some three months before their departure for France, and the other, undated, at Streatham, while Johnson was staying with the Thrales. The Oxford letter (400), which is of minor consequence, complains of Mrs. Thrale's failure to answer a previous one, as well as of boredom, and of the inconvenient times of coaches going back to London. It also refers to Johnson's intervention with the Vice-Chancellor, on behalf of a man named Carter, a protégé of Mrs. Thrale's, for whom she hoped to find a position as riding master at the University. As there is nothing in the letter of a confidential sort, it is difficult to account for its being written in French, except as a bit of practice for the forthcoming tour. The Streatham letter (307.1), on the other hand, is of very great interest. First published in 1932, with annotations by J. D. Wright, in the *Bulletin of the John Rylands Library*,[25] it has gained a certain notoriety as a result of Katharine C. Balderston's article, "Johnson's Vile Melancholy," which appeared in the festschrift to Chauncey Brewster Tinker, *The Age of Johnson*, in 1949.[26]

Describing this letter as "the most problematic" in the Rylands Library collection, Wright pointed out that an undated communication of Mrs. Thrale's to Johnson, in English (she apparently felt less competent to write to him in French), but also intended for delivery to him within the house at Streatham, appears to be a response to his pleas and complaints. In *his* letter, Johnson asks for guidance as to whether he may roam freely through the house, or must confine himself to his room. If the latter, he requests that she turn the key in his door twice a day, and so, by her vigilance and protection, help him out of his weakness. "There is nothing difficult in that for you," he says (in French); "you will be able to invent a *régime* that is practicable without fuss, and efficacious without risk."

He goes on to complain of her inconsistency and neglect in "the execution of her own laws," and adds that she has "forgotten so many promises, and condemned [him] to so many reiterated pleas that the recollection horrifies [him]." Finally, he insists, "it is essential to remember what is agreed upon. I wish, my protector, that your authority might always be clear to me, and that you might hold me in that bondage which you know so well how to render happy."[27] In the apparent reply (311.1a) to this strange missive, which Chapman conjecturally dates as May 1773, Mrs. Thrale protests that she has done everything in her power to keep her promises and to pay constant attention to Johnson's "Complaint"—his melancholy, secret brooding, and she advises him to "shake off these uneasy Weights, heavier to the Mind by far than Fetters to the body. Let not your fancy dwell thus upon Confinement and Severity."

If we go on together your Confinement shall be as strict as possible except when Company comes in, which I shall more willingly endure on your Account.

Dissipation is to you a glorious Medicine, and I believe Mr. Boswell will be at last your best Physician. For the rest you really are well enough now if you will keep so; and not suffer the noblest of human Minds to be tortured with fantastic notions which rob it of all its Quiet.

"Dissipation" she appears to be using in the sense of "diversion," and the reference to Boswell no doubt anticipates the journey to Scotland and the Western Isles, which would begin on 6 August 1773. If Chapman's dating of the mysterious letter, and of Mrs. Thrale's putative reply, is accurate, the northern jaunt was just over two months away. Its therapeutic results, certainly, were to prove even better than she had forecast.

This is not the time or place for a rehashing of the "vile melancholy" issue. Balderston may well have been right in believing that Johnson was something of a masochist with a desire to be enslaved, perhaps even manacled and padlocked, in order to be relieved of his mental anguish and his nagging fears for his sanity. In the present context, however, in which we are examining the reasons for his expressing his intimate requests in French, it is important to recall a few pertinent facts:

1. The "solitude profonde" of which he complains in that letter was inevitable. Mrs. Thrale's mother was desperately ill with cancer and needed her daughter's almost constant attention.[28]

2. Extensive renovations were going on at Streatham, involving some excavation, and Johnson's room was one of those to be rebuilt and refurbished.[29]

3. Perpetual anxiety hovered around Mrs. Thrale's young children (Harry, aged 6; Hester Maria [Queeney], almost 9; Lucy Elizabeth, in precarious health and doomed to die in November of the same year, aged 4; Sophia [Sophy], aged 2; Susanna Arabella, aged 3; and another child, Ralph, shortly to be born). A measles epidemic in 1773 affected nearly all of them, and Johnson was warned to stay away if he had not had the disease. All of these things must have created great strains on the household, and it is hardly necessary to seek psychiatric explanations for the confusion and emotional disturbance that must have reigned during this very difficult period. The need for a clear-cut and practicable régime, for a system that would regularize the routine of the ménage without fuss and noise, was what Johnson appears to have been asking for, in the interests of his hostess's sanity as well as his own.[30]

4. In the final paragraph of the letter, he pleads, "Is it too much to ask of a soul such as yours, that, mistress of the others, she might become mistress of herself, and that she might overcome this inconsistency?" This, surely, is hardly the demand of a flagellant for more of the scourge and the manacles, but rather the request of a troubled and disquieted guest for the restoration of order in the household.

Why, then, was the letter written in French? There are several plausible explanations. There were workmen about the house, and maidservants, at least one of whom might have been able to read a letter in English. Henry Thrale, though engaged in his brewery business most of the time, might have intercepted such a letter, but it is unlikely that he had much knowledge of French. Young Queeney, who would be 9 on September 17 of that year, was by all accounts a precocious child, "exceedingly bright but hard to control," to use Mary Hyde's phrase.[31] Well versed already in English literature, and about to be taught Italian by Baretti,[32] she could certainly have understood any note of Johnson's in English, but French was as yet beyond her grasp.

Balderston makes much of Johnson's fear that Mrs. Thrale would not "make her rule severe enough," and she infers from this and other internal evidence that the letter is "a pathological document, the product of a sick mind," and argues that Johnson's "fantasies" were "erotic in nature." Part of her argument hinges on the word *régime*, which she associates, along with allusions to padlocks and manacles and the kissing of feet, with masochism and other "phenomena fairly commonplace in the records of sex pathology."[33] A more recent, and in some ways friendlier, study of Johnson's problems, by the late George Irwin, traces the origin of Johnson's difficulties to a deep-seated hatred of his mother, and the process by which he subconsciously sought to resolve his guilt and allay his anxieties becomes, on this theory, a kind of association transference to Mrs. Thrale.[34]

Perhaps, in the end, we ought to leave psychiatry to the psychiatrists. For my part, I find it difficult to believe that a man so obsessed would go on, later in the same year, to have such a delightful holiday in the company of James Boswell, and to record his adventures in what must surely stand as a literary masterpiece of the first order of magnitude.

4

It is clear from what I have said that Johnson had an undoubted command of the French language, which he exercised creatively, amusingly, and purposefully, as the situation required. A professor of French whom I consulted on this subject, and to whom I showed samples of his translations and his French compositions, expressed the opinion that his skill in the language was well above the standard of undergraduate French. "It is undoubtedly the French of a well-educated Englishman," she said, "but it also shows a strong vocabulary and a reasonable grasp of idiom, together with a courtliness of expression that would be considered rare at the present time."

Where, when, and how did Johnson acquire these abilities? My answer must be partly conjectural and partly logical, rather than factual, since we have no firm knowledge of any special training or tuition in Johnson's experience. What we do know may be simply stated:

1. His first extensive exercise in rendering French into English dates back to the early 1730s, when he dictated to Hector his translation of the Le Grand version of Lobo, a book he had first encountered as an undergraduate at Oxford.

2. Gilbert Walmesley, in his letter of recommendation to the Rev. John Colson, dated 2 March 1737, in which he praises the abilities of both Garrick and Johnson, refers particularly to the latter's talent for translation from French as well as Latin.[35]

3. When Johnson was growing up in Lichfield, there were, in addition to the Garrick family, a number of Huguenot refugees capable of giving French instruction.[36]

4. Both Walmesley and Cornelius Ford, who had a considerable say in his education, were men of the world who almost certainly read and understood French.

5. Johnson possessed a copy of Abel Boyer's *Dictionnaire Royal Français et Anglais*, and at least one other work by the same authority.[37]

6. At Oxford, in his time, an experiment was under way for the teaching of French and other modern languages to a selected group of undergraduates and graduates. Although there is no evidence that Johnson, or anyone else from Pembroke, participated in it, it is not unreasonable to suppose that an alert and highly intelligent student such as he would have been aware of it. There is some reason to believe, moreover, that some Oxford tutors did indeed teach French, if only on an informal basis.[38]

7. Johnson acquired, quite early in his career, a considerable knowledge of the work of French writers—knowledge of a kind that he was able to apply, not only in his duties for the *Gentleman's Magazine*, but in his editorial work on Shakespeare as well. To cite one example, in his *Miscellaneous Observations on Macbeth* (1745), commenting on the lines,

> Come Fate into the lists,
> And champion me to th'utterance[,]

he notes, "This passage will be best explained by translating it into the language from whence the only word of difficulty in it is borrowed. *Que la destinée se rendre en lice, et qu'elle me donne un défi à l'outrance.* (His note was repeated and slightly expanded in the 1765 edition of Johnson's Shakespeare).[39] This impressive instance of Johnson's ability to recall an appropriate French usage is not by any means an isolated one. When editing the text of *Hamlet*, for example, he rejected a conjectural emendation of Warburton's ("sign" for "sigh" at IV.vii.122) by saying that it was so ingenious that "to criticize it is like drawing a bow against a hero, or as Voltaire writes to the Empress [in his *Ode à la reine de Hongrie, Marie-Thérèse d'Autriche*]

> Le genereux François
> Te combat et t'admire."

Though he has slightly misquoted Voltaire here, inverting the word order in the first line, the fact that he remembered an apt passage from the French is interesting.[40] As I have noted elsewhere, even when his recollection is imperfect, he is able to identify the French source and its author. In his Shakespeare, indeed, he refers to a number of French authors whose works he evidently knew at first hand, such as Scarron, Brantôme, Rabelais, and Scudéry, as well as Voltaire.

8. He formed in his early years a habit, which became lifelong, of reading French literature. In the *Lives of the Poets*, for instance, there are references to nearly thirty French authors, including Boileau, Fénelon, Montesquieu, Racine, Rousseau, and Voltaire. That his study was linguistic as well as literary is plainly discerned when he comments on Boileau's *Satires* from a grammatical as well as a stylistic point of view.[41]

I believe that Johnson acquired his knowledge of French largely through self-instruction, and that he used two of the works of Abel Boyer in the process: the *Dictionnaire Royal* already mentioned, and *The Compleat French Master*, which had appeared as early as 1694, and which was probably on the shelves of Michael Johnson's bookshop. This popular handbook of Boyer's was not the first of its kind.[42] An anonymous grammar, called *A Plaine Pathway to the French Tongue*, had preceded it by at least a century. Aimed particularly at merchants, it was designed to teach the language by means of dialogues, such as business conversations between dealers, grocers, tailors, booksellers, bookbinders, linen drapers, and shoemakers.[43] Boyer's *Compleat French Master*, while using similar techniques, was directed at a higher level of society, being proudly described on its title page as intended "for the use of His Highness the Duke of Gloucester." It, too, employs "familiar dialogues" as one of its chief means of instruction, but this time they are much less business oriented, taking the form of witty and humorous colloquies, some of them quite racy, on the subject of love and other human relationships. In the second edition (1699), which I examined (the edition most likely to be available to Johnson), 180 pages are devoted to what Boyer calls "A New Methodical French Grammar," covering articulation, orthography, prosody, analogy, and syntax, and these are followed by a sixty-three-page vocabulary (two columns to the page) of "all the most necessary words to speak either language," thirty-three pages of familiar phrases, 153 pages of the familiar dialogues, seven pages of proverbs, and twelve pages of French songs, with music, all on love themes. The familiar phrases include some rather belligerent ones, such as

Vous serez foüetté: you shall be whipt
Vous meritez le foüet: you deserve to be whipt
Je vous rosserai: I'll pommel you
Je vous battrai dos et ventre: I'll beat you back and side
Prenez ce Garçon, et fouettez le d'importance: Take up this Boy, and whip him soundly

—intended, no doubt, for the use of a schoolmaster.[44]

This, at any rate, was the content of *The Compleat French Master*. In general, an intelligent student could indeed pick up a fair knowledge of French from this book, together with Boyer's *Dictionnaire Royal*, which was published a little later, in 1702, and a copy of which, as has been stated, Johnson possessed. That *Dictionnaire*, incidentally, was claimed by its author to be a more comprehensive *English* dictionary than any previous one, the English words and idioms in it being defined and explained as well as translated into their French equivalents.

In his Preface, Boyer expresses his thanks to a Mr. Savage, an English *gentilhomme d'esprit et de mérite*, who had generously augmented his vocabulary with more than a thousand additional words. The Dictionary of National Biography entry for Boyer, who, by the way, had left France during the Huguenot persecutions about the same time as Garrick's grandfather, identifies the Mr. Savage as Richard Savage, Johnson's friend, but, since Savage was only five years old in 1702, a more likely candidate would be John Savage (1673–1747), who translated a number of French texts into English.[45]

There is, however, a valid historical link between Boyer and Johnson. In 1713 Boyer began publication of a monthly periodical, *The Political State of Great Britain*, which contained reports of parliamentary debates, based on notes given to him by members of both Houses, the names of Lords being confined to initials or other abbreviations in order to avoid legal action, but surprisingly, with the full names of the members of the House of Commons frequently listed. Thus, the precedent for the publication of parliamentary debates, compiled by Guthrie and Johnson at a later date for the *Gentleman's Magazine*, had been set by Abel Boyer.[46]

One of the reasons for the popularity of Boyer's *Dictionnaire* and *Compleat French Master* and other books of the kind in Britain was the growing awareness of educated citizens of the need to communicate with their contemporaries in Europe, where French was the essential language of commerce and diplomacy. While it is clear that the teaching of modern languages was not a high priority in the grammar schools or in the universities in Johnson's time, and that most of the language instruction was performed by resident and travelling tutors for the benefit of those who could afford it, several moves were afoot to remedy the situation. I mention two of these in particular.

First, in a book titled *Of Education with respect to Grammar Schools, and the Universities*, published in 1701, eight years before Johnson was born, the Rev. Francis Brokesby advanced, among other things, the rather revolutionary proposal that young people be trained up "in such useful learning as may render them beneficial to themselves and the Community." Ahead of his time, perhaps, he advocated language instruction at an early age, with emphasis on Latin, Greek, and Hebrew, but with exercises, also, "in some Modern Language, which it is the interest of the Scholar to be acquainted with, and able to write therein."

In this book, Brokesby appears to believe that regular modern language instruction was already available in the universities, but there is little supporting evidence of this.[47] In a fairly determined attempt to uncover information on this point, the only scrap I found was a set of manuscript notes in the Balliol College Library, made by a student of French in the late seventeenth century—translations of stock phrases and a pattern of conjugations that would suggest rote learning. Limited though they are, these notes show that at least one student was learning French at Balliol.[48]

Of interest in this context is my second piece of intelligence with regard to attempts to improve the situation. It comes in Sir Charles Firth's *Modern Languages at Oxford, 1724–1929* (1929), which contains some information on the teaching of French at Oxford in Johnson's day. Pointing out that the Revolution of 1688 had brought Great Britain "again into close contact with Europe," and that the long continuing struggle between England and France had involved the country in coalitions and wars that "brought her into hostile relations with one half of Europe and alliances with the other," Firth observes that the British government had at last faced up to the need for officials to be given appropriate training in modern languages, and particularly in French, which Voltaire had been right in describing as "almost the universal language." Thus, in 1724,

the experiment of introducing the teaching of Modern Languages at Oxford and Cambridge was tried by the Government. Why should not the Universities supply a national need by supplying men trained to use living languages as well as men skilled in Latin and Greek?[49]

Under the scheme introduced by the Government, twenty young men in each of the two universities were to be instructed gratuitously in Modern History and Modern Languages "to fit them for the service of the State, and to be given employment at home or abroad if they proved their proficiency."[50] To provide the necessary instruction for these students, George I endowed a Professor of Modern History with a salary of £400 a year, out of which he was to pay two teachers of modern languages to work under his direction. The Letters Patent setting forth the pertinent regulations, largely the work of Lord Townshend, Walpole's Secretary of State, and Edmund Gibson, Bishop of London, are dated 28 September 1724. A young M.A. of Christ Church, David Gregory, was appointed to the Professorship at Oxford, and took up his duties on 26 October 1724. Fifteen of the twenty scholars were selected early in 1725, and the remaining five were added on 21 January 1726. Care was taken to make the list contain representatives from as many of the colleges as possible. The scholars were nominated for three years, and each was required to learn two languages.

One of Gregory's functions was to report annually on the progress of the students. Copies of his reports, with frank appraisals of each of them, are in the Public Record Office. They clearly demonstrate that the major intention of the program was to encourage them to speak and write in the chosen languages, and that the Modern History element was of minor importance. Indeed, the only teaching required of Gregory consisted of four public lectures in the year.[51]

His reports show that the scholars, most of whom had a solid background in classical languages, performed well on the whole. Nearly all of them made French their first choice, and either German, Italian, or High Dutch their second. Some of them, like Warren of Balliol (of whom more anon) and Wyndham of Wadham, had difficulty in sparing enough time from their other studies to cope with the linguistic work.[52]

For a variety of reasons, the experiment failed. Not all of those selected were strongly motivated to language learning. By the time of Johnson's matriculation in 1728, only one of the original twenty was still in residence. In a letter to Lord Townshend, dated 24 May of that year, Gregory hints that the conservatism of the University, which was consistently hostile to the House of Hanover and to the Whig party, and therefore reluctant to accede to recommendations from the throne or the government, had something to do with the imperfect progress that had been made. Nevertheless, he urges Townshend to appoint more scholars to the foundation. Gregory continued in the Professorship until 1736, when he became a Canon of Christ Church (he later became Dean). He still had the duty of appointing and paying the two teachers of language their £25 per annum, but, as Firth observes, "Beyond the fact that they existed nothing is known about them."[53]

Firth attributes the failure of the language experiment, in part, to the fact that there was, as yet, no organized Civil Service in Britain. The attempt to train civil servants at the universities met with the same kind of resistance as had been noted by Francis Brokesby against anything that smacked of "useful learning."[54]

From the point of view of my present inquiry, however, the existence of French language teaching in Oxford just before and during Johnson's time may well be linked to the fact that he studied there the Le Grand translation of Father Lobo's *Voyage to Abyssinia*. Although none of the scholars mentioned in Gregory's reports was a Pembroke man, there were several at nearby Christ Church, and it is not impossible that Johnson, who had made contact with that college through his friend, John Taylor, and who knew a good deal about that College before Taylor's arrival, was acquainted with some of those, including Gregory, who were involved in the experiment. Certainly, Oxford was small enough at the time for the news of such an innovation to be spread about.[55]

While my tracing of the subsequent careers of the twenty-four students on whom David Gregory reported is not yet complete, I would like to note at this time one possible, and two certain, links with Samuel Johnson. One of the participants in the experiment was a Balliol man called Thomas Warren, and you will recall that it was one Thomas Warren who edited the *Birmingham Journal* and, together with Edmund Hector, persuaded Johnson to translate the French version of Father Lobo's *Voyage*. The possibility of a connection here is, however, quite remote.[56]

A second, and more plausible, link is with a Christ Church participant, Gilbert West, whom Gregory rated very highly, and who was given immediate employment on graduation with the then Secretary of State, Lord Townshend, himself.[57] Though he had so early in his career become an expert in international law, as well as a proficient writer of French, West decided to retire in 1729 to a pleasant house in Wickham in Kent, where, in Johnson's words in the *Lives of the Poets*, "he devoted himself to learning and to piety," and produced some translations of Pindar that Johnson described as "too paraphrastical."[58]

The third and most important link (indeed the missing link I had hoped to find) is with a man for whom Johnson had a high personal regard, Robert James, M.D., inventor of the controversial, kill-or-cure pills and powders, and author of James's *Medicinal Dictionary*. James, who was born in Kinvaston, Staffordshire, and educated at Lichfield Grammar School, was four years Johnson's senior, but, nonetheless, a lifelong friend. He matriculated at St. John's College, Oxford, in 1722, and graduated with a B.A. on 5 July 1726, but went on to study medicine and to be admitted an extra-licentiate of the College of Physicians. He ultimately settled in London, but first practiced in Sheffield, Lichfield, and Birmingham, and was in the Lichfield-Birmingham area at the time of Johnson's employment under Thomas Warren. Incidentally, James's language facility and training paid off in later years, for he translated a number of medical texts from French and Italian.[59]

In Gregory's reports to the Secretary of State James is given an even warmer commendation than West. "He writes and speaks both French and Italian very well," notes Gregory, "and has the peculiar happiness that with his good parts he has the most diligence and assiduity imaginable."[60]

Whether Johnson encountered James at Oxford we do not know. What is of importance in this context is that a fellow Lichfeldian, and a known friend of Johnson's, had set the pace in French studies just before Johnson's time at the University, with consequences that I have attempted to demonstrate.

To conclude, let me recall a scene in Boswell's *Life*, recorded at the Thrales' on 7 April 1778:

> He was for a considerable time occupied in reading
> *Memoires de Fontenelle*, leaning and swinging upon the
> low gate into the court, without his hat.[61]

If I were wearing a hat, I would now gladly doff it in his direction.

NOTES

1. Boswell, *Life*, IV, 21 and n.

2. Hesther Lynch Piozzi, "Anecdotes of the Late Samuel Johnson LL.D." in *Johnsonian Miscellanies*, ed. G. B. Hill, 2 vols. (Oxford: Clarendon Press, 1897), II, 193–98, 261–62, et passim.

3. Ibid., I, 334.

4. *The French Journals of Mrs. Thrale and Dr. Johnson*, ed. M. Tyson and H. Guppy (Manchester: John Rylands Library, 1932), p. 79.

5. Ibid., pp. 217–18 (18 Sept. 1775).

6. Ibid., pp. 85–86 and n.1.

7. Ibid., p. 169.

8. Ibid., p. 175.

9. Ibid.

10. Ibid., p. 177.

11. Ibid., p. 181.

12. Ibid., p. 186.

13. Ibid., p. 78.

14. Ibid., p. 131.

15. Ibid., pp. 96, 106–107; F. A. Hedgcock, *A Cosmopolitan Actor: David Garrick and his French Friends* (London: Stanley Paul, [1912]), p. 218 et passim; R. A. Barrell, *Chesterfield et la France* (Paris: Nouvelles Editions Latines, 1968), pp. 37 ff.; R. A. Barrell, ed., *French Correspondence of the Fourth Earl of Chesterfield*, 2 vols. (Ottawa: Borealis Press, 1980), passim. Barrell notes (I, 1) that, of the 2,600 Chesterfield letters extant, approximately one-ninth are in French, including 150 addressed to his natural son and to his godson.

16. See John L. Abbott, "Samuel Johnson and 'The Life of Dr. Richard Meade,'" *Bulletin of the John Rylands Library*, 54, 1 (1971), 14–15.

17. *Letters*, 58.1 and n. 3.

18. *The Greek Theatre of Father Brumoy*, trans. Charlotte Lennox et al. 3 vols. (London, 1759). The French original is *Le Théâtre des Grecs*, par le R. P. Brumoy, de la Compagnie de Jésus à Paris, 3 tomes. (Paris, 1730).

19. *The Greek Theatre*, III, 138; *Le Théâtre*, III, xxiv. Here I must acknowledge my indebtedness to Professor John Abbott for his assistance and advice, and for his generous provision of copies of his writings on the subject of Johnson's translations from the French. In particular, his unpublished doctoral dissertation (Michigan State University, 1963), "Dr. Johnson's Translations from the French," contains a chapter (Chapter IX, pp. 150–68) on the Brumoy translation. While agreeing with Abbott's conclusion that this is one of the most literal of Johnson's translations, I have noted some examples of passages in which the renderings are perhaps a little freer than he allows.

20. Abbott, "Dr. Johnson's Translations from the French," p. 155.

21. Johnson, *Works*, II, 217 (*Idler* 69).

22. *Life*, I, 86–87. See also note 2 above.

23. For the four letters, see *Letters*, 213, 248, 307.1, and 400; for the French phrases, ibid., 79, 93, 258, 311, 419, 423, 539, 779.5, 857, 954, 955.

24. Barrell, *French Correspondence*, I.1.

25. J. D. Wright, "Some Unpublished Letters to and from Dr. Johnson," *Bulletin of the John Rylands Library*, 16 (1932), 33–34, 61–65.

26. Katharine C. Balderston, "Johnson's Vile Melancholy," *The Age of Johnson: Essays Presented to Chauncey Brewster Tinker* (New Haven: Yale Univ. Press, 1949), pp. 3–14.

27. The translation of this letter, with which no paraphrastic liberties have been taken, is my own.

28. Mary Hyde, *The Thrales of Streatham Park* (Cambridge, Mass.: Harvard Univ. Press, 1977), pp. 60–61.

29. Ibid., pp. 48, 52, 69, 73.

30. Ibid., p. 73 et passim.

31. Ibid., p. 79.

32. Ibid., p. 76.

33. Balderston, pp. 8, 11.

34. George Irwin, *Samuel Johnson: A Personality in Conflict* (Auckland, N.Z.: Auckland Univ. Press, 1971), pp. 127–28. Irwin's argument is not without its ambiguities, however. Not content with the theory of transference to Mrs. Thrale, he writes of her

mother, Mrs. Salusbury, "Johnson seems unconsciously to have transferred to her the feelings he had once towards his own mother." On this reasoning, one might claim that the world is full of threatening, domineering mothers.

35. *Life*, I, 102.

36. Mary Alden Hopkins, *Dr. Johnson's Lichfield* (New York: Hastings House, 1952), p. 22, notes that many of the clergy in Lichfield spoke French, and that there were others there, besides the Garricks, who were of Huguenot origin or descent. There is evidence, too, that French was taught in Lichfield by prisoners of war. See Rosemary Parnaby, "Murals Found in a Bird St. Shop," *Transactions of the Lichfield Archaeological and Historical Society*, 2 (1960–61), 53.

37. *The Sale Catalogue of Samuel Johnson's Library*, ed. J. D. Fleeman (Victoria, B.C.: Univ. of Victoria, 1975), Lot 502; and *Samuel Johnson's Library, An Annotated Guide*, ed. Donald Greene (Victoria, B.C.: Univ. of Victoria, 1975), pp. 40–41.

38. See pp. 91–92 below, and note 48; and Sir Charles Firth, *Modern Languages at Oxford 1724–1929* (Oxford: Clarendon Press, 1929), pp. 1–19.

39. *Macbeth*, III.ii (in later editions III.i.71–72), and Johnson, *Works*, VII, 26.

40. *Works*, VIII, 1000.

41. See, e.g., James Gray, "'Swear by my Sword,' A Note in Johnson's Shakespeare," *Shakespeare Quarterly*, 27 (1976), 205–208; and Johnson, *Lives*, I, 224–25 (Life of Rochester) for his particular knowledge of Passerat and Boileau.

42. Nor was it the last. In the *Gentleman's Magazine* Register of Books for April 1735 (p. 222), e.g., there is an announcement of "A New French Grammar teaching a person of an ordinary Capacity, without the help of a Master, to read, speak and write that Tongue, in less than half the usual Time, in an entire new and easy Method. By J. E. Tandon. Printed for J. Fox, pr. 2s."

43. Only one copy of *A Plaine Pathway*, printed in London by Thomas East in 1575, is known to have survived. It was reprinted between 1575 and 1600, but only the title page of the "newly-corrected" edition is extant (BL Hartley 5936/360). A facsimile reprint was published by Scolar Press in 1968.

44. A. Boyer, *The Compleat French Master for Ladies and Gentlemen* (London: Printed for R. Sare at Gray's-inn-gate in Holbourn, etc., 1699).

45. The DNB author notes that Boyer's *Dictionnaire* "was much superior to every previous work of the kind, and has been the basis of very many subsequent French-English dictionaries."

46. Boyer had been provided by members of both Houses of Parliament, among whom he mentioned Lord Stanhope, with reports of their speeches (DNB entry).

47. F.B.B.D. [The Rev. Francis Brokesby], *Of Education with respect to Grammar Schools, and the Universities; concluding with Directions to Young Students in the Universities*. . . . (London, 1701), Table of Contents (unpaginated), and pp. 81, 131.

48. I am grateful to the former Balliol Librarian, Mr. Vincent Quinn, for drawing these uncatalogued manuscript notes to my attention, and for other helpful information.

49. Firth, *Modern Languages*, pp. 2–4.

50. Firth, *Modern Languages*, pp. 4–5.

51. Firth, *Modern Languages*, p. 6.

52. Firth, *Modern Languages*, pp. 8–10.

53. Firth, *Modern Languages*, pp. 14–15.

54. Brokesby, pp. 130–31.

55. *Life*, I, 76. John Taylor's tutor at Christ Church, Edmund Bateman, whom Johnson admired and recommended, was a colleague of David Gregory. According to Thomas Hearne, Bateman and Gregory shared an interest in architectural history. Bodleian Library, Western MSS: *Hearne's Diaries*, Vol. 127, f. 40 (entry for Wednesday, 2 Sept. 1730).

56. Though the earlier years of Thomas Warren the printer's life are obscure, it is unlikely that he went to university. The only Thomas Warren recorded in *Alumni Oxonienses, 1715–1886* as a gentleman of Balliol College in the Johnson years became Rector of Halwell, Devon, in 1735. W. Musgrave's *Obituary Prior to 1800* (London: Harleian Society, 1899–1901) gives details for only one Thomas Warren, who died of the stone in Warminster, Wilts., on 20 September 1767, at the age of 80, but Joseph Hill, *The Book Makers and the Book Sellers of Old Birmingham* (Birmingham: Shakespeare Press, 1907), p. 45 n., informs us that Thomas Warren the printer was buried at St. Philip's in Birmingham. By coincidence, both Warrens died in the same year. See also *A Dictionary of the Printers and Booksellers who were at work in England Scotland and Ireland from 1726 to 1775*, ed. H. R. Plomer et al. (Oxford: Clarendon Press, 1932), p. 257.

57. Firth, pp. 8–11.

58. *Lives*, III, 329, 331 (Life of Gilbert West).

59. James's translations included those of Prosper Alpinus, *The Presages of Life and Death in Diseases*; F. Hoffman, *Halle, the Younger: A Dissertation on Endemical Diseases*: T. Mouffet, *Health's Improvement*; S. Paulli, *A Treatise on Tobacco*; B. Ramazzini, *Health Preserved*; and *The Modern Practice of Physic*, a translation of the aphorisms of Hermann Boerhaave and the commentaries of F. Hoffman.

60. Firth, *Modern Languages*, p. 10. Copies of Gregory's three reports on the participants in the experiment are in the Public Record Office.

61. *Life*, III, 247.

MARTINE WATSON BROWNLEY

6 · Samuel Johnson and the Writing of History

Fuelled by various unfortunately memorable conversational remarks and a few passages in his writings, the common view of Samuel Johnson has long been that he was at best uninterested in and at worst hostile to history. Yet many of his works and his projects, his library, and much of his reading show his respect for historical study and his belief in its importance. The discrepancies in his recorded stances have been explained mainly in terms of Johnson's personality and his contemporary context. From the beginning, Boswell related some of Johnson's more pungent comments to his habit of talking for victory, while later commentators recognized his tendency to use history occasionally as a stalking horse for biography. Critics have also pointed out Johnson's dislike of the Scots and of deism and atheism, which made him unsympathetic to Gibbon, Hume, and Robertson, his hesitancy about the general utility of history, and his reactions against historical analogies misused for Whig political purposes or fashionable conversational cliches.[1] Although all of these are valid explanations for Johnson's occasional negativity about history itself, they do not account for his attitude toward the writing of history. On this subject, contrary to his usual habit, the reductionism sometimes characteristic of his conversation is not offset by more balanced views developed in his writing. He constantly portrays historical composition as an undemanding endeavor; the description in *Idler* 94 is typical: "He that writes the history of past times, undertakes only to decorate known facts by new beauties of method or of style, or at most to illustrate them by his own reflections."[2] Such oversimplification is particularly puzzling in view of the clarity with which Johnson recognized the manifold difficulties facing the historian. Indeed, in his most extended discussion of historical writing, after glowingly depicting the authorial advantages of "the happy historian," he admits that "very few in any age have been able to raise themselves to reputation by writing histories."[3] Johnson's views on historical truth, narrative, and style not only show why he persisted in reducing the historian to a compiler with literary skill, but they also reveal larger and more basic concerns about historical content and form that contributed to the contradictory opinions he expressed about history itself.

Boswell praised Johnson's narrative of public affairs in the *Life of Waller,* and suggested "how nobly he might have executed a *Tory History* of his country."[4] Johnson did possess many of the attributes of a good historian. Strict and literal truth in history, as in everything else, was always primary with Johnson. However, he was also echoing the first point made in every critical discussion of historical writing since classical times when he emphasized that "the first law of History" is "the Obligation to tell Truth" and that "the first qualification of an historian" is "the knowledge of the truth."[5] Because he was so deeply concerned that "Many falsehoods are passing into uncontradicted history,"[6] he constantly stressed the importance of absolute accuracy in historical writing. He himself lacked much patience for adjusting "minute events,"[7] but he was eager for others to do so. He wrote to Charles Burney that he was glad that publication of his *Account of the Musical Performances in Commemoration of Handel* had been delayed, "since you have gained an opportunity of being more exact."[8] He sneered at "that Bulk, at which modern Histories generally arrive" by "adopting flying Reports, and inserting unattested Facts."[9]

Johnson had learned well many of the lessons which the seventeenth-century English antiquarian movement had taught historians, particularly the need for reliable sources and for proper evaluation of them. He recognized the importance of documentary evidence, stressing the superiority of written history over tradition and complaining to Boswell that "it was but of late that historians bestowed pains and attention in consulting records, to attain to accuracy."[10] In his writings on the Seven Years' War in the *Literary Magazine,* which have been described by Donald Greene as Johnson's attempt to develop "a piece of substantial and serious historiography," he included full texts of various diplomatic and political documents, in order to preserve *"materials for the history of the present time."*[11] He was a discriminating evaluator of historical evidence, whether written or oral. On their travels in Scotland, Boswell lauded "Dr. Johnson's peculiar accuracy of investigation," which "detected much traditional fiction, and many gross mistakes"—a positive view of the systematic and relentless demolitions of local lore and legend that often enraged his hosts. With written records Johnson could be equally impressive. In a breakfast conversation on the trip, for example, he pointed out that Bacon's history was not a primary source for the reign of Henry VII, but simply an amalgam of other historians' accounts and tradition. Not until after the middle of the nineteenth century would historians, aided by German source criticism, come to exactly the same conclusion.[12]

Johnson possessed in abundance the "distrust" that he termed "a necessary qualification of a student in history."[13] His thoroughgoing scepticism was more similar to French historical thought of the period than to English. Like the Pyrrhonists, he saw only too clearly the many obstacles in the search for historical truth, although he stopped short of their conclusions. For example, in his review of *The Account of the Conduct of the Duchess of Marlborough*, after considering all of the problems raised by eyewitness accounts, he writes that the only viable option might seem to be to "distrust every relation, and live in perpetual negligence of past events; or . . . in perpetual suspense." Nevertheless, he finally affirms that "truth, though not always obvious, is generally discoverable."[14] His rigorous approach to historical evidence, however, led him to emphasize the limitations of factual validity. In answering conversational cant about the utility of reading history, he pointed out that "We must consider how very little history there is; I mean real authentick history. That certain Kings reigned, and certain battles were fought, we can depend upon as true; but all the colouring, all the philosophy, of history is conjecture."[15] For Johnson, these basic facts of history, the only totally reliable elements in any historical account, were also the least useful. He pointed out that historical facts generally did not supply motives.[16] They supplied "few lessons applicable to private life,"[17] the direct moral instruction Johnson desired in all writing. The kind of history that Johnson valued—the history necessary "to judge rightly of the present," the history which he believed self-interest alone made it "not prudent" to neglect, and the history that in education he ranked second in importance only to "the religious and moral knowledge of right and wrong"[18]—had to offer more than factual evidence.

At the same time, what Johnson understood more clearly than most other commentators of his era, and what concerned him most of all about historical writing, was that the most rudimentary attempt to interpret the bare facts of the past necessarily moved the historian away from the absolute truth essential to history. Again and again, he expressed his concern over how the imposition of form on factual evidence endangers historical accuracy. He realized that a historian can very easily "imagine himself to know what he only guesses." He opposed "systematic dogmatism," when historians "hastily improve hints into systems."[19] Johnson was extremely sensitive to the volatility and vulnerability of historical evidence. He noted that in many cases, the extant records could support opposite interpretations. He worried that modern historians "often deceive themselves and their readers when they attempt to explain by reason that which happened by chance, when they search for profound policy and subtle refinement in temporary expedients."[20] More than most in the eighteenth century, Johnson was aware of the differences between the past and the present. He emphasized the limitations that present vision imposes on evaluations of the past, complaining that "Our political historians too often forget the state of the age they are endeavoring to describe," and suggesting that the accounts of many ancient historians were unfairly dismissed as false because modern times offered no parallels.[21] His own sturdy common sense proved an invaluable tool for historical inquiries, in part because, unlike Voltaire, he never elevated it into an absolute standard for judgment. Finally, from his knowledge of the human mind and heart, Johnson knew how often truth was violated through "inveterate prejudice and prevailing passions." Patriotism created problems, because "every historian discovers his country."[22] Shame might lead historians who wrote from the losing side to exaggerate the power of their conquerors.[23] There was the natural desire of both historians and readers to prefer pleasure to instruction in historical accounts and to believe what flattered them.[24] Human memory itself he viewed as fallible and untrustworthy.[25] In all of these instances, Johnson's basic emphasis falls on the ways that the human imagination could insinuate itself and obtrude at every point in the process of creating history, between the event and the oral or written evidence about it, between the evidence and its various interpreters, and even between the historian's work and the reader. He recoiled from the inevitable damages that the imagination could inflict on historical truth.

Johnson's insistence on absolute truth in history, and his gloomy recognition of all the obstacles to obtaining that truth, once led Boswell to accuse him of reducing "all history to no better than an almanack, a mere chronological series of remarkable events."[26] Boswell's remark accurately describes the only kind of record that Johnson totally trusted, but such regressions to chronicle could not offer what Johnson wanted from historical writing. His primary concern might be truth, but he also required art. Swift's achievement—in Johnson's view, relating "what he had to tell distinctly enough"—was not sufficient, for in history Johnson was equally concerned with "the merit of the composition." He sneered that the "strong facts" that marked Swift's history were equally characteristic of "the Sessions-paper of the Old Bailey."[27] In a letter to Cave in 1743 discussing an abortive and still obscure "Historical Design" in which the two were involved, he opposed "Naked Papers, without an Historical treatise interwoven."[28] The reference reflects the formal practices of most of the early English antiquarians, whose histories were simply series of documents. Johnson wrote that

"No active or comprehensive mind can forbear some attention to the reliques of antiquity," and he encouraged and supported various antiquarian endeavors.[29] But one of his letters describes "A mere antiquarian" as "a rugged being,"[30] and he viewed many of their productions similarly. Leland's *Itinary* he criticized as "an unpleasant book of mere hints."[31] He several times effusively praised Lord Hailes's *Annals of Scotland* for offering all the accuracy he so often vainly sought in history—"such a stability of dates, such a certainty of facts, and such a punctuality of citation"—and he even had some positive things to say about Hailes's narrative. Nevertheless, in the end he admitted that the "mere dry particulars" which the *Annals* contained left them "to be considered as a Dictionary."[32]

If for Johnson collections of evidence alone did not create history, neither did chronology. He considered it along with geography as "necesary preparatives and attendants of history," and wrote that without it, "History is little more than romance."[33] But in his view the "chronological series of actions or preferments" insufficient for biography[34] was no better for history. Like Gibbon, who believed that only those who composed narratives from evidence of the past could be considered historians, Johnson considered narration essential to history. The first two of the three definitions of "history" in his *Dictionary* focus on narrative. He distinguished between journals, which had "regard only to time," and history, which "ranges facts according to their dependence on each other, and postpones or anticipates according to the convenience of narration."[35] His two main requirements for historical narrative were generality and rapidity. He disliked excessive particularity in history, because "the Spirit of History . . . is contrary to minute exactness."[36] Knolles, who he felt "displayed all the excellence that narration can admit," was "without minuteness."[37] In contrast, Thomas Birch's *History of the Royal Society of London* was more "a diary than a history," because it proceeds "so minutely" and "so slowly."[38] A certain amount of compression, but not too much, was necessary for the effects he admired. Carte's material was "diffused in too many words," but because of Tacitus's excessive compactness, Johnson commented that the Roman "seems to me rather to have made notes for an historical work, than to have written a history."[39]

Johnson was well aware that narrative, like any other interpretation imposed on historical evidence, could distort the truth. Although he praised Voltaire as "a good narrator" and considered his *Charles XII* "one of the finest pieces of historical writing in any language," he pointed out that Voltaire's love of "a striking story" had led him into falsehood.[40] But as a whole, in criticizing historical writing, particularly that of his contemporaries, his emphasis was on stylistic distortions. Johnson reflected classical and Renaissance commonplaces by favoring a historical style between the overly poetic and the overly prosaic, or, as Edward Gibbon described it, "the middle tone between a dull Chronicle and a Rhetorical declamation."[41] Bishop Burnet's writing, for example, Johnson condemned as "mere chit-chat"; he was equally unhappy with "the foppery of Dalrymple." Sheffield, lacking "the fire and fancy of a poet," found the middle way in his history and earned Johnson's praise.[42]

Johnson was very much of his age in insisting that historical writing display both solid factual evidence and literary art. His contemporaries were finally closing the gap between the two that had developed during the seventeenth century, when legitimate concerns about eliminating rhetorical distortions in history had led to such excessive emphasis on content rather than form that effective expression was at best distrusted and at worst spurned in historical composition. This rigid separation lessened in the early eighteenth century as the antiquarian enthusiasm and political fury that had fuelled it died down, but not until Hume's and Robertson's histories in the 1750s and the 1760s did the rift start to narrow in practice. Beginning in 1776, when Gibbon synthesized the scholar, the philosopher, and the literary stylist, joining seventeenth-century research with Enlightenment philosophy in inimitable prose, factual evidence and literary art were fused as closely as they had ever been in England. But this merger of evidence and style in historical writing, the achievement of the great British triumvirate of historians, exacerbated many of Johnson's deepest concerns about the ways in which any imposed form could distort historical truth. He disliked dry antiquarian writing, but he feared that the very virtues of his contemporaries represented a movement too far in the opposite direction.

The problems that chiefly concerned Johnson emerge clearly in his detailed review of Thomas Blackwell's *Memoirs of the Court of Augustus*, where he criticizes not "the facts of this history, but the style; not the veracity, but the address of the writer."[43] Always sensitive to the historical context, Johnson condemns Blackwell's anachronistic use of modern terms. But the bulk of his criticism concerns Blackwell's failure to maintain the middle style proper for history. Blackwell mingles the grand and the burlesque "with most unlucky dexterity," and uses jocular and light words "with great solemnity." In general, Johnson blames overwriting—the "luxuriant style," the "gaudy or hyperbolical epithets"—for most of Blackwell's deviations from the mean. Having "heated his imagination," Blackwell expects to do the same for his readers. But his "exclamations," "zeal," and "declamations" only show his political partiality—Johnson sneers at "the *lawless Caesar*, whom this author, probably, stabs every day and night in his sleeping or waking dreams"—while at the same time retarding his narrative. Sometimes Blackwell's stylistic excesses not only obscure historical truth, but sense itself; Johnson points out certain "sonorous sentence[s]" which are meaningless "noise."

In what he termed the "garden of eloquence"[44] of a minor writer like Blackwell, Johnson saw the flaws he considered characteristic of most contemporary historical styles. Among the greater historians of his time, William Robertson, the only one of the three whom Johnson liked personally, bore the brunt of his attack. Johnson complained that Robertson "paints," criticizing him for his "pretty words" and his "tinsel." He objected to Robertson's "*verbiage.*" He told Boswell that "I always thought Robertson would be crushed by his own weight,— would be buried under his own ornaments."[45] Boswell was so concerned that some of Johnson's remarks about Robertson were unfair to Robertson's work and inaccurately represented Johnson's real opinions of it, that after recording them, he twice editorially insisted that Johnson actually recognized Robertson's merits.[46] Murphy, too, wrote that Robertson's *History of Scotland* was the subject of Johnson's "constant praise."[47] At one point Johnson himself even went so far as to blame his own influence for Robertson's stylistic faults—"having too many words, and those too big ones."[48]

Given his general respect for the man and his works, that Johnson would comment as harshly as he did about Robertson's style indicates the depth of his concern about the issues he saw at stake—in this case, historical truth itself. Robertson's art brought to the fore all of Johnson's fears that "real authentick history" would be confused with or compromised by conjectural elements in the narrative, "all the colouring, all the philosophy." He vigorously asserted the point when Boswell praised Robertson's "penetration" and "painting":

> "Sir, you must consider how that penetration and that painting are employed. It is not history, it is imagination. He who describes what he never saw, draws from fancy. Robertson paints minds as Sir Joshua paints faces in a history-piece: he imagines an heroick countenance. You must look upon Robertson's work as romance, and try it by that standard. History it is not."[49]

Every contrast developed in the remark reinforces Johnson's initial distinction between historical and imaginative writing. "Imagination" is the first definition of "fancy" in his *Dictionary*. The juxtaposition of history with romance, which Johnson connected with fiction, falsehood, and unreality—with "wild strain[s] of imagination"—constantly recurs in his writing and conversation.[50]

In reaction to the increasing fusion of fact and art that he saw in contemporary historiography, Johnson focused on the restraints necessary for the historical writer by emphasizing the limits of historical fact itself and the resulting need for careful control of style. He favored Hume, the less ornamental writer, over Robertson, and liked Clarendon, whose stylistic "negligence" he recognized, better than either of his contemporaries. Despite Clarendon's flaws, Johnson pointed out that he had managed to achieve "inartificial majesty" without "the nicety of laboured elegance."[51] His infamous preference for Goldsmith over Robertson as a historian also rests primarily on Robertson's stylistic shortcomings rather than on Goldsmith's strengths. Johnson's actual claim was that "Goldsmith's History is better than the *verbiage* of Robertson." His comments are not especially flattering to Goldsmith; he called the Roman history an "abridgement," and judged it superior to Lucius Florus and Eutropius, minor Roman epitomizers. Johnson's whole point is that Goldsmith's plain, concise, and competent treatment lacked all of the stylistic excesses that so bothered him in Robertson.[52]

Behind some of Johnson's later attacks on the styles of Robertson and others is probably the unacknowledged specter of Gibbon. The greatest historian of the age wrote in a style that made Robertson appear relatively subdued. Johnson's retaliation was silence. With perhaps some displacement, he directly commented on Gibbon's ugliness, but his only reference to the history that Boswell records centers on the author more than the work: "now that he has published his infidelity, he will probably persist in it."[53] Nor was the *Decline and Fall* in Johnson's library. (Significantly, however, he did own Henry Edwards Davis's attack on the history—an incompetent production whose sole distinction was to have elicited Gibbon's only formal reply to the many critics of his work.[54]) Yet it was surely the publication of Gibbon's history in February of 1776 and its immediate success—Gibbon wrote to a friend that his "ancient history . . . has succeeded like the novel of the day"—that led Johnson in May of that same year to refer to "that painted form" as the taste of the age in historical writing.[55] Gibbon himself had praised Robertson's "bold imagination,"[56] but Johnson surely recognized that it paled in comparison to Gibbon's own.

Johnson, too, had a very good historical imagination. Twice in *A Journey to the Western Islands* he includes paragraphs showing that "the fictions of romantick chivalry had for their basis the real manners of the feudal times."[57] At least once in conversation he seemed to acknowledge that historians should be allowed some imaginative latitude:

> "There are (said he) inexcusable lies, and consecrated lies. For instance, we are told that on the arrival of the news of the unfortunate battle of Fontenoy, every heart beat, and every eye was in tears. Now we know that no man eat [*sic*] his dinner the worse, but there *should* have been all this concern; and to say there *was*, (smiling) may be reckoned a consecrated lie."

But, as Boswell noted, Johnson was speaking "jocularly,"[58] deflecting with humor his deep and continuing uneasiness about the part that the imagination assumed in historical writing.

Direct references to the imagination occur in most of Johnson's comments which seem to denigrate historical writing or style. For example, after calling on the historian to stop at a "mediocrity of style," he immediately demands confinement of the mind to an "even tenour of imagination."[59] Similarly, his comments reducing the historian to a compiler emerge not so much as deprecations of the task itself, but as attempts to ensure that writers will strictly control distortions of fact with form. His desire is to exclude the imagination as completely as possible from the composition of history:

> "Great abilities . . . are not requisite for an Historian; for in historical composition, all the greatest powers of the human mind are quiescent. He has facts ready to his hand; so there is no exercise of invention. Imagination is not required in any high degree; only about as much as is used in the lower kinds of poetry. Some penetration, accuracy, and colouring will fit a man for the task, if he can give the application which is necessary."[60]

In such comments Johnson is in effect dividing the historian's task by segregating the collection and verification of evidence from the presentation of that evidence in written form. The Italian city-states in the early Renaissance had often operated similarly, appointing their public historiographers mainly for their literary skills to write up the researches of others into formal histories.[61] But the Italians separated the two endeavors because of their belief in the primary importance of literary art in historical writing; Johnson's motive was different. It is true, as Godfrey Davies notes, that Johnson tended to underestimate the amount of exact information available to the historian and also failed to recognize how much could legitimately be inferred from such data.[62] But by treating the accumulated facts as a given, and thereby momentarily ignoring all of his own insights about the difficulties with such evidence, he could highlight the literary restraint that his own era had made him see as crucial for the historian. In his view, although the imagination would inevitably taint historical evidence, the literary distortions which it created in the process of writing history could perhaps be more easily controlled.

Johnson's tendency to depict historical writing as simply compilation has been correctly defended as characteristic of his age. George Birkbeck Hill quotes similar sentiments in a letter from Hume to Robertson;[63] even Gibbon's greatness lies not in improved historical methodology or new research, but in his ability to synthesize existing materials. However, even at his most reductive, Johnson was never satisfied with history as compilation, because such work lacked the novelty so important for him in all writing. He complained that Boswell for his Corsican history used no materials unavailable to others; emphasizing Blackwell's failure to provide "many novelties" in the *Memoirs of the Court of Augustus*, he pointed out that "after all, to inherit is not to acquire; to decorate is not to make."[64] His strong preference for eyewitness accounts despite his awareness of their shortcomings, which has been criticized, derived mainly from the fact that participants offered both unique perspectives and a kind of reliability unavailable to later historians. In Johnson's case the rhetorical equation of historical writing with compilation was one way of trying to come to terms with his deeper concerns about distortions created by the imagination in history.

Starting from the great classical premises that the content of history must be truthful and that it should be presented in a middle style, Johnson added his knowledge of historical research and methods, his understanding of the fallible human mind and heart, and his perceptions of the dangers posed by the movement of late eighteenth-century historiography in a more literary direction. The result was a clear and uncompromising vision of historical fact and its limitations, and a fear that stylistic excesses could blur the distinctions between historical truth and fiction. His reaction was to focus on the restraints necessary for historians, particularly on limiting the exercise of the imagination in their works. Johnson's understanding of the inevitability of fictional elements in history shows in embryonic form the kind of perception which in the later twentieth century would lead writers to fuse genres, mixing history, autobiography, and biography with the novel to highlight the elusive nature of "fact" itself and its formal permutations. In history, the same perceptions as they developed during the nineteenth century would push practitioners through increasing positivism almost to despair about the possibility of objectively knowing any historical truth at all. Only in the twentieth century would some historians, and particularly philosophers of history, begin to try directly to come to terms with the literary ramifications of historiography, addressing some of the same kinds of basic stylistic problems that had concerned Johnson two hundred years before.

Thus Johnson's attitudes toward the writing of history are some of the earliest reflections in England of the kind of thinking that ultimately resulted in the collapse of the Aristotelian dichotomy between poetry and history. Seventeenth-century writers had feared stylistic distortions of truth, but they had believed that the problems could be solved simply by banishing literary art from history. Despite his many affinities with that century, Johnson nevertheless affirmed the older classical tradition that historical writing required art. Even as he did so, however, he saw more clearly than most other seventeenth- or

eighteenth-century writers and theorists that style was only one manifestation of the ubiquitous intrusion of the imagination that could
render historical truth fictional. His reactions, particularly to contemporary historians, were in certain instances overstated or naive, but
they reflect a complex vision of the innumerable obstacles to ascer-
taining and presenting any truth at all about the past. Indeed, given
the extent of Johnson's understanding of the fictionalization inherent
in any historical writing, what is impressive about his thought is not
his occasional negativity and reductiveness, but his continuing belief
in the importance of history itself and his unwavering insistence that
Clio remain a Muse.

N O T E S

1. *Life*, II, 238; William R. Keast, "Johnson and Intellectual History," in *New Light on Dr. Johnson*, ed. Frederick W. Hilles (New Haven: Yale Univ. Press, 1959), pp. 247–48; Godfrey Davies, "Dr. Johnson on History," *Huntington Library Quarterly*, 1 (1948), 3–4, 9–10, 14–15. John A. Vance's useful study, *Samuel Johnson and the Sense of History* (Athens: Univ. of Georgia Press, 1984), appeared too late to be considered in this essay; although some of our interpretations and conclusions overlap, others differ significantly.

2. *Idler* 94, *Works*, II, 291.

3. *Rambler* 122, *Works*, IV, 288.

4. *Life*, IV, 39; see also I, 354–55.

5. Allen T. Hazen, *Samuel Johnson's Prefaces and Dedications* (New Haven: Yale Univ. Press, 1937), p. 211; *Idler* 84; *Works*, II, 263.

6. *Letters*, II, 314.

7. *Lives*, I, 368. See also *Life*, III, 359, n. 2; IV, 36, n. 3; 51, n. 2.

8. *Life*, IV, 361.

9. "The Life of Boerhaave," *Early Biographical Writings of Dr Johnson*, ed. J. D. Fleeman (Westmead: Gregg International, 1973), p. 25.

10. Samuel Johnson, *A Journey to the Western Isles of Scotland, Works*, IX, 111; here-after cited as *Journey*. James Boswell, *The Journal of A Tour to the Hebrides with Samuel Johnson, LL. D.*, in *Life*, V, 220; hereafter cited as *Tour*.

11. Donald J. Greene, ed., *Samuel Johnson: Political Writings, Works*, X, 126, 127.

12. *Tour*, in Boswell, *Life*, V, 336, 220; F. J. Levy, ed., *The History of the Reign of King Henry VII, by Francis Bacon* (Indianapolis: Bobbs-Merrill, 1972), pp. vii, 51–52.

13. "Review of *The Account of the Conduct of the Dutchess of Marlborough*," *Works* (1825), VI, 5. See also *Letters*, I, 137.

14. "Review of *The Account of the Conduct of the Dutchess of Marlborough*," *Works* (1825), VI, 5, 6. On the Pyrrhonists, see David Jordan, *Gibbon and His Roman Empire* (Urbana: Univ. of Illinois Press, 1971), pp. 42–46, 83–84.

15. *Life*, II, 365–66.

16. *Life*, II, 79.

17. *Rambler* 60, *Works*, III, 319.

18. *The History of Rasselas, Prince of Abissinia: A Tale*, ed. R. W. Chapman (Oxford: Clarendon Press, 1927), pp. 136, 137; *Lives*, I, 99–100. See also "An Account of the Harleian Library," in *Works* (1825), V, 184.

19. E. L. McAdam, Jr., *Dr. Johnson and the English Law* (Syracuse: Syracuse Univ. Press, 1951), pp. 92, 99, 92.

20. McAdam, *Johnson and English Law*, pp. 98, 92.

21. McAdam, *Johnson and English Law*, p. 92; *Idler* 87, *Works*, II, 270; see also *Journey, Works*, IX, 97.

22. *Idler* 20, *Works*, II, 62.

23. *Journey, Works*, IX, 98.

24. *Idler* 20, *Works*, II, 62; see also *Life*, II, 221–22.

25. *Letters*, II, 242; I, 186.

26. *Life*, II, 366.

27. *Life*, II, 65.

28. *Letters*, I, 20; see also Greene, *Political Writings, Works*, X, xxv, n. 1.

29. Hazen, *Prefaces and Dedications*, p. 167; see also *Letters*, I, 101–102, 279–80, 402–403; II, 172–73, 314, 432, and *Diaries, Prayers, and Annals*, ed. E. L. McAdam, Jr., Donald and Mary Hyde, *Works*, I, 91.

30. *Letters*, II, 247.

31. *Works*, I, 195.

32. *Life*, III, 58, 404; *Letters*, I, 409; II, 83, 95, 105. Johnson praised Percy for equalling Hailes in research, but excelling him in elegance, crediting "Percy's attention to poetry" for giving "grace and splendour to his studies of antiquity" (*Letters*, II, 247).

33. "An Account of the Harleian Library," *Works* (1825), V, 186; Hazen, *Prefaces and Dedications*, p. 88.

34. *Rambler* 60, *Works*, III, 362.

35. *A Dictionary of the English Language* (1755; rpt. New York: Arno Press, 1979); *Letters*, I, 20.

36. *Letters*, I, 20.

37. *Rambler* 122, *Works*, IV, 290.

38. "Review of the *History of the Royal Society of London*," in *Works* (1825), VI, 76.

39. *Tour*, Boswell, *Life*, V, 296; *Life*, II, 189.

40. *Life*, II, 125; *Anecdotes by William Seward, F. R. S.*, in *Johnsonian Miscellanies*, ed. George Birkbeck Hill, 2 vols. (Oxford: Clarendon Press, 1897), II, 306; *Letters*, II, 314.

41. *Memoirs of My Life*, ed. Georges A. Bonnard (New York: Funk and Wagnalls, 1969), p. 155.

42. *Life*, II, 213; II, 236–77; *Lives*, II, 177.

43. "Review of *Memoirs of the Court of Augustus*, in *Works* (1825), VI, 12–13. All references in this paragraph are from this review, in the following order: pp. 11, 14, 11, 15, 13, 15.

44. *Ibid.*, p. 16.

45. *Life*, II, 237; III, 404; *Anecdotes by the Rev. Dr. Thomas Campbell*, in *Johnsonian Miscellanies*, II, 48; *Apophthegms, Sentiments: Opinions, & Occasional Reflections*, in *Johnsonian Miscellanies*, II, 10; *Life*, III, 173; II, 236, 237.

46. *Life*, II, 53, 238.

47. "An Essay on the Life and Genius of Samuel Johnson, LL.D.," in *Johnsonian Miscellanies*, I, 429–30. The *History of Scotland* is Robertson's earliest work, perhaps a little less ornate in style than his later histories. A copy of this work was in Johnson's library, along with three copies of Robertson's *History of America*. In a scene in Scotland, Robertson "fluently harangued to Dr. Johnson on the spot, concerning scenes" from the *History of Scotland* (Donald Greene, *Samuel Johnson's Library: An Annotated Guide*, ELS Monograph Series, No. 1 [Victoria, B.C.: Univ. of Victoria, 1975], p. 98; *Tour*, Boswell, *Life*, V, 43).

48. *Life*, III, 173.

49. *Life*, II, 237–38.

50. *Rambler* 4, *Works*, III, 20, 21; *Idler* 84, *Works*, II, 261; see also the definitions in Johnson's *Dictionary* under "romantick."

51. *Anecdotes by the Rev. Dr. Thomas Campbell*, p. 48; *Rambler* 122, *Works*, IV, 289; see also *Life*, III, 257–58.

52. *Life*, II, 236, 237. It should be noted, however, that Johnson also says that Goldsmith excels Vertot, three of whose historical works he recommended to the Rev. Daniel Astle in advising him on his studies (*Life*, IV, 311).

53. *Life*, IV, 73; II, 448. One other exception to Johnson's silence on the *Decline and Fall* may be *Life*, III, 238, which Hill terms a "jocular allusion" to the work (*Life*, VI, 142), but the reference is questionable. See also *Life*, III, 244–45.

54. Greene, *Samuel Johnson's Library*, p. 53.

55. J. E. Norton, *A Bibliography of the Works of Edward Gibbon* (1940; rpt. New York: Burt Franklin, 1970), pp. 37, 41; *Life*, III, 58.

56. *Gibbon's Journal to January 28th, 1763: My Journal, I, II & III and Ephemerides*, ed. D. M. Low (New York: Norton, 1929), p. 103.

57. *Journey*, *Works*, IX, 155–56, 77.

58. *Life*, I, 355.

59. *Rambler* 122, *Works*, IV, 289.

60. *Life*, I, 424–25.

61. Felix Gilbert, "The Renaissance Interest in History," in *Art, Science, and History in the Renaissance*, ed. Charles S. Singleton (Baltimore: Johns Hopkins Univ. Press, 1967), p. 378.

62. Davies, "Dr. Johnson on History," pp. 19–20, see also 6–7.

63. *Life*, II, 237–38, n. 4.

64. *Letters*, I, 191, 230; "Review of *Memoirs of the Court of Augustus*," *Works*, (1825) VI, 9–10. See also *Idler* 85, *Works*, II, 264–65.

ELIZABETH R. LAMBERT

7 · *Johnson on Friendship: The Example of Burke*

Those who know Samuel Johnson need not be told of the importance he attached to friendship. The evidence is everywhere in his life and writings. "To love all men is our duty," Johnson wrote in *Rambler* 99, "But to love all equally is impossible." Thus, out of the many, an individual selects a few "for intimacy and tenderness" and in so doing, improves "the condition of his existence by superadding friendship to humanity and the love of individuals to that of the species."[1]

Johnson also details other aspects of friendship in *Ramblers* 64, 89, and 160 where he discusses the requisites of true friendship— "Friendship is seldom lasting but between equals"[2]—the benevolence that operates between friends, and the elements that go into the choosing of friends. According to Johnson, such elements are varied: "He that can contribute to the hilarity of the vacant hour, or partake with equal gust the favourite amusement, he whose mind is employed on the same objects . . . will be welcomed with ardour and left with regret. . . ."[3]

However accurate Johnson was in calculating the advantages of friendship, he also took into account its darker aspects. "How many friendships have you known formed upon principles of virtue?" he asked Boswell. "Most friendships are formed by caprice or by chance, mere confederacies in vice or leagues in folly."[4] On the same somber note he wrote in *Idler* 41 of the death of friends and in *Idler* 23 of the elements that work against lasting friendships: "opposition of interest, suspicion," and long separation without contact.[5]

Sir John Hawkins, James Boswell, and Hester Thrale, among others, report Johnson's various remarks concerning the nature and qualities of friendship which he made in the company of friends. Moreover, Johnson's letters over a lifetime, to many and varied individuals, echo the sentiments expressed in his writings and in conversation. In the twentieth century, biographers such as John Wain, James Clifford, and W. J. Bate have dealt with the multiplicity of Johnson's friendships, and the indexes to their volumes indicate the extent of their task. In compiling his exhaustive index to Johnson's letters, R. W. Chapman classified Johnson's friends according to the various Johnsonian circles to which they belonged; these circles number some twenty-two. One of Chapman's categories was "intimate friends"—a select list of those who were also named in other circles. In setting apart a group as Johnson's "intimate friends," Chapman used a distinction that Johnson himself frequently made between acquaintances, companions, and, simply, friends.

One day in conversation with Sir Joshua Reynolds, Johnson observed that an individual wishes "to have an intimate friend with whom to compare minds."[6] This special dimension—intellectual exchange—operated in conjunction with specific traits necessary to any friendship. However, Johnson did not consider all those who shared his amusements, or his frustrations, or even his life, as intimate friends. Mrs. Anna Williams lived in his house for thirty years, attending to him late in the evenings, managing his household, and listening to his counsel. When she died in 1783, Johnson wrote to Dr. Burney of his loss: "My domestick companion is taken from me. She is much missed, for her acquisitions were many, and her curiosity universal; so that she partook of every conversation."[7] In letters to others, he used the same term with respect to Mrs. Williams—"domestick companion." In spite of all they shared, Anna Williams was a companion and not an intimate friend. Johnson was not deprecating the relationship between himself and Mrs. Williams; rather, he was describing it for what it was. For intimate friendship, intellectual equality was needed.

However, intellectual equality of itself did not produce intimate friendship; on the contrary, while veneration, respect, and admiration could result when intellectual equals met, there was also the possibility of bitter competition, hostility, and jealousy. But intimate friendship, or "love," as Johnson wrote in *Rambler* 89, "is only to be excited by that levity and chearfulness which disencumbers all minds from awe and solicitude." Thus intellectual exchange which is the product of intimate friendship does not take place in a sterile, stultified atmosphere but in a situation where there is "easy freedom and familiarity of intercourse." The conversation which takes place among familiars, Johnson added, tends to yield "useful hints . . . nor can one converse on the most familiar topicks without some casual information."[8] At times, conversation on familiar topics involved the participants in heated discussion—and in such an atmosphere Johnson thrived. The tavern chair is the "throne of human felicity," he told Hawkins. Among the reasons for his preference, Johnson noted "the free conversation and interchange of discourse with those whom I most love; I dog-matize and am contradicted, and in this conflict of opinions and senti-ments I find delight."⁹

In addition to intellectual equality and exchange, there is yet an-other dimension to Johnsonian intimate friendship. In the remark to Sir Joshua quoted earlier, Johnson added that intimate friends "cherish private virtues" as well as "compare minds." Johnson elabo-rates on the distinction in *Rambler* 64: "That friendship may be at once fond and lasting, there must not only be equal virtue on each part, but virtue of the same kind . . ."

> We are often, by superficial accomplishments and accidental endear-ments, induced to love those whom we cannot esteem; we are sometimes, by great abilities and incontestable evidences of virtue compelled to es-teem those we cannot love. But friendship compounded of esteem and love, derives from one its tenderness, and its permanence from the other; and therefore requires not only that its candidates should gain the judgment, but that they should attract the affections . . . the great effect of friendship is beneficence.¹⁰

Thus, while the intellect judges one to be worthy of friendship vir-tue must also attract the affections. This point comes up repeatedly as when Johnson speaks of the friendship of "a wise and good man"¹¹ or, in his poem on friendship, of the great pleasure "When Virtues kindred Virtues meet/And sister souls together join."¹² In his empha-sis on virtue as intrinsic to intimate friendship, Johnson was adhering to the Aristotelian distinction between perfect and inferior friend-ship. Perfect friendship is that which exists between men who are good and alike in virtue, but inferior friendship is based on pleasure or utility.

For Johnson, as for Aristotle, virtue was a prerequisite for intimate friendship because only the virtuous could be trusted with one's ambi-tions, hopes, intellectual discoveries, and even one's irrational fears. When Mr. Fitzherbert hanged himself in 1777, Johnson commented, "Everybody liked him; but he had no friend, as I understand the word, nobody with whom he exchanged intimate thoughts." Johnson judged that Fitzherbert's suicide "was owing to imaginary difficulties in his affairs, which had he talked with any friend would soon have vanished."¹³

Just as Johnson's perception of the intellectual exchange operating in a friendship is dynamic, so also is his concept of a virtuous man. That beneficence which is the great effect of friendship is not simply *being* good; it is concerned with *doing* good, with kindness in action. There were many who came to Johnson out of genuine personal need, out of vanity, curiosity, or even veneration, but only the few could, as he said of those who came to Socrates, offer "union of minds . . . sincere kindness or steady fidelity."[14] In spite of Johnson's bear-like manner, which at times made him abruptly unkind, he did not tolerate cruelty in himself or in others, and he quickly sought to make amends for his own shortcomings.[15] Moreover, kindness was expected of members of his cherished Literary Club. As we know, Sir John Hawkins was made to feel unwelcome because of rude behavior to Edmund Burke. We have no idea of the specific discourtesy, but it was enough to merit Johnson's judgment that Hawkins was "unclubable."[16]

Closely associated with intimate friendship is the other intimate relationship which is sexual. Johnson's most explicit statements contrasting intimate friendship and sexual relationships are found in the 1743 poem noted above, "Friendship: An Ode." For once eschewing the middle of the road, Johnson speaks only of the vast differences between the two relationships. In the poem he limits his use of the word "love" to refer only to sexual passion—the drive that we share with lower creation. There is no mention of love as Christian charity or as the romantic attachment that commonly leads to marriage. On the other hand, Johnson uses the term "friendship" in the context of the ideal—the spiritual—and the moral opposite of sensual love. Just as "love," in the context of the poem, refers to the lowest elements of sexual passion, "friendship" connotes the ideal form of that relationship.

Johnson sets up the dichotomy between love and friendship in the very beginning of the ode when he speaks of friendship as "to men and Angels only giv'n," and sexual passion as shared by savages and lower nature—"The human and the savage breast,/Inflames alike with raging fires." Driving home his point, he states that the objects of sensual emotion are transitory and indiscriminate while only the favored few are given the tranquility of friendship, "With bright, but oft destructive gleam,/Alike o'er all his lightnings fly;/Thy lambent glories only beam,/Around the fav'rites of the sky."

If the origin of friendship is heavenly, Johnson continues, it thus follows that those of dubious moral character cannot experience friendship. It is here that Johnson introduces, by implication and direct statement, the notion that trust and honesty are as inherent to friendship as they are the antithesis of sensual love: "Thy gentle glows of guiltless joys/On fools and villains ne'er descend/In vain for thee the monarch sighs/And hugs a flatterer for a friend." In effect, intellectual vacuity and moral indigence preclude any ability to experience friendship, and power is hard put to find any sincere manifestation of it.

The dangers of sensual love, Johnson notes in the ode, are all too apparent, but the dangers to which friendship are prone are more subtle because, like friendship itself, they originate in the mind. Ignoring the damage caused by separation, misunderstandings, or unintentional neglect, Johnson addresses only one hazard. Invoking friendship as "directress of the brave and just," Johnson asks "let the tortures of mistrust/On selfish bosoms only prey."

The spiritual aspect of friendship is the note upon which Johnson opens the ode, and he concludes by returning to the same theme. A relationship, such as love, based on passion is likely to end when the body tires and grows old, or when another object of passion takes the place of the present one. But a relationship involving the mind will share in its eternity—"What rais'd our Virtues here below/Shall aid our Happiness above." It is upon this positive note that Johnson ends the poem.

"Friendship: An Ode" was first printed in *The Gentleman's Magazine* in July 1743 and is supposed to have been written by Johnson at the request of Elizabeth Porter, his future wife. If so, it is unfortunately prophetical. His marriage to Tetty was, for the most part, fraught with frustration, guilt, and loneliness. Nor were his relationships with other women free of sexual problems. For example, with the publication of Boswell's notes labelled "tacenda," we now know that Johnson, in his relationship with Mrs. Desmoulins, had to contend with the forces he described so vividly in the ode.[17] Johnson once told Boswell that in the best of all possible worlds, that is, one free from duty and fear of damnation, "I would spend my life in driving briskly in a post-chaise with a pretty woman," but, he added, "she would be one who could understand me and would add something to the conversation."[18]

As we listen to Johnson's words describing the intellectual and moral equality needed for intimate friendship, our minds scan the individuals seated at a meeting of the Literary Club. These people, remember, were the ones he classified as "those whom I most love." Who could, with any real equality, compare minds with Johnson? Johnson himself supplies us with a name. On one occasion when he was ill, visitors at his bedside mentioned Edmund Burke. Johnson exclaimed, "That fellow calls forth all my powers. Were I to see Burke now, it would kill me."[19] At first glance, the intellectual exchange in the Johnson-Burke relationship might seem to consist of Johnson's need to challenge Burke's Whig affiliations. However, Johnson's admiration of Burke surmounted their irreconcilable political differences and went far beyond them.

Johnson had been attracted by the quality of Burke's mind from their first meeting on Christmas Day 1758 at David Garrick's home. At that time, Burke, twenty years Johnson's junior, corrected Johnson on the subject of Bengal. Arthur Murphy reports that on the following day Johnson approached him and said, "I suppose Murphy, you are proud of your countryman. *Cum talis sit utinam noster esset!*"—"If this be the kind of man he is, would that he were ours"—wishing, no doubt, that Burke's talents could be better employed in Tory circles. Later Johnson told Murphy that "a man of sense could not meet Mr. Burke by accident, under a gateway to avoid a shower, without being convinced that he was the first man in England."[20] Other contemporaries such as Mrs. Thrale, Fanny Burney, Boswell, Reynolds, and Dr. Brocklesby record the same compliment. Perhaps it is Hester Thrale Piozzi who best describes Johnson's love for Burke. In her *Anecdotes* she writes: "He had always a very great personal regard and particular affection for Mr. Edmund Burke, as well as an esteem difficult for me to repeat, though for him only easy to express."[21] But Mrs. Piozzi's puzzle need not be ours. As we have seen, intimate friendship, for Johnson, involved more than intellectual affinity; it also involved the reciprocal recognition of virtue by which the affections were attracted. What was there in Burke that elicited Johnson's "particular affection" for him?

For one thing, both men shared a practical, operative knowledge of human nature which found expression in concrete ways. Someone once complained to Johnson that it was useless to give money to beggars, as they only spent it on gin. Johnson rejoined, "Gin and tobacco are the only Pleasures in their power, let them have the enjoyments within their reach without Reproach."[22] Burke sounded very much like Johnson when he too was admonished for giving a shilling to a beggar because it would only be spent on gin: "He is an old man," Burke replied, "if gin be his comfort, let him have gin."[23]

It is related of both Johnson and Burke that their charity to the unfortunate was more personal than giving money to beggars. Boswell records a touching instance when Johnson found a poor woman lying in the street so much exhausted that she could not walk. Johnson "took her upon his back and carried her to his house" where he learned that she was a prostitute. Boswell notes that Johnson "instead of harshly upbraiding her, had her taken care of with all tenderness for a long time at considerable expence, till she was restored to health, and endeavoured to put her into a virtuous way of living."[24]

Burke, too, once befriended a prostitute who approached him. Upon his questioning her, she expressed a desire to change her way of life. Taking her into his home, he put her under the charge of Mrs. Webster, an old servant of the family, who trained the woman for domestic service. Later Burke found a position for her.[25]

Nor were these single instances in the lives of both men. Mrs. Thrale notes that Johnson "has more tenderness for Poverty than any other Man I know; and . . . in consequence of these principles he has now in his house whole nests of People."[26] Throughout his life, Burke

too, took into his house "whole nests of people"—Irish relations, political allies, French emigrés fleeing for their lives—and these various
personalities frequently set Burke's household at odds much in the
same way as the quarrels of Mrs. Desmoulins and Mrs. Williams made
Johnson wary of going home. For example, in 1785 the Comtesse De
Genlis visited the Burkes at Beaconsfield. She claimed that she could
not sleep if the least bit of light filtered into the room. By the time she
left three days later, the window shutters on the darkest bedroom in
the house had been refitted, additional window curtains added, dense
bed curtains drawn, and, since none of this was effective, every evening the carpenter nailed blankets against every crevice in the room
and removed them every morning.[27]

The virtues shared by Johnson and Burke also include personal
courage of an extraordinary sort. Boswell notes that while Johnson
feared death "he feared nothing else," and, among the several instances cited, Boswell repeats the story that Johnson told him concerning the night he was attacked in the street by four men, to whom "he
would not yield, but kept them all at bay till the watch came up and
carried both him and them to the roundhouse."[28]

Witnesses also report similar conduct on the part of Burke during
the Gordon Riots. "Mr. Burke," one report went, "was in great danger
this morning—he took up two rioters himself and went to ask the mob
what they would have. 'If you want me,' he said, 'here I am but never
expect I shall vote for a repeal of the Act I supported.'"[29]

Intimate friendship is reciprocal, and Burke's esteem for Johnson
equaled Johnson's for him. As noted earlier, Johnson had judged a
contributing cause of Fitzherbert's suicide to be the lack of a friend to
whom he might have confided imaginary difficulties. The political
storms that raged around Burke in 1783 were not imaginary, nor was
he suicidal, but it was to Johnson that he confided his frustration and
his sense of failure. The circumstances were these: on 2 April 1783
the King had given into pressure and had formed the coalition government by appointing the Duke of Portland to be the first Lord of
the Treasury; Lord North and Charles Fox, former adversaries, to
be Principal Secretaries of State, and Burke to be Paymaster of the
Forces. As Paymaster of the Forces, Burke regained a position that
he had held under the second Rockingham Administration. No sooner
had he come back into office than a scandal erupted concerning John
Powell and Charles Bembridge, two clerks in the Pay Office who had
been dismissed for misconduct. Burke, believing them to be innocent,
had reinstated them while they were still under indictment. Powell resigned, but before his case came to trial, committed suicide. The en-
suing criticism of Burke made him talk of retiring and he stated as
much to Johnson. Johnson dissuaded him saying, "Never think of

that." According to Boswell, who discreetly omitted Burke's name in the *Life of Johnson* account, "The gentleman urged, 'I should then do no ill.' Johnson replied, 'Nor no good either, Sir, it would be civil suicide.'"[30]

Burke did not often reveal his personal reactions to situations, having from the age of sixteen resolved "to keep within" his opinions of others, of himself, and of his affairs.[31] Thus his confiding in Johnson was unusual, and Johnson's advice, considering their political differences, was significant because, two weeks earlier, Boswell had complained to Johnson that Burke's detractors were "actually representing him as mad." On that occasion, Johnson had no sympathy, saying that if one emoted as Burke did on the floor of the House of Commons, "can he wonder that he is represented as mad?"[32] Johnson's remark is sometimes taken to support the notion that Burke was actually mad. However, it was just two weeks later that the incident above occurred during which Johnson urged Burke not to resign. Johnson's vote of confidence in Burke would seem to indicate that, however close to a nervous breakdown Burke may have been, he was not mad.

Johnson was also one of the few to whom Burke confided; he "spontaneously denied," as Johnson said, that he was Junius.[33] In 1771 when rumor was making Burke the author of the letters, and not always in flattering terms, Burke wrote to Charles Townshend, "My friends I have satisfied; my enemies shall never have any direct satisfaction from me."[34]

One of the salient features of the relationship between Johnson and Burke was their public conversation. As a matter of fact, they were known as conversational rivals and frequently took each other on in public for the sheer intellectual exhilaration of it. Johnson wrote to Mrs. Thrale of one such incident:

> But Montague and you have had with all your adulations nothing finer said of you than was said last Saturday night of Burke and Me. We were at the Bishop of St. Asaph's . . . and towards twelve we fell into talk, to which the Ladies listened, just as they do to you, and said, as I heard, *there is no rising unless somebody will cry fire.*[35]

Moreover, it seems that, at times, they deliberately took opposing sides. One evening before Joseph Baretti's trial, Johnson and Burke differed somewhat heatedly concerning some part of the defense. Later George Steevens admonished Johnson for arguing with "too much warmth." "It may be so, Sir, (replied the Doctor) for Burke and I should have been of one opinion if we had had no audience."[36]

Burke's and Johnson's styles were much different. To Sir Joshua Reynolds, Johnson once explained his extraordinary accuracy in talk— "to impart whatever he knew in the most forcible language he could put it in; and that by constant practice, and never suffering any careless expressions to escape him, or attempting to deliver his thoughts without arranging them in the clearest manner, it became habitual to him."[37] Boswell once succinctly commented that Johnson's opponents had "been tossed and gored" that evening.[38]

On the other hand, Burke's style was more deliberate; Goldsmith noted that Burke wound "into a subject like a serpent."[39] Burke's manner had been developed by years in the House of Commons where, by habit, he was the last to speak and then held the floor for hours, marshalling fact upon fact, qualifying, explaining, and illustrating all the while. In commenting upon each other's talk, Burke told Sir Joshua that if Johnson "had come early into parliament, he certainly would have been the greatest speaker that ever was there." When told of Burke's compliment, Johnson did not deny the truth of it and said that he would like to try his hand at it.[40] In turn, when Johnson was asked by the Scotsman MacLeod to describe the particular excellence of Burke's eloquence, he answered, "copiousness and fertility of allusion; a power of diversifying his matter by placing it in various relations. Burke has great knowledge and great command of language."[41]

Not all of the interaction between Johnson and Burke took place in the public arena. The two men often spent quiet evenings together. Johnson reported several such instances to Mrs. Thrale, on one occasion noting, "Two nights ago Mr. Burke sat with me a long time, he seems much pleased with his journey. We had both seen Stonehenge this summer for the first time."[42]

However, all was not perfect at all times, and Johnson's friendship with Burke did have its difficult moments. Aside from a light comment or two, the men did not seriously discuss politics in each other's presence. According to Boswell, Johnson went so far as to deny Burke political honesty because of Burke's adherence to party "right or wrong," as Johnson said.[43]

Their disagreement as to the American question was a public matter. On 8 March 1775, Johnson published *Taxation No Tyranny*, and, two weeks later, on 22 March, Burke spoke in Commons in behalf of conciliation with the colonies. His speech was published on 22 May. Burke's speech was not an answer to Johnson's pamphlet; the two pieces are different in fundamental ways. Burke's speech was an effort to stem the movement toward war with the American colonies by offering a plan for conciliation. On the other hand, Johnson's pamphlet was, as Donald Greene describes it, "'a Declaration of Rights' of the British subject (and taxpayer) as against those of the Americans."[44] In spite of the differences, the two pieces reveal the writers' deeply held and opposing convictions concerning the legitimacy of the colonists' complaints. This was one instance when the two men most decidedly would not have been of one opinion if they had no audience.

Also a matter of public record is Johnson's poor opinion of Burke's wit based on Burke's habit of punning. As readers of the *Journal of a Tour to the Hebrides* and *The Life of Johnson* know, Johnson's opinion on that score was contradicted by Boswell and Malone, and, in fact, by many others.[45] While there is no record of Johnson's telling Burke, point-blank, what he thought of his punning, Burke knew of Johnson's opinion and was sensitive on the subject. Mrs. Thrale records a dinner party during which Lord Mulgrave rebuked Burke for "some vile quibble" saying, "Why Burke! Why you riot in puns today now Johnson is not at hand." Mrs. Thrale describes Burke's reaction: "Burke changed color and looked like death. Lord Mulgrave did not, however, seem to perceive it tho' I did."[46]

Johnson's judgments of Burke's wit and his politics were harsh, but Burke's were no less so when he said that Johnson "*knew*" his charge against the Opposition was false when he said that they were "endeavouring to involve the nation in a War on account of the Falkland's Islands."[47]

However, the two men did not allow such factors to stand in the way of their solid friendship. Burke was accustomed to opposition from some of his closest friends, as was Johnson, and Johnson did not expect perfection of any man. Johnson once told Boswell, who spoke of testing a friendship by asking for money that was not needed: "That is very wrong, Sir. Your friend may be a narrow man, and yet have many good qualities: narrowness may be his only fault. Now you are trying his general character as a friend, by one particular single in which he happens to be defective, when, in truth, his character is composed of many particulars."[48] It is apparent why Johnson could overlook Burke's Whig connections, for at the heart of it, Burke's virtues had no political labels. Johnson would have certainly concurred with Burke's stand on the French Revolution, a stand that defied political lines. In an unpublished letter of 1792, Burke spoke of the animosities roused by his expression of "sincere opinions" respecting the situation in France. He noted: "Whether they are allowed to be Whig principles or not is a very small part of my concern. I think them exactly such as the sober, honourable, and intelligent in that party have always professed . . . If they are Tory principles, I shall always wish to be thought a Tory."[49]

When all is taken into account, Johnson and Burke were more alike than they were different. Their powers of mind, their convictions regarding the nature of human folly and pain, and their personal involvement with the unfortunate of the world were the elements that held the relationship together for twenty-six years without a break. In a touching letter to Mrs. Thrale, Johnson spoke of the quality of such a relationship:

Those that have loved longest, love best . . . that fondness which length of time has connected with many circumstances and occasions, though it may for a while be suppressed by disgust or resentment with or without a cause, is hourly revived by accidental recollections . . . esteem of great powers or amiable qualities newly discovered may embroider a day or a week, but a friendship of twenty years is interwoven with the texture of life.[50]

Boswell, using Langton's account, describes Burke's last visit to the dying Johnson. Burke, in the company of others, was one of the last to visit him. Noting the number of men in the room, Burke said to Johnson, "'I am afraid, Sir, such a number of us may be oppressive to you.' 'No, Sir, (said Johnson) it is not so; and I must be in a wretched state, indeed, when your company would not be a delight to me.'" Obviously affected, Burke replied, "'My dear Sir, you have always been too good to me.' Immediately afterwards, he went away."[51] After Johnson's death, Burke left Beaconsfield, his country retreat, to be first pall bearer at Johnson's funeral.

In 1792 Burke spoke publicly of what Johnson's friendship meant to him. His remark came in the midst of fierce parliamentary debate on Fox's motion to send a minister to Paris to deal with the provisional government of France. Burke noted that Erskine, the preceding speaker, had quoted Johnson in arguing against foreign war. Although he reminded Erskine that Johnson had not been against war with the colonies in 1776, the rest of his remarks echo the numerous references Burke made to their relationship over the thirteen years he outlived Johnson. "Dr. Johnson was a great and a good man," Burke said, and continued, "his virtues were equal to his transcendent talents, and his friendship I value as the greatest consolation and happiness of my life."[52]

NOTES

1. Johnson, *Works*, IV, 166.
2. *Works*, III, 344.
3. *Works*, V, 89.
4. *Works*, IV, 280.
5. *Works*, II, 73.
6. Sir Joshua Reynolds, *Portraits: Sir Joshua Reynolds*, ed. Frederick W. Hilles (London: Heinemann, 1952), p. 82.
7. *Letters*, No. 882.
8. *Works*, IV, 108–109.
9. Sir John Hawkins, *The Life of Samuel Johnson, LL. D.* (London, 1787), p. 48.
10. *Works*, III, 341–42.
11. *Works*, IV, 108.
12. *Works* (1787), XIV, 547. This is not to say that all of Johnson's friends were models of virtue or even that he demanded they be (see below, p. 15). For example, the rakish

propensities of Boswell and Beauclerk were public knowledge; however, both men suppressed conversation about their escapades when in Johnson's presence. Boswell was also circumspect when he discussed licentiousness with Edmund Burke, putting his question in the context of one man's advice to a son: "As to [what he would say to] a son [of his pursuit] of women." (See James Boswell, *Boswell: Laird of Auchinleck, 1778–1782*, ed. Joseph W. Reed and Frederick A. Pottle [New York: McGraw-Hill, 1977], p. 63).

13. Boswell, *Life*, III, 149. See also II, 228.

14. *Works*, III, 340.

15. See *Life*, IV, 115 n. 4 and Appendix A, pp. 431–33.

16. *Life*, I, 27 n. 2.

17. James Boswell, *Boswell: The Applause of the Jury, 1782–1785*, ed. Irma S. Lustig and Frederick A. Pottle (New York: McGraw-Hill, 1981), pp. 110–13.

18. *Life*, III, 162.

19. *Life*, II, 450.

20. Arthur Murphy, *An Essay on the Life and Genius of Samuel Johnson* (London, 1792), p. 96.

21. Hester Lynch Thrale Piozzi, *Anecdotes of the Late Samuel Johnson, LL. D.*, ed. S. C. Roberts (Cambridge: Cambridge Univ. Press, 1925), p. 155.

22. Hester Lynch Piozzi (Mrs. Thrale), *Thraliana: The Diary of Mrs. Hester Lynch Thrale (Later Mrs. Piozzi), 1776–1809*, ed. Katharine C. Balderston, 2nd ed., 2 vols. (Oxford: Clarendon Press, 1951), I, 185.

23. Sir James Prior, *Life of the Rt. Hon. Edmund Burke* (London, 1872), p. 242.

24. *Life*, IV, 321.

25. Peter Burke, *The Public and Domestic Life of the Right Hon. Edmund Burke* (London: Nathaniel Cooke, 1854), p. 135.

26. *Thraliana*, I, 184.

27. Prior, *Life of Burke*, pp. 349–50.

28. *Life*, II, 299.

29. Edmund Burke, *The Correspondence of Edmund Burke*, ed. Thomas W. Copeland, 10 vols. (Cambridge: Cambridge Univ. Press, 1958–78), IV, 246.

30. *Life*, IV, 223. See also *Cobbett's Parliamentary History of England*, 36 vols. (London, 1806–20), XXIII, 919.

31. Arthur P. S. Samuels, *The Early Life, Correspondence and Writings of the Rt. Hon. Edmund Burke, LL. D.* (Cambridge: Cambridge Univ. Press, 1923), p. 88.

32. *Applause of the Jury*, pp. 153 and 219, n. 4. Johnson once also likened Burke to "a lion who lashes himself into a fury with his own tail" (*Life*, V, 575).

33. *Life*, III, 376.

34. Burke, *Correspondence*, II, 249–50.

35. *Letters*, No. 669.

36. *Life*, IV, 324. In fact, contemporaries argued as to which one was the better speaker. Thomas Copeland discusses this issue in "Johnson and Burke" in *Statesmen, Scholars, and Merchants: Essays in Eighteenth-Century History Presented to Dame Lucy Sutherland*, ed. Anne Whiteman et al. (Oxford: Clarendon Press, 1973), p. 394.

37. *Life*, I, 204.

38. *Life*, II, 66.

39. *Life*, II, 260.

40. *Life*, II, 138–39.

41. James Boswell, *Journal of a Tour to the Hebrides with Samuel Johnson*, ed. Frederick A. Pottle and Charles H. Bennett (New York: McGraw-Hill, 1936), p. 172.

42. *Letters*, No. 669.

43. *Life*, II, 223 and 348. See also III, 45.

44. *Works*, X, 402.

45. See Boswell, *Tour* (London, 1785 [1st ed.]), p. 19; *Tour* (London, 1785 [2nd ed.]), pp. 24–26. For Burke's reaction, see *Correspondence*, V, 248–50. For a discussion of the nature of Burke's wit, see John C. Weston, "Edmund Burke's Wit," *Review of English Literature*, 4 (1963), 95–107.

46. *Thraliana*, I, 149. Mrs. Thrale records this incident twice. In the second account, she writes: "I never saw a Man so over whelmed with Anger and Shame" (I, 27).

47. James Boswell, *Private Papers of James Boswell from Malahide Castle in the Collection of Lt. Colonel Ralph Heyward Isham*, ed. Geoffrey Scott and Frederick A. Pottle, 18 vols. (Mount Vernon, N.Y.: Privately printed, 1928–34), XVII, 9.

48. *Life*, III, 238.

49. Edmund Burke to Sir David Dalrymple, 16 April 1792. National Library of Ireland, Morrison MSS.

50. *Letters*, No. 900.

51. *Life*, IV, 407.

52. *Parliamentary History*, XXX, 109. See also *Life*, IV, 407 n. 3.

Part Three

INTERPRETATIONS
of
JOHNSON'S
WORKS

JOHN L. ABBOTT

8 · The Making of the Johnsonian Canon

Two hundred years after his death, students of Samuel Johnson have a clearer sense of the texture of his life, one increasingly defined without exclusive dependence on Boswell. Similarly, they are developing a clearer sense of what he wrote, the real dimensions of the Johnsonian canon.[1] There are, in fact, not one but several Johnsonian canons, or at least a single canon composed of several distinct parts. The primary canon consists of the major writings by which Johnson's literary genius is best assessed: *The Rambler*, *A Dictionary of the English Language*, *Rasselas*, *The Plays of William Shakespeare*, and *Prefaces Biographical and Critical* to the works of various English poets. Less well known and certainly less often read are numerous significant works that can be confidently attributed to him. These include, among others, the lives of Father Paul Sarpi, Dr. Herman Boerhaave, Admiral Blake, Sir Francis Drake, and John Philip Barretier that he composed in the 1730s and 1740s, lives that clearly anticipate the mature biographer of the English poets. The canon is greatly enlarged by works that Johnson never intended as known demonstrations of his talent, the numerous prefaces and dedications and other compositions he wrote for friends and others who sought out the most gifted writer in the nation to assist them. While these have been identified and properly attributed to Johnson, he has been more tentatively linked with other works. Did he assist Saunders Welch, for example, in a text entitled *A Proposal to Render Effectual a Plan to Remove the Nuisance of Common Prostitutes from the Streets of the Metropolis* . . . (1758); what connection did he have with Robert James's volume entitled *A Treatise on Canine Madness* (1760); what role did he play in revising Fanny Burney's *Cecilia* (1782); was there any link between Johnson and a text published in 1783 entitled *A System of Vegetables*; and did he actually write and have published fabricated newspaper items concerning foreign affairs in order to tease Mrs. Salusbury?[2]

The range suggested by the few texts mentioned here is remarkable; there is plenitude and variety, one that connects Johnson to the fullest concerns of his age and the largest issues affecting our humanity. There is a demonstration throughout the canon, not simply in major works, of the literary excellence and the moral and philosophical depth that we summarize by the term Johnsonian. Consider the following excerpts:

1. The reader will here find no regions cursed with irremediable barrenness, or blest with spontaneous fecundity; no perpetual gloom or unceasing sunshine; nor are the nations here described either devoid of all sense of humanity, or consummate in all private and social virtues: here are no Hottentots without religion, polity, or articulate language; no Chinese perfectly polite, and completely skilled in all sciences: he will discover what will always be discovered by a diligent and impartial inquirer, that wherever human nature is to be found, there is a mixture of vice and virtue, a contest of passion and reason; and that the Creator doth not appear partial in his distributions, but has balanced in most countries their particular inconveniences by particular favours.

2. These lines, therefore, are impious in the mouth of a Christian, and nonsense in that of an atheist. . . . Irreligion has corrupted the present age, but let us not inscribe it on marble, to be the ruin or scorn of another generation. Let us have some regard to our reputation amongst foreigners, who do not hold either fools or atheists in high veneration, and will imagine that they can justify themselves in terming us such from our own monuments. Let us therefore review our public edifices, and, where inscriptions like this appear, spare our posterity the trouble of erasing them.

3. Statesmen and generals may grow great by unexpected accidents, and a fortunate concurrence of circumstances, neither procured nor foreseen by themselves, but reputation in the learned world must be the effect of industry and capacity.

4. May it not be opposed to this soft language that the vices of the great ought to be more severely censured, because they are committed in open day, because they set fashion on the side of wickedness, corrupt whole nations by their influence, and are out of reach of any other punishment?

5. He that has delivered his country from oppression, or freed the world from ignorance and error, can excite the emulation of a very small number; but he that has repelled the temptations of poverty, and disdained to free himself from distress at the expense of his virtue, may animate multitudes, by his example, to the same firmness of heart and steadiness of resolution.

The above passages are, respectively, from Johnson's Preface to *A Voyage to Abyssinia* (1735), *On Gay's Epitaph* (1738), *The Life of Dr Herman Boerhaave* (1739), Annotations to Crousaz's *Commentary* on Pope's *Essay on Man* (1739), and *An Essay on Epitaphs* (1740).[3] Even the casual student of Johnson would see in these passages the literary, philosophical, and moral qualities that define his established works. Such excerpts demonstrate what a full exploration of the canon itself provides, the realization that Johnson's genius was never narrowly focused in a few masterworks but liberally expressed in much that he put pen to. Johnson will best be assessed through a knowledge of all that he wrote, from a canon as carefully defined as evidence and debate will allow. Although concern with the larger Johnsonian canon has been a feature of much recent scholarship, it has always been a preoccupation of serious students of the writer.

Boswell comments early in the *Life* that although Johnson had been often "solicited by his friends to make a complete list of his writings, and talked of doing it, I believe with a serious intention that they should all be collected on his own account, he put it off from year to year, and at last died without having done it perfectly." Boswell doubts, however, whether Johnson himself "could have remembered every one of them, as they were so numerous, so various, and scattered in such a multiplicity of unconnected publications; nay, several of them published under the names of other persons, to whom he liberally contributed from the abundance of his mind." He concludes, with a sense of resignation, that "we must, therefore, be content to discover them partly from occasional information given by him to his friends, and partly from internal evidence."[4]

I do not invoke Boswell here to suggest that he must remain central to a discussion of the Johnsonian canon. This is not the case. His control of the canon in the *Life* is something of an illusion, his enumeration of Johnson's works highly derivative. But Boswell's zeal to define the canon is genuine and persistent; his *Life* is the work that suggests to most readers that Johnson's writings were indeed "numerous," "various," and "scattered in . . . a multiplicity of unconnected publications." In Boswell, too, we see demonstrated the mode of attribution used to this day to define the canon—the use of external and internal evidence in such a way that attribution is rooted more in fact than in mere intuition.

Here, though, I would like to look not so much at the canon's past, but its present and future. I would like to make the following points:

1. New evidence suggests that the canon will continue to expand. We have not yet determined all that Johnson wrote.
2. The canon will contract as some items are reexamined and rejected.

3. New knowledge of the literary history of the age will help in defining the canon.

4. A more complete understanding of Johnson's literary style will help in defining the canon.

Collectively, these four points suggest that we are less able at this century's end to provide a definitive canon of Johnson's writing than a list of attributions to Johnson. The latter, however, will enable us to see in progress a history of the making of the canon; it will serve, along with definitive biographies of Johnson and definitive texts and critical studies of his known writings, to determine his contributions to English literary history.

We have all witnessed the growth of the canon over the years as Johnson's numerous works have been identified in a "multiplicity of unconnected publications." Many twentieth-century students of Johnson have heeded the advice of Donald Greene, who urged the "'canonical' investigator to do his own driving," to work independently of the various authorities of the past. Libraries have been overturned and a wide range of texts has been examined in efforts to recover all that Johnson wrote. This tendency persists. Let me give one example to show how the Johnsonian canon will continue to grow. Consider, for example, the following lines:

> The Moral that is convey'd us by every Incident of his Life, is such as may be expected from a Philosopher and a Christian. We every where find Satisfaction arising from Villany transitory and delusive, and the virtuous Man rising in the Home-felt Joy of Mind and Conscience, in Proportion as he sinks in the Eyes of the Vulgar and the Mean. . . . The Great may here view how transitory their State may prove; the Oppressed may learn, that there is no Condition of Life so abject, but that Virtue and Patience may soften and retrieve.

Thomas Kaminski, who has completed a study of Johnson's early writing, argues that Johnson is the author of these lines, which originally appeared as a preface to a translation of the Abbé Prevost's *Memoires et Aventures d'un Homme de Qualité*.[5] If this is the case, Johnson's early career is further clarified and the canon is enriched by several hundred more words that seem to have a distinctive Johnsonian style at the same time they speak to issues of known concern to him. Although there must come a time when we will reach the end of Johnson's literary production, one suspects that other new items similar to this one will be proposed for debate and possible admission to the canon.

There is a contrary tendency, however, one that suggests the canon will also contract as various items are reexamined and possibly rejected. This fact is demonstrated in examining Johnson's "secret collaboration" with Sir Robert Chambers, his relationship with Dr.

Robert James and his *Medicinal Dictionary*, and his involvement with the *Gentleman's Magazine*.

Thomas Curley has already detailed the secret collaboration between Samuel Johnson and Robert Chambers, a joint venture that produced *A Course of Lectures on the English Law*, a work that deserves comparison with Blackstone's *Commentaries*. Curley has kindly shared with me his long introduction to his edition of Chamber's *Lectures*, a work that will have a direct bearing on our understanding of the Johnsonian canon. It will, in fact, require us to reexamine some of the conclusions reached by E. L. McAdam, Jr., in his *Dr. Johnson and the English Law*. What Curley suggests is that passages McAdam assumed to be Johnson's if only through dictation, could be assigned to Chambers himself, a learned man capable of writing material that seems Johnsonian in style and content. Curley argues that the "difficult task of going beyond McAdam's assertions and assessing all of the Lectures for a careful and comprehensive evaluation of Johnson's possible contributions remains to be done." Such an examination may well reduce the Johnsonian canon.[6]

In "Johnson, James, and the *Medicinal Dictionary*," O M Brack and Thomas Kaminski argue that most of Allen Hazen's attributions to Johnson in James's volumes, chiefly biographies, are not by Johnson. Hazen was not alone in seeing Johnson's hand in James's *Dictionary*: Johnsonians generally accepted them as authentic; I used them to show how Johnson translated from the French.[7] Although Brack and Kaminski proceed conventionally enough in their examination of these disputed pieces—theirs is essentially based on internal and stylistic evidence—their assumption about proving authorship differs from that of earlier scholars. Instead of arguing for Johnson's authorship, they ask us to join them in building a case against it: in something of an indirect challenge to the scholarship of the past that asked "why not by Johnson?" they ask "why by Johnson?" demanding that we disprove their negative. Such a technique may serve us well in the future as we attempt to make definitive judgments about the canon.

Perhaps no publication enriched Johnson's personal and literary life so much as the *Gentleman's Magazine*. He told Boswell that when he first saw St. John's Gate he "beheld it with reverence." Johnson's contributions to Cave's periodical practically frame his literary career: in no other context do we find such a large body of Johnson's miscellaneous writing; in no other place did we expect to find more possible additions to the canon. New knowledge about the rise of the *Gentleman's Magazine* during the mid-eighteenth century suggests, however, that Johnson's role in the periodical was less than previously imagined. Some works attributed to him seem more likely to be the product of his friend, John Hawkesworth. Considerable evidence points to

Hawkesworth's active participation in the magazine, including service as its literary editor; from the late 1740s to 1773, the year of his death, Hawkesworth is a strong candidate for the authorship of material in the publication that might be linked with Johnson, especially the many drama and book reviews that were published during this time.[8]

The difficulty of sorting out Johnson's contributions to the *Gentleman's Magazine* during this time is compounded by the fact that Hawkesworth was seen then and ever after as a successful imitator of Johnson's style. Consider, for example, his conclusion to his last *Adventurer*, a periodical paper he wrote with Johnson and other contributors:

> Time, who is impatient to date my last paper, will shortly moulder the hand that is now writing it in the dust, and still the breast that now throbs at the reflection: but let not this be read as something that relates only to another; for a few years only can divide the eye that is now reading from the hand that has written. This awful truth, however obvious, and however reiterated, is yet frequently forgotten; for, surely, if we did not lose our remembrance, or at least our sensibility, that view would always predominate in our lives which alone can afford us comfort when we die.

Fluency of this kind caused John Courtenay in his "Moral and Literary Character of Dr. Johnson" to write: "Ingenious HAWKESWORTH to this school [Johnson's] we owe, /And scarce the pupil from the tutor know." Johnson himself acknowledged his literary powers in a gracious comment on Hawkesworth's life of Swift, if not his debt to his friend's biography, when he came to compose his commentary on the Dean. He writes: "I cannot, therefore, be expected to say much of a life concerning which I had long since communicated by thoughts to a man capable of dignifying his narration with so much elegance of language and force of sentiment." Johnson could have been thinking of any number of passages in Hawkesworth's life of Swift; few, though, are so eloquent as his summary of the writer's last days:

> Such was Dr. *Jonathan Swift*, whose writings either stimulate mankind to sustain their dignity as rational and moral beings, by shewing how low they stand in mere animal nature, or fright them from indecency, by holding up its picture before them in its native deformity: and whose life, with all the advantages of genius and learning, was a scale of infelicity gradually ascending till pain and anguish destroyed the faculties by which they were felt; while he was viewed at a distance with envy, he became a burden to himself; he was forsaken by his friends, and his memory has been loaded with unmerited reproach: his life, therefore, does not afford less instruction than his writings, since to the wise it may teach humility, and to the simple content.[9]

Excerpts such as these, which demonstrate clearly that Hawkesworth was capable of writing Johnsonian-sounding prose, soon cloy, but they are useful to keep in mind as the authorship of items in the *Gentleman's Magazine* is examined. The January 1754 issue of the periodical included, for example, lengthy coverage of Hogarth's *Analysis of Beauty*. While there is little original commentary in this review, the summary is striking in its fluency:

> Such are the principles which Mr *Hogarth* has established, explained, and applied to practice in his analysis of beauty; a book, written with that precision and perspicuity, which can only result from a perfect knowledge of his subject in all its extent. . . . The player and the dancing-master, whom others consider as patterns of just action and genteel deportment, are not less instructed than the statuary and the painter; nor is there any species of beauty or elegance that is not here investigated and analyzed.
>
> A book, by which the author has discovered such superiority, could scarce fail of creating enemies; those who admit his analysis to be just are disposed to deny that it is new, . . . The work however will live when these cavils are forgotten; and except the originals, of which it is pretended to be a copy, are produced, there is no question but that the name of the author will descend to posterity with that honour which competitors only can wish to withhold.

The comments above caused Arthur Sherbo, one of the most important shapers of the Johnsonian canon, to link it and a brief review of the same volume in the December 1753 issue of the *Gentleman's* to Johnson. Given the general tenor of the passage, not to mention the stylistic specifics that parallel Johnson's favored constructions (it is almost overburdened with the doublet he so often employed), it is not difficult to share in this conclusion. But this was before Hawkesworth's major role in the publication had been determined, one that on the face of it makes him a more likely author of these items. In this particular case external evidence, provided by Sherbo himself, confirmed Hawkesworth's authorship: John Nichols and George Steevens in their *Genuine Works of William Hogarth* assign the 1754 review to Hawkesworth; by implication, at least, it seems as if he wrote the one in the preceding month as well.[10]

Other pieces, once linked to Johnson in the *Gentleman's Magazine*, now seem more likely to be Hawkesworth's property. During the late 1740s the magazine capitalized on and certainly helped sustain the great interest in William Lauder's case against Milton, his charge that *Paradise Lost* was not an original work. Johnson's role in Lauder's unmasking is quite well known; there is reason to credit him with the *Gentleman's* apology and explanation concerning this case, which appeared in the December 1750 issue. James L. Clifford says that "perhaps" Johnson wrote this explanation, a view shared by other Johnsonians. I am not so sure. Hawkesworth might have had the final editorial word in this case, not Johnson, though we lack the evidence that would settle the issue. A knowledge of the literary terrain of the magazine at this time—the fact that Hawkesworth played an important role in the publication—must be taken into account.[11]

In other cases involving the *Gentleman's Magazine*, however, changes in the Johnsonian canon definitely seem in order. The magazine for April 1768 featured an unusually long review of Richard Deane's *Essay on the Future Life of Brute Creatures*, a book that is discussed in the *Life* between Johnson and by "a gentleman who seemed fond of curious speculation," obviously Boswell himself. Johnson had no use for such speculation and deems Boswell "a very foolish *fellow*" for raising the issue. John Wilson Croker in his edition of Boswell's *Life of Johnson* finds the *Gentleman's* review "in style very like Johnson's." Croker's tentative linking of Johnson with this review has merit, especially because of Johnson's response to Deane's text. The *Gentleman's* reviewer is also hostile to the volume. In this case, though, Croker is probably wrong. He did not know that by 1768 Hawkesworth was deeply involved in reviewing for the *Gentleman's* and did not know that this review carried the "X" signature that Hawkesworth regularly used at this time. Evidence for Hawkesworth's primary role in Cave's magazine during midcentury continues to mount: letters exchanged by Thomas Birch and David Henry on 27 March 1760 and 21 May 1760—I found these in the Birch Collection in the British Library too late to refer to them in my biography of Hawkesworth—prove that Hawkesworth reviewed, and to Birch's displeasure, his book entitled *Some Particulars of the Life of Henry Prince of Wales*. This review appeared in the *Gentleman's* for February through May 1760. While such evidence obviously proves authorship only of a particular piece, it clearly shows Hawkesworth's wide participation in the periodical. Johnson's activities in the magazine during this period have not been similarly documented.[12]

A reexamination of Johnson's relationship with Sir Robert Chambers, with Dr. Robert James, and with the *Gentleman's Magazine* suggests, then, the value of a careful review of the items in the canon that are connected with these relationships. The canon that results from such reassessments will be a more accurate reflection of what Johnson actually wrote.

In most discussions of the making of the Johnsonian canon there is a direct or implied address to Johnson's style. Boswell's reference to a Johnsonian "aether" suggests an atmosphere that we all detect, though we are never quite sure how to describe it.[13] Ever since the eighteenth century many have claimed a special sensitivity to Johnson's style, the ears of some detecting a signature that the eyes of others would prefer to see. But twentieth-century students of the canon have admitted to difficulties in detecting Johnson's style with certainty. Allen Hazen modestly asserted in his introduction to *Samuel John-*

son's Prefaces & Dedications that a critical appraisal of Johnson's prose style "is a task reserved for maturity." R. W. Chapman, a seasoned reader of Johnson, confessed to confusion when Johnson's style had to be distinguished from that of his able imitator. Ignorant of the key that indicated authorship in the *Adventurer*, Chapman commented that "by the end of the day [he] was at a loss to tell Hawkesworth from Johnson." W. K. Wimsatt, Jr., in his classic studies of Johnson's prose style and vocabulary, pointed the way to a more scientific assessment of Johnson's prose that might yield the ways that style could genuinely determine authorship. But Wimsatt's almost algebraic formulations seem in the end better able to describe than definitively characterize Johnsonian prose. In Appendix B of *The Prose Style of Samuel Johnson* he reveals that there is no real counting of even fairly discreet elements—doublets and triplets, for example—because readers work from differing definitions of these terms. Brian McCrea, in an article entitled "Style or Styles: The Problem of Johnson's Prose," asks us, in fact, to stop shadowboxing with Wimsatt, to acknowledge a flexibility in Johnson's writing that precludes any definition of a single Johnsonian style.[14]

Wimsatt cites a professor who in the late nineteenth century determined the average length of each sentence in Macaulay's *History of England*—it was 23.43 words. I invoke this detail here to show how far Wimsatt and others have come as they have moved to some meaningful quantification of Johnson's prose style, McCrea's objections aside. I invoke it as a reminder, too, that we should always examine data carefully to see if it provides mere facts with no point or direction. This should be kept in mind as the Johnsonian canon receives more sophisticated applications of computer technology than it has enjoyed in the past. Such assessments could have value, at least as they provide another kind of evidence with which attribution can be made. Consider, for example, the following paragraph addressed "To the Public" in an Advertisement for *The World Displayed*, which appeared in the *London Chronicle* for 13 November 1759:

> Curiosity is seldom so powerfully excited, or so amply gratified, as by faithful Relations of Voyages and Travels. The different Appearances of Nature, and the various Customs of Men, the gradual Discovery of the World, and the Accidents and Hardships of a naval Life, all concur to fill the Mind with expectation and with Wonder; and as Science, when it can be connected with Events, is always more easily learned, and more certainly remembered, the History of a Voyage may be considered as the most useful Treatise on Geography; since the Student follows the Traveller from Country to Country, and retains the Situation of Places by recounting his Adventures. It is hoped that this Collection will be favorably received, as none has hitherto been offered so cheap or so commodious.[15]

Even those who might not recall from this single paragraph Johnson's connection with the compilation this commentary highlights would probably conclude that the prose could belong to Johnson himself, with the exception of the last labored sentence. While few would disagree with Allen Hazen's view that this "must surely be by Johnson," they might offer reasons that would resist easy conversion into that peculiar language (at least for the humanist) by which computers speak to us and to each other. In any electronic definition of Johnson's prose we should keep in mind two important problems: on the one hand, the larger qualities of discourse that we see and hear to be Johnsonian—the special syntactical structures, the special flow and rhythms of his language—resist mechanical quantification. On the other hand, the most discrete aspects of style—peculiarities of spelling, punctuation, and other mannerisms—must be seen to reflect Johnson's intentions and not those of his compositor if they are to be used to argue for authorship. I suspect that best results will flow from assessments of diction from substantial prose samples. Would the *Parliamentary Debates* in the *Gentleman's Magazine* be a likely locus for such computer application? Possibly. Here we have known writings of Samuel Johnson in apparent intersection with those of John Hawkesworth. If Johnson's prose could in some way be distinguished from that of his cleverest imitator, we might solve at once a problem of authorship that has lingered for years at the same time we might demonstrate conclusively the value of electronic definitions of authorship.[16]

Perhaps the way I have characterized the canon in this brief study seems somewhat discouraging: we still contend with the problems Boswell and others confronted; the canon has an organic quality about it, at once growing and decaying; our methods of contending with it are still imprecise. The difficulties that we face in defining the canon need not lead, however, to some sort of scholarly agnosticism. The canon simply proves James Gray's observation that "work on Samuel Johnson must always be work in progress." It might not be too great a claim to say that the Johnsonians of this century have identified many of the probable sources of Johnson's writings and have learned to pose the right questions in order to make reasonable attributions. We know the proper applications and limitations of internal and external evidence; we are closer now than ever before to fixing the exact nature of Johnson's writings. Although we must wait for the definitive bibliographic study of Johnson's writings that J. D. Fleeman and others will provide, we can look forward in the near future to the completion of Donald Greene's *Check List of the Writings Attributed to Samuel Johnson*.[17]

The *Check List* is not meant to be a canon, in the sense of an authorized or definitive list of Johnson's writings; rather, it is a chronological list of works attributed to Johnson over the years with an appendix of "Erroneous or Highly Doubtful Attributions." The *List* is a sensible solution to the problem of establishing a canon of Johnson's works before all the returns are in, before we have had a chance to reexamine and debate a number of attributions. As it provides convenient access to all writings attributed to Johnson, the *List* should encourage just this kind of debate. It will have other uses as well: it will serve as an informal history of the making of the Johnsonian canon until a more formal account can be provided; it will provide an extensive record of the way we have responded to Johnson over the years in attributing works to him, or refusing to do so, on the basis of style and content. The *List* will show, in fact, that defining the canon is not a technical exercise, but a means, like biography and literary criticism, of determining Johnson's real contributions to English literary history.

NOTES

1. There is no definitive list of Johnson's writings, though there is abundant commentary on the canon itself. A very partial listing follows. The best review of the canon is by Donald Greene, "The Development of the Johnson Canon," in *Restoration and Eighteenth-Century Literature: Essays in Honor of Alan Dugald McKillop*, ed. Carroll Camden (Chicago: Univ. of Chicago Press, 1963), pp. 407–42. Hereafter cited as Greene, "Johnson Canon." A major source of information about the canon is *Boswell's Life of Johnson*. Boswell's mastery of the canon, while impressive, is not complete: there are inconsistencies between the "Chronological Catalogue" of Johnson's prose works in the *Life* and references to Johnson's writing in the narrative itself; Boswell's use of "acknowl.," "intern. evid.," and the asterisk are similarly inconsistent and create hierarchies of attribution where none really exist. Greene, "Johnson Canon," is to be consulted here. Boswell must be supplemented by other important accounts of the canon: Thomas Davies, ed., *Miscellaneous and Fugitive Pieces* (London, 1773–74); Thomas Tyers, "A Biographical Sketch of Dr. Samuel Johnson," *Gentleman's Magazine*, 54 (1784), 899–911, 982; "Additions," 55 (1785), 85–87 (revised and reissued as a pamphlet in 1785; reprinted with an introduction by Gerald D. Meyer [Los Angeles: Augustan Reprint Society, 1952—Publication No. 34]; "An Account of the Writings of Dr. Samuel Johnson, including some Incidents of his Life," *European Magazine*, 6 (1784), 411–13; 7 (1785), 9–12, 81–84, 190–92, 249–50. Sir John Hawkins's *The Life of Samuel Johnson, LL.D.* (London, 1787) and his 1787 edition of Johnson's *Works* together with the 1788 and 1789 supplements demonstrate, with the works noted above, that a Johnson canon was well established before Boswell's list. The growth (and decay) of the canon can be seen in examining later editions of the *Works* and the *Life*. While nineteenth-century commentaries on the canon should be considered with caution, some provide valuable information. Johnson's involvement in the *Gentleman's Magazine* is discussed in "The Autobiography of Sylvanus Urban," *GM*, n.s. 46, pt. 2 (1856), 3–9, 131–40, 267–77, 531–41, 667–77; n.s. 47, pt. 1 (1857), 3–10, 149–57, 282–90, 379–87. Twentieth-century scholarship is marked by a number of serious attempts to define what Johnson wrote. These include: W. P. Courtney and D. N. Smith, *A Bibliography of Samuel Johnson* (Oxford: Clarendon Press, 1915. Reissued with facsimiles, 1925—hereafter cited as Courtney); R. W. Chapman and Allen T. Hazen, "Johnsonian Bibliography: A Supple-

ment to Courtney," *Proceedings of the Oxford Bibliographical Society*, 5 (1939), 119–66. The accounts of Johnson's writing in the *CBEL* for 1940 by D. N. Smith and (unsigned) in the *New CBEL* for 1971 are useful but cannot be considered definitive. Other surveys of the canon are found in *Samuel Johnson: A Survey and Bibliography*, ed. James L. Clifford and Donald J. Greene (Minneapolis: Univ. of Minnesota Press, 1970), which can be updated by issues of *The Eighteenth Century: A Current Bibliography* and the *Johnsonian News Letter*. Important specialized studies and listings are: Allen T. Hazen, *Samuel Johnson's Prefaces & Dedications* (New Haven: Yale Univ. Press, 1937—hereafter cited as *Prefaces*); J. D. Fleeman, *A Preliminary Handlist of Documents & Manuscripts of Samuel Johnson* (Oxford: Oxford Bibliographical Society, 1967); and Donald P. Eddy, *Samuel Johnson: Book Reviewer in the Literary Magazine: or, Universal Review 1756–1758* (New York: Garland Publishing, Inc., 1979). Definitive editions of Johnson's writing, especially his major works, are now available in the Yale editions. These may be supplemented by *Early Biographical Writings of Dr. Johnson*, introduced by J. D. Fleeman (Westmead: Gregg International Publishers, Ltd., 1973). Forthcoming from AMS Press, New York, is *Shorter Prose Writings of Samuel Johnson*, ed. Donald Greene and O M Brack.

2. See E. L. McAdam, Jr., "Dr. Johnson and Saunders Welch's *Proposals*," *Review of English Studies*, n.s. 4 (1953), 337–45. McAdam states: "In this pamphlet, I believe, Johnson assisted, though there is no external evidence available" (p. 337). I plan to provide external evidence in an essay that more closely links Johnson with this text. J. D. Fleeman suggested Johnson's connection with James's text. For Johnson's connections with *Cecilia* see *Life*, IV, 223 n.5. See Courtney for Johnson's involvement with *A System of Vegetables* (p. 156), a dubious attribution. The date of the fabricated newspaper items is not clear; they may not exist. See *Johnsonian Miscellanies*, ed. G. B. Hill, 2 vols. (Oxford: Clarendon Press, 1897), II, 391–92.

3. I quote from *Samuel Johnson*, ed. Donald Greene (Oxford: Oxford Univ. Press, 1984), pp. 40, 53, 68, 84, 101. This is the first "school" edition of Johnson's writings that gives a real sampling of the full range of the Johnsonian canon.

4. *Life*, I, 112.

5. Greene, "Johnson Canon," p. 427. Thomas Kaminski kindly shared with me his forthcoming study entitled *The Early Career of Samuel Johnson*. The lines quoted here appear in the *Gentleman's Magazine*, 10 (1740), 251.

6. See Curley, "Johnson's Secret Collaboration" in *The Unknown Samuel Johnson*, ed. John J. Burke and Donald Kay (Madison: Univ. of Wisconsin Press, 1982), pp. 89–110, and McAdam's book (Syracuse, N.Y.: Syracuse Univ. Press, 1951). I quote from Curley's Introduction to *A Course of Lectures on the English Law* (p. 4, typescript).

7. Allen T. Hazen, "Samuel Johnson and Dr. Robert James," *Bulletin of the Institute of the History of Medicine*, 4 (1936), 455–65, and "Johnson's Life of Frederick Ruysch," *ibid.*, 7 (1939), 324–34; John L. Abbott, "Dr. Johnson, Fontenelle, Le Clerc, and Six 'French' Lives," *Modern Philology*, 63 (1965), 121–27; Brack and Kaminski, *Modern Philology*, 81 (1983–84), 378–400.

8. *Life*, I, 112. John L. Abbott, *John Hawkesworth: Eighteenth-Century Man of Letters* (Madison: Univ. of Wisconsin Press, 1982), Chap. V., "Hawkesworth and The *Gentleman's Magazine*, 1747–1773," pp. 86–111. Hereafter cited as *Hawkesworth*.

9. *The Adventurer* (London, 1793), IV, 244; *Life*, I, 223; "Swift," in *Lives*, III, 1. *The Works of Dr. Jonathan Swift*, ed. John Hawkesworth (London, 1766), I, 70–71.

10. See *Gentleman's Magazine*, 23 (1753), 593 and 24 (1754), 11–15; Sherbo, "Samuel Johnson and The *Gentleman's Magazine*, 1750–1755," in *Johnsonian Studies*, ed. James L. Clifford and Donald Greene (Cairo: Oxford Univ. Press, 1962), pp. 146, 150; and *Genuine Works of William Hogarth*, ed. Nichols and Steevens (London, 1808), pp. 231–33.

11. The best student of the Lauder controversy is Michael Marcuse. See "The *Gentleman's Magazine* and the Lauder/Milton Controversy," *Bulletin of Research in the Hu-*

manities, 81 (1978), 179–209. The apology and explanation is *GM*, 20 (1750), 535–36. See James L. Clifford, *Dictionary Johnson* (New York: McGraw-Hill, 1979), p. 65. Donald Greene argues for Johnson's connection with this piece in "Some Notes on Johnson and the *Gentleman's Magazine*," *PMLA*, 74 (1959), 83–84.

12. *Gentleman's Magazine*, 38 (1768), 177–80. Cf. *Life*, II, 54; Boswell, *Life*, ed. John Wilson Croker (London, 1876), III, 44. *Hawkesworth*, pp. 93–100; BL Add. MS. 4310, fols. 33, 35v, 36. Birch's book is reviewed in the *GM*, 30 (1760), 78–82, 124–27, 181–86, 227–30.

13. *Life*, I, 421.

14. *Prefaces*, p. xxiii. Chapman's comment is in his review of Hazen's study in *Review of English Studies*, 14 (1938), 361. See W. K. Wimsatt, *The Prose Style of Samuel Johnson* (New Haven: Yale Univ. Press, 1941), pp. 150–52, hereafter cited as *Prose Style*. Also central in his *Philosophic Words* (New Haven: Yale Univ. Press, 1948). For McCrea's essay, see *Style*, 14 (1980), 201–15.

15. *Prose Style*, p. 24 n. 1. Wimsatt refers to L. A. Sherman, "On Certain Facts and Principles in the Development of Form in Literature," *The University Studies of the University of Nebraska*, 1 (1892), 350–53. He comments: "Such, and only such, can be the conclusion reached by counting items chosen without reference to meaning" in response to Sherman's conclusion that the sentence average "was the resultant of the forces which made Macaulay's literary character." I quote from the *London Chronicle*.

16. *Prefaces*, p. 217. Hazen quotes all but the final sentence, "which is hardly Johnson's." The application of computer technology to the Johnsonian canon deserves fuller commentary than I am able to give here. If only in storing and retrieving material relating to the canon, the computer will have practical application; in determining authorship it may have even greater use, though caution should be exercised. The problems and hazards of computer application in defining and detecting Johnson's prose have been explained by Arthur Sherbo in "The Electronic Computer and I," *University College Quarterly* (Michigan State University), 7 (1962), 8–11 and Part II, 9 (1963), 18–23. These essays recount the background of an unpublished study he did of Johnson's and Hawkesworth's prose styles, which he kindly shared with me, entitled "Counting Words: The Prose Styles of Samuel Johnson and John Hawkesworth." Sherbo's methodology is sound; this kind of study should be undertaken with the use of computer capacity not available twenty years ago. For a brief review of the applications of computer technology in humanistic studies see Robert L. Oakman, *Computer Methods for Literary Research* (Athens, Georgia: Univ. of Georgia Press, 1984).

17. *Johnson's Sermons: A Study* (Oxford: Clarendon Press, 1972), p. 6. The *Check List* will be published by AMS Press, Inc., New York.

WILLIAM H. EPSTEIN

9 · Patronizing the Biographical Subject: Johnson's Savage and Pastoral Power

—"it was therefore impossible to pay him any Distinction, without the entire Subversion of all Oeconomy, a Kind of Establishment which, wherever he went, he always appeared ambitious to overthrow" (Johnson's *Life of Savage*)[1]

1

"The modern Western state," asserts Michel Foucault, "integrated in a new political shape, an old power technique which originated in Christian institutions." Because Christianity "postulates in principle that certain individuals can, by their religious quality, serve others not as princes, magistrates, prophets, fortune-tellers, benefactors, educationalists, and so on, but as pastors," Christianity "proposed and spread . . . a very special form of power," which Foucault calls "pastoral power." As its "ultimate aim is to assure individual salvation in the next world," pastoral power "does not look after just the whole community, but each individual in particular, during his entire life." Hence it "cannot be exercised without knowing the inside of people's minds, without exploring their souls, without making them reveal their innermost secrets." Moreover, Foucault insists, "a new distribution, a new organization of this kind of individualizing power" began in and around the eighteenth century, when the "ecclesiastical institutionalization" of pastoral power "lost its vitality" and "suddenly spread out into the whole social body," where "it found support in a multitude of institutions," all of which were integrated into and dominated by the "state," which emerges now "as a modern matrix of individualization, or a new form of pastoral power." Medicine, psychiatry, education, the family, the police, and other public and private institutions became the means by which pastoral power changed "its objective," by which "a series of 'worldly' aims," promising salvation "in this world" rather than the next, "took the place of the religious aims of the traditional pastorate."[2]

Although Foucault does not mention literature in this context, we have long recognized that, in one way or another, various eighteenth-century literary genres also participated in the redistribution of this new "individualizing 'tactic.'"[3] For instance, the notion of a trans-social redistribution of pastoral power's knowledge of the individual informs such influential studies as Ian Watt's analysis of the rise of the English novel or John Sitter's exploration of literary loneliness in mid-century poetry. The study of eighteenth-century English biography can also be approached as an individualizing tactic which exploits and is exploited by pastoral power. English life-writing, it can be claimed, has always been concerned with the complex relationship between the secular and the sacred. Indeed, in its most common early form—saints' lives and other modes of hagiography—it can be described as a discursive practice completely dominated by traditional pastoral power: the sacred plot of individual revelation through sacrifice and salvation reproduces over and over again a life-story, the *only* life-story, which Christianity authorizes. In fact, throughout its development, English biography can be shown to have inscribed and institution-alized pastoral power's distribution of "each individual in particular, during his entire life," to have considered itself to be, as Foucault maintains pastoral power must be, "coextensive and continuous with life" and "linked with a production of truth—the truth of the individual himself."[4]

The modern state's appropriation of biography as a discursive practice which institutionalizes a new individualizing tactic can be traced in Johnson's *Life of Savage* (1744), one of English biography's most well-known and admired texts, perhaps because, as Paul Fussell has remarked, we can discern in it "Johnson's archetypal Portrait of the Artist."[5] Indeed, throughout Johnson's biographical narrative, Savage tries to use the institutions of authorship and literature as an individualizing tactic through which he can reclaim his cultural identity. As the biography constantly demonstrates, many of Savage's poems, such as *The Author to be Let, The Volunteer Laureate*, and *The Bastard*, are autobiographical works proclaiming, lamenting, and exploiting his marginal status in English society. For instance, the publication of *The Bastard*, Savage's most famous poem, is presented in Johnson's narrative as a powerful instrument of revenge that individualizes its author as it generalizes and depersonalizes his reputed mother, whom it forces to leave Bath and "shelter herself among the Crouds of London" (pp. 72–73). Yet, as we know, Johnson's Savage is more often an unsuccessful, frustrated participant in the mid-eighteenth-century institutions of authorship and literature—and his fruitless effort to sustain a literary career, and to define himself in terms of it, suggests one way that biography has accommodated and disobliged pastoral power. For he represents, somewhat more obviously perhaps than many other biographical subjects, a threat to the individualizing tactic of the modern state. If Savage, a marginal figure if there ever was one, can be brought into the center of the institutional matrix, then (despite the intimations of discontinuity which his anomalous situation implies) English biography can still function as a discursive practice through which cultural authority can produce and reproduce individual lives. To appreciate the kind of problem Savage offers in this respect, and how that problem is treated in Johnson's narrative, we turn now to the concept and practice of patronage, another cultural institution through which the sacred was transformed into the secular and with which both Savage and biography were intimately associated.

2

Here is how the scholarship on English literary patronage in the late Middle Ages and early Renaissance describes the situation in which the pre–Gutenberg hagiographer produced biography: " 'he wrote the lives of saints who inspired the foundation of, or themselves founded, religious orders . . . for the heads of religious houses to be read by the inmates of those houses.' "[6] Thus the early English patron is not only a royal or aristocratic connoisseur of literature who influences and supports the production of literary texts, but also, as the OED and Johnson's *Dictionary* remind us, "a founder of a religious order," or a "special tutelary saint of a person, place, country, craft, or institution" (that is, a patron saint), or "one who holds the right of presentation to an ecclesiastical benefice," in all of which functions the patron is expected to act as "advocate and defender" (the earliest sense of the term in English usage) of the Church.[7] Hence patronage is a practice closely allied to the ecclesiastical institution that governed the distribution of traditional pastoral power. The hagiographer's writing lives of the founding patrons or patron saints of particular religious orders for the heads of religious houses to be read by the inmates of those houses perfectly encapsulates the hermetic character of the conditions under which early English biography was produced.

Although the recent scholarship of Peter Lucas, Elizabeth Eisenstein, and others[8] has informed our concept of the early development of English literary patronage and has pushed back our sense of when it began to change, students of English literary history still tend to identify the traditional system of patronizing literature with the classic studies of Elizabethan authorship undertaken by Phoebe Sheavyn and her followers.[9] Governed by the ancient genealogical and class-oriented sociopolitical structures of authority vested in the crown, the church, and the nobility, traditional patronage was essentially hermetic and self-authenticating. Like a religious order or a craft guild, it can be described as a closed, privileged, preserving cell which established and enforced its own rules, and which jealously guarded and sponsored the processes of admission and advancement. Further, because the reading public was relatively limited and because access to the materials and opportunities associated with both reading and writing were relatively restricted, authors and readers tended to share a small, specially informed community in which formal publication was only one (and often not the most significant) means of distribution. One of the most common patterns of the literary career (and there were many variations on it) involved access to the circulation of literary texts in manuscript; a university or private tutorial education; the opportunity to travel and broaden knowledge and contacts (often as the result of domestic and foreign civil or ecclesiastical service); membership in an exclusive circle of poets, a peerage of talent, like the "Sons of Ben," which considered itself the only appropriate judge of literary merit; the selection of a suitably classical topic and poetic convention; the acquisition of a royal, noble, or ecclesiastical patron; and the occasional publication of text surrounded and authorized by dedicatory poems from previously established authors and by lists of similarly authenticated and authenticating literary peers.

As the work of A. S. Collins and, more recently, of Paul J. Korshin suggests,[10] this hierarchical system was changing throughout the eighteenth century. Korshin notes that "*direct* crown support for intellectuals" dwindled away almost entirely under the Georges; that "job-oriented public patronage, paid for out of Treasury funds," offered "few places . . . specifically designated for literary men and scholars"; that "very few" peers "were interested in supporting literature and scholarship on a large scale"; and that "there is practically no evidence of large or continuous literary patronage from members of the rising mercantile class."[11] Yet, as both Collins and Korshin make clear, hierarchical patronage gradually lost its influence over literature not because it ceased to support authorship (indeed, its subsidizing of individual authors seems to have been about the same, numerically, as during the Renaissance) but because the size of the reading public and the number of authors or potential authors increased dramatically. There were simply too many authors to support and too large and diverse a readership to influence. The old hermetic cell had been broken open.

Of course, hierarchical patronage did not die out overnight; rather, as Korshin and others suggest, it was dispersed, somewhat haphazardly, over a wider territory. Although the soliciting of subscriptions to individual works (which began in the early seventeenth century but was much more prevalent in the eighteenth) "democratized literary patronage" to some extent, both this method and the nearly universal practice of gathering "incidental bounty" through a dedication directed to someone with whom the author was, in most cases, unacquainted and from whom he or she could expect little or no reward,[12] was hardly sufficient to influence what was becoming a vast, nearly anonymous reading and writing public. Literature and authorship were now patronized primarily by the booksellers, by what was called "the trade," a consumer-oriented mercantile monopoly that acted as agent for both readers and writers. The new trade grew in prominence because, unlike the old order or guild, which flourished within a small, recognizable, hierarchical, self-authenticating community of common interests, accomplishments, and opportunities, the trade could service an expanding, diversifying, democratizing, consuming culture.

Hence mid-eighteenth-century authorship was no longer a way of announcing or reaffirming one's acceptance or position in the traditional sociopolitical structures of authority. The celebrated observation appended to one of Johnson's *Dictionary's* definitions of "patron" ("Commonly a wretch who supports with insolence, and is paid with flattery") points to this cultural shift. Indeed, we can find signs of this ambiguous and changing situation distributed throughout the text of Johnson's literary career. For instance, the revised version of *The Vanity of Human Wishes* depicts the contemporary scholar assailed by "Toil, Envy, Want, the Patron, and the Jail."[13] The replacement of the word *Garret* with *Patron* is a powerful symbolic gesture. The original wording locates the scholar in the two places, the garret and the jail, where he characteristically toils, envies, and wants. The revised wording disrupts this parallelism: instead of the place, the levee, or its "outward Rooms,"[14] the revision offers the person who dominates the place— and whose neglect, the new wording suggests, is responsible for the scholar's ills. The patron also now dominates the line: customarily isolated from his potential client in a privileged inner space which garret- and jail-dwellers may not enter, the patron can be glimpsed in the middle (the inner space) of this line, where he momentarily reassumes an institutional agency and cultural authority that, as we have seen, the mid-eighteenth century was increasingly reluctant to recognize. In stressing the patron's isolation and neglect, the revised *Vanity of Human Wishes* acknowledges the decline of the old patronage system's enveloping authority. No longer able to control the production and consumption of literature on behalf of a devitalized form of pastoral power, it is classed now among the forces that assail literature, its diminished authority directed against the institution that it once governed.

Johnson's famous letter to Chesterfield, which, it has often been claimed, prompted the garret/patron revision, is another example from Johnson's own literary career of the ambiguous and changing relationships between authorship, patronage, and cultural authority. Recent scholarship has suggested that the letter ought to be read as a direct response to papers Chesterfield published in *The World*, papers that invited the conclusion that he was still patronizing the *Dictionary* long after the two men had broken and that promoted views on language that Johnson had abandoned.[15] Nevertheless, as we know, Johnson's letter (to which Chesterfield never responded and to which subsequent readers have customarily reacted as if it were a general observation and not a specific response) has often been treated as the modern author's declaration of independence from the old, hierarchical patronage system. Its description of a patron is well known and frequently quoted: "one who looks with unconcern on a Man struggling for Life in the Water and when he has reached ground encumbers him with Help." Its depiction of an impoverished, unknown Johnson waiting vainly in Chesterfield's "outward Rooms" is engraved in art and memory. And its characterization of the letter's writer, emerging now as Dictionary Johnson, a figure who will himself dominate mid- and late-eighteenth-century cultural discourse, suggests the new attitude with which the mid-century author confronts the traditional structures of authority: "The notice which you have been pleased to take of my Labours, had it been early, had been kind; but it has been delayed till I am indifferent and cannot enjoy it, till I am solitary and cannot impart it, till I am known and do not want it."[16] Indifferent, solitary, and known, adjectives which might describe the patron, are used here to characterize the New Author, whose appropriation of the patron's attitude indicates that he has become (or has the illusion of becoming) his own patron.

That the self-patronizing author is but an illusion is evident from Johnson's own extensive efforts to act as a patron of literature. Holladay and Brack have recently catalogued and enumerated many instances of Johnson's "writing reviews, signing subscription lists, influencing booksellers, contributing to others' works, revising others' works, and [ghost]writing Prefaces and Dedications." They conclude: "Johnson did whatever he could to gain for other authors the attraction of aristocrats, booksellers, subscribers, and the public, all potential sources of income in a period of transition from court to private patronage to purely commercial publication reliant on mass consumption."[17] Thus the autonomous public posture Johnson occasionally assumed ("No man who ever lived by literature, has lived more independently than I have done")[18] was constrained by his patronage of other writers, whose dependence and distress he both relieved and shared.

This situation is implicated in a satirical piece, a letter to the editor subsequently entitled "A Project for the Employment of Authors," which Johnson wrote for the *Universal Visiter* in 1756, the year after the Chesterfield letter. This essay ironically suggests that the recent prodigious increase in the number of authors, who "are spread over all the town and all the country, and fill every stage of habitation from the cellar to the garret," can be alleviated by pressing them into military service, "for which they may seem particularly qualified" by their familiarity with "want" and uncertainty and by their willingness "to obey the word of command from their patrons and their booksellers." The essay's conclusion ("if they should be destroyed in war, we shall lose only those who had wearied the public, and whom, whatever be their fate, nobody will miss") reinforces its major premise ("If I were to form an adage of misery, or fix the lowest point to which humanity could fall, I should be tempted to name the life of an author"). Although this observation can be treated as an overstatement supporting the satire, its sting is not easily salved. The author emerges here not as the indifferently independent self-patronizer of the Chesterfield letter, but, as is more customary in Johnson's work, as "an adage of misery," neglected by his patron, deserted by the public, "worried by critics, tormented by his bookseller, and hunted by his creditors." No longer entailed in the landed estate of hierarchical patronage, the author is now the public's performer, plaything, and pet—"teazed like a bear at the stake, tormented like a toad under a harrow; or hunted like a dog with a stick at his tail."[19]

3

The biographical subject of a text which refers to itself in its opening paragraphs as one of those "mournful Narratives" that "has been written only to enumerate the Miseries of the Learned" (p. 4), Johnson's Savage also becomes an "adage of misery" as he turns to authorship and literature in an effort to reenter the hierarchical system which has, he claims, inappropriately excluded him. This turning from genealogy to authorship is powerfully and directly presented in Johnson's narrative, where Savage's "Discovery of his real Mother" (the Countess of Macclesfield) prompts "his frequent Practice to walk in the dark Evenings for several Hours before her Door, in Hopes of seeing her as she might come by Accident to the Window, or cross her Apartment with a Candle in her Hand." Banished to the dark but seeking the light of entry, he finds that "he could neither soften her Heart, nor open her Hand," and, in the next sentence, without any previously delineated desire or preparation, determines "He was therefore obliged to seek some other Means of Support, and having no Profession, became, by Necessity, an Author" (p. 12). This relationship between necessity and authorship is sketched throughout Johnson's narrative. For instance, Savage's inconstant "Supply" of funds and increasing friendships "necessarily leading him to Places of Expence, he found it necessary to endeavour once more at dramatick Poetry" (p. 21). Conversely, his selling *The Wanderer* for a mere ten guineas "was not to be imputed either to Necessity by which the Learned and Ingenious are often obliged to submit to very hard Conditions, or to Avarice by which the Booksellers are frequently invited to oppress that Genius by which they are supported" (p. 58). In a sense, such necessity is responsible for the habitual predicament of a common, secular authorship disinherited by genealogy or excommunicated by religion; neither a person who writes for bread nor a client who writes for patronage can be trusted to seek the truth. "The name of an Author would never have been made contemptible, had no Man ever said what he did not think, or misled others, but when he was himself deceived" (p. 46).

Of course, "the Discovery of his real Mother" implies the discovery of Savage's real father (the Earl Rivers), but the father has been long dead and his will thwarted. Savage cannot reach his father, the pater who can act as his patron and authenticate his place in the hierarchy. The shared philological root [20] suggests one reason why, in Johnson's narrative, Savage's mother does not acknowledge him: to do so would be to patronize him, to assume the father's role. But her role is to maintain the separation of father and son, and hence to force Savage into authorship and literature, through which she will become the subject and victim of his writing, and through which he will discover the futility of his quest for patronage and learn to resign himself to the divine will, to the supreme Father of all our Being and the original Patron of all our words. Johnson's narrative acknowledges the pater/patron relationship in various ways. To Richard Steele, himself an established author who is one of the many patrons and father figures Savage acquires and then loses, is attributed the statement: "*the Inhumanity of* [Savage's] *Mother had given him a Right to find every good Man his Father*" (p. 13). In a poem by Savage reprinted in Johnson's narrative, Aaron Hill, "an Author of an established Character" (p. 23) who patronizes Savage's early efforts at playwriting, is addressed as "Thou Brother, Father, nearer yet—thou Friend" (p. 22). Here and elsewhere Johnson's narrative suggests that Savage has a natural right to seek paternity and patronage wherever he can find it. As the Duke of Dorset, one of the many noble personages to whom Savage attaches himself, remarks: "it was just to consider [Savage] as an injured Nobleman, and . . . the Nobility ought to think themselves obliged without Solicitation to take every Opportunity of supporting him by their Countenance and Patronage" (p. 20). That Savage seeks this natural right through authorship, that he tries to establish a literary career in terms of the old, eroding system of patronage—and thereby reenter the nobility, is a significant narrative structure which, as we shall see, Johnson's biography symbolically appropriates and then frustrates.

Johnson's earliest surviving comment on Savage is a Latin epigram published in the *Gentleman's Magazine* in April 1738, about the time of their first meeting and six years before the initial publication of the biography. Although "the epigram cannot be taken to show more than slight and recent acquaintance,"[21] it intimates that, in one way or another, the notion of patronage (and of its uncertain application and authority) was deeply and presuppositionally embedded in Johnson's writing on Savage. The epigram reads: "Humani studium generis cui pectore fervet, / O! colat humanum Te foveatque genus!"[22] Clarence Tracy, who observes that the epigram implies an "antithesis [that] rings through" the *Life of Savage*, translates it as "Devotion to mankind burns in your breast! O! may mankind in turn cherish and protect you!"[23] Tracy's translation suggests the community's responsibility to support Savage, an injunction enriched and implemented by the knowledge that the verb *foueo* in the epigram's second line can also mean to patronize, as well as to make warm, give comfort to, soothe, relieve, fondle, caress, nurse, foster, nurture, minister to, favor, support, encourage, befriend, promote, cherish, and cultivate.[24] Indeed, we might claim that, in its various senses, this verb informs the biography's depiction of Savage's treatment by the changing patronage system, for Johnson's narrative employs nearly all these meanings as it elaborates and particularizes the many patron–client relationships it traces.[25]

For instance, Steele and Robert Wilks the actor are presented as patrons "by whom [Savage] was pitied, caressed, and relieved" (p. 13). Elsewhere, a client is somewhat generally described as "one whom [a patron] has relieved and supported, whose Establishment he has laboured, and whose Interest he has promoted" (p. 16). Connotations of *foueo* emerge also in the differences among the various women with whom Savage is involved. "Instead of supporting, assisting, and defending him," his mother would "delight to see him struggling with Misery" (p. 6); in contrast, the actions of the Countess of Hereford, who intercedes with the Queen after the murder trial, provoke the observation that it is "much more amiable to relieve, than to oppress" (p. 39). Several senses of the Latin verb characterize Lord Tyrconnell's patronage. At first, this is "the Golden Part of Mr. *Savage's* Life," during which he is "courted" and "caressed" (p. 44). Yet, upon their falling out, it comes to typify the inevitable situation of all client–patron relationships: "he was only a Dependent on the Bounty of another, whom he could expect to support him no longer than he endeavoured to preserve his Favour, by complying with his Inclinations" (p. 66).

The group of subscribing friends, who eventually replace Tyrconnell, fare no better. Jailed for debt in Bristol, Savage discovers that "his Friends, who had hitherto caressed and applauded, . . . all refused to preserve him from a Prison, at the Expence of eight pounds" (p. 124). Finally, in the narrative's summary character sketch, Savage emerges as one who "appeared to think himself born to be supported by others, and dispensed from all Necessity of providing for himself" (p. 137). This is an echo of Savage's preface to the 1726 *Miscellaneous Poems*, an autobiographical account reprinted in Johnson's narrative: "Thus however ill qualified I am to *live by my Wits*, I have the best Plea in the World for attempting it; since it is too apparent, that I was *born to it*" (because he has been "thrown, friendless on the World, without Means of supporting *myself*; and without Authority to apply to those, whose Duty I know it is to support me") (p. 28).

Born to live by his wits, born to be supported by others—this is the Savage we have been tracing. Unlike another recipient of "Mr. *Wilks's* Generosity" whom the narrative briefly describes—a failed author named Smith who saves the money he receives from a benefit organized by Wilks, uses it to study medicine at Leyden, and eventually becomes "one of the chief Physicians at the *Russian* court" (p. 17)—Savage is unable to capitalize on the several benefits Wilks stages for him or, for that matter, on any patronage arrangement into which he enters. "He was very ready to set himself free from the Load of an Obligation; for he could not bear to conceive himself in a State of Dependence" (p. 138). The biography studiously catalogues the various patrons to whom Savage is such a disobliging client; contempt, dissatisfaction, and neglect characterize the behavior of both parties. Savage cannot abide his patrons' condescension, but he will not allow them to ignore what he sees as their duty to him. The narrative is constantly following Savage's movement from one unsatisfactory patronage scheme to another: "To despair was not, however, the Character of *Savage*, when one Patronage failed, he had recourse to another" (p. 90). Steele is a "Patron [who] had many Follies" (p. 16); Mrs. Oldfield, the actress who comes closest to the ideal combination of substitute mother and undemanding patron, dies; Wilks, the actor, and Hill, the author, cannot provide him access to the nobility; his various aristocratic patrons, like Hereford, Middlesex, and Tyrconnell, presume on the relationship and are in turn abused by their client, who insists on acting as willfully as a "real" nobleman; political and royal patrons, like Walpole, the King, the Queen, and the Prince of Wales, are either unreliable and niggardly or unapproachable and unavailing; the group of subscribing friends organized by Pope are "*Little Creatures*" (p. 111) who provide him with "a Pension less than that which Mrs. *Oldfield* paid him without exacting any Servilities"

(p. 114); the Bristol merchants, "sufficiently studious of Profit," cannot countenance Savage's "Neglect of Oeconomy" (pp. 120–21).

Finally, there is Abel Dagg, the Keeper of Bristol Newgate Gaol—"a Pattern of Benevolence . . . whose Heart has not been hardened by such an Employment" (p. 127). Dagg is generous, patient, and undemanding. As the client of this "Pattern" or patron (the two words not only share a common Latin root and French derivation but, until the sixteenth century, were both spelled, and apparently pronounced, "patron"—hence the sense, as here and in Johnson's *Dictionary*, of "pattern" as an exemplar to be copied), Savage can write in a letter to a friend: "I am now all collected in myself, and tho' my Person is in Confinement, my Mind can expatiate on ample and useful Subjects, with all the Freedom imaginable . . . if, instead of a *Newgate* Bird, I may be allowed to be a Bird of the Muses, I assure you, Sir, I sing very freely in my Cage" (p. 125). With this totemic image of eighteenth-century authorship (Sterne's Yorick, we remember, emblazons a caged starling on his family arms), Johnson's Savage ends his quest to reenter the nobility, to regain paternity and patronage through the old self-authenticating system of hierarchical authority. This disintegrating arrangement for producing literature can no longer confer anything but a revokable symbolic status—what the narrative calls "uncertain Patronage" (p. 43), a phrase that not only describes Savage's specific situation but also characterizes the general condition of the new, emerging institution of literature, which authorizes authorship not by enmeshing the writer and his text in a self-authenticating, hierarchical context of privileged and private production and consumption but by forcing the writer to assert his independence and isolation from both the hierarchical authority structures and the reading public. Indeed, it is in the mid-eighteenth century that the reading public clearly establishes itself as the consumer which does not produce, as the authority which endorses authorship (in concert with the booksellers, its agents) through the brute fact of its massive anonymity. In such a situation, the writer aspiring to be transformed into an author can deny his essential humanity in two ways—by embracing either the immaterial or the material. That is, he can invoke, as Johnson does here and in many of his works, the residual authority and individualizing tactic of the old form of pastoral power, by renouncing the material world and resigning himself to the divine will in order to seek salvation and self-definition in God's eternal and immaterial realm—as Savage does just before he dies by declaring that he is "all Resignation to the *divine Will*" (p. 123) and by singing very freely in his cage. Or the aspiring author can reside, temporarily and provisionally, in the transient individuality promised to everyone by the new secular form of pastoral power, can become a mere name, a material nexus of acceptability and marketability in a commodity culture that canonizes self-advertisement and secularizes salvation.

4

Biography, itself a form of writing aspiring to literary status, is in a similar situation. By the mid-eighteenth century it is no longer patronized exclusively or dominantly by the structures of hierarchical authority through which traditional pastoral power is distributed. For the most part, mid eighteenth-century biography must seek patronage and authority from the reading public, the vastness and anonymity of which threaten to consume it, that is, both read it and exhaust it, use it and use it up. For the reading public's appetite is enormous, and yet the stipulative supply of biographical subjects (the received and recognized gods, saints, heroes, and leaders of traditional hierarchical culture) is limited. If biography is to survive it must generate more and different biographical subjects, must learn how to exploit the individualizing tactic authorized by the new, secular form of pastoral power.[26] As I have suggested, Johnson's Savage is a powerful sign of this transitional situation. A self-proclaimed bastard son of nobility, a convicted and nearly executed murderer, a self-advertised "volunteer laureate" and "author to be let," he is a biographical subject in flux—the subject simultaneously and ambiguously presented and authorized by traditional hierarchical biography, by the new subcultural criminal biography, and by the emerging magazine biography (which Johnson helped to initiate in the *Gentleman's Magazine* and which sought to link high and low culture). A successful failure more notorious than famous, a creation of the exploding subculture of hack-writing (which discovered him at his murder trial, variously supported and disobliged him throughout his subsequent public careers, and in the service of which he battled anonymously and pseudonymously as one of Pope's allies in the War of the Dunces), Savage is a classic transitional figure, a fatherless, unpatronized, disestablished, self-promoting author who became (to use the phrase with which Goldsmith dubbed Beau Nash) a "child of the public."[27]

As Neil McKendrick, John Brewer, and J. H. Plumb have recently shown, eighteenth-century England gave birth to "the first of the world's consumer societies." "Bourgeois consumerism" was a crucial precondition for the shift from a "client economy" serving the aristocracy to an "open market" in which Mandevillian tradesmen manipulated luxury as a "great chain of enterprise." McKendrick quotes from the *London Tradesman* of 1747, a kind of early trade journal: a tradesman "must be 'a Perfect Proteus, change Shapes as often as the Moon, and still find something new'; for 'the continual Flux and Reflux of

Fashion, obliges him to learn something new almost every day,'" obliges him, McKendrick later asserts, to produce and manipulate agents of supply and demand in his "pursuit of new levels of consumption from an ever-widening market."[28] In this "Perfect Proteus" we glimpse not only a Wedgwood or a Boulton merchandising pottery or buttons but the booksellers (the Trade) and their factories of hack writers producing, publishing, and distributing reading material to an expanding, seemingly insatiable mass public, whose demand for new, diverse biographical subjects must be supplied. Indeed, McKendrick's description of the modification, during the course of the eighteenth century, in one of the fashion industry's agents of change, the fashion doll, is strikingly similar to the transformation which, I have been suggesting, the biographical subject undergoes during the same period.

The fashion dolls of the early part of the century were wooden, often life-sized mannequins outfitted in the elaborate costuming of the French court. Accurate down to details of hairstyle, underclothing, and the other accessories of fashion, they were sent annually to the English court and then passed on "to the leading London fashion makers." But by the end of the century the English had developed "a flat fashion model cut out of cardboard," which "cost only three shillings . . . and later only a few pence, . . . was printed by the thousand," and was "specifically aimed at different classes and professions." McKendrick comments: "Where the French fashion doll of the first decades of the century served only an *élite*, the English fashion doll of the last decades of that century served a mass consumer market. . . . Its role was now the manipulation and extension of consumer demand. Its dramatic metamorphosis in the course of the century nicely confirms the change from a world where fashion was not only designed to serve the few but was designed to mark them off from the rest of society, to a world where fashion was being deliberately designed to encourage social imitation, social emulation, and emulative spending."[29]

Here, minus some of the more overt conspiratorial and manipulative features McKendrick proposes, and enriched by the influence of the Church, is the shift in patronizing the biographical subject which I have been tracing. Like the fashion doll, the biographical subject moves out of the client economy of the elite and into the mass consumer market over the course of the eighteenth century. Moreover, like the fashion doll, it marks a new tactic of individualization: the selection and production of biographical subjects are no longer the sole responsibility and privilege of a patronage arrangement dominated by the traditional structures of hierarchical authority. A biographical subject like Johnson's Savage signifies that biography too has become an agent in the great chain of enterprise, another institutional channel through which the modern state can materially produce or reproduce the individual in this world. On the reading public's behalf biography can now authorize practically anyone (or anything) as a biographical subject. Indeed, Johnson, Boswell claims, "is reported to have once said, that 'he could write the Life of a Broomstick.'"[30]

Thus Johnson's *Savage* reveals and conceals the individualizing tactic through which mid eighteenth-century cultural discourse institutionalizes the shift from a sacred to a secular form of pastoral power. It grants to the biographer the authority to act as father/patron of his biographical subject, an emergent generic convention which has been occasionally acknowledged—for instance, when the Johnsonian narrator has been treated as a kind of benign father figure for a disinherited, "artificial bastard," or when Johnson has been chastised for defending the convicted murderer too vigorously (vindicator or legal advocate is one of the senses of the Latin word *patronus* that Johnson's *Dictionary* also ascribes to its English derivative). Yet, because one text (con-)textualizes another which (con-)textualizes another in an infinite process of discursive reencoding, this authority can and will be revoked over and over again. If the fatherless, patronless Savage can become Johnson's *Savage*, then Dictionary Johnson can become Boswell's *Johnson*, a (con-)textualization in which Johnson's status as father/patron of biography is recognized and then usurped by a biographer whose self-conscious desire to exert the new pastoral power consumes his biographical subject. Hence this generic shift in eighteenth-century English biography is itself subject to "continual flux and reflux": in the discourse of consumerism, everyone soon comes to realize what Johnson's Savage can never quite accept, "that his Opinion in Questions of Criticism [is] no longer regarded, when his Coat [is] out of Fashion" (p. 101).

If Johnson's Savage is a transitional agent of change, an English fashion doll or child of the public demonstrating that the traditional three estates are no longer the sole patrons and beneficiaries of English biography, then Boswell's Johnson is the modern state itself—an infinitely reproducing matrix of individualization, a technological marvel of interchangeable parts, a self-patronizing, self-advertising, self-consuming economy of biography that perfectly encapsulates the secular form of pastoral power and which thus situates itself at the conventionally acknowledged center of generic authority. Consequently, the epigram with which this essay begins—"it was therefore impossible to pay him any Distinction without the entire Subversion of all Oeconomy, a Kind of Establishment which, wherever he went, he always appeared ambitious to overthrow" (p. 98)—can refer not only to Savage's neglect of domestic management but also, in and through Johnson's narrative, to his role as a biographical subject who heralds a new economic, political, social, and literary distribution of the conditions that produce biography and reproduce individuals.

N O T E S

1. Samuel Johnson, *Life of Savage*, ed. Clarence Tracy (Oxford: Clarendon Press, 1971), p. 98—hereafter cited parenthetically in the text.

2. Michel Foucault, "Afterword: The Subject and Power," in *Michel Foucault: Beyond Structuralism and Hermeneutics*, ed. Hubert L. Dreyfus and Paul Rabinow, 2nd ed. (Chicago: Univ. of Chicago Press, 1983), pp. 213–15.

3. Foucault, "Afterword," p. 215.

4. Foucault, "Afterword," p. 214.

5. Paul Fussell, *Samuel Johnson and the Life of Writing* (New York: Harcourt Brace Jovanovich, 1971), p. 264. The scholarship on Johnson's *Life of Savage* is too vast and diverse to be summarized here. Among the many studies which I have found particularly instructive, I will mention only a few: Robert Folkenflik, *Samuel Johnson, Biographer* (Ithaca: Cornell Univ. Press, 1978), esp. pp. 195–213; Patrick Parrinder, "Samuel Johnson: the Academy and the Marketplace," in *Authors and Authority: A Study of English Literary Criticism and its Relation to Culture 1750–1900* (London: Routledge and Kegan Paul, 1977), pp. 5–31; and John Dussinger, "Style and Intention in Johnson's *Life of Savage*," *ELH*, 37 (1970), 564–80, revised as "Johnson's *Life of Savage*: the Displacement of Authority," in Dussinger's *The Discourse of the Mind in Eighteenth-Century Fiction*, Studies in English Literature, vol. 80 (The Hague and Paris: Mouton, 1974), pp. 127–47. Of course, Johnsonian scholarship owes a huge debt to Clarence Tracy for his edition of the *Life of Savage* (cited above) and *The Artificial Bastard: a Biography of Richard Savage* (Cambridge, Mass.: Harvard Univ. Press, 1953).

6. Peter J. Lucas, "The Growth and Development of English Literary Patronage in the Later Middle Ages and Early Renaissance," *The Library*, 6th ser., 4 (1982), 237. Lucas is quoting here from J. Capgrave, *Ye Solace of Pilgrimes*, ed. C. A. Mills (London and New York: H. Frowde, 1911), p. 1. Lucas's omnibus article is a gold mine of information and sources, enhanced by an extensive bibliography.

7. Defining patronage as a formal, theoretical operation has been dominated in recent years by anthropologists, sociologists, and political scientists. For a survey of the scholarship in this area see S. N. Eisenstadt and Louis Roniger, "Patron–Client Relations as a Model of Structuring Social Exchange," *Comparative Studies in Society and History*, 22 (1980), 42–77, which also enumerates the "core analytical characteristics" of patron–client relations and posits a "'clientistic' model of structuring the relations between generalized and specific exchange" as an explanation of these characteristics. Eisenstadt and Roniger lack a historical perspective and tend to stress Mediterranean and Third World societies in their analysis.

8. See Elizabeth Eisenstein, *The Printing Press as an Agent of Change: Communications and Cultural Transformations in Early Modern Europe*, 2 vols. (Cambridge: Cambridge Univ. Press, 1979), which complements and supersedes such older studies as Marjorie Plant, *The English Book Trade: An Economic History of the Making and Sale of Books*, 2nd ed. (London: Allen and Unwin, 1965), David T. Pottinger, *The French Book Trade in the Ancien Regime, 1500–1791* (Cambridge, Mass.: Harvard Univ. Press, 1958), and Frank Arthur Mumby, *Publishing and Bookselling: a History from the Earliest Times to the Present Day*, 4th ed. (London: Jonathan Cape, 1956).

9. See Phoebe Sheavyn, *The Literary Profession in the Elizabethan Age*, 2nd ed., rev. J. W. Saunders (Manchester: Manchester Univ. Press, 1967) as well as Edwin Haviland

Miller, *The Professional Writer in Elizabethan England: a Study of Nondramatic Literature* (Cambridge, Mass.: Harvard Univ. Press, 1959), J. W. Saunders, *The Profession of English Letters* (London: Routledge and Kegan Paul, 1964) and Gerald Eades Bentley, *The Profession of Dramatist in Shakespeare's Time 1590–1642* (Princeton: Princeton Univ. Press, 1971). To these should be added such recent historical and critical studies as *Patronage in the Renaissance*, ed. Guy Fitch Lytle and Stephen Orgel (Princeton: Princeton Univ. Press, 1981), French R. Fogle and Louis A. Knafla, *Patronage in Late Renaissance England*, (Los Angeles: Clark Library, 1983), Richard Helgerson, *Self-Crowned Laureates: Spenser, Jonson, Milton, and the Literary System* (Berkeley and Los Angeles: Univ. of California Press, 1983), and Stephen Greenblatt, *Renaissance Self-Fashioning: from More to Shakespeare* (Chicago: Univ. of Chicago Press, 1980).

10. A. S. Collins, *Authorship in the Days of Johnson; Being a Study of the Relation between Author, Patron, Publisher and Public 1726–1780* (London: R. Holden, 1927), and *The Profession of Letters: a Study of the Relation of Author to Patron, Publisher, and Public, 1780–1832* (London: Routledge, 1928); Paul J. Korshin, "Types of Eighteenth-Century Literary Patronage," *Eighteenth-Century Studies*, 7 (1973–74), 453–73. Also of interest here are Alexandre Beljame, *Men of Letters and the English Public in the Eighteenth Century, 1660–1744, Dryden, Addison, Pope*, ed. Bonamy Dobrée, trans. E. O. Lorimer, International Library of Sociology and Social Reconstruction, ed. Karl Mannheim (London: Kegan Paul, Trench, Trubner, 1948); Michael Foss, *The Age of Patronage: the Arts in Society 1660–1750* (London: Hamish Hamilton, 1971); *Books and their Readers in Eighteenth-Century England*, ed. Isabel Rivers (Leicester: Leicester Univ. Press, 1982), esp. Terry Belanger, "Publishers and Writers in Eighteenth-Century England," pp. 5–25, and W. A. Speck, "Politicians, Peers, and Publication by Subscription 1700–50," pp. 47–68; and a recent special issue of *Eighteenth-Century Studies*, 17 (Summer 1984), "The Printed Word in the Eighteenth Century," ed. Raymond Birn, esp. John Feather, "The Commerce of Letters: the Study of the Eighteenth-Century Book Trade," pp. 405–24, and Martha Woodmansee, "The Genius and the Copyright: Economic and Legal Conditions of the Emergence of the 'Author,'" pp. 425–48. In addition, the work of contemporary historians and critics like Robert Darnton, Lawrence Lipking, and Jerome Christensen has altered our notions of the conditions for producing literature in and around the eighteenth century. For Darnton, see *The Business of the Enlightenment: a Publishing History of the Encyclopédie, 1775–1800* (Cambridge, Mass.: Harvard Univ. Press, 1979), and *The Literary Underground of the Old Regime* (Cambridge, Mass.: Harvard Univ. Press, 1982). For Lipking, see *The Life of the Poet: Beginning and Ending Poetics Careers* (Chicago: Univ. of Chicago Press, 1981). Christensen's deconstructionist study of Hume as the quintessential Enlightenment man of letters will appear soon; the opening chapter is forthcoming in the journal *Representations*.

11. Korshin, "Types of Patronage," pp. 457, 459, and passim.

12. Korshin, "Types of Patronage," pp. 464, 467.

13. Johnson, *Works*, VI, 99, l. 160. See also *The Poems of Samuel Johnson*, ed. David Nichol Smith and Edward L. McAdam, 2nd ed. (Oxford: Clarendon Press, 1974), p. 122, l. 160.

14. The phrase is from Johnson's famous letter to Chesterfield, 7 February 1755, *Letters*, I, 64 (no. 61).

15. See Howard Weinbrot, "Johnson's *Dictionary* and *The World*: the Papers of Lord Chesterfield and Richard Owen Cambridge," *Philological Quarterly*, 50 (1971), 663–69. There has always been intense interest in the Johnson-Chesterfield relationship and the scholarship continues to grow; see, for instance, the exchange between Paul Korshin and Jacob Leed in *Studies in Burke and His Time*, 12 (1970), 1676–90, 12 (1970–71), 1804–11, and 13 (1971), 2011–15.

16. *Letters*, I, 64–65 (no. 61).

17. Gae Holladay and O M Brack, Jr., "Johnson as Patron," *Greene Centennial Studies,* ed. Paul J. Korshin and Robert R. Allen (Charlottesville: Univ. Press of Virginia, 1984), pp. 177, 199–200.

18. Boswell, *Life,* I, 443.

19. "To the Visiter," *The Universal Visiter and Monthly Memorialist,* 4 (April 1756), 159–66. The new title emerges in *Works* (1825), V, 355–62. For a discussion of this essay in the context of Johnson's satiric writing see Carey McIntosh, *The Choice of Life: Samuel Johnson and the World of Fiction* (New Haven: Yale Univ. Press, 1973), pp. 73–75.

20. Lucas, "The Growth of Patronage," pp. 223–24, also explores the connection between patron and *pater,* which, he claims, implies an "imbalanced relationship" that "comes about in a society where wealth is unevenly distributed."

21. *Poems,* ed. Smith and McAdam, p. 56; *Works,* VI, 44, concurs and adds that the epigram should be read as "part of a campaign for recognition in the pages of the *Gentleman's Magazine,* if not employment."

22. "Ad Ricardum Savage," *Gentleman's Magazine,* 8 (April 1738), 210; see also *Poems,* ed. Smith and McAdam, pp. 56–57, and *Works,* VI, 43–44.

23. *Savage,* ed. Tracy, pp. xvii–xviii.

24. See the *Oxford Latin Dictionary* (Oxford: Clarendon Press, 1968–82), p. 729.

25. The one sense of *foueo* that Johnson's narrative never seems to evoke is "minister to," a significant omission that reinforces the notion that eighteenth-century biography participated in the shift from a sacred to a secular form of pastoral power.

26. The democratizing of the biographical subject in the course of the eighteenth century is apparently paralleled by the choice of subjects in other aesthetic modes. For instance, John Brewer has pointed out that the first depiction of an individually identifiable common man did not occur in English political cartoons until the 1780s ("Georgian Political Cartoons: Images of Popular Politics," Midwest American Society for Eighteenth-Century Studies, 29 October 1982, De Kalb, Illinois), although certainly Hogarth and others were depicting such individuals in other types of prints much earlier in the century.

27. *Collected Works of Oliver Goldsmith,* ed. Arthur Friedman, 5 vols. (Oxford: Clarendon Press, 1966), III, 360. See also Dussinger, "Style and Intention," p. 570, where Johnson's narrative shows Savage's attempt "to translate his quest for a legitimate filial relationship to the poet's role as 'the child of the public.'"

28. Neil McKendrick, John Brewer, and J. H. Plumb, *The Birth of a Consumer Society: the Commercialization of Eighteenth-Century England* (Bloomington: Indiana Univ. Press, 1982), pp. 13, 33, 50, 197–200, 202.

29. McKendrick et al., *Birth of a Consumer Society,* pp. 43–45.

30. *Life,* II, 389.

ROBERT DEMARIA, JR.

10 · The Theory of Language in Johnson's Dictionary

1

One of the most common and durable questions about Johnson's *Dictionary* is whether Johnson was concerned faithfully to record English or in some way or other to fix it, adjust it, or reform it.[1] The short answer to this question is that Johnson is chiefly a faithful recorder of English. In truth, however, this short answer is acceptable only if one includes numerous exceptions and reservations. In a variety of ways Johnson departs from the absolute, zero degree of historical lexicography—to which no dictionary has ever unfalteringly adhered. Like other lexicographers, even Sir James Murray and Phillip Gove, who achieved higher degrees of science, Johnson interprets and forms the language as he registers it. Johnson is rarely the authoritarian lexicographer that some have imagined, and his interpretation of language is only on rare occasions an expression of his personality. However, there is a theory of language implicit in Johnson's *Dictionary*, as in every other dictionary, and an examination of Johnson's departures from pure, historical registration is one way of revealing his theoretical commitments.

Far from being a matter of personal whimsy or idiosyncrasy, Johnson's interpretation of language in the *Dictionary* rests on a view of the subject that was commonly received at his time and is fundamentally Lockean,[2] though like Locke's own view it is mixed with shades of other seventeenth-century linguistic theories. The received theory distinguishes sharply between the form and the function of language. As the only adequate vehicle and receptacle of knowledge, language has the highest possible importance, but apart from its supremely important function, language has no value at all. Words are nugatory in themselves but crucially important as the containers of ideas. Moreover, the only way in which form has anything to do with the functioning of language is by means of conventional assignment. The connection between form and meaning is merely arbitrary, yet language is so important to communication that the conventions should be regularized and strictly controlled. Language would be better if it were organized on strictly logical principles—like etymology and analogy—and it would be best if it could be reduced to the unequivocal symbolism of mathematics. As Locke and others recognized, however, no such artificial organization of language can ever be instituted over the existing power of usage. The obscurity of ambitious, well-meaning schemes, like Bishop Wilkins's *Philosophical Language,* and the failure of even modest orthographical reforms prove the point. Part of the Lockean theory of language, therefore, is a stoical acceptance of the fundamentally unalterable though imperfect condition of language. But such acceptance does not change the basic view of language; the wish for a better arrangement survives a realistic acquiescence to the power of usage because the primary focus of attention in this theory of language is on the meaning rather than outward form of language.

Johnson's illustrative quotations contain an exposition of the Lockean theory of language in excerpts from Locke, Isaac Watts, William Holder, Robert South, Henry Felton, and others.[3] What I wish to show in this essay is that Johnson's practice as a lexicographer embodies the theory that it expresses in its illustrative quotations. In particular, by talking about some of Johnson's most important deviations from the absolute ideal of recording English I hope to show that his book adheres to various aspects of the Lockean view of language I have just outlined, especially its emphasis on the function of language.

2

The widest restriction that Johnson imposes on the ideal of recording English is in his selection of sources. Despite his characterization of his research as "fortuitous and unguided excursions into books"[4] Johnson clearly emphasizes some writers, some periods of English, and some kinds of writing at the expense of others. Most of the illustrations in the *Dictionary* and most of the vocabulary come from writers of acknowledged literary merit who flourished in the years between the birth of Shakespeare and the death of Pope. Johnson's preference for great literature written in this period is a philological statement, and his book would have been very different if it had given writers like Chaucer and Henryson or Nash and Webster some of the space occupied by Shakespeare, Dryden, and Milton. But Johnson's choice of literary texts also reveals a philosophical commitment to the Lockean conception of language as "the conduit of knowledge." Johnson's selection of texts for inclusion in the *Dictionary* is influenced by a sense that his word book should also be a kind of encyclopedia responsible for transmitting important knowledge. Johnson indicates his encyclopedic intentions often in the preface, perhaps nowhere more pointedly than toward the end when he says, "I shall not think my employment useless or ignoble, if by my assistance foreign nations, and distant ages, gain access to the propagators of knowledge, and understand the teachers of truth; if my labours afford light to the repositories of science, and add celebrity to Bacon, to Hooker, to Milton, and to Boyle" (par. 92).

Johnson presents a round of knowledge in the *Dictionary*, and to some extent he chose his texts for this purpose. Although there are certainly some "fortuitous" inclusions,[5] Johnson more often deviates from writers of acknowledged literary merit in order to present knowledge of various kinds and to pursue the dream "that my book might be in place of all other dictionaries whether appellative or technical" (par. 72).

The earliest documents relative to Johnson's *Dictionary*, as well as the history of the genre, suggest that Johnson directed his work partly to an audience of students.[6] His sense of his audience and his educational purpose, rather than strictly philological reasons, explain why Johnson made basic educational texts so conspicuous in his illustrative quotations. The most important educational works in the *Dictionary* are Locke's and those of his disciple, Isaac Watts, but these are supplemented by numerous others, including an elementary geography book by George Abbot called *A Brief Description of the World*, Ascham's *Scholemaster*, two works by Richard Allestree, a prominent author in Locke's recommended syllabus, Henry Felton's *Dissertation on Reading the Classics*, addressed "to a young Nobleman of sprightly Parts, and a lively imagination" (p. x), William Derham's *Physico-Theology*, which Johnson recommended to students on other occasions, Bishop Wilkins's *Mathematical Magick*, a copy of which Johnson gave to a youngster on his tour of the Hebrides, Milton's essay "Of Education," the only one of Milton's prose works that Johnson quotes in the *Dictionary*, Peacham's *Art of Limning* and some of his other instructional books, William Walker's *Syntaxis* and George Cheyne's *Philosophical Principles of Religion: Natural and Reveal'd*, written "for the Use of Younger Students of Philosophy, who while they were taught the most probable account of the *Appearances of Nature* from the Modern Discoveries, might thereby have the *Principles* of *Natural Religion* insensibly instill'd into them at the same time."[7]

Johnson may have half believed the felicitous Renaissance theory that the books with the best language are also the books with the best contents, and he was quite often able to satisfy verbal and material ends with the same texts, but I think it is clear that many of Johnson's choices are more sensitive to purity of meaning than purity of language. The very extensive inclusion of religious and moral works, for example, is partly attributable to Johnson's sense of his educational mission. These tend, with very few exceptions, to be works of fundamental moral teachings and middle-of-the-road or Latitudinarian Anglicanism. A book of basic knowledge is no place for the knotty or dubious parts of theology. Accordingly, Rogers, Tillotson, and Atterbury are three of the prime speakers on religion. Johnson mostly leaves out the less orthodox divines, even those he admired, like William Law.[8]

Some other inclusions and exclusions seem very pointed; for example, Hobbes is excluded, and the works of Bishop Bramhall, which are dedicated to attacking Hobbesian determinism, are widely cited. As a mass of other quotation in the *Dictionary* shows, Johnson wished to drive home the importance of human freedom to morality.[9] Overall, the desire to combine religion and learning in his book draws Johnson to the same sort of curriculum he was always recommending. The *Dictionary* is designed to transmit a message like the one that appears in Johnson's educational fable, "The Vision of Theodore." The message is the inevitability of human ignorance and the vanity of human learning without the assistance of revealed religion. What Johnson performs with a fable in "Theodore" he does in the *Dictionary* with numerous citations from Glanville's *Scepsis Scientifica*, Thomas Baker's *Reflections upon Learning wherein is shewn the Insufficiency thereof*, and the many other works he cites that allude to these themes.

Johnson's determination to make his word book a thesaurus of useful knowledge suggests a commitment to a basically Lockean view of the relations between language and knowledge. That view is perhaps most appropriately expounded in the Preface to Chambers's *Cyclopædia*, a work upon which Johnson claims to have formed his style (Boswell, *Life*, I, 218–19). Chambers maintains that "The business of knowledge is cantoned out among the body of words," and "The whole compass of words, in all their cases, is supposed equivalent to the whole system of possible science."[10] Going beyond Locke, Chambers imagines the father of lexicography as "a priest or mystagogue": "this was in the early days of the Egyptian sages, when words were more complex and obscure than now; and mystic symbols and hieroglyphics obtained; so that an explication of their marks or words, might amount to a revelation of their whole inner philosophy" (I, xvi). Chambers clearly believes that modern lexicography carries some of this same interpretative burden, and Johnson inherits a sense of this responsibility from Chambers. In his article on "Encyclopédie" in the *Encyclopédie* Diderot translated Chambers's Preface, and in Diderot's article Michel Foucault finds "glowing into life the luminous element in which language and learning, correct discourse and knowledge, universal language and analysis of thought, the history of mankind and the sciences of language freely communicate."[11] Johnson wrote his book in the light of such a "luminous element," and it had been "glowing into life" generations before Diderot's redaction of Chambers. Chambers himself received the concept from Locke, but it was apparent to Edward Phillips thirty years earlier and to other lexicographers before him. J. A. Comenius, for example, sought "the marriage of things and words" and believed this could best be done in a dictionary. Comenius himself looked back to Ludovico Vives for support and cited his opinions that, "the taske or worke of defining belongs to some great and excellent man, who not only hath searcht out the whole nature of the thing which he is about to define, but even is not ignorant of all other things."[12] In a famous passage of the preface Johnson says he is "not yet so lost in lexicography, as to forget that *words are the daughters of earth, and that things are the sons of heaven*. Language is only the instrument of science, and words are but the signs of ideas" (par. 17). Part of what lexicography means in this passage and throughout Johnson's *Dictionary* is a tendency to identify language and knowledge. Johnson's deprecatory definition of "lexicographer" and his acts of self-satire under "Grubstreet" and a few other words belittle his work, but these instances are acts of humility, like his poem "Γνῶθι Σεαυτόν," which correct the strong sense of important responsibility that, for Johnson, attended the production of dictionaries.

3

Like the selection of texts, the vast number of extracts that Johnson reprints from them is attributable to the obligation he felt to provide knowledge along with mere words. The selection of texts has a great but somewhat invisible effect on the presentation of language in the *Dictionary*. Johnson was able to find much of the important knowledge he wished to convey in the works of great writers, the supremacy of whose language was recognized. The effect of extensive quotation, however, is more apparent. Early critics of the *Dictionary*, like Thomas Edwards and Noah Webster, complained about the "needless number of authorities,"[13] and Johnson himself confessed in the preface that "authorities will sometimes seem to have been accumulated without necessity or use, and perhaps some will be found, which might without loss, have been omitted" (par. 65). However, by quoting so much Johnson did not only heap up instances or accumulate knowledge; he also expressed a philosophical commitment.

Charles Richardson, who wrote the *New Dictionary of the English Language* on philosophical principles very different from Johnson's, correctly complained in his preface that Johnson's method tends "to interpret the import of the context, and not to explain the individual meaning of the word." [14] Unlike Richardson and like Locke, Johnson finds that every meaning of a word requires separate treatment, almost as though it were a separate word. To put it another way, the definition of "word" is contingent upon meaning. Robert South provides a radical version of the theory in Johnson's illustration of "equivocally": "Words abstracted from their proper sense and signification lose the nature of words, and are only *equivocally*[1] so called." Johnson's own defense of his extensive quotation implies a similar understanding of words:

> those quotations which to careless or unskilful perusers appear only to repeat the same sense, will often exhibit, to a more accurate examiner, diversities of signification, or, at least, afford different shades of the same meaning. . . .
>
> Some senses however there are, which, though not the same, are yet so nearly allied, that they are often confounded. Most men think indistinctly, and therefore cannot speak with exactness; and consequently some examples might be indifferently put to either signification: this uncertainty is not to be imputed to me, who do not form, but register the language; who do not teach men how they should think, but relate how they have hitherto expressed their thoughts. (pars. 65 and 75)

The project of registering language is for Johnson inseparable from the task of registering thoughts, and his commitment faithfully to record English is inseparable from a wish to record what has been thought in English. This particular commitment is so fully accepted in the forms adopted by lexicographers after Johnson that it looks inevitable to us. But Richardson's point that it interprets context and sees words themselves as having no formal integrity is well taken. To prove the point he should have adduced the nine consecutive quotations from Addison under the twentieth sense of "to have," the fifty-six illustrations of "ill" used as an adverb, or the four consecutive quotations from Milton under the first sense of "he." In each case Johnson's extensive quotation reveals his linguistic philosophy in two ways: it shows his interest in the content of language, and it suggests that every usage of a word makes for a different meaning. The particular meanings that Johnson was interested to make prominent in his book also appear in cases where the amount of quotation is clearly exuberant. The last of the nine quotations from Addison under the twentieth sense of "to have," for instance, clearly does little to improve the reader's knowledge of how the word works, but it does inculcate one of the *Dictionary*'s fundamental moral themes: "That excellent author *has* shewn how every particular custom and habit of virtue will, in its own nature, produce the heaven, or a state of happiness, in him who shall hereafter practice it." The message in the fourth of Milton's quotations under the first sense of "he" is equally fundamental: "Extoll/*Him* first, *him* last, *him* midst."

4

Because so many particular usages of words constitute separate meanings under a single formal unit, the great infirmities of language are equivocality and ambiguity. Unlike Romantic and post-Romantic works that delight in ambiguity and see it as a source of energy in literary works, Johnson's *Dictionary*, like Locke's works, contains a persistent lamentation about the errors into which we fall on account of uncertain meanings. The best solution to the problem is proposed by Isaac Watts in illustration of the word "single": "If one *single*[2] word were to express but one simple idea, and nothing else, there would scarce be any mistake." Unfortunately, as Locke points out under "name," "If every particular idea that we take in, should have a distinct *name*[2], *names* must be endless." Johnson reflects this Lockean view when he says in the preface, "names, therefore, have often many ideas, but few ideas have many names" (par. 48).

The ambiguity of language is an evil that cannot be cured, but it should be palliated. Hooker prescribes the way to lessen the evil under the crucial word "distinction": "The mixture of those things by speech, which by nature are divided, is the mother of all error: to take away therefore that error, which confusion breedeth, *distinction*[7] is requisite." Johnson is deeply responsive to this advice, and the most salient feature of his book, besides the amount of quotation, is the number of senses into which he divides each definition. In the preface Johnson prepares his readers for the multiplicity of distinctions: "some faults will at last appear to be the effects of anxious diligence and persevering activity. The nice and subtle ramifications of meaning were not easily avoided by a mind intent upon accuracy, and convinced of the necessity of disentangling combinations, and separating similitudes" (par. 74).

Johnson's multiplicity of sense divisions represents a commitment to recording usage, but careful ordering of the different uses under distinct rubrics reveals a wish for greater stability and precision than the vagaries of usage can supply. Johnson says outright that he uses scholastic categories to make some distinctions (par. 74), and he admits that some quotations "might be indifferently put to either signification" (par. 75) in a chain of senses. His categories are therefore more orderly, logical, and distinct than the language they record. In a way, Johnson's carefully numbered senses resemble the efforts of twentieth-century analytical philosophers to achieve an ideal of "reference" with a combination of letters and numbers. Johnson's overexacting divisions of words into senses amounts to a wish that each word become so many distinct unambiguously referential words.

Furthermore, Johnson follows certain principles in the way he organizes and numbers the senses of each word. Some of these principles are linguistic; others are more broadly philosophical; but they all add up to a style of registering the language that is some degrees removed from the absolute ideal of making an historical record. Every lexicographer who wishes to distinguish senses must divide them up in some way or other; it is impossible to let usage speak for itself in this matter. Like other lexicographers, Johnson has his way of dividing senses, and a consideration of it reveals aspects of his linguistic philosophy.

First of all, like his definitions, Johnson's orderings of the senses show a predilection for etymology and analogy—two principles according to which language can be made to seem logical and regular, like the unambiguous language of mathematics, which Locke, as a philosopher of language, specifically envied. Johnson tries to tie words to their etymologies in the way he defines them: "trivial," for instance, is not only "Vile; worthless; vulgar;" but also "such as may be picked up in the highway." "Seminary" is "5. Breeding place; place of education, from whence scholars are transplanted into life," and "Terrier" is a "dog that follows his game under ground." Likewise, in his handling of words with highly ramified branches of meaning, Johnson tries to keep the whole series of definitions rooted in a basic etymological sense; sometimes he even adds a note that does this explicitly. Under sense 27 of "to break," for instance, Johnson says, "It is to be observed of this extensive and perplexed verb, that, in all its significations, whether active or neutral, it has some reference to its primitive meaning, by implying either detriment, suddenness, or violence." Similarly, under sense 64 of "to fall" Johnson says, "This is one of those general words of which it is very difficult to ascertain or detail the full signification. It retains in most of its senses some part of its primitive meaning, and implies either literally or figuratively descent, violence, or suddenness." When irregular usage must be recorded Johnson sometimes protests in terms of his predilection for etymology as a source and test of meaning. For instance, under the third sense of "to prejudice" he writes, "This sense, as in the noun, is often improperly extended to meanings that have no relation to the original sense; who can read with patience of an ingredient that *prejudices* a medicine?" (See also "to riddle.") Etymological meanings, especially those based on Latin and Greek, are often in the *Dictionary* equivalent to what Locke praises under "to rest" as the "philosophical use of words." Using terms that Johnson adapted for his description of truth in the preface to Shakespeare, Locke says, "The philosophical use of words conveys the precise notions of things, which the mind may *rest*[8] upon, and be satisfied with, in its search after knowledge."

Both Johnson's logical divisions of words into numbered senses and his preference for "philosophical" usage represent a tendency to follow through on the wishes of seventeenth-century linguistic projectors. As W. K. Wimsatt says, "The vocabulary of 'hard' words is a kind of basic English, like the language of integers and particles proposed by Bishop Wilkins."[15] However, it is important to remember that this reforming tendency in Johnson is continually mitigated by his fundamental adherence to the standard of usage and his sense of himself as a recorder of English. Indeed, the illustrative quotations under the word "etymology" itself undercut the faith in this principle that Johnson frequently expresses. None of the quotations sees etymology as a guarantee of meaning, and Collier explicitly states the competing and, I think, prevalent view in the *Dictionary*: "When words are restrained, by common usage, to a particular sense, to run up to *etymology*[1], and construe them by dictionary, is wretchedly ridiculous."

Johnson's reliance upon quotation to complete his definitions, or in some cases to take their place,[16] is also a commitment to usage, although, as I tried to show earlier, it is often more than this. Along with Johnson's reliance on quotation comes a general despair about the efficacy of definition, despite the skill with which he performs it. Sometimes important authors appear to express Johnson's despair in an explicit fashion. For instance under the verb "to define" Locke is adduced to say, "Though defining be thought the proper way to make known the proper signification, yet there are some words that will not be *defined*[1]." In a few cases, Johnson gives up and resorts to foreign languages to get around the problem of definition. The fourth sense of "to seem" is "It Seems. A phrase hard to be explained. It sometimes signifies that there is an appearance though no reality; but generally it is used ironically to condemn the thing mentioned, like the Latin *scilicet*, or the Old English *forsooth*. *Id mihi datur negotii* scilicet. *This*, it seems, *is to be my task*." More often, however, Johnson depends upon his examples to take care of hard definitions, and he has a predilection for examples that point out the complexity of a word and the resultant difficulty for the lexicographer. Under the first sense of "to bear," for instance, Johnson says simply, "This is a word used with such latitude, that it is not easily explained," and he cites Watts: "We say to *bear* a burden, to *bear* sorrow or reproach, to *bear* a name, to *bear* a grudge, to *bear* fruit, or to *bear* children. The word *bear* is used in very different senses." Perhaps the most extreme example of John-son's tendency to print examples that present the bewildering variety of usage is his entry under "twister":

> Twister. . . . One who twists; a ropemaker. To this word I have annexed some remarkable lines, which explain twist in all its senses.

> When a *twister* a-twisting will twist him a twist
> For the twisting of his twist, he three twines doth intwist;
> But if one of the twines of the twist do untwist,
> The twine that untwisteth untwisteth the twist.
> Untwirling the twine that untwisteth between,
> He twirls with his *twister* the two in a twine;
> Then twice having twisted the twines of the twine,
> He twitcheth the twine he had twined in twain.
> The twain that in twining before in the twine,
> As twins were intwisted, he now doth untwine,
> 'Twixt the twain intertwisting a twine more between,
> He, twirling his *twister*, makes a twist of the twine.

This tongue twister comes from Wallis's *Grammatica Linguae Angli-canae*; it appears in a section called "Praxis Grammatica," which Wallis included, with copious notes, "in order to display the genius of En-glish." [17] As an illustrative quotation, however, it provides a satirical demonstration of the inadequacy of general definition and the inex-haustible variety of usage.

5

Generally speaking, there are two main kinds of definition in John-son's *Dictionary*. One is philosophical and adheres to a seventeenth-century dream of ideal lexicography. The other works mostly by syn-onomy and tends to explain words in a more desperate and often a more emotional way. Most of the famous "Johnsonian" definitions are philosophical definitions of simple words. These sound like parodies of "dictionary definitions," and I believe Johnson was conscious of their nearness to parody. To give a couple of infrequently cited ex-amples: "to roll" is "To move any thing by volutation, or successive application of the different parts of the surface, to the ground," and "to sip" is "To drink by small draughts; to take at one apposition of the cup to the mouth no more than the mouth will contain." Likewise, "to rattle" is "To make a quick sharp noise with frequent repetitions and collisions of bodies not very sonorous: when bodies are sonorous, it is called jingling." In the philosophical kind, definition tends to be more precise than usage, to idealize it at the same time that it collects and summarizes it. Many of these definitions Johnson completely remands to experts on the subject comprehended by the word. In these instances it is clear that he regards the meaning of words as determined only by the most philosophical sense. Johnson's wish for a philosophical language is even clearer in entries, like "ardour," where there is no exemplification for the philosophical, first sense of the word.

The other kind of definition, the one that works by synonymy, is at least as common in Johnson as the philosophical definition, but it leans towards, rather than away from, usage. This is especially evident in the many cases where the synonymy seems exuberant, and Johnson seems to be interpreting the "feeling" of the word rather than the precise meaning. "To plague," for example, is in the second sense, "To trouble; to teaze; to vex; to harrass; to torment; to afflict; to distress; to torture; to embarrass; to excruciate; to make uneasy; to disturb." "Sluggish" is "Dull; drowzy; lazy; slothful; idle; insipid; slow; inactive; inert," and "mild" in the first sense, means "Kind; tender; good; indulgent; merciful; compassionate; clement; soft; not severe; not cruel." In each case the definition is a response to the word, almost an associational response, rather than an attempt to define it in a separate logical language. In words with this sort of definition, the examples of usage are the more specific and precise parts of the entry.

In a large number of entries in the *Dictionary* Johnson directly expresses the conflict between the claims of usage and the wish for a more philosophical language by making editorial comments. In many of these entries Johnson invokes the principle of analogy and thereby expresses his wish for a more logical language, before bowing stoically to the authority of usage. Perhaps the best example is Johnson's discussion of "latter." He says, "This is the comparative of *late*, though universally written with *tt*, contrary to analogy, and to our own practice in the superlative *latest*. When the thing of which the comparison is made is mentioned, we use *later*; as, *this fruit is* later *than the rest*; but *latter* when no comparison is expressed; as, *those are* latter *fruits.*" Johnson thinks it necessary to point out the deviation from the principle of analogy, but he nevertheless records the usage. To express his stoic acceptance of usage despite his knowledge of a better way Johnson finishes the entry under "latter" with a quotation from Horace: "—*Volet usus/ Quem penes arbitrium est, et vis, et norma loquendi.*" [18]

This conflict of lexicographical ideals happens frequently in entries for compound words. Under "disannul," for instance, Johnson says, "This word is formed contrary to analogy by those who not knowing the meaning of the word *annul*, intended to form a negative sense by the needless use of the negative particle. It ought therefore to be rejected as ungrammatical and barbarous." The barbarians who use the word are Hooker, Bacon, Sandys, and Herbert. Such awesome authority may have forced Johnson to include the word, but his remark shows that he has linguistic principles besides usage. In order to further his wish that English might be, as he says in the preface, "less apt to decay," Johnson again expresses his ideals in the face of great authority in his entry under "to dissever": "In this word the particle *dis* makes no change in the signification, and therefore the word, though supported by great authorities, ought to be ejected from our language." Quotations follow from Sidney, Raleigh, Shakespeare, and Pope.

The strength of Johnson's appeals to etymology or analogy varies widely in different instances. In deciding most cases of orthography, for instance, Johnson follows etymology or analogy only when the precedent of usage is ambiguous. But with newly formed or barely naturalized words Johnson is often more dictatorial in his insistence upon an etymological basis for correct spelling.[19] "Phiz," for instance, should, "if it be written at all, be written phys," but the older word "pander" draws only the lament that contemporary spellers have forgotten the word's eponymous original, Pandar. Other new words are branded "barbarous" or blasted with another remark for their failures of analogy, redundancy, or impurity—all standards that can be upheld only in opposition to the pure ideal of recording English.[20]

New words, unprotected by custom, rouse his respect for linguistic principles more than old words, but Johnson is most apt to invoke such logical principles and to issue warnings when the philological question at hand involves important meaning. Language is valuable chiefly as a vehicle for knowledge, and the most important knowledge is religious and moral. A sense of this priority seems to drive Johnson to deplore the "gradual corruption of the phrase, *would God*" and the resulting eighth sense of "would" meaning "I wish." The fact that the usage is supported by Shakespeare, Milton, Bacon, Daniel, Ben Jonson, and Dryden does not deter Johnson from regretting its development. Being more authoritarian, Johnson gives a second sense of "immaterial"—"Unimportant; without weight"—but he gives no illustrations. The second sense is so inimical to the first—"Incorporeal"—and the word is so important to the language of spirit that Johnson raises his voice to say, "This sense has crept into the conversation and writings of barbarians; but ought to be utterly rejected." The editors of the OED cite Johnson's remark under their sense 4 of "immaterial," and they object, "it is, however, the opposite of material in the sense of 'important' found from 1528 onwards." Johnson himself lists this sense of "material" and illustrates it amply. What the editors of the OED fail to notice are Johnson's extraphilological, religious motives.

6

To a much greater extent than the OED, Johnson's lexicography serves a variety of standards that are not purely historical. Johnson is concerned about logic in language and the way logic might permeate language through etymology and analogy; he is concerned to support literary usage and a standard of English purity; in his concern for none of these philological principles, however, does he forsake his commitment to the standard of usage. But Johnson's most important commitment of all is to the principle that language is valuable only insofar as it conveys meaning, and he believes that certain meanings, certain uses of language, are more important than others. This belief comes out on every page of the *Dictionary*; it is reflected in Johnson's selection of sources, his selection of quotations from his sources, his definitions, his ordering of the senses of words, and his editorial remarks.

In a very obvious way, Johnson's commitment to meaning influences his presentation of language in his definitions of words that are important to religion and morality. Johnson's first definition of "pious," for instance, is "Careful of the duties owed by created beings to God; godly; religious; such as is due to sacred things." Johnson's definition is also an expression of piety. The OED brackets Johnson's sense of the word by putting his first clause within quotation marks, signs of its closure in history; the OED then adds, "reverence to God (or the gods)." *Webster's III* replaces "God" with "deity." Each dictionary bears its cultural assumptions, and the three together show something about the extension of religious and moral meaning, its gradual broadening and loss of intensive strength. Cultural differences appear also in a comparison among the three dictionaries' respective treatments of the word "appetite." Johnson's first definition is "The natural desire of good; the instinct by which we are led to seek pleasure." The second definition distinguishes a sense of the word that is morally degraded in relation to the first: "The desire of sensual pleasure." The OED distinguishes a general sense, "inclination" in 1 and 2, from "The determinate desire to satisfy the natural necessities, or fulfil the natural functions, of the body." *Webster's III* makes the last its first definition and depresses to the second sense a more general meaning, but morally charged words like Johnson's "good" and "pleasure" are absent. Meaning is not most importantly religious and moral meaning in *Webster's III*, though it too undoubtedly has its bias, which, with the passage of cultural time, will become more and more evident.

Johnson's particular moral and religious orientation is recognizable in his judgmental definition of "suicide" as "the horrid crime of destroying one's self." But whether or not this remark reveals Johnson's personal feelings, the important point is that a received, religious view of human life permeates Johnson's treatment of the language, and this is proper because the function of language is to reveal, as Chambers puts it, "the inner philosophy" of the people who speak the language. Accordingly, Johnson's definition of "trance" is "An extasy; a state in which the soul is rapt into visions of future or distant things; a temporary absence of the soul from the body." "Swoon," "suspension of consciousness," and "suspended animation" are the key words in the definitions of later dictionaries, and only an etymological vestige of the language of soul and body remains. Likewise, Johnson reveals the inner philosophy of his culture in the way he organizes the definition of "life" itself. The first definition is "Union and co-operation of soul with body." In the succeeding fourteen senses Johnson gradually works his way downward on the chain of being until he is out of the realm of mere humanity; he concludes in sense fifteen with a glance at "Animated existence; animal being." This order is altogether different from what one finds in the post–Darwinian concatenations in the OED and *Webster's III*. These later choices also harbor assumptions, although the editors were trying to achieve a more purely philological goal than Johnson. For Johnson, however, such an achievement, even if it were possible, would not have been desirable because it would have meant the dereliction of a duty tied up with lexicography but infinitely higher than it or any other merely verbal study.

NOTES

1. The durability of the question is shown in some recent letters exchanged in the *Times Literary Supplement* between Donald Greene and John Barrell: 27 May 1983 (p. 545) and 10 June 1983 (p. 603). See also my reply of 24 June (p. 667). For an account of the whole question of authority in English lexicography, including its relation to Johnson's *Dictionary*, see Ronald A. Wells, *Dictionaries and the Authoritarian Tradition* (The Hague: Mouton, 1973).

2. Among those who have noticed this view, I should especially mention John H. Middendorf; see his "Ideas vs. Words: Johnson, Locke, and the Edition of Shakespeare," in *English Writers of the Eighteenth Century*, ed. John H. Middendorf et al. (New York: Columbia Univ. Press, 1971), pp. 249–72. Practically all the papers on the *Dictionary* presented at the Oxford Conference commemorating the two hundredth anniversary of Johnson's death (1984) noted the Lockean character of Johnson's linguistic operation.

3. For a list of the key linguistic terms in the *Dictionary* and some account of how Johnson presents the subject, see Robert Carroll Miller's doctoral dissertation, "Johnson's *Dictionary* Categorized: A Selection for Eighteenth-Century Studies," (Diss., Texas A&M Univ., 1975), pp. 1–20, 404–406. I have made my own index to the linguistic material in the *Dictionary* in which I locate 659 quotations relevant to the subject.

4. *A Dictionary of the English Language*, 2 vols. (London: W. Strahan, 1755), preface, par. 28. In quotations from the *Dictionary*, the word under which the quotation appears is italicized and, unless given in my text, the sense number is indicated as a superscript number within square brackets. Quotations from the preface are cited in the text with a paragraph number.

5. The many authors and works from which there are only a few citations suggest that Johnson may have incorporated some of his casual reading into the *Dictionary*. Some of the rarely cited are Oldham ("to poach"), Duncomb ("polytheist"), Jane Col-

lier's *Essay on the Art of Tormenting* ("to prink"), Mrs. Mulso ("quatrain"), Manwood's *Lawes of the Forest* ("pricket"), Shelvocke's *Voyages* ("to swab"), Dodsley's *Miscellany* ("to find[3]"), Andrew Bourde's *Fyrst Boke of the Introduction to Knowledge* ("to sit[2]"), Samuel Boyse "The Olive: An Ode" ("predal"), and "Children in the Wood" ("redbreast"). However, it is incorrect to assume that Johnson read every author and book cited in the *Dictionary* because fragments of authors quoted within other books are sometimes cited with their own proper names.

6. See the MS "A Short Scheme for compiling a new Dictionary of the English Language," facs. in *The R. B. Adam Library Relating to Dr. Samuel Johnson and his Era*, 4 vols. (London and New York: Oxford Univ. Press, 1929–30), vol. II.

7. George Cheyne, *Philosophical Principles of Religion*, 2nd ed. (London, 1715), Preface, Sig. A4ʳ.

8. But Law is cited a few times. See "gewgaw," for instance.

9. The most overt display of this intention occurs in Johnson's entry under "caitiff," where he concludes his etymological remarks with the observation, "so certainly does slavery destroy virtue" and a (slightly misquoted) quotation, which he attributes to Homer:

Ἥμισυ τῆς ἀρετῆς ἀποάινυται δούλιον ἦμαρ.
The day of slavery despoils the better half of virtue.

10. Ephraim Chambers, *Cyclopædia: or, an Universal Dictionary of the Arts and Sciences*, 4th ed. (London, 1741), I, xi.

11. Michel Foucault, *The Order of Things: An Archeology of the Human Sciences* (New York: Pantheon Books, 1970), p. 88.

12. J. A. Comenius, *A Patterne of Universall Knowledge, in a plaine and true Draught*, trans. Jeremy Collier (London, 1651), p. 129.

13. Edwards to D. Wray, 23 May 1755. Bodleian MS 1012, f. 208; see James H. Sledd and Gwin J. Kolb, *Johnson's Dictionary: Essays in the Biography of a Book* (Chicago: Univ. of Chicago Press, 1955), p. 135. See Webster to David Ramsay, *Letters of Noah Webster*, ed. Harry Warfel (New York: Library Publishers Service, 1953), p. 288. Webster also complained about the heterogeneity and impurity of Johnson's sources; see Wells, *Dictionaries and the Authoritarian Tradition*, p. 90.

14. See *A New Dictionary of the English Language*, 2 vols. (London: Pickering, 1839), I, 38.

15. W. K. Wimsatt, *Philosophic Words* (New Haven: Yale Univ. Press, 1948), p. 110.

16. The only definition for the first sense of "tune" as a noun is a quotation from Locke. "Pyramid," "quartile," and many other technical terms are likewise defined only by John Harris's *Lexicon Technicum*. In other cases Johnson's definition follows the illustrative quotation so closely as to make it redundant. Johnson's first definition of "quantity," for example is "That property of any thing which may be encreased or diminished"; the illustration from Cheyne that follows is "*Quantity* is what may be increased or diminished."

17. John Wallis, *Grammatica Linguae Anglicanae* (1653), rpt. in *Opera quaedam miscellanea* (Oxford, 1699), pp. 61, 70.

18. *Ars Poetica*, lines 72–73. Brink and other modern editors have *ius* where Johnson prints *vis*. In the translation of Francis:

If custom will, whose arbitrary sway,
Words, and the forms of language, must obey.

See *The Works of Horace*, trans. Philip Francis (London, 1807), p. 347.

19. I hasten to add that his entry under "show," among others, indicates that Johnson also gave pronunciation consideration in establishing orthography.

20. See Harold B. Allen, "Samuel Johnson and the Authoritarian Principle in Linguistic Criticism," (Diss., Univ. of Michigan, 1940), for a complete list of words that Johnson branded with labels such as "low," "burlesque," and "barbarous."

PETER SEARY

11 · The Early Editors of Shakespeare and the Judgments of Johnson

Upon publication of Johnson's *Shakespeare* in 1765, it was generally recognized that a major contribution of the edition was to be found in its preface, where, as Boswell rightly observes, Johnson's critical appraisal "was like the grave, well considered, and impartial opinion of the judge, which falls from his lips with weight, and is received with reverence."[1] Johnson's criticism of Shakespeare's plays in his preface also extended to their first editors, and it is with Johnson's magisterial assessments of Pope, Theobald, and Warburton that I am concerned in this essay.

The modern tradition of editing renaissance English classics begins with Nicholas Rowe's *Shakespear* (1709), but it was Pope's *Shakespear* (1725) and Theobald's *Shakespeare Restored: or, A Specimen of the Many Errors, as well Committed, as Unamended, by Mr. Pope in his Late Edition of this Poet* (1726) that raised the question of editorial practice as a subject for detailed consideration. Almost immediately, however, this matter was obscured by the shadow cast by the *The Dunciad Variorum* (1729), which demonstrated once again Pope's excellence as a poet, even as it created confusing impressions of his ideas of scholarship. According to Johnson in his *Proposals for Printing . . . The Dramatick Works of William Shakespeare* (1756), both Rowe and Pope "were very ignorant of the ancient English literature."[2] This, of course, is a severe criticism of Pope's scholarly qualifications as an editor of Shakespeare; but Johnson also had great respect for Pope as a poet, and we are subsequently told: "The observation of faults and beauties is one of the duties of an annotator, which some of Shakespeare's editors have attempted, and some have neglected. For this part of his task, and for this only, was Mr. Pope eminently and indisputably qualified."[3] Johnson, however, immediately proceeds to observe of Pope's asterisks and commas marking passages he approved of:

But I have never observed that mankind was much delighted or improved by their asterisks, commas, or double commas; of which the only effect is, that they preclude the pleasure of judging for ourselves, teach the young and ignorant to decide without principles; defeat curiosity and discernment, by leaving them less to discover; and at last shew the opinion of the critick, without the reasons on which it was founded, and without affording any light by which it may be examined.[4]

Here we have a sequence of criticism followed by praise followed by criticism. But the thinking of the paragraph as a whole, although appearing to be judicious and balanced, is, in fact, badly founded. If Pope began his task of editing Shakespeare with an assumption that it would be considerably easier to perform than his commentary on *Homer*, he was soon to discover his mistake. Eustathius, Madame Dacier, and the other scholiasts he consulted may not have given much insight into Homer as a poet, as he complained, but they had provided a scholarly base from which accurate criticism might begin. No equivalent scholarship devoted to Shakespeare existed, as Pope discovered when he began casting about for assistance; his difficulties were essentially the same as those of Francis Atterbury, whose help he sought:

I protest to you, in an hundred places I cannot construe him, I dont understand him. The hardest part of Chaucer is more intillegible to me than some of those Scenes, not merely thro the faults of the Edition, but the Obscurity of the Writer: for Obscure he is, & a little (not a little) enclin'd now & then to Bombast whatever Apology you may have contriv'd on that head for him. There are Allusions in him to an hundred things, of which I knew nothing, & can guess nothing. And yet without some competent knowledge of those matters there's no understanding him. I protest Æschylus does not want a Comment to me, more than he does: so that I begin to despair of doing you any considerable Service.[5]

Consequently, instead of a systematic commentary on Shakespeare comparable to that devoted to Homer, readers of Pope's edition discovered only the preliminaries to such a work, that some of "The more obsolete or unusual words are explained" and that "Some of the most shining passages are distinguish'd by comma's in the margin; and where the beauty lay not in particulars but in the whole, a star is prefix'd to the scene." This is justified on the grounds that it seemed "a shorter and less ostentatious method of performing the better half of Criticism (namely the pointing out an Author's excellencies) than to fill a whole paper with citations of fine passages, with *general Applauses*, or *Empty Exclamations* at the tail of them."[6] Pope's solution to the problem of a commentary does indeed obviate the criticisms he himself had levelled at Madame Dacier's commentary on Homer,[7] but it is most probable that Pope's decision not to comment on particular passages in Shakespeare as he had in Homer came from a realization that he would expose himself to very serious charges of having misunderstood his author. He was by no means able to explain all the "obsolete or unusual words" in his text, and without this ability it would have been folly to engage in commenting on Shakespeare as a poet; Johnson was mistaken in his belief that "For this part of his task, and for this only, was Mr. *Pope* eminently and indisputably qualified."[8] Johnson's sanguine expectations of Pope as a commentator on beauties and faults seem similar in their foundations to those of George Sewell: "When a Genius of similar Fire and Fancy temper'd with a learned Patience, sits down to consider what SHAKESPEAR would *Think*, as well as what he could *Write*, we may then expect to see his Works answer to our Idea of the Man."[9] But whereas Johnson appears to believe that Pope's taste could compensate entirely for his lack of scholarly understanding, Sewell recognizes the need for "learned Patience."

In the Preface to *Shakespeare*, Johnson's harshest criticism is reserved for Lewis Theobald, the most controversial of the early editors of Shakespeare, and David Nichol Smith in his Preface to *Eighteenth Century Essays on Shakespeare* tells us: "On the question of Theobald's qualifications as an editor, it would appear that we must subscribe to the deliberate verdict of Johnson."[10] By the time of Johnson's writing, vituperation among Shakespearian scholars was well established, and, for example, Warburton's reference in his own preface[11] to letters from Pope urging him to edit Shakespeare prompted the Cambridge scholar, Styan Thirlby, to note in the margin of his copy of Warburton's edition: "You might as well have said See my arse in a band box."[12] Nonetheless, Johnson's comments on Theobald *are* harsh:

> *Pope* was succeeded by *Theobald*, a man of narrow comprehension and small acquisitions, with no native and intrinsick splendour of genius, with little of the artificial light of learning, but zealous for minute accuracy, and not negligent in pursuing it. He collated the ancient copies, and rectified many errors. A man so anxiously scrupulous might have been expected to do more, but what little he did was commonly right.[13]

Elsewhere Johnson characterizes Theobald as weak, ignorant, mean, faithless, petulant, and ostentatious.[14]

At best Theobald must appear an enigmatic figure to those who would acknowledge with most modern editors of Shakespeare the brilliance of his emendations while accepting the unflattering accounts of his intellect given by Pope, Warburton, and Johnson. Johnson's statements about Theobald have been a decisive factor in shaping his later reputation, and Nichol Smith has attempted to justify them by attributing the acknowledged excellence of Theobald's edition of Shakespeare to Warburton.[15] But Smith makes no real attempt to explain the generally accepted inferiority of Warburton's performance in his own edition of 1747, a work in which, it has been said, "Warburton reveals himself . . . as without doubt the stupidest man ever to edit Shakespeare."[16]

Johnson's account of Theobald was affected by a sense of gratitude to Warburton, which, as a concomitant, entailed acceptance of Warburton's portrayal of his predecessor. In 1745 Johnson's *Miscellaneous Observations on the Tragedy of Macbeth* appeared, and Warburton, now famous as the friend of Pope and as a polemicist, went out of his way in his preface to *Shakespear* (1747) to praise Johnson's work:

> as to all those Things, which have been published under the titles of *Essays, Remarks, Observations*, &c. on *Shakespear*, (if you except some critical Notes on *Macbeth*, given as a Specimen of a projected Edition, and written, as appears, by a Man of Parts and Genius) the rest are absolutely below a serious Notice.[17]

Johnson felt that Warburton had praised him "when praise was of value to me."[18] As Sir John Hawkins observed: "Of Warburton he always spoke well. He gave me, says he, his good word, when it was of use to me."[19] But it was in the same Preface that Warburton had written:

> Mr. *Theobald* was naturally turned to Industry and Labour. What he read he could transcribe: but, as what he thought, if ever he did think, he could but ill express, so he read on; and, by that means got a Character of Learning, without risquing, to every Observer, the Imputation of wanting a better Talent. By a punctilious Collation of the old Books, he corrected what was manifestly wrong in the *latter* Editions, by what was manifestly right in the *earlier*. And this is his real Merit; and the whole of it. For where the Phrase was very obsolete or licentious in the *common* Books, or only slightly corrupted in the *other*, he wanted sufficient Knowledge of the Progress and various Stages of the *English* Tongue, as well as Acquaintance with the Peculiarity of *Shakespear*'s Language to understand what was right; nor had he either common Judgment to see, or critical sagacity to amend, what was manifestly faulty. Hence he generally exerts his conjectural Talent in the wrong Place: He tampers with what is sound in the *common* Books; and, in the *old* ones, omits all Notice of Variations the Sense of which he did not understand.[20]

The extent of Warburton's misrepresentations of Theobald, who had died in 1744, is readily apparent in an examination of their Shakespearian correspondence.[21] But, if Theobald's industry in collation is disregarded, Warburton has provided a convenient summary of his own editorial shortcomings, as was demonstrated at length in the eighteenth century by Thomas Edwards in *The Canons of Criticism* (first published in 1747 as *A Supplement to Mr. Warburton's Edition of Shakespear*).

Johnson's gratitude to Warburton and his prolonged experience of both Warburton and Theobald as editors produced a conflict that continued to influence him from the publication in 1756 of his *Proposals* to the eventual appearance of his edition in 1765. Although it will easily be granted that as a polemicist Theobald commands less respect than Warburton, it is very doubtful whether, as Johnson once said, Warburton, cut into slices, would make "two-and-fifty Theobalds." This extravagance in favor of Warburton occurred in 1758 and followed an observation by Dr. Burney that Johnson (in "some volumes of his Shakespeare already printed, to prove he was in earnest") "seemed to be more severe on Warburton than Theobald." [22] In fact, Burney was accurate, since Johnson's notes on *The Merchant of Venice*, the play in question, generally quote Theobald without comment, but reprint Warburton to correct him. In addition to this testimony of Johnson's opinion of Warburton as an editor, there is the evidence of his cancelled notes to *Shakespeare*, in which, as William Seward remarked, he "was inclined to treat Warburton's Notes upon that Author very roughly. At the solicitation of Mr. Tonson and Mr. Millar, the sheets that contained any abuse upon the Bishop's Notes were cancelled." [23] Contemporary support for this anecdote is found in William Kenrick's preface to his *Review of Doctor Johnson's Edition of Shakespeare* (1765), where it is said Johnson was "prevailed on by his printer prudentially to cancel several annotations, in which he had strongly expressed his dissent from that learned scholiast." [24] Edmond Malone has a MS note by this passage in his copy of Kenrick's work: "This is true." [25] In 1938 there appeared a study of Johnson's cancelled notes, which had survived in Bishop Percy's set of Johnson's edition. [26] Although even in his cancelled notes Johnson was no more severe upon Warburton than Warburton habitually was in his treatment of rivals, there can be no doubt of Johnson's low opinion of Warburton's editorial practice.

There is really no question that as an editor of Shakespeare Theobald is infinitely superior to Warburton, and this was generally recognized in the eighteenth century. In *The Companion to the Play-house* (1764), David Erskine Baker says of Theobald's *Shakespeare* that it "is still in great Esteem; being in general prefered to those Editions published by *Pope*, *Warburton*, and *Hanmer*." [27] Even after the publication of Johnson's edition, Theobald's *Shakespeare*, according to John Nichols, was pronounced by Joseph Warton "to be *the best* till those of Steevens and Malone appeared." [28] The reading public evidently agreed, since "of the various Editions of Theobald . . . no less than 12,860 copies were sold." [29] Malone's summary of Warburton's reputa-

tion as an editor of Shakespeare stands in marked contrast: "His un-
bounded licence in substituting his own chimerical conceits in the
place of the author's genuine text, has been so fully shewn by his
revisers, that I suppose no critical reader will ever again open his
volumes."[30] In the nineteenth century the editors of the Cambridge
Shakespeare comment that "Theobald, as an Editor, is incomparably
superior to his predecessors, and to his immediate successor, Warburton, although the latter had the advantage of working on his materials. . . . Many most brilliant emendations . . . are due to him." On
Johnson's assertion that Warburton would make "two-and-fifty Theobalds" they state: "From this judgment, whether they be compared as
critics or editors, we emphatically dissent."[31] More recently, John
Dover Wilson has paid witty tribute: "no editor should pass Lewis
Theobald without a salute—'*splendid-emendax*.'"[32] And in *Shakespeare:
The Critical Heritage, Volume 2, 1693–1733* Brian Vickers goes so far as
to call Theobald "the best all-round editor of Shakespeare in this period or any other."[33]

As an editor of Shakespeare Johnson is closer to Theobald than
to any other of his predecessors, and certainly Johnson found Theobald more useful than Warburton. It is not surprising that after Theobald's death his copy of the second folio, with his marginalia, passed
eventually into Johnson's hands. Of much greater importance is that
Johnson, having begun his edition of Shakespeare by using Warburton's
edition as his copytext (thereby following the usual eighteenth-century
practice of emending the text of one's immediate predecessor), "abandoned Warburton's edition beginning with *The Taming of the Shrew*, the
eleventh play in his edition and the first play in volume three."[34] It was
at this point that he adopted the 1757 edition of Theobald's *Shakespeare*,
which may have been set up from a set of Theobald's second edition
(1740) containing MSS corrections by Theobald.[35] Johnson used Theobald's 1757 edition for twenty-three of the plays and vacillated between Theobald's and Warburton's texts in eleven others.[36] Many
restorations of Shakespeare's text previously attributed to Johnson
now have to be attributed to the editor of the 1757 edition.[37]

Johnson's respect for Theobald as an editor, as revealed in his aban-
doning Warburton's edition in favor of Theobald's, is more solidly
complimentary than his praise of Warburton. When his own editorial
work was concluded, Johnson remarked in his Preface:

> The part of criticism in which the whole succession of editors has la-
> boured with the greatest diligence, which has occasioned the most ar-
> rogant ostentation, and excited the keenest acrimony, is the emendation
> of corrupted passages, to which the publick attention having been first
> drawn by the violence of the contention between *Pope* and *Theobald*, has

been continued by the persecution, which, with a kind of conspiracy, has been since raised against all the publishers of *Shakespeare*.[38]

And of his own attempts at conjectural emendation, he added: "As I practised conjecture more, I learned to trust it less; and after I had printed a few plays, resolved to insert none of my own readings in the text. Upon this caution I now congratulate myself, for every day encreases my doubt of my emendations."[39] Yet in his accounts of Theobald, the most successful of all the practitioners of conjectural emendation, Johnson seems either guilty of misrepresentation, or callous: "'O poor Tib.! (said Johnson) he was ready knocked down to my hands; Warburton stands between me and him.'"[40]

In his *Proposals* (1756) Johnson asserts:

> Mr. *Theobald, if fame be just to his memory* considered learning only as an instrument of gain, and made no further inquiry after his authour's meaning, when once he had notes sufficient to embellish his page with the expected decorations.[41]

Johnson may have thought Theobald mercenary, but it is unfortunate that such a statement should occur in a paragraph concerned with the elucidation of obscure words and phrases in Shakespeare by means of parallel readings, since Theobald was the first consistently to use this very important technique in the study of an English author, both in *Shakespeare Restored* and in his edition.[42] This Johnson must have known, since Theobald's illustrations were of use to him in his *Dictionary* (1755), but it is not surprising that his representation of Theobald is biased since his source was again Warburton's Preface: "As to Mr. Theobald, who wanted Money, I allowed him to print what I gave him for his own Advantage: and he allowed himself in the Liberty of taking one Part for his own, and sequestering another for the Benefit, as I supposed, of some future Edition."[43]

Nichol Smith is indubitably right when he says that Warburton's "statement of the assistance he rendered to Theobald is rude and cruel, but it is easier to impugn his taste than his truthfulness."[44] However, an examination of Theobald's correspondence with Warburton on the subject of notes to Shakespeare clearly reveals that Warburton's truthfulness was no better than his taste. What is of more immediate interest is Johnson's loyalty to Warburton, despite his obvious mistrust of Warburton as an editor. As might be expected, Johnson's views were formed by an entirely non-Shakespearian matter, for, in addition to praising Johnson's *Miscellaneous Observations on Macbeth* in 1747, Warburton praised Johnson on the occasion of another performance that was much nearer his heart. In a letter to Boswell, Dr. William Adams, the Master of Pembroke, related that, shortly after Johnson had sent his famous letter (7 February 1755) to Lord Chesterfield on patronage:

> While this was the talk of the town . . . I happened to visit Dr. Warburton, who finding that I was acquainted with Johnson, desired me earnestly to carry his compliments to him, and to tell him, that he honoured him for his manly behaviour in rejecting these condescensions of Lord Chesterfield, and for resenting the treatment he had received from him, with a proper spirit. Johnson was visibly pleased with this compliment.[45]

Warburton had reasons of his own for resenting Chesterfield: he had dedicated an edition of *The Alliance of Church and State* to Chesterfield prior to inquiring about livings at Chesterfield's disposal. Chesterfield had replied (14 September 1749) that he regretted he could not be of any assistance.[46]

Warburton's praise of Johnson's rebuff of Chesterfield, when Johnson was still recovering from the stress and debilitation of concluding the *Dictionary*, perhaps accounts for Johnson's loyalty to Warburton and for his consequent acceptance of Warburton's denigration of Theobald. However, when Johnson attempted a formal evaluation of Warburton's *Shakespear* he was hard-pressed to be complimentary:

> Of the last editor it is more difficult to speak. Respect is due to high place, tenderness to living reputation, and veneration to genius and learning; but he cannot be justly offended at that liberty of which he has himself so frequently given an example, nor very solicitous what is thought of notes, which he ought never to have considered as part of his serious employments, and which, I suppose, since the ardour of composition is remitted, he no longer numbers among his happy effusions.[47]

On another occasion Johnson remarked to Dr. Adams:

> If . . . I had written with hostility of Warburton in my Shakespeare, I should have quoted this couplet:
>
> 'Here Learning, blinded first, and then beguil'd,
> Looks dark as Ignorance, as Fancy wild.'[48]
>
> You see they'd have fitted him to a *T*," (smiling.)
> DR. ADAMS. "But you did not write against Warburton."
> JOHNSON. "No, Sir, I treated him with great respect both in my Preface and in my Notes.[49]

In an even more expansive mood, Johnson had declared in "The Life of Pope" that Warburton supplied the best notes to Theobald's *Shake-*

speare.[50] Warburton, however, thought Johnson's comments "full of insolence and malignant reflections."[51]

Johnson's loyalty to Warburton is attractive. Indeed, because he had no knowledge of Theobald, Dr. Samuel Parr believed Johnson had accomplished the impossible and had spoken well of Warburton without insulting those whom Warburton despised.[52] But, of course, when Johnson himself was still an aspiring scholarly hack, his views of Theobald were very different. In the *Miscellaneous Observations on Macbeth* he had said of Theobald: "some of his amendments are so excellent, that, even when he has failed, he ought to be treated with indulgence and respect."[53] Johnson's thought here is echoed and expanded in his Preface to *Shakespeare*, but without reference to Theobald:

> an emendatory critick would ill discharge his duty, without qualities very different from dulness. In perusing a corrupted piece, he must have before him all possibilities of meaning, with all possibilities of expression. Such must be his comprehension of thought, and such his copiousness of language. Out of many readings possible, he must be able to select that which best suits with the state, opinions, and modes of language prevailing in every age, and with his authour's particular cast of thought, and turn of expression. Such must be his knowledge, and such his taste. Conjectural criticism demands more than humanity possesses, and he that exercises it with most praise has very frequent need of indulgence.[54]

When comparing Pope and Theobald as editors in the Preface, he says:

> *Theobald*, thus weak and ignorant, thus mean and faithless, thus petulant and ostentatious, *by the good luck of having* Pope *for his enemy*, has escaped, *and escaped alone*, with reputation, from this undertaking.

The sentence meiotically acknowledges the justice of contemporary views that as an editor of Shakespeare Theobald was superior to both Pope and Warburton—but it is the conclusion of Johnson's paragraph that is interesting:

> So willingly does the world support those who solicite favour, against those who command reverence; and so easily is he praised, whom no man can envy.[55]

There is an evident ambivalence in Johnson's attitudes to scholars and scholarship that at times, perhaps, we all feel. By 1765, he also wished to command respect—not as a commentator beating "his little gold to a spacious surface," nor as a "retired and uncourtly Scholar," nor yet as "a harmless drudge" providing parallel readings to illustrate words, but as a commanding personality in the larger arenas of life. This vitiates his judgment of one who was content simply to be a scholar.

Taken altogether there are sufficient contradictions and complications behind Johnson's "deliberate verdict" on Theobald to prevent any easy acceptance of Johnson's assessment of him, especially when, as with Nichol Smith, it is necessary to add plausibility by supposing that the acknowledged merits of Theobald's *Shakespeare* are to be ascribed to Warburton.

NOTES

1. *Life*, I, 497.
2. *Works*, VII, 56.
3. *Works*, VII, 57.
4. Ibid.
5. *Correspondence of Alexander Pope*, ed. George Sherburn, 5 vols. (Oxford: Clarendon Press, 1956), II, 78–79.
6. Preface, *The Works of Shakespear*, 6 vols. (London, 1725), I, xxii–xxiii.
7. See "Observations on the First Book," *The Iliad of Homer* (Quarto ed.; London, 1715), I, 47–49.
8. *Proposals* (1756), *Works*, VII, 57.
9. Preface, *The Works of Mr. William Shakespear. The Seventh Volume* (London, 1725), p. viii.
10. Preface to the first edition (Glasgow, 1903), repr. 2nd ed. (Oxford: Clarendon Press, 1963).
11. *The Works of Shakespear*, 8 vols. (London, 1747), I, xix, n.
12. Folger Library: PR 2752 1747a c.2.
13. *The Plays of William Shakespeare*, 8 vols. (London, 1765), I, sig. D^r (*Works*, VII, 95–96).
14. Ibid., I, sigs. D1^v–D2^r (*Works*, VII, 96). The Yale editors comment (VII, 95, n. 7): "Lewis Theobald, one of the best of the eighteenth-century editors of Shakespeare, was much misunderstood and contemned."
15. Introduction, *Eighteenth Century Essays on Shakespeare*, 2nd ed. (Oxford: Clarendon Press, 1963), pp. xlv, lvi–lvii.
16. Leading article, "Shakespeare and the Judgments of Johnson," *Times Literary Supplement*, 22 May 1969, p. 545.
17. I, xiii. The Folger Library possesses a set of Warburton's *Shakespear* (PR 2752 1747a c. 5) annotated by the editor for a second edition (which was never printed). The compliment to Johnson has been crossed out.
18. *Life*, I, 175–76.
19. *Apophthegms* in *Johnsonian Miscellanies*, ed. G. B. Hill, 2 vols. (Oxford: Clarendon Press, 1897), II, 7.
20. *The Works of Shakespear*, 8 vols. (London, 1747), I, xi.
21. Printed by John Nichols in *Illustrations of the Literary History of the Eighteenth Century*, Vol. II (London, 1817) and supplemented by R. F. Jones in *Lewis Theobald: His Contribution to English Scholarship, with some Unpublished Letters* (New York: Columbia Univ. Press, 1919).
22. *Life*, I, 329.

23. *European Magazine*, 24 (1793), 296. Warburton was consecrated Bishop of Gloucester in 1760.

24. P. 15.

25. Bodleian Library: Malone 142.

26. See Allen T. Hazen, "Johnson's *Shakespeare*, a Study in Cancellation," *Times Literary Supplement*, 24 September 1938, p. 820.

27. David Erskine Baker, *The Companion to the Play–house* (London, 1764), Vol. II, Art. "Theobald." Sir Thomas Hanmer, sometime Speaker of the House of Commons, edited Shakespeare for the Clarendon Press in 1744 at his own expense. His sumptuous edition was based on Pope's and has unsupported emendations.

28. Nichols, *Illustrations*, II, 714n. Cf. Warton's *Essay on the Genius and Writings of Pope*, 4th ed., corr., 2 vols. (London, 1782), II, 235–36.

29. Ibid. Nichols's estimate is, perhaps, conservative; Edmond Malone, in a MS note ("Shakespeariana," I, 238, Bodleian Library: Malone 14), believed Theobald's first edition numbered 1,360 copies and that there were 10,000 more copies from 1740 to 1774.

30. Preface to *The Plays and Poems of William Shakespeare*, 10 vols. in 11 (London, 1790), I, i, lxvii.

31. *Cambridge Shakespeare* (Cambridge, 1863), I, xxxi, xxxiv, n.

32. General Introduction, *The Tempest*, New Cambridge Shakespeare (Cambridge, 1921), p. xv.

33. (London: Routledge & Kegan Paul, 1974), II, 1.

34. G. Blakemore Evans, "The Text of Johnson's *Shakespeare* (1765)," *Philological Quarterly*, 28 (1949), 426.

35. This was suggested by R. F. Jones; see Evans, "Johnson's *Shakespeare*," p. 428, n. 10.

36. See Arthur M. Eastman, "The Texts from which Johnson printed his *Shakespeare*," *Journal of English and Germanic Philology*, 49 (1950), 182–91.

37. For example, concerning *1 Henry VI*, Blakemore Evans writes: "In *1 Henry VI* alone thirty-two readings which would otherwise be credited (or discredited) to Johnson must now be assigned to the anonymous reviser of the 1757 text. Of these thirty-two readings, seven may be considered worthwhile either as restorations or emendations, five of the seven finding a place in all modern editions. Johnson's total of two restorations and six emendations (only one later accepted) does not compare favorably" (Evans, "Johnson's *Shakespeare*," p. 426).

38. Preface, *The Plays of William Shakespeare*, 8 vols. (London, 1765), I, sig. D7ʳ (*Works*, VII, 104).

39. Ibid., I, sig. Eᵛ (*Works*, VII, 108).

40. *Life*, I, 329 (ap. 1758).

41. *Works*, VII, 56; italics added.

42. See *Shakespeare Restored* (London, 1726), pp. viii, 128; Preface, *The Works of Shakespeare*, 7 vols. (London, 1733), I, xliii. The potential of this technique, which was borrowed from classical scholarship, was recognized, but scarcely realized, by John Urry and Timothy Thomas in the compilation of a glossary to Chaucer; see *The Works of Geoffrey Chaucer* (London, 1721), sig. mᵛ and the glossary.

43. *The Works of Shakespear*, 8 vols. (London, 1747), I, x–xi.

44. Introduction, *Eighteenth Century Essays on Shakespeare*, p. xlvi.

45. *Life*, I, 263.

46. British Library: Egerton MS. 1955, f. 11ʳ–11ᵛ.

47. Preface, *The Plays of William Shakespeare*, 8 vols. (London, 1765), I, sigs. D2ᵛ–D3ʳ (*Works*, VII, 98).

48. Richard Savage's *Wanderer*, II.167–70. L. F. Powell notes that the original reads: "as Frenzy wild."

49. *Life*, IV, 288 (ap. 1784).

50. *Lives*, III, 167.

51. See *Literary Anecdotes of the Eighteenth Century*, ed. John Nichols, V (London, 1812), 595, n.

52. See Boswell, *Life*, IV, 47, n. 2.

53. Note III, *Works*, VII, 8.

54. *The Plays of William Shakespeare* (London, 1765), I, sig. C8^v (*Works*, VII, 94–95).

55. Ibid., I, sigs. D1^v–D2^r (*Works*, VII, 96); italics added.

THOMAS M. CURLEY

12 · Johnson, Chambers, and the Law

Samuel Johnson's keen interest in the law as an intellectual discipline
and as an essential profession for the well-being of society is well
documented. Not only had he seriously contemplated becoming a lawyer, but his writings, from the *Parliamentary Debates* of the early 1740s
to his *Political Tracts* of 1776, often involve fundamental matters of
law. Less well recognized is the fact that, with the large exception of
The Lives of the English Poets (1779–81), almost all the literary labors
of the last two decades of his life were decidedly legal and political
in orientation. Indeed, at Oxford in 1776, he even found himself
prodded to publish a history of English government by the Master of
University College, Dr. Nathan Wetherell. Within Johnson's hearing,
Wetherell talked up the proposal with Boswell: "I would have given
him a hundred guineas if he would have written a preface to his
'Political Tracts,' by way of a Discourse on the British Constitution."[1]
Johnson refused the sly invitation with a growl: "Why should *I* be
always writing?" At that moment Johnson might have silently recol-
lected that through his assistance, Wetherell's own nephew, Sir Robert
Chambers, had practically accomplished this project in a valuable survey of the entire British constitution, entitled *A Course of Lectures on the
English Law*, in the previous decade. Since these law lectures first appeared in 1985, the friendship between Johnson and Chambers and
its impact on the great writer's legal concerns and literary canon have
long remained unstudied.[2] In this essay, I shall discuss an intellectual
partnership that marks an important discovery in the legal history of
the age, accounts for a noteworthy addition to Johnson's writings, and
provides a fresh biographical perspective on his later life and literary
achievement.

That their friendship should have languished in such obscurity for
two centuries is surprising when one considers its significance. John-

son's association with Chambers was probably more intimate and prolonged than any other similar relationship between the aging author and a young man. In fact, in depth and duration, Boswell's more celebrated connection with Johnson pales by comparison. Born the son of a Newcastle attorney in 1737, Chambers first met Johnson at the commencement of his legal training at the Middle Temple in London in the summer of 1754—approximately a decade before Johnson's more famous acquaintances with Boswell and the Thrales began. Somehow this seventeen-year-old Newcastle schoolboy, bright but self-effacing, crossed paths with the century's most fascinating personality in English literature and found a steadfast companion and guide in Johnson. The reputation of the *Rambler* may have induced the novice templar to visit nearby Gough Square. Here Johnson completed the monumental *Dictionary of the English Language* and introduced Chambers to a moody Italian comrade, Joseph Baretti, and to two odd boarders, the blind spinster Anna Williams and the ugly and taciturn Robert Levett. Whatever their eccentricities, all of them took an immediate liking to this lonely stranger in London and maintained the attachment for the rest of their lives. Johnson himself took the initiative to keep the new friendship alive. Not a month passed after Chambers's departure for Lincoln College, Oxford, in the fall term of 1754 before Johnson communicated his warm regards very much in the style of the young man's mentor: "I hope, dear Sir, that you do not regret the change of London for Oxford. Mr. Baretti is well, and Miss Williams, and we shall all be glad to hear from you whenever you shall be so kind as to write."[3]

At this early date Johnson would certainly have tendered considerable advice to Chambers about his plans to combine legal training at the Middle Temple and a liberal education at Oxford. Chambers, later on, paid poetic tribute to the formative influence of Johnson upon his early manhood:

> Johnson, whose kind attractive Call
> Led me at Learning's Shrine to bend,
> Since Happiness is sought by all,
> How best to attain that wish'd for End
> O teach your Pupil and your Friend.[4]

This sense of discipleship was something more than mere rhetorical flattery. It stemmed from Johnson's supervision of Chambers's academic ambitions from the time of the younger man's matriculation at Lincoln College to his tenure as Vinerian Professor at Oxford, beginning in the mid-1760s when together they collaborated in the composition of *A Course of Lectures on the English Law*. Theirs was a harmonious conjunction of often distinct personalities. Chambers was

a shy, fastidious scholar, slight of build, decorous in deportment, conservative in politics, and learned in the classics and the law. Fatherless
since early adolescence, he needed and nurtured the companionship
of stronger men with more energetic intellects to rouse his lethargic
mind and pen into fruitful activity. Mrs. Thrale conceded that he
"made Virtue amiable" and yet wondered why he was so popular with
Johnson's circle of friends.[5] But Johnson, like most other contemporary witnesses, recognized his erudition, his kindly manners, and his
attractive modesty. In Chambers Johnson possibly found the promise
of legal eminence that he once coveted for himself, the gracious
breeding and academic excellence that he always prized, and the filial
attachment that he may well have craved in lonely middle age.

Chambers for his part took immense pride in having formed such
an intimate bond with England's foremost living author. Cherishing
the relationship, he was responsible for preserving the primary evidence of their friendship and collaboration on the Vinerian law lectures by saving almost every letter that Johnson ever wrote to him.
Even as an Oxford undergraduate, he could not resist transmitting
the good news of having made Johnson's acquaintance to his beloved
Newcastle schoolmaster, Rev. Hugh Moises, who was eager to hear
more about the rumored publication of the *Dictionary*: "your Friend
Johnson's (I should hope) will be a valuable Book: is it come abroad
yet? if it be w[ha]t is the Price?"[6] Not long after the *Dictionary*
appeared, a depressed and weary Johnson permitted himself a brief
holiday at Oxford in August 1755, when he renewed his ties with
Chambers and felt close enough already to request some trifling
errands in an invitation for a reunion in London: "As you are soon to
come to town I shall be glad if you will pay my Barber whom I forgot
for a weeks shaving &c and call at Mrs Simpson's for a box of pills
which I left behind me, and am loath to lose."[7] A year later when managing *The Literary Magazine*, Johnson had enough respect for the undergraduate's abilities to include Chambers's biographical article on
Ben Jonson in the fourth issue of the new periodical during the summer.[8] As it turned out, the anonymous essay probably represented the
only specimen of Chambers's voluminous writings ever to appear in
print with his authorization during his lifetime. Appropriately,
Johnson was his publisher.

The Vinerian Chair of English Law at Oxford was established in
1758 to redress serious deficiencies in contemporary legal training by
giving undergraduates a systematic introductory study of their country's laws. Chambers's instructor in the law, Sir William Blackstone, was
elected first Vinerian Professor; his annual course of law lectures became the classic *Commentaries on the Laws of England* (1765–69). Just a
year before the Vinerian Professorship came into being, Chambers

had attended Blackstone's private lectures on the common law and began a long friendship with the foremost eighteenth-century teacher of English law. Blackstone impressed on his pupil's mind a conception of English law as one of the legitimate liberal arts, amenable to scientific classification and worthy of serious historical research within the university curriculum. Chambers's intellectual gifts must have endeared him to Blackstone, who supported his pupil's nomination as one of the two original Vinerian Scholars for the new Oxford chair of law. As Blackstone competed for the Vinerian Professorship, Chambers hoped to safeguard his prospects for a scholarship by capitalizing on the illustrious endorsement of "Dictionary" Johnson. A bundle of letters of recommendation was duly sent to the university authorities on Chambers's behalf, even though Johnson privately cautioned his friend against accepting an academic prize which paid only thirty pounds a year and would retard a lucrative legal practice in London:

> Of what value do you expect any of these new benefactions to be. The great fault of our constitution is that we have many little things which may support idleness, but scarcely any thing great enough to kindle ambition. So that very few men stay in the houses who are qualified to live elsewhere. A professorship of the common law is at least decent, but I do not expect it to be of much use; it will not be worth the acceptance of any practical Lawyer, and a mere speculatist will have no authority. However I am glad it is thought on.[9]

Despite his reservations, Johnson soon sent his congratulations upon hearing of Chambers's election to the honor without opposition. Even at the outset of his connection with the Vinerian foundation, Chambers hoped one day to become the second Vinerian Professor, but, as Johnson hinted, he would have to delay his call to the bar in London by binding himself as a Vinerian Scholar to a needlessly repetitive attendance at Blackstone's entire course for two years.

Thus it happened that Chambers's pursuit of the new legal scholarship inaugurated Johnson's involvement in one of the most innovative academic programs at Oxford of the century. The Vinerian Chair represented a substantial deviation from conventional legal instruction and the traditional university curriculum of classical learning inherited from the Continent. Of the approximately twenty professorships already existing at Oxford, not one confined itself to the study of England's own intellectual heritage. Even the Regius Professorship of Civil Law focused on Roman jurisprudence. Johnson himself in 1748 had urged that more of his countrymen become familiar with the fundamentals of English law: "This Knowledge by peculiar Necessity constitutes a Part of the Education of an *Englishman* who professes to obey his Prince according to the Law, and who is himself a secondary Legislator, as he gives his Consent by his Representative, to all the Laws by which he is bound, and has a Right to petition the great Council of the Nation, whenever he thinks they are deliberating upon an Act detrimental to the Interest of the Community. This is therefore a Subject to which the Thoughts of a young Man ought to be directed." [10] In permitting Blackstone to offer a literate and encyclopedic survey of the British constitution annually, Oxford took a first tentative step in providing undergraduates a practical preparation for a more active role in the legal and political establishment. The Vinerian foundation indicated at least Oxford's willingness to recognize the academic soundness of a purely native body of knowledge even though the university's officials obstructed Blackstone's enterprising leadership and prevented the establishment of anything approaching a professional school of law. The rise of modern law schools would occur later, in the newly created United States of America. Nevertheless, that Samuel Johnson indirectly played a part in the history of the Vinerian Chair fully suited his patriotic labors on behalf of England's language, literature, and culture.

Probably owing in part to the lax management of so many of the university professorships, the regulations drawn up for the new chair were rigorously enforced, especially during Blackstone's tenure. In 1758, for example, Chambers petitioned in vain for a relaxation of a rule requiring a Vinerian Scholar's daily presence at two complete Vinerian courses before the eighth year of his matriculation at Oxford. [11] Chambers, having taken up residence in 1754 and having already attended Blackstone's lectures on the common law in 1757, would have to hear virtually the same law lectures twice again before 1762. However, these confining regulations ultimately worked to Chambers's advantage by assuring him preferential consideration for promotion to higher offices on the Vinerian foundation. In 1761, three years after he took his B.A. degree from Lincoln College, Chambers supplemented his Vinerian stipend with an annual income of sixty pounds from a Percy Fellowship at University College. Awarded his M.A. degree and called to the bar in the same year, he began practicing law in London and on the northern circuit each summer and, in 1762, strengthened his ties with the university by his election as first Vinerian Fellow. The new rank boosted his Vinerian salary to fifty pounds and virtually guaranteed his eventual elevation to the professorship.

Throughout the 1760s the lives of Johnson and Chambers became increasingly intertwined, so much so that the aging author looked to Chambers almost as much as he depended upon the Thrales for help in surviving a depressing and often unproductive decade. For at the time it was Chambers who introduced Johnson not only to a new generation of mutual acquaintances at Oxford but also to the major intellectual project preoccupying the writer after his edition of Shakespeare's plays appeared, namely, his supervision of Chambers's *A Course of Lectures on the English Law*. If Pembroke College qualifies as Johnson's youthful alma mater, then University College is the site of his principal connection with Oxford in later life because Chambers taught there from 1761 to 1771. As early as 1762, Johnson first visited the college in order to seek Chambers's advice about a proper schoolmaster for George Strahan, the son of a favorite publisher. Two years later Johnson returned to oversee Strahan's matriculation at Chambers's college and could already affirm, "The College is almost filled with my friends, and he will be well treated." [12] Strahan went on to become a fellow of University College and a vicar, ministering to Johnson on his deathbed and afterwards publishing the author's *Prayers and Meditations*.

Many others at University College came to know Johnson through Chambers and to share in alleviating the loneliness of the writer's final years. At the head of this group of dons and undergraduates was Chambers's kinsman and major academic patron, Dr. Nathan Wetherell, the Master of University College and a Vice-Chancellor of Oxford. Wetherell presided over the college's golden age of distinguished matriculants and tutors, many of whom imbibed the conservative intellectual atmosphere of the place in preparation for honorable public service on Britain's behalf during the French Revolution. [13] Here it was that Johnson sent the appreciative dons a gift copy of his philippic against the American Revolution, *Taxation No Tyranny*. Of the oldest teaching fellows, Samuel Swire and John Coulson revered Johnson's company. But the finest tutor, William Scott, destined to win legal renown as Baron Stowell, relied on the introduction of his boyhood comrade, Chambers, to enter the inner circle of Johnson's friends as a member of the Literary Club and the Essex Head Club and as an executor of the writer's estate. Scott's younger brother, John, the future Lord Chancellor Eldon, owed to Chambers both his acquaintance with Johnson and his own initiation into the legal profession. [14] Among Chambers's other students, Herbert Croft would contribute a biography of Edward Young to *The Lives of the English Poets*, and William Windham went on to enjoy Johnson's deepest affection in the Literary Club and the Essex Head Club. By far the most brilliant undergraduate, William Jones, entered the Literary Club on Chambers's recommendation and rejoined his former tutor in India on the bench of the Bengal Supreme Court. In the forefront of oriental scholarship as the founder of the Asiatic Society of Bengal, Jones would, at a meeting of that organization in Calcutta, duly memorialize one "of the most sagacious men in this age who continues, I hope, to improve and adorn it, Samuel Johnson." [15]

University College was to provide a very congenial setting for Johnson's collaboration on *A Course of Lectures on the English Law*. When Chambers was elected second Vinerian Professor on 7 May 1766, he should have quickly undertaken an original lecture series that would meet the high standards set by Blackstone's first Vinerian course. He went so far as to announce that he would begin running the second Vinerian series in November 1766 with the aim of completing his delivery of a complete course by the following spring. Unfortunately, laziness, a law practice, and the formidable research necessary for a new course delayed him. Even worse, Blackstone's *Commentaries* were now being published and exposed the unproven professor to invidious comparison with his famous teacher. Chambers panicked and produced no lectures in the fall term. In this emergency Johnson generously came to his aid in October 1766 and inaugurated a collaboration that would continue at irregular intervals for approximately three more years.

The two men would have puzzled over a major obstacle at the outset of their deliberations, namely, the problem of composing a lecture series that would neither slavishly repeat Blackstone's nor foolishly avoid basic subject matter for the sake of arcane novelties useless in an introductory study of the law. Their solution entailed a drastic simplification of Blackstone's survey, primarily by deleting his lengthy discussion of judicial process, by reducing his four divisions of English law to three major sections, and by concentrating on constitutional history for a unique political perspective that stresses the human need for law and order rather than the protection of individual liberties in government. Their joint labors eventually yielded a full set of fifty-six lectures, later expanded to the mandatory number of sixty lectures, dealing with the fundamental concepts, traditions, and statutes making up the British constitution.[16] An eloquent introduction of four lectures sets forth the metaphysical and quasi-utilitarian foundations of all law as well as the Saxon and Norman roots of the common law. Then follows part I on the public law of English government in sixteen lectures, which, like the introduction, have legal assumptions found in Johnson's political writings. The fourteen lectures of part II catalogue the criminal law but, except for the underlying thesis of human malignity, show little of Johnson's farsighted humanitarianism. Finally, part III surveys the private law of property in twenty-two technical lectures of limited relevance to Johnson's canon.

Only recently recovered from poor health, Johnson loyally stayed at Oxford for a month of the fall term of 1766 to make sure that the recipient of his earlier recommendations for a Vinerian Scholarship in 1758 did not now fail his duties in the highest station of the academic chair. But back in London he had to continue urging Chambers to work on the lectures throughout the winter: "I suppose you are dining and supping, and lying in bed. . . . Come up to town, and lock yourself up from all but me, and I doubt not but Lectures will be produced. You must not miss another term. . . . Come up and work, and I will try to help you."[17] This coaxing drew Chambers into London possibly for a week or two in January 1767 and again through most of February until mid-March when Johnson, honored by an interview with George III, might have been conducting legal research in the Queen's Library at Buckingham House. By 17 March 1767, Chambers at last began delivering what turned out to be only half a course of lectures during the first academic year of his Vinerian Professorship.

To guarantee that all went according to schedule, Johnson visited the university himself, noting in his diary entry of 9 April, "I returned from helping Chambers at Oxford."[18] An arrogant undergraduate, who documented Chambers's intention to give "only half a course this year," complained about the professor's lengthy absence in London and sourly recorded Johnson's presence at University College on 5 April: "We had Johnson, the Author of the Dictionary, etc., to dine with us to-day. He seems to be a Man of very strong sense & deep Judgment, but not remarkably bright or of quick apprehension. He is also fond of Sarcasm, which has a double portion of Gall flowing from the most disgusting Voice & person you almost ever beheld."[19] Johnson would stop by briefly at Chambers's Oxford residence at New Inn Hall in May and again in October as the half-course ever so slowly expanded into a complete series. Certainly more meetings occurred, some of them of considerable duration, before the second Vinerian course neared completion in 1769. During these sessions they presumably pooled their ideas and legal research before Chambers resumed drafting his belated course and assimilated any argumentation that Johnson may have dictated or written for the professor's use in at least a few lectures. No doubt, in periods of Johnson's absence, Chambers independently carried on the composition of the lion's share of his course.

Such was the prolonged collaboration that provided the intellectual backdrop of Johnson's nomination of Chambers for election as the twelfth member of the Literary Club—its first barrister and the first to see public service in the empire—on 15 February 1768. This event, which was to be Chambers's entrée to a whole new set of London celebrities, may have represented Johnson's return for the good fellowship extended to him at University College through the second Vinerian Professor. Whatever the nature of Johnson's specific contributions to the course, he surely oversaw its creation until possibly as late as January 1770. He therefore knew at least portions of the lecture series well enough to be able to draw on them for inspiration in his own writings. After all, the second Vinerian course offered a conservative, historically pragmatic interpretation of the British constitution that agreed with Johnson's avowed political principles. Assisting Chambers would have augmented Johnson's already considerable knowledge of English government and imparted a panoramic vision of its constitutional development for use in his political publications of the 1770s. Other friends like Boswell and the Thrales may have been instrumental in evoking *A Journey to the Western Islands of Scotland* and his *Political Tracts*, but in all likelihood it was Johnson's earlier interaction with Chambers that shaped the actual content of these works. Furthermore, there remain rich possibilities of thematic ties between the law lectures and Johnson's literary criticism and philological essays. For to Johnson, literature like statecraft embodied a common law of fortuitous adaptation and progressive correctness which the second Vinerian course summarily traced in the political history of England.

The precise relationship between Chambers's lectures and Johnson's canon is not easy to assess. The publication of *A Course of Lectures on the English Law* will make possible an extensive examination of the issue by legal and literary scholars. Readers should be warned that at least a few passages formerly ascribed to Johnson have been discovered almost verbatim in Chambers's private papers written before and after the composition of the lectures. The creation of the course from 1766 to 1770 may have entailed more than Johnson's general supervision of Chambers's writing process. At times it may have amounted to a truly joint authorship resulting in legal discourses whose style and thought are neither solely Chambers's nor purely Johnson's. Moreover, as some scholars have argued, it may even have involved Chambers's incorporation of groups of paragraphs or entire lectures dictated or drafted by Johnson.[20] At least this much can be stated with safety: Johnson was sufficiently familiar with the course to have remembered certain lectures for use in his own writings and to have been influenced in his political and literary themes by a comprehensive, cohesive, and congenial survey of the British constitution. A sampling of parallel passages from the lectures and Johnson's works, with a specimen of Chambers's writing, strikingly suggests some of the possibilities and difficulties involved in an evaluation of specific links between Chambers's Vinerian course and Johnson's canon.

The collaboration probably reinforced for Johnson two doctrines central to the course and to his own notions of government. The first of these tenets is the principle of human necessity behind the formation of political societies, a principle originating in the basic psychological demands of human nature for the protective restraints of a strong ruling authority. As the *Lectures* stress:

> There is therefore a necessity of some *governing* power, by which those who are inclined to be happy at the cost of others may be compelled to their part of the general task,—and of a *public wisdom*, by which private judgement shall be directed and controlled. Those to whom this power is entrusted, and this wisdom is imputed, are the governors of society; the first care therefore of every new society must be to select and establish governors, and its first law must constitute the power, by which future laws are to be made.[21]

In *The False Alarm* (1770) Johnson too would appeal to the "pregnant principle of political necessity" in examining the foundation of the English body politic:

> The first laws had no law to enforce them, the first authority was constituted by itself. The power exercised by the House of Commons is of this kind, a power rooted in the principles of government, and branched out by occasional practice, a power which necessity made just, and precedents have made legal. . . . All government supposes subjects, all authority implies obedience.[22]

The rigorously realistic historiography of the Lectures would have suited Johnson's own pragmatic view of British antiquities. Part I, Lecture 7 makes a memorable apologia for reputable antiquarian scholarship that transcends a biased Whig interpretation of English history:

> It is therefore not by searching into past times, but by searching superficially and deciding hastily that just censure is incurred. Knowledge is always promoted by inquisitive industry, and almost always retarded by systematic dogmatism. To these studies may be eminently applied that important axiom "*Qui pauca considerat facile pronunciat*," and of antiquaries, as of other scholars, I suppose it will be found that often as their knowledge increases their confidence grows less.[23]

This disavowal of historical dogmatism bears comparison with Johnson's criticism of philosophical optimism in his review of Soame Jenyns's *A Free Inquiry into the Nature and Origin of Evil* for *The Literary Magazine* (1757):

> Thus it appears how little reason those who repose their reason upon the scale of being have to triumph over those who recur to any other expedient of solution, and what difficulties arise on every side to repress the rebellions of presumptuous decision. *Qui pauca considerat, facile pronunciat.*[24]

One of the most remarkable passages in the course, also in Part I, Lecture 7, attacks Whig historians for their anachronistic idealization of the supposedly liberty-loving House of Commons in ancient times. It sums up the pragmatic philosophy of historical development not only in the *Lectures* but also in Johnson's writings on the maturation of English politics, language, and literature:

> We now live at a time when by diffusion of civility and circulation of intelligence the manners of the whole nation are uniform, when by determinations of acknowledged authority, the limits of all jurisdictions are fixed, when a long course of records and precedents has furnished models for almost every civil transaction, and experience has supplied what reason wanted in the art of government. To us therefore it is natural to think that former ages glided on with the same regular and uniform tranquillity. But when we search into early times this idea must be carefully driven from our minds. We must remember, that in every compound the proportion of the components must be settled by successive trials; that there was a time when every thing polished was rough, when every thing artificial was rude; that the essays of a new government were experimental; that the public affairs were at first conducted by extemporaneous prudence, and regulated by such expedients as opportunity supplied and necessity enforced; that authority was more connected with personal than political characters; that power was undefined, and practice unsettled.[25]

The premises in this passage recall a fundamental political proposition enunciated in Johnson's parliamentary debate on spirituous liquors in the early 1740s: "All the schemes of government, my lords, have been perfected by slow degrees, and the defects of every regulation supplied by the wisdom of successive generations. . . . [T]he first essay of a new regulation is, therefore, only an experiment made, in some degree, at random, and to be rectified by subsequent observations." [26] Similarly, in *The False Alarm*, Johnson stressed the fortuitous and expedient nature of the historical development of government:

> Governments formed by chance, and gradually improved by such expedients, as the successive discovery of their defects happened to suggest, are never to be tried by a regular theory. They are fabricks of dissimilar materials, raised by different architects, upon different plans. We must be content with them as they are; should we attempt to mend their disproportions, we might easily demolish, and difficultly rebuild them.
>
> Laws are now made, and customs established; these are our rules, and by them we must be guided.[27]

Chambers echoes the lecture passage in his *Observations on Mr. Hastings's Plan for the Administration of Justice* in explaining the historical growth of an Anglo-Indian law for British India in 1776:

> I readily agree with my Lord Chief Justice that "the local laws and customs of these provinces proved in court, are rules by which we are to administer justice,"—even as the law now stands; but we must remem-

ber that the time is not very long past when in this country, authority was more connected with personal than political characters, when power was undefined and practice unsettled and that the first essays of the English government must have been experimental, and that all public business and the collection of the revenue, was for some time conducted by extemporaneous prudence and regulated by such expedients as opportunity supplied and necessity enforced. It is therefore probable that some modes of proceeding which are now supposed to be fixed and which it would be inconvenient to condemn, can neither be proved like customs, by evidence of constant and immemorial usage, nor established as law by reference to books of authority.[28]

Besides comparable constitutional principles, more specific similarities exist between the lectures and Johnson's publications. For example, the introduction, Lecture 2 contains an astute explanation of ancient migrations that approximates Johnson's analysis of Highland emigration in *A Journey to the Western Islands of Scotland* (1775). This lecture speculates about the reasons for the formation of feudal governments in Europe in the Dark Ages:

> Few questions are more difficult to be solved than that which enquires for what reason a nation should . . . transport themselves . . . into countries . . . utterly unknown. . . . It has . . . been generally supposed that at a certain period of time the regions of the north were overstocked with inhabitants and *Temple* denominates the Gothic invasions as the *swarming of the northern hive.* But this cause has always appeared to me to be assumed without proof, only because no other could be found. It may be doubted whether there is not now room in Scandinavia and Sarmatia for all their present inhabitants and all the other nations of Europe put together. . . . The superstitious opinions of the northern nations were such as disposed them to hazard and adventure. Peace was regarded by them as . . . inglorious, and they considered the man who suffered himself to waste away with the pains of sickness or languor of age, not only as neglecting his *fame* but his *duty.* . . . A single chief was perhaps contented to . . . plunder villages on the coast. But if many united together and formed a great army, they marched onward with avowed hostility, till . . . weariness disposed them to rest in some fruitful country.[29]

Alarmed by the dwindling population of feudal Scotland, Johnson may well have revived the lecture discussion in his search for a cogent historical analogy to the current crisis. If the lecture explains ancient migration as a cataclysmic response to military invasions by fierce Germanic tribes, so too Johnson's travel book treats Highland emigration as a violent reaction to economic encroachments of rapacious landlords:

> It has been a question often agitated without solution, why those northern regions are now so thinly peopled, which formerly overwhelmed with their armies the Roman empire. The question supposes what I believe is not true, that they had once more inhabitants than they

could maintain, and overflowed only because they were full. . . . An adventurous projector heard of a fertile coast unoccupied, and led out a colony; a chief of renown for bravery, called the young men together, and led them out to try what fortune would present. . . . The religion of the North was military; if they could not find enemies, it was their duty to make them: they travelled in quest of danger, and willingly took the chance of empire or death. . . . The Gothick swarms have at least been multiplied with equal liberality. . . . Their country was not deserted for want of room. . . . In a country fully inhabited, . . . evident marks will remain of its former populousness. But of Scandinavia and Germany, nothing is known but that as we trace their state upwards into antiquity, their woods were greater, and their cultivated ground was less.[30]

The later influence of the *Lectures* seems most dramatically evident in the final and most fiery political tract of his old age, *Taxation No Tyranny* (1775). This pamphlet appears to have synthesized information about ancient and modern migrations, parliamentary sovereignty, the House of Commons, and the British empire found in various passages throughout the introduction and part I of the course. Part I, Lecture 15 especially bears comparison with both *Taxation No Tyranny* and *The Patriot* (1774); the concluding lecture discussion about the mother country's right to tax her settlements is directly relevant to a major thesis of Johnson's last two pamphlets:

> Those who increase the expenses of the public, ought to supply their proportion of the expenses increased. The payment of fleets and armies may be justly required from those for whose protection fleets and armies are employed. No state intends to place its colonies in a condition superior to its own, to afford protection without the return of obedience, or to be satisfied with obedience so easy and unexpensive as every man suffered to be his own judge would prescribe to himself. If by forsaking our native country we could carry away all its happiness and leave its evils behind, what human being would not wish for exile? If the name of a colonist conferred a right to live in plenty and security at the expense and hazard of the mother country, to refuse all contribution to the necessities of the public, or to proportion his share by his own interest or humour, a colonist would then obtain more than sovereignty. He would obtain sovereignty exempt from the care of its own preservation. In such a state it never was yet the intention of one man to place another, and to this state therefore our colonies can have no reasonable claim.[31]

The Patriot virtually repeats this rhetorically effective argument in a succinct form:

> To suppose, that by sending out a colony, the nation established an independent power; that when, by indulgence and favour, emigrants are become rich, they shall not contribute to their own defence, but at their own pleasure; and that they shall not be included, like millions of their fellow subjects, in the general system of representation; involves

such an accumulation of absurdity, as nothing but the shew of patriotism could palliate.

He that accepts protection, stipulates obedience. We have always protected the Americans; we may therefore subject them to government.[32]

Taxation No Tyranny similarly grounds Britain's taxing authority in the
colonial obligation to share some economic responsibility for imperial
protection:

> Of every empire all the subordinate communities are liable to taxa-
> tion, because they all share the benefits of government, and therefore
> ought to furnish their proportion of the expence.
>
> This the Americans have never openly denied. That it is their duty to
> pay the cost of their own safety they seem to admit; nor do they refuse
> their contributions to the exigencies . . . of the British empire; but they
> make this participation of the public burden a duty of very uncertain
> extent, and imperfect obligation, a duty temporary, occasional, and
> elective, of which they reserve to themselves the right of settling the de-
> gree, the time, and the duration, of judging when it may be required,
> and when it has been performed. . . .
>
> This claim, wild as it may seem, this claim, which supposes dominion
> without authority, and subjects without subordination, has found among
> the libertines of policy many clamorous and hardy vindicators.[33]

A comparison of other passages in the lecture and the pamphlet confirms their common viewpoint and invites readers to draw the same
reasonable conclusion that a dispassionate scholarly assessment of the
taxation issue in the late 1760s previews Johnson's inflammatory pro-
nouncements in *Taxation No Tyranny*, published on the eve of a revolution that permanently decided in America's favor the philosophical
debate over the right to imperial rule, taxation, and representation.

Many questions about Chambers's tenure as second Vinerian Professor remain unanswered. Neither collaborator ever specified the
exact nature and extent of Johnson's contributions to the course. Even
Chambers's own original copy of a complete series of sixty private lectures and four public lectures has vanished without a trace. Only the
manuscript of approximately fifty-six private lectures, more than
2,000 pages in length and prepared by several scribes as Chambers's
gift to George III, has survived in the British Library. Were the *Lectures* well received at Oxford? Chambers's wife did assert, years later,
that her husband's "Vinerian Lectures were attended by many pupils,
who have since done honour to the profession of the law or to other
public situations."[34] Moreover, John Scott in his old age claimed to
have read Chambers's lectures before "about one hundred and forty
boys and young men," a possibly exaggerated enrollment far exceed-
ing the peak number of fifty students that Jeremy Bentham found attracted to Blackstone's "formal, precise, and affected" delivery of the

first Vinerian course.[35] Why had so much needless delay clogged Chambers's performance in the Vinerian Chair? Blackstone, according to William Scott's rumor, had only some hearty port to fire his disciplined labors on the *Commentaries*. Chambers had the sober counsel of Johnson for encouragement but, despite successive annual fines for failing to deliver sixty lectures each year, did not offer a complete Vinerian course until the academic year of 1769–70. In addition to his indolence, timidity, and cautiousness in legal matters and research, another problem of a more serious and chronic nature must have obstructed him. The fact is that he was far too unsettled about the future direction of his career to put his whole heart into his Vinerian duties. A poetic "Epistle from R. C. to Doctor Samuel Johnson on the Choice of Life," probably composed in the summer of 1767, betrays Chambers's vexing indecision about continuing at Oxford, engaging in foreign service, or even plunging into marriage one day:

> Say, shall I haunt th'ambitious Bar?
> Where modest worth must often fail,
> Where Justice is with Form at War:
> Shall I for this quit Isis' Vale?
> Shall I for this grow nightly pale?
>
> Shall I, by Fashion's Torrent borne,
> Wildly resolve abroad to rove?
> Where Wealth breeds Fear and Want breeds Scorn:
> Shall I for this leave New Inn Grove
> and each sequester'd Scene I love?
>
> Shall I, to enjoy my *Hall* and Wife,
> Shun Splendour, Gaiety and Power,
> And pass in Household Cares my Life?
> Or shall I wear out Hour by Hour
> A solitary Batchelour?[36]

Within seven years of writing these verses, Chambers would find all those questions answered by a judicial appointment in British India that would induce him to marry a beautiful fifteen-year-old, Frances Wilton, and would force him to abandon New Inn Hall and part forever from Samuel Johnson. Primarily because of the collaboration, Chambers shares with the Thrales some of the credit for lightening the burden of Johnson's old age. But even when the collaboration ended and Johnson's visits to Oxford noticeably declined by 1770, their friendship remained intact. Mulling over the government's offer of a judgeship in Bengal in the spring of 1773, Chambers gradually relinquished his Vinerian duties but temporarily continued his law practice at 6 King's Bench Walk, Inner Temple. There a mutual friend, Bennet Langton, dropped by on 10 May to draw up a will bequeathing his estate to three sisters rather than to the nearest male relation. This violation of feudal succession led to a famous episode in Boswell's *Life*, a hilarious incident involving one of Chambers's last professional assignments as a barrister. Chambers was a fussbudget about health and was given to prescribing remedies for Johnson's chronic disorders. When an ailing Johnson stopped by at the time of Langton's transaction, Chambers's unwelcome solicitousness provoked an outburst of anger and then of merriment at the expense of lawyer and client. "Pr'ythee don't teaze me," Johnson told Chambers in a fit of pique, "Stay till I am well, and then you shall tell me how to cure myself."[37] Perceiving the vanity of mortal human wishes in Langton's business, Johnson eventually recovered his sense of humor and whimsically upheld feudal conventions against the upstart "*testator*" and his three "*dowdies*." Langton, Johnson laughed, "thinks he has done a mighty thing. . . . [H]e'll call up the landlord of the first inn on the road; and, after a suitable preface upon mortality and the uncertainty of life, will tell him that he should not delay making his will; and here, Sir, will he say, is my will, which I have just made, with the assistance of one of the ablest lawyers in the kingdom; and he will read it to him. . . . He believes he has made this will; but he did not make it: you, Chambers, made it for him. I trust you have had more conscience than to make him say, 'being of sound understanding'; ha, ha, ha! I hope he has left me a legacy. I'd have his will turned into a verse, like a ballad." Chambers, a serious man annoyed by Johnson's boisterous sense of human absurdity, impatiently shooed his troublesome guest out into the street while the peals of laughter, as Boswell so vividly remembered, resounded through the Inns of Court from Temple-bar to Fleet-ditch. Chambers bore Johnson no grudge, but Langton, failing to appreciate the joke, nursed feelings of resentment for weeks. "Is not this very childish," Johnson commented with tongue in cheek, "Where now is my legacy?"[38]

The laughter would soon subside into sadness when Johnson had to contemplate the distressing thought of taking a permanent leave of his friend. As Chambers prepared to vacate the Vinerian Chair for a seat on the Supreme Court of Judicature in India during the summer of 1773, he accompanied Johnson on that famous journey to Scotland as far as Newcastle so that they could have one long last reunion to themselves. In early August Chambers sent a letter to his mother—a letter never before published—in order to make sure that his birthplace provided a warm welcome for their illustrious guest:

Honoured Madam
    As I have now quitted the Bar, it is almost needless to tell You that I shall not appear on the Northern Circuit as a Barrister; but on Friday or Saturday Morning I shall set out for Newcastle in Company with my Friend Dr. Johnson, who is going into Scotland to pay a Visit to Boswell.

We shall, I hope, get to Newcastle on Monday Night, or on Tuesday before Dinner, and I must beg that You will endeavour to accommodate my Friend with a Bed, during the two or three Days that he may probably stay with Us.

If it will not put You to any great Inconvenience I should be glad to have some of my Circuit Friends to dine with me on Wednesday, and some more on Thursday. . . .

> Yours
> with all Duty & Affection
> Robt. Chambers [39]

Although Newcastle proved something of a disappointment for Johnson, his subsequent separation from Chambers in Scotland bothered him very much. Stranded by stormy seas in the Hebrides a few weeks later, Johnson actually anguished over the possibility of never seeing Chambers before the voyage to India took place. So he wrote from Skye:

This restraint, which has all the alleviations that courtesy and hospitality can afford, is made very painful to me by the fear of not being able to take leave of you, before your departure. If I am detained from you by insuperable obstructions, let this be witness that I love you, and that I wish you all the good that can be enjoyed through ⟨the⟩ whole of our Existence. You are going where there will be many opportunities of profitable wickedness, but you go with good principles, a confirmed and solid Christian. I hope to see you come back with fortune encreased, and Virtue grown more resolute by contest. [40]

Fortunately, a delay in the departure of the voyage did permit a final leavetaking on 30 March 1774. Chambers, newly married and harassed by last-minute preparations for the long trip, evidently arrived late for the visit. Johnson, who had not been invited to the private wedding ceremony and whose own indisposition had not permitted him to see Chambers for some time, already suffered from a self-inflicted sense of injury and neglect. He now began to suspect that Chambers had failed him in this final rendezvous and hastily scribbled a bleakly understated note that hangs at the present time in the Johnson House at Gough Square:

Dear Sir
I have waited for you to three this afternoon. I suppose something unexpected has hindred you and am sorry, though I have nothing to say to you which I have not said. I would have been glad to see you once more. I pray God to bless you for Jesus Christs Sake.
> Farewel. [41]

This note—without a signature, a date, or a postmark—was never mailed to Chambers. Chambers, though late as usual, did keep his appointment and received from Johnson one last paternal blessing, a magnificent letter of introduction to Governor-General Warren Hastings in India, and a set of the rare Edinburgh edition of the *Rambler*. To this cherished gift of moral essays distilling the essence of Johnson's wisdom about life, Chambers appended an inscription in memory of this poignant interview: "Given to Robert Chambers, as a Token of Remembrance, by his beloved Friend, the ingenious and learned Authour of the Rambler. 1774." They were destined never to meet again.

Chambers's appointment as one of the four new judges of the Supreme Court of British India created by the Regulating Act of 1773 radically changed his life and made him a participant in the momentous undertaking of formally introducing English law to the subcontinent. It also reignited Johnson's interest in the politics and culture of India. Johnson not only would daydream about taking a "ramble" to Bengal in 1775 but also became an influential proponent of oriental studies spearheaded by the Asiatic Society of Bengal under Chambers's colleague on the Supreme Court bench, Sir William Jones.[42] Largely because of Chambers, Johnson renewed an acquaintance with Hastings and Joseph Fowke at Calcutta and kept himself informed about dissensions within the English government at Bengal that ruined Fowke and threatened Hastings and Chambers with parliamentary recall in the 1780s. Johnson, in fact, knew of Chambers's personal opposition to Hastings's administration and followed some especially controversial Supreme Court cases that affected the future course of Anglo-Indian Law. Concerning the infamous trial and execution of Rajah Nandakumar for forgery in 1775, Johnson, like Chambers on the bench, suspected the perpetration of a grievous miscarriage of justice that would go far in disgracing the Bengal court at home: "The effects of English Judicature are not believed here to have added any thing to the happiness of the new dominions. Of you, Sir, I rejoice to say that I have heard no evil."[43]

In 1776 Chambers directed his father-in-law, the sculptor Joseph Wilton, to deliver "Dr. Johnson's Copy" of the judge's *Observations on Mr. Hastings's Plan for the Administration of Justice, with additional Proposals, including a Plan of Legislative and Executive Magistracy.*[44] This lengthy manuscript would have summarized for Johnson, if he read the work, a series of enlightened colonial reforms sometimes echoing passages in the Vinerian law lectures. He always refused to become involved in schemes for governmental reorganization or to take sides in the distant political quarrels, despite the urging of Fowke abroad and the agitation of Edmund Burke at home. Reports of corruption in India only confirmed Johnson's misgivings about British imperialism in his final years but did not induce him to indulge in speculations about any radical retreat from the political *status quo*. Reacting to Fox's East India Bill championed by Burke for reforming British India in 1783, an aging and weary Johnson displayed very little enthusiasm: "Mr Burke has just sent me his speech upon the affairs of India, a volume of above an hundred pages closely printed. I will look into it; but my thoughts now seldom travel to great distances."[45]

Fortunately, Johnson would live to see Chambers escape parliamentary censure for his acceptance of an additional judgeship from Hastings in the captured Dutch settlement of Chinsura in 1781. Moreover, Johnson would foresee Chambers's promotion to the Chief Justiceship of the Bengal Supreme Court, from 1791 to 1798, and would send a moving letter of fond farewell that ranks among the longest and most heartfelt performances in his collected correspondence. The former collaborator on a lecture series extolling English government did not forget to reassure Chambers of his patriotic political principles in this letter of 19 April 1783: "I have at least endeavoured to preserve order and support Monarchy."[46] Johnson then reviewed the lives of their mutual acquaintances in the Literary Club and exhorted his absent friend to advance oriental studies, a request that Chambers obeyed during his twenty-five years in India even to the end of his life in 1803. Lastly, in keeping with the funereal tone of a letter filled with intimate revelations of failing health and fading friendships, Johnson concluded on a religious note of fatherly advice for the salvation of Chambers's soul. The benediction was an apt memorial to the durability and intensity of their forgotten friendship:

> One of my last wishes for you, at a gay table was ἀ ρετήν τε καὶ ὀλβόν.[47]
> Let me now add in a more serious hour, and in more powerful words—
> Keep innocency, and take heed to the thing that is right, for that shall
> bring a Man peace at the last. . . .
> Nothing now, I think, remains but that I assure you, as I do, of my
> kindness, and good wishes, and express my hope that you do not forget
>   Your old Friend and hum-
>   ble servant,
>   Sam: Johnson.

News of Johnson's death did not reach the obituary pages of *The Calcutta Gazette* until 9 June 1785, too late for Chambers ever to reply again to a letter from his old friend who lay buried in Westminster Abbey. A mutual friend of University College, Sir William Scott, reported the details of Johnson's demise to Chambers in 1787. A portion of this letter, printed for the first time, follows:

> Dr. Johnson you must have heard, died above two years and a half ago, leaving Sir Joshua, S[ir]. J[ohn]. Hawkins & myself his Executors. Poor Man! He felt the Approaches of Death with a keen Sensibility of Mind & was extremely tenacious of his Life. A vast inundation of Matter respecting his Life and Character has found its Way into the World. You will be amused with the Writings of Mrs Thrale, Boswell & Sir John

Hawkins, tho' You will not read every thing that has been written with Approbation. Boswell is compiling a larger book of his history. Mrs. Thrale is publishing two Volumes of his Letters; and many of his Friends are fearful that his Reputation may suffer in more Ways than one by such a Publication; and then one considers the free Things which Johnson indulged Himself occasionally in saying of his Friends, it seems not improbable that some of our Reputations may not be the better for it.[48]

As it happened, Chambers had no reason to fear for his reputation by a disclosure of his secret collaboration with Johnson years before at Oxford. Only Mrs. Thrale knew of the relationship, and she kept this knowledge to herself.

The discovery of *A Course of Lectures on the English Law* in the twentieth century fills a large gap in the life of Johnson and sheds new light on the political and literary ideals found in his final writings. His dealings with Chambers afford a glimpse of Johnson's paternal protectiveness, generosity, and political conservatism noted by Boswell and other contemporary observers. Even more, their friendship elucidates concerns of Johnson inadequately documented by previous biographers, namely, his lively curiosity about British history and interest in British India which left this John Bull of English literature respectively prouder of English civilization and angrier about European colonialism. Then, too, their partnership in performing the duties of the second Vinerian Professorship helps to correct the Boswellian portrait of Johnson as a marmoreally changeless and self-sufficient intellect. The author who promoted Chambers's work as an academic lawyer displayed an unusual capacity in old age to learn from another mind and to refine conceptions of country and culture for an unprecedented outburst of political writing at the end of a remarkably diverse literary career. If Johnson was a writer possessed with truly encyclopedic knowledge, he was, after all, a man with a restless and probing intelligence who richly benefited from the learning and loyalty of "my friend Mr Chambers, a man whose purity of manners and vigour of mind are sufficient to make every thing welcome that he brings."[49]

NOTES

1. *Life*, II, 441.
2. *A Course of Lectures on the English Law Delivered at the University of Oxford, 1767–1773*, by Sir Robert Chambers, Second Vinerian Professor of English Law, and Composed in Association with Samuel Johnson, ed. Thomas M. Curley, 2 vols. (Madison, Wisconsin: Univ. of Wisconsin Press, 1985). Hereafter cited as *Lectures*.
3. *Letters*, I, 57 (no. 54).
4. Sir Robert Chambers, "An Epistle from R. C. to Doctor Samuel Johnson on the

Choice of Life, written about the Year 1766," ed. Herman W. Liebert, "'The Choice of Life': A Poem Addressed to Dr. Samuel Johnson" (printed at the Carl Purington Rollins Printing-Office of Yale University Press for the Annual Dinner of The Johnsonians, September 19, 1969), p. 4. Chambers enrolled at Lincoln College on 30 May 1754 and was admitted to the Middle Temple on the following 28 June.

5. *Thraliana: The Diary of Mrs. Hester Lynch Thrale, 1776–1809*, ed. Katherine C. Balderston, 2 vols. (Oxford: Clarendon Press, 1942), I, 473–74 and 329–30.

6. Hugh Moises to Robert Chambers, 30 January 1755 (Oxford University Archives, MS Don. C56, f. 104).

7. *Letters*, I, 76 (no. 75.1).

8. "The Life of Ben Jonson," *Literary Magazine*, 4 (1756), 169–71. Herman W. Liebert, in his edition of Chambers's poetic "Epistle," p. 2, also ascribes this anonymous magazine article to him.

9. *Letters*, I, 107–108 (no. 114.1).

10. "The Preceptor," *Samuel Johnson's Prefaces & Dedications*, ed. Allen T. Hazen (New Haven: Yale Univ. Press, 1937), pp. 187–88. For Blackstone's election to the Vinerian Chair and his frustrated effort to create a school of law at Oxford, see Lucy Sutherland, "William Blackstone and the Legal Chairs at Oxford," *Evidence in Literary Scholarship: Essays in Memory of James Marshall Osborn*, ed. René Wellek and Alvaro Ribeiro (Oxford: Clarendon Press, 1979), pp. 229–40, and James Clitherow's "Memoir," published as "Preface to First Edition," in Sir William Blackstone, *Reports of Cases Determined in the Several Courts of Westminster-Hall from 1746 to 1779*, ed. Charles Heneage Elsley, 2 vols. (London: S. Sweet, 1828), I, xvi–xvii. Reacting against objections to his manner of appointing deputy lecturers, Blackstone, on 10 July 1761, vented his mounting vexations as Vinerian Professor in a printed reply: "With regard to himself—he is not conscious of having given just Cause (or any Cause that dares be avowed) for the Series of peevish Opposition and personal Insult which he has met with in the Execution of his present Employment" (Oxford University Archives, V/3/5/16).

11. The "Postscript" in Blackstone's *A Discourse on the Study of Law; Being an Introductory Lecture, Read in the Public Schools, October XXV, M.DCC.LVIII* (Oxford, 1758), pp. 35–49, details the statutory requirements of the Vinerian Chair. For criticism of the Vinerian Scholars' request for an exemption from attending Blackstone's course annually, see *A Reply to Petition to Request in the Last Convocation*, 20 November 1758 (Oxford University Archives, V3/5/12). There is no evidence to suggest that the regulation regarding the Vinerian Scholars' duties was relaxed during Blackstone's tenure.

12. *Letters*, I, 170 (no. 167). According to the "Register of University College" (Vol. II, 1729–1842), Chambers received a Percy Fellowship there on 23 December 1761 and remained a tutor at the college for approximately ten years.

13. William Carr, *University College* (London: F. E. Robinson, 1902), pp. 185–92.

14. Horace Twiss, *The Public and Private Life of Lord Chancellor Eldon*, 3 vols. (London: John Murray, 1844), I, 86–88, 91.

15. Sir William Jones, Annual Discourse before the Asiatic Society of Bengal, 24 February 1785, quoted in *Life*, II, 125 n. 4.

16. The fact that George III wanted a personal copy for the royal library is responsible for the survival of a complete manuscript of fifty-six lectures (with an extra Lecture 6a of Part I dealing with the royal family) drafted by several scribes and running to about 450,000 words. The manuscript was discovered in the 1930s by the late E. L. McAdam in the British Museum, to which the king's library had been donated (King's MS 80–97).

17. *Letters*, I, 193 (no. 187.2); see also I, 192–93 (no. 187.1) and I, 193–94 (no. 187.3). A more detailed account of the collaboration can be found in Thomas M. Curley, "Johnson's Secret Collaboration," *The Unknown Samuel Johnson*, ed. John J. Burke, Jr., and Donald Kay (Madison: Univ. of Wisconsin Press, 1983), pp. 91–112.

18. *Works*, I, 113, 120. For other evidence of a collaboration continuing possibly until January 1770, see *Letters*, I, 196 (no. 189.1), I, 200 (no. 191.1), I, 222–23 (nos. 211, 211.1), I, 225 (no. 214), and I, 233 (no. 226.1). See also *Life*, II, 68 n. 1. Mrs. Thrale, in *Thraliana*, I, 204, lists among Johnson's works "Law Lectures for Chambers."

19. Walter Spencer Stanhope to John Stanhope, March 1767 and 5 April 1767, in *Annals of a Yorkshire House*, ed. A. M. W. Stirling, 2 vols. (London: John Lane, 1911), I, 205, 208. "Viner's Accounts" (Oxford University Archives, UC/A3/1) records annual Vinerian payments from 1757 to 1874 and documents by successively diminishing fines the gradual growth of the second Vinerian course from 1767 to 1770. Not until the academic year ending in July 1770 were sixty lectures at last delivered. For a list of starting dates for all seven annual presentations of Chambers's course, see E. L. McAdam, "Dr. Johnson's Law Lectures for Chambers, II," *Review of English Studies*, 16 (1940), 159–61.

20. McAdam was the first to claim a collaboration in "Dr. Johnson's Law Lectures for Chambers: An Addition to the Canon," *Review of English Studies*, 15 (1939), 385–91, and went so far as to quote lecture passages attributed to Johnson without much proof in *Dr. Johnson and the English Law* (Syracuse: Syracuse Univ. Press, 1951), pp. 65–122; hereafter cited as McAdam. Only two works, Sir (later Lord) Arnold McNair's *Dr. Johnson and the Law* (Cambridge: Cambridge Univ. Press, 1948), and Harold Greville Hanbury's *The Vinerian Chair and Legal Education* (Oxford: Basil Blackwell, 1958), have disputed the claim. Otherwise, a succession of distinguished scholars of Johnson—L. F. Powell, R. W. Chapman, W. J. Bate, James L. Clifford, and Donald Greene, to name a few—have accepted Johnson's authorship of at least portions of the law lectures. Greene's anthology, *Samuel Johnson* (1984), in The Oxford Authors Series, includes an entire Vinerian lecture as part of Johnson's canon, and John Vance's *Samuel Johnson and the Sense of History* (Athens, Ga.: Univ. of Georgia Press, 1984) takes into account Johnson's part in composing the lecture series. So far the most comprehensive study of the intellectual content of the lectures is James E. Reibman, "Dr. Johnson and the Law" (Diss., Univ. of Edinburgh, 1979). See also my introduction to Volume I of the *Lectures* for cautions about making specific attributions merely on the basis of a supposedly Johnsonian thought and style.

21. *Lectures*, Introduction, Lecture 1, par. 12. McAdam attributes this passage to Johnson, p. 83.

22. *Works*, X, 322, 325.

23. *Lectures*, Part I, Lecture 7, par. 7. McAdam attributes this passage to Johnson, p. 99.

24. *The Works of Samuel Johnson, L.L.D.*, 2 vols. (New York: George Dearborn, 1837), II, 606.

25. *Lectures*, Part I, Lecture 7, par. 2. McAdam attributes this passage to Johnson, pp. 97–98.

26. Parliamentary Debate on Spirituous Liquors, 23 February 1743, in *Works* (1825), XI, 464.

27. *Works*, X, 328.

28. Chambers, *Observations on Mr. Hastings's Plan for the Administration of Justice, including a Plan of Legislative and Executive Magistracy*, British Museum Add. MS. 39,998, ff. 288–303, completed originally by 24 January 1776 and sent to Johnson and other English friends from Calcutta on 29 March 1776. Capitalization of common nouns has been silently reduced to lower case in this quotation, as in all lecture passages.

29. *Lectures*, Introduction, Lecture 2, pars. 3, 4, 6. McAdam attributes this passage to Johnson, pp. 86–87.

30. *Works*, IX, 97–99.

31. *Lectures*, Part I, Lecture 15, par. 25. McAdam attributes this passage to Johnson, p. 105.

32. *Works*, X, 397.

33. *Works*, X, 418.

34. Frances Chambers, "Memoir of the Late Sir Robert Chambers, Knt.," in *Catalogue of the Sanskrit Manuscripts, Collected During His Residence in India, by the Late Sir Robert Chambers, Knt., Chief Justice of Bengal* (London: G. Roworth and Sons, 1838), p. 29.

35. Twiss, *Lord Chancellor Eldon*, I, 91, and John Bowring, *Memoirs of Bentham*, in Bowring's edition of *The Works of Jeremy Bentham*, 11 vols. (London, 1838–43), X, 45.

36. Chambers, "An Epistle from R. C. to Doctor Samuel Johnson on the Choice of Life," pp. 4–5.

37. *Life*, II, 260–62.

38. *Letters*, I, 334 (no. 313).

39. Robert Chambers to Ann Chambers, 3 August 1773, in The Hyde Collection.

40. *Letters*, I, 374 (no. 329.1).

41. *Letters*, I, 404 (no. 353.1); see also I, 402–404 (no. 353).

42. *Letters*, II, 62 (no. 417).

43. *Letters*, III, 19 (no. 835.1); see also III, 15 and n. 2 (no. 834).

44. Robert Chambers to Joseph Wilton, 29 March 1776, in The Hyde Collection.

45. *Letters*, III, 127 (no. 928). Despite an abiding admiration for Burke, Johnson, who was opposed to the Fox ministry, was certainly unsympathetic to an East India Bill that was widely considered to be an encroachment on the King's prerogatives.

46. *Letters*, III, 17–20 (no. 835.1).

47. ὀλβόν should be ὄλβον: "virtue and wealth." Johnson here contrasts an earlier valediction from the pagan Homeric Hymn 15 with a present blessing from the Christian-Hebraic tradition in Psalms 37.38 better suited to the solemnity of this final parting.

48. Sir William Scott to Sir Robert Chambers, 1787, in the possession of a descendant of Chambers, Mr. Richard A. Boyle of Hermongers Barn, Sussex, England, who generously gave me access to the letter.

49. *Letters*, I, 402 (no. 353).

ISOBEL GRUNDY

13 · The Techniques of Spontaneity: Johnson's Developing Epistolary Style

It was a critical truism of the eighteenth century that the familiar letter ought to be modeled on conversation. William Walsh gave a lead in 1692: "The Stile of letters ought to be free, easy and natural; as near approaching to familiar Conversation as possible." Steele popularized Walsh in an early *Tatler*: "I said there was no Rule in the World to be made for writing Letters, but that of being as near what you speak Face to Face as you can."[1] Literary opinion unanimously followed Steele.

This was a new departure in the theory of the letter. Katherine Gee Hornbeak has made it plain that even before English literary circles began to admire the French seventeenth-century masters of preciosity (Voiture, Balzac, and Scarron) the models of epistolary style recommended for humble imitators were elaborate, sententious, and antithetical. Confirmed by the French influence, this style persisted with "incredible longevity," in some cases past the close of the eighteenth century.[2]

Alongside it, however, flourished the identification of letters with talk, made usually without any analysis of what talk consists of. Though Lady Mary Wortley Montagu dismissed Mme de Sévigné's letters as "tittle tattle," the earliest instance that I know of rebellion against the well-worn analogy between letters and conversation comes from Mary Brunton in 1810:

> This letter-writing is but a poor affair after all. It carries on just such a conversation as we should do, if you were not to answer me till I had forgotten what I had said; turning your back to me too all the while you were speaking. A *triste* enough *confab.* you will allow![3]

Actual talk, of course, involves much more closely connected answering: the two voices alternate in a true exchange, with a rapidity unknown to letters. Those of us who are academics habitually write—or lecture—in longer sentences, more complete and extensive units of meaning, than we could use in even pedagogical talk without being vulnerable to a charge of rudely monopolizing it. The letter writer has no means of evading monologue.

The inevitable differences between letters and talk were not really confronted by those Restoration and eighteenth-century critics who so readily likened the one to the other. Still, among epistolary setters of fashion, French elaboration and preciosity gave way to an ideal to which, over and over again, two metaphors were applied: that of talking on paper and that of the mind (or heart) undressed. This generally meant not naked but *en negligé*, though it also offered scope for *doubles entendres*. (Pope put both metaphors together and seized the opportunity for bawdy implication throughout his correspondence with the safely distant Lady Mary, beginning with his opening letter.)[4] An air of relaxation became the polite ideal in correspondence as in talk. Any evidence of "study" (whether rigorous logic, or formality of structure, or flamboyant ornament) was out; intimacy and apparent carelessness were in.

But Johnson's talk, at least as reported by Boswell and other biographers, was not at all in this style: never even apparently careless. This is not to say that he was a monologuist, or failed to allow plenty of space for the other side of his conversations. Even when he ends a debate with a winning smash, he has generally allowed or encouraged a long rally beforehand. But, as we all know, he was always playing his best. Boswell recorded the comment that his spoken sentences were "so neatly constructed" that they "might have been all printed without any correction." A Miss Beresford who met him on a coach journey exclaimed: "How he does talk! Every sentence is an essay"[5]—and if suitable as a potential essay it would, according to the new orthodoxy, be unsuitable as a potential letter. Our impression of Johnson's talk may be less of structure or polish than of purposefulness and fierce concentration on its object; but that conversational utilitarianism is as remote from genteel ease as is the baroque elaboration of the seventeenth-century French.

Johnson, in his *Rambler* essay about epistolary style (no. 152; 31 August 1751), calls those Frenchmen "despicable" for their "adulatory professions" and "servile hyperboles." But he is no better pleased with Walsh's remarks on the equivalence of letters and talk. Walsh wrote that since the "two best Qualities in Conversation, are good Humour and good Breeding; those Letters are therefore certainly the best that shew the most of those two Qualities." Johnson, although he was to quote this remark under *letter* in the *Dictionary*, in the *Rambler* calls it a fit introduction to Walsh's "pages of inanity." The snub, I believe, is due to something more than Johnson's usual antiaristocratic stance. Though we may not readily associate him with good breeding, he often mentioned its importance, and just six months earlier had devoted *Rambler* 98 to inculcating it. Whatever Walsh's crime, it was not being on the side of good breeding.

Ramblers 98 and 152, on good breeding (chiefly in conversation) and on letter-writing, are, naturally enough, very much alike. Each betrays some anxiety about how to maintain dignity while descending from questions of obvious moral significance to "the minuter duties of social beings." Each asserts that little things and even trivial things *are* useful and even important—but each maintains the classification "little-and-trivial," and just as no. 98 applies this classification to social custom, no. 152 applies it to familiar letters.[6] That so few personal letters have been published in England, Johnson maintains, "must be imputed to our contempt of trifles, and our due sense of the dignity of the publick." To write a good letter, he says, "it is necessary to learn how to become little without becoming mean, to . . . fill up the vacuities of action by agreeable appearances," to grasp "the art of decorating insignificance."

His 1751 advice about epistolary style comes down, in defiance of contemporary orthodoxy, strongly on the side of decoration. While he agrees that the letter's basic purpose is to give pleasure, he denies that this implies spontaneity, let alone carelessness: "Wherever we are studious to please, we are afraid of trusting our first thoughts, and endeavour to recommend our opinion by studied ornaments, accuracy of method, and elegance of style." The epigrammatic as well as the lyrical, he points out, is a form of embellishment. He vigorously defends the letter's more specialized uses—its right to engage in highly structured narrative, or logical disputation, or rhetorical persuasion—and its right, therefore, to the particular styles appropriate to each. Even apart from these special occasional purposes, the letter aims "to preserve in the minds of the absent" not only love but also esteem—and "to excite love we must impart pleasure, [but] to raise esteem we must discover abilities." Not ease therefore but strenuousness, even display, is called for. In letter writing "words ought surely to be laboured" since "Trifles always require exuberance of ornament; the building which has no strength can be valued only for the grace of its decorations."

Johnson's early letters (those that have survived) are obviously written to this recipe: if they resemble talk, it is talk with those qualities which contemporaries found remarkable and unusual in Johnson's own. Their formality puts them quite out of step with current epistolary theory and practice.[7] The very earliest in Chapman's edition, from

1731, has a neatness of construction well worthy of print, and its subject matter (apology for long silence), though peculiarly the province of letters, is one well adapted to flourish and ornament:

> I can indeed make no apology but by assuring you that this delay, whatever was the cause of it, proceeded neither from forgetfulness, disrespect, nor Ingratitude; Time has not made the Sense of the Obligation less warm, nor the thanks I return less sincere.[8]

Dryden never structured a sentence in a dedication with more evident skill, or more care to rouse esteem rather than love. Four years later, writing to urge a correspondent to abandon ceremony, Johnson himself sounds prodigiously ceremonious, constrained, and stiff:

> Solitude is certainly one of the greatest obstacles to pleasure and improvement, and as he may be justly said to be alone, who has none to whom he imparts his thoughts, so he, who has a friend, though distant, with whom he converses without suspicion of being ridicul'd or betray'd, may be truly esteem'd to enjoy the advantages of Society.[9]

If we were to imagine this as spoken, I'm afraid the voice we should hear would be the voice of Joseph Surface.

As late as 1763, in his first letter to Boswell, Johnson mapped out formal rather than familiar requirements for his correspondence. Though he loved every aspect of talk with his friends, he says, he would not attempt to capture these pleasures on the page. He would never write just to share the details of his daily life or to put Boswell in mind of his affection: when absence prevented his doing these things in person they would not be done. His letters to Boswell would never be what he had seemed to expect letters to be in *Rambler* 152, "written only for the sake of writing" and for the promotion of friendship. Instead they would be restricted to those which might enable him to do an important duty or a real kindness.[10]

Despite their difference from each other, these statements of intent (*Rambler* 152 and the letter to Boswell) each tally with much that Johnson the letter writer put into practice. His letters encompass a wide range of special purposes (narrative, description, debate), but more frequent than any other purpose (in the letters to Boswell as much as any) is that of giving advice. In this Johnson was following ancient epistolary tradition, but following it with an energy and versatility all his own. He issues by letter theological persuasion, practical instruction (on every kind of literary project, on choosing books, on the economics of publishing, and on surviving divorce), and moral advice on every imaginable human dilemma. He is one of the very few writers who can make something worth reading out of advice to a young child to be good. Never in later life would he remind anyone of

Joseph Surface, but he continues to fill his letters with aphorisms and with general positions to which he relates the particular case under consideration.[11] His epistolary sentences continue to make it quite clear that thought and choice have gone into their ordering. They have not flowed unconscious from his pen.

Yet the *kind* of thought and choice do change, as we shall see at once when we come to consider the kind of effect Johnson aims at in his later letters. From his letters to Hester Thrale we know that—at least in the 1770s and 1780s, the brief span that produced the vast majority of all his letters that we have—Johnson did wholeheartedly adopt the "topicks with which those letters are commonly filled which are written only for the sake of writing." The subjects which he told Boswell in 1763 that he would *not* write on—

> that I am or am not well, that I have or have not been in the country, that I drank your health in the room in which we sat last together, and that your acquaintance continue to speak of you with their former kindness

—are exactly those which later make up the bulk of his epistolary material, outweighing practical instruction and even moral advice. And there is clearly some connection between this new commitment to common topics and a shift in Johnson's style.

The remarks I quoted about Johnson's "method of conversation" have another side to them. Having noted the correctness and printworthiness of Johnson's talk, they continue: "At the same time, it was easy and natural; the accuracy of it had no appearance of labour, constraint, or stiffness." In other words, Boswell's informant here does claim for Johnson the expected qualities of the letter writer, and disclaims the qualities that I find in Johnson's earliest letters.[12] The Johnson we know so well from Boswell, Hester Thrale, and Fanny Burney spoke with *both* formality and ease, and his late letters likewise encompass both.

In conversation Johnson "never sought to please till past thirty years old, considering the matter as hopeless";[13] it was still later before he formed a letter writing style in which to please. The opening pages of Chapman's edition, the all too few letters remaining from Johnson's youth, exhibit no stylistic features which are purely epistolary, or any less appropriate to any other genre: no rhetorical questions that seem to imply exchange even in what is actually a monologue, no private allusions or private jokes, no "negligence of transition" or ellipsis or incomplete syntax, no unconventional directness or assumption of intimacy (any of which would go far to dissipate the impression of labor). Johnson's one surviving letter to his wife is just as formal and measured in style as any other from the 1740s, despite its use of "thou" and "thee." The business-like letters to Edward Cave make just the very faintest, most distant approach to becoming familiar when they become colloquial or elliptical: "nothing in it is well," Johnson writes about something or other in Latin, and again (as an exclamation) "If I had but good Pens"—which is doubly obscure because only doubtfully legible.[14]

It is not until July 1749 that we first hear the accents of speech from Johnson's pen, as he bursts out to Lucy Porter: "You frighted me, you little Gipsy, with your black wafer . . ." This opens the third and last paragraph of a letter which up to there was brisk and not informal; the first two paragraphs sound written, but this sounds spoken. The colloquial word "frighted," the humorous abuse cloaking affection and depth of emotion, the reference to an event occurring privately between his correspondent and himself, are all hallmarks of the genuinely familiar style. The black wafer had made Johnson think for a moment that his mother had died: he was frightened; then he must have been relieved; *then* he wrote two business paragraphs of his answer in just the way he would have done without the fright, and without referring to it. But when he has once expressed his fear, that leads him away from his sequences of carefully planned subordinate clauses into a string of loose, brief, and simple coordinates suggestive of a naive stylist like Defoe: "I long to know how she dos [*sic*] and how you all do. Your poor Mamma is come home but very weak yet I hope she will grow better, else she shall go into the country. She is now upstairs and knows not of my writing." There is something here of Johnson's earlier directness to Cave, something of the bareness of his expression at times of emotional stress (as in his surviving note to Taylor on his wife's death), something too of his later simplicity to children: everything most characteristic of his letters and quite uncharacteristic of his printed works.[15]

During the 1750s we can trace Johnson's gradual development of a style for intimate friendship in his letters to the Warton brothers. These are not revealing to the same degree as the letter to Lucy Porter, but they are immensely more revealing than any earlier ones that have survived. Writing on 8 March 1753 to invite Joseph Warton to contribute to the *Adventurer*, Johnson makes the element of compliment (which he had found objectionable in the French, and had used himself objectionably in 1731) both subordinate to and indistinguishable from the business aim of the letter. The element of apology, which had been so obtrusive in 1731, is offhandedly disposed of at the beginning with "Dear Sir / I ought to have written to you before now, but I ought to do many things which I do not." This, I think, is a deliberate flouting of an epistolary convention that Johnson had earlier observed. Now he *assumes* both Warton's honest recognition of his own value and his tolerance for his correspondent's minor failings; he both states these things and understates them. The result is that his whole letter, while concentrating on its practical task, breathes a spirit of friendly trust, and therefore even of intimacy, precisely by the way it avoids any more elaborately fashioned compliment or apology.[16]

In this correspondence, without very much detail about his own or the Wartons' activities, with hardly any anecdote, Johnson nevertheless hits the tone of warmth, humor, and freshness that was to characterize his later, best-known letters. The style he writes is not far from the business one developed in notes to Cave (closely related, therefore, to the "vital" but also "humdrum" indigenous models of purely practical epistolary composition which Hornbeak sees as growing up alongside the still flourishing ornate models).[17] With the Wartons as with Cave Johnson has literary business to transact: here and there prose gives way to lists, but also the exhilaration of the scholarly search blends effortlessly with the thread of pathos supplied by repeated expressions of anxiety for the mutually beloved Collins.

The personal holds its own with the professional: this correspondence provides us with examples of practically every trick of style that discriminates the epistolary from all other manners: what we may call the techniques of spontaneity. These few and short letters incorporate reference to the moment of writing ("Dear Sir / I am sat down to answer your kind letter"), unattached exclamation ("Poor dear Collins—"), friendly mockery ("Your Brother, who is a better correspondent than you, and not much better"), and self-mockery:

> I have a great mind to come to Oxford at Easter, but you will not invite me, shall I come uninvited or stay here where nobody perhaps would miss me if I went. a hard choice but such is the world to / Dear Sir, Your most humble servant / Sam: Johnson[18]

This last passage again mocks an epistolary convention: the weaving of the concluding salutation into the structure of the final sentence which Chapman calls "the syntactical conclusion." These "studied varieties of phrase" were seen by informalists like Boswell as a "species of affectation in writing"; they were admired by proponents of epistolary elaboration like Johnson, who called them "more elegant, and, in addressing persons of high rank . . . likewise more respectful" than something less studied or capable of variation.[19] Johnson wove this conclusion for Thomas Warton just six weeks after a more famous example for a person of high rank, none other than Lord Chesterfield:

> I have been long wakened from that Dream of hope, in which I once boasted myself with so much exultation, My lord Your Lordship's Most humble Most Obedient Servant, / Sam: Johnson[20]

The ostentatious respect which is conveyed by the tradition when exercised appropriately on a noble patron, albeit a rejected one, becomes matter for jest when directed with elaborate self-mockery to an equal. Though the ending he composes for his friend is in itself studied or affected, his words are short, his syntax simple (the phrase "a hard choice" manages without syntax altogether) and the manner childishly direct.

Expressions of affection, and more particularly of praise and gratitude, play a large part in these letters, but almost always mingled with teasing: "Though not to write when a man can write so well is an offence sufficiently heinous yet I shall pass it by"; "That way of publishing without acquainting your friends is a wicked trick"; "You might write to me now and then, if you were good for any thing, but *honores mutant mores*. Professors forget their friends." (This to Thomas, who was now Professor of Poetry.)[21]

These letters make much of their own insignificance. "Dear Mr Warton let me hear from you, and tell me something I care not what so I hear it but from you." If one of Johnson's should be lost, "the miscarriage of it will be no great matter, as I have nothing to send but thanks."[22] Much of their subject matter has no existence outside the letter, but is invented for the occasion, as talk so often is. Johnson not only quotes widely, in keeping with his correspondents' scholarly interests—Homer, Virgil, Lucretius, Ariosto, Horace, Polydore Vergil, Pope—but also plays with his quoted authors. He deliberately adapts Virgil to aggrandize himself or his *Dictionary*; he hijacks a dignified claim of disinterestedness from Pope's *Epistle to Dr. Arbuthnot* to make a present of it to Thomas Warton (who, he says, can sleep without a modus as Pope could "sleep without a Poem in my head" and without worry about hostile critics.[23] He presents "Professors forget their friends" as if it were a bungled attempt at translating a much more general Latin statement, so that the moral aphorism is burlesqued.

When Johnson does use any elaborated effect in these letters he generally turns it to nonformal or antiformal, that is, to specifically epistolary uses. Early in 1755, nearing completion of the *Dictionary*, he writes, "I now begin to see land, after having wandered, according to Mr Warburton's phrase, in this vast sea of words." He develops the image to foresee his critical reception as a landing of Ulysses who may face either acclaim or condemnation, "a Calypso that will court or a Polypheme that will eat me." All this, though in its way apt, has also the humor of deliberate incongruity and irresponsible imaginative play. Johnson would hardly have written it for print, and Thomas Warton, copying it out, seems to have felt it was too much, since he changed "eat me" to "resist." The fun reaches a climax as Johnson exclaims, "But if Polypheme comes to me have at his eyes." (Chapman in a footnote expresses surprise at Johnson's "inadvertence" in ascribing "'eyes' to the notoriously monocular Cyclops"; myself I should be inclined to suspect the presence of one of those private jokes or deliberate errors that make the editing of letters such a minefield.) [24]

It is also entirely characteristic that this fantasy should be followed by a naked admission of an emotional weak spot: Johnson does not fear the critics' skill or strength, but "I am a little afraid of myself, and would not willingly feel so much ill-will in my bosom as literary quarrels are apt to excite." The playful manner is not inimical to direct expression of feeling: far from it. Johnson has already felt free to write to Joseph, "I enter my name among those that love, and that love you more and more in proportion as by writing more you are more known." [25]

This correspondence alone shows us, without adducing those with Bennet Langton and Hill Boothby and others, that ten years or so before Johnson abjured petty epistolary subject matter in writing to Boswell he was already a master of it, and that *Rambler* 152 was written almost if not quite simultaneously with letters in a newly relaxed, heterogeneous and playful style. The essay coincides pretty nearly with the watershed which apparently divides Johnson's early, formal letters from his far more numerous later ones.

We might easily conclude from this that in its vindication of "studied ornaments" and "accuracy of method" in letters it looks backwards, not forwards. But that I think would be wrong. Johnson's mature letters are also in their own way remarkable for "exuberance of ornament." Whenever he wrote with friendship as his primary end, he continued to illustrate his *Rambler* observations that the letter writer who "has no present to make but a garland, a ribbon, or some petty curiosity, must endeavour to recommend it by his manner of giving it," and that pleasure will be communicated as well as esteem raised "by scenes of imagery, points of conceit, unexpected sallies and artful compliments." This group of four categories effectively embraces the means he uses to interrupt directness and simplicity, and to make up the variety of his own epistolary style. (It is not true, of course, that *all* his letters employ these methods at any period of his life, for practical business is often uppermost. Often Johnson's letters are so direct that their style seems indistinguishable from saying the simplest thing in the shortest manner—not his habit in works for the printer.) But just as "scenes of imagery, points of conceit, unexpected sallies and artful compliments" are displayed in his early, formal letters, so we can identify a new kind of each of these in his later, informal letters, as my quotations from those to the Wartons exemplify.

This truly epistolary style, which would be inappropriate outside the confines of a letter, reaches its apogee in Johnson's letters to Hester

Thrale, which in many ways repeat more fully and richly the elements of those to the Wartons. In preferring these letters to any of Johnson's other correspondences, I concur with many common readers but differ from Chapman. Valuing most highly in Johnson's letters his "success in accommodating their matter and their manner to the character and abilities of his correspondents," he thought the most interesting correspondence that with Boswell,

> who had good reason to be proud of being thus admitted to a share in his master's deepest meditations. The letters to Mrs. Thrale are on a different plane, and show a facet of Johnson hardly ever seen in the *Life*. Though they are never patronizing they are limited by her power of appreciation. On the other hand they are enriched by her feminine intuitions, which permitted an allusiveness that would have been out of keeping if addressed to a Boswell or a Langton.[26]

This seems to be a misapprehension of allusiveness, which does not demand intuition (whether feminine or not) for its decipherment, but rather shared areas of knowledge. It is an important tool for the creation of epistolary intimacy, that sense of sharing which the most skillful letter writers are able to conjure up on their solitarily written pages. Johnson's letters to the Wartons are packed with allusion to their shared experience of books; Hester Thrale shared less with Johnson in this area than they, but still a great deal, and in addition she shared the whole expanse of knowledge which a common daily life offers—knowledge of the same routine, people, animals, opinions, anecdotes, and jokes.

The writing of letters, it seems to me, is governed by a paradox related to that which Johnson put forward about biography: it demands an intimate knowledge the possession of which will usually prevent writing at all. The best letters are written between those who not only have sufficient talent or intellectual capacity but who also "have eat and drunk and lived in social intercourse" together;[27] but that intercourse must normally be broken before letters will be written. According to this criterion we should expect Johnson to write his best letters to Hester Thrale, and of his letters to Boswell we should expect the best to be those written after the shared experience of the Scottish journey.

This I believe is the case: not that these letters are simply the most charming, but that they are the most epistolary—epistolary, that is, in the new manner. The high proportion of advice in most of Johnson's letters to Boswell puts them in the center of the tradition as he inherited it; it is qualities shared with the Hester Thrale letters—allusiveness and conscious imaginative shaping of friendship as well as passive recording of it—that relate them also to the tradition as he passed it on. With the publication of many of his letters by these two not long after his death, Johnson became an influence on the development of the new letter writing which, like other relaxed eighteenth-century styles (landscape gardening, realistic fiction, naturalistic acting), is a product of the art which conceals art. This kind of writing implicitly recognizes its differences from conversation as a two-dimensional canvas recognizes its differences from the painter's three-dimensional subject matter, and has evolved methods for representing conversation rather than mimicking it.

These are Johnson's techniques of spontaneity, the methods by which he uses letters themselves to create a relationship which is similar to but not identical with the real-life relationship on which the correspondence is based. He regularly summons his absent correspondent to take an imaginary place in the letter by supposedly responding to its contents or supplying a contrasting view. This is a rich source of "scenes of imagery, points of conceit, unexpected sallies and artful compliments." He pictures Thomas Warton confined by duty to his students, Hester Thrale electioneering, Boswell making Johnson himself matter for discussion in his own domestic circle. At the same time the fancifulness of this proceeding is recognized: Johnson not only sketches but caricatures his intimate correspondents, as he does with himself in the vignette of his Ulyssean arrival from the sea of words.

The fact that the letter writer is constantly at work on such imaginary scenarios makes misquotation and misapplication the most serviceable kind of literary allusion for his purposes. The quotations or citations in the Warton correspondence include only one used with perfect seriousness, in the sense that Johnson wishes to call into his letter the full intellectual and emotional force of the original: this is an obscure line from Euripides, applied to his continuing sorrow after his wife's death.[28] The ten or a dozen other allusions (they are difficult to count, some being very general references to a well-known trope or proverb and others multiple, like simultaneous involvement of Ariosto and Homer, or Warburton and Pope) are all at least partly in jest. Most of them apply to Johnson's own affairs (notably the appearance of his *Dictionary*), words invented for more glamorous contexts. They not only perform a specifically mock-heroic or reductive function but also create an atmosphere in which implications are multiple, puzzling, or ambivalent. Through them Johnson presents the happenings of his own life in such a doubtful light as to appeal for his correspondent's response, for comment and interpretation, and so to contribute to the effect of exchange.

The method of allusiveness and multiplicity is seen at its peak in two passages Johnson sent Hester Thrale on the subject of letter writing.[29] They catch in their fire his correspondent (as competitor), himself (as boaster) and the genre of letter writing (as mirror of the naked soul, as embodiment of Nature and Friendship, as equal of Shakespeare and the ancients, and as exemplar of the miscellaneous, the irregular, and the meandering). In each case Johnson is thinking of letters as *writing upon nothing*, the ultimate test of creativity. In each case critical praise is lavished; ironical reserve is only hinted.

> Nothing is inverted, nothing distorted, you see systems in their elements, you discover actions in their motives. . . . The original Idea is laid down in its simple purity, and all the supervenient conceptions, are spread over it stratum super stratum, as they happen to be formed.

This expresses Johnson's sardonic enjoyment of the theory that spontaneity guarantees communication. He was actually so far from believing that an "original Idea" and its "supervenient conceptions" can be conveyed entire from one brain to another without toil and trouble, just "as they happen to be formed," that he had evolved a specialized rhetoric which creates just those nonce words and nonce scenes that exist only for the purpose of sharing. Yet the rhetoric that must create its own material is also the subject of his mockery.

> Can you write such a letter as this? So miscellaneous, with such noble disdain of regularity, like Shakespeare's works, such graceful negligence of transition like the ancient enthusiasts. The pure voice of nature and of friendship.

The delight of this passage lies in its communication of energy and enjoyment; the joke is, of course, that to achieve naturalness requires so much effort. To savor the joke quite perfectly, we might have to be Hester Thrale—to share the memory of particular past conversations which Johnson is undoubtedly drawing on here—but, more practicably, we also need to share some knowledge of eighteenth-century theories of the relation of literature to nature, and especially of letter writing to nature.

This kind of multiple allusiveness—to specific, unexplained, shared private memories, to particular writers, to the whole both venerable and mockable literary tradition, the minuter epistolary tradition, and to a broad intellectual background which may also be treated among friends with playful exasperation—marks Johnson's letters to the Wartons and many others, but more particularly those to Hester Thrale. It makes them the finest of all Johnson's remarkable letters, both because they are the most epistolary, the least like any other genre of writing, and because they are—by conscious choice and effort, not by handing over to an automatic pilot—the most fully reflective of a complex, self-conscious, private mind.

NOTES

1. William Walsh, *Letters and Poems, Amorous and Gallant* (London, 1692), preface, Sig. A2ᵛ; Richard Steele, *Tatler* 30, 16–18 Jan. 1709.

2. Hornbeak, *The Complete Letter Writer in England, 1568–1800* (Northampton, Mass., 1934), pp. 41ff, 74.

3. Montagu to Lady Bute, 20 July 1754 (*Complete Letters*, ed. Robert Halsband, 3 vols. [Oxford: Clarendon Press, 1965–67], III, 62, also 215); Brunton to Mrs. Izett, 30 Aug. 1810, in her husband's "Memoir of Her Life" (*Emmeline, With Some Other Pieces* [Edinburgh, 1819], p. xxxvii).

4. Pope to Lady Mary, 18 Aug. [1716], *Correspondence*, ed. George Sherburn, 5 vols. (Oxford: Clarendon Press, 1956), I, 352–53). She also used the same images, e.g. to Sir James Steuart, 18 Oct. [1758], 19 July 1759: III, 182–83, 221.

5. Boswell, *Life*, IV, 236, 283–84.

6. *Works*, V, 42–47; IV, 159–64.

7. R. W. Chapman, discussing the special case of the salutations and closes used by Johnson, concludes that he is "a little, but only a little, more formal and stately than the average of his kind"—that is, of scholars or academics ("The Formal Parts of Johnson's Letters" in *Essays on the Eighteenth Century Presented to David Nichol Smith in Honour of his Seventieth Birthday* [Oxford: Clarendon Press, 1945], p. 153).

8. To Gregory Hickman, 30 Oct. 1731 (*Letters*, I, 1 [no. 1]).

9. To Richard Congreve, 25 June 1735 (*Letters*, I, 6 [no. 3.2]).

10. *Letters*, I, 164 (no. 163).

11. Cf. Isobel Grundy, "Samuel Johnson: Man of Maxims?" (*Samuel Johnson: New Critical Studies*, ed. Isobel Grundy [London: Vision Press, 1984], pp. 13–30).

12. *Life*, IV, 237.

13. Hester Lynch Piozzi, *Anecdotes of the Late Samuel Johnson, LL.D., during the Last Twenty Years of His Life*, ed. Arthur Sherbo (London: Oxford Univ. Press, 1974), p. 145.

14. 31 Jan. 1740, Autumn 1743 (*Letters*, I, 15–17, 21 and n. 6 [nos. 12, 15]).

15. 12 July 1749; I, 31 (no. 25).

16. I, 47–48 (no. 46).

17. Hornbeak, *Complete Letter Writer*, pp. 77, 86.

18. *Letters*, I, 60, 58, 63, 67 (nos. 57, 55, 60, 64 [20 March 1755]).

19. Chapman, "The Formal Parts of Johnson's Letters," p. 152; Boswell, *Life*, V, 238–39.

20. 7 Feb. 1755 (*Letters*, I, 64 [no. 61]).

21. *Letters*, I, 67, 90, 103 (nos. 65, 96, 109).

22. *Letters*, I, 67, 60 (nos. 64, 57).

23. *Letters*, I, 66 (no. 64); Pope, *Arbuthnot* (1735), lines 269–70.

24. 1 Feb. 1755 (*Letters*, I, 61 and n. [no. 58]). Some years later "Polyphemus" was the Hawkins children's nickname for Johnson; see Laetitia-Matilda Hawkins, *Memoirs, Anecdotes, Facts, and Opinions* (London, 1824), I, 86.

25. 8 March 1754; *Letters*, I, 53–54 (no. 51).

26. *Letters*, I, xix.

27. *Life*, II, 166.

28. 21 Dec. 1754 (*Letters*, I, 59 [no. 56]). For a particularly useful discussion, see William Kinsley, "'Allusion' in the Eighteenth Century: The Disinherited Critic," in *Man and Nature: Proceedings of the Canadian Society for Eighteenth-Century Studies*, III, ed. Robert James Merrett (Edmonton, Alberta: Academic Printing and Publishing, 1984), pp. 23–46.

29. 25 Oct. 1777, 11 April 1780: *Letters*, II, 228–29, 340–41 (nos. 559, 657). No. 559 especially has been a target of critical debate. William Henry Irving denied Johnson

was being facetious and ironical, though he found the resultant message out of character; see *The Providence of Wit in the English Letter-Writers* (Durham, N.C.: Duke Univ. Press, 1955), pp. 289–90. Howard Anderson and Irvin Ehrenpreis disagree; see "The Familiar Letter in the Eighteenth Century: Some Generalizations," in *The Familiar Letter in the Eighteenth Century*, ed. Anderson, Philip B. Daghlian, and Ehrenpreis (Lawrence, Kan.: Univ. of Kansas Press, 1966), p. 272.

BRIAN CORMAN

14 · Johnson and Profane Authors:
The Lives *of Otway and Congreve*

The wickedness of a loose or profane author is more atrocious than that
of the giddy libertine, or drunken ravisher, not only because it extends
its effects wider; as a pestilence that taints the air is more destructive
than poison infused in a draught, but because it is committed with cool
deliberation. By the instantaneous violence of desire a good man may
sometimes be surprised before reflection can come to his rescue; when
the appetites have strengthened their influence by habit, they are not
easily resisted or suppress'd; but for the frigid villany of studious lewdness, for the calm malignity of laboured impiety, what apology can be
invented? What punishment can be adequate to the crime of him who
retires to solitudes for the refinement of debauchery; who tortures his
fancy, and ransacks his memory, only that he may leave the world less
virtuous than he found it; that he may intercept the hopes of the rising
generation; and spread snares for the soul with more dexterity?[1]

As this passage (from *The Rambler* 77) clearly indicates, the very concept of a profane author offended Johnson deeply, in part, no doubt
because of his pride in his own profession. Yet when he considers individual cases, he often allows his compassion to soften his moral response to human frailty. Dryden's works, for example, "afford too
many examples of dissolute licentiousness and abject adulation; but
they were probably, like his merriment, artificial and constrained—
the effects of study and meditation, and his trade rather than his pleasure."[2] Admirers of the *Lives* rightly "wonder" with Lawrence Lipking
at how "much clear-eyed condemnation can coexist with a regard for
the poet."[3]

Ralph Rader has remarked that the greatness of Johnson the biographer lies in the "universality of judgment" he is able to achieve
rather than in the "inherent universality" of his subjects. "The pleasure of Johnson's *Lives* is Johnson, not Pope or Addison."[4] The emphasis, then, is on the process of judgment rather than in the presentation

of those facts which lead to judgment. I would add that the *Lives* are most thoroughly triumphant when they reveal the internal dialogue between the profound moralist and the sympathetic student of human nature in the very formation of the Johnsonian judgment. The process of judgment informs Johnson's inquiries into the lives of Otway and Congreve, but since his moral principles so thoroughly overpower his more humane instincts, *Otway* and *Congreve* are not among Johnson's most successful biographies. The critical sections of these *Lives*, however, offer an interesting contrast, for here Johnson reveals the kind of balanced judgment that characterizes his finest discussions of literary texts.

Johnson wastes little time before establishing the tenor of his judgment of Otway. The *Life of Otway* begins: "Of Thomas Otway, one of the first names in the English drama, little is known; nor is there any part of that little which his biographer can take pleasure in relating" (*Lives*, I, 241). What little Johnson knows about Otway characteristically comes from secondary sources. An examination of his use of his sources reveals how thoroughly he has managed, despite his ignorance, to judge Otway. Because there is the predictably high percentage of overlap among these sources (often virtually word for word), it is difficult to determine with certainty where Johnson got much of his information; nonetheless he seems to have worked most closely with the *Lives of the Poets*, ghostwritten for Cibber by Johnson's old friend and amanuensis Robert Shiels.[5] Shiels, to cite a single example, is the only one of Otway's earlier biographers to provide an explanation for Otway's failure as an actor: "he is said to have failed in want of execution, which is so material to a good player, that a tolerable execution, with advantage of a good person, will often supply the place of judgment, in which it is not to be supposed Otway was deficient."[6] Shiels's distinction between execution and judgment, though not his use of it in defense of Otway, may well be the only aspect of his treatment of Otway that genuinely interested Johnson. The result is a lengthy reformulation of Shiels's argument, which is probably the most engaging passing in the *Life of Otway*.[7]

Further comparison with Shiels's Otway reveals more about Johnson's attitude toward Otway the man. Both, for example, discuss Otway's brief military career. Shiels's version of the anecdote notes his commission and the brevity of his service, and then tries to explain this embarrassing fact:

> It is not natural to suppose that it proceeded from actual cowardice, or that Mr. Otway had drawn down any disgrace upon himself by misbehaviour in a military station. . . . Yet we have some reason to conjecture that Mr. Otway felt a strong disinclination to a military life, perhaps from a consciousness that his heart failed him, and a dread of

misbehaving, should he ever be called to an engagement; and to avoid the shame of which he was apprehensive in consequence of such behaviour, he, in all probability, resigned his commission.[8]

Johnson's version alters the tone from advocacy to impartial—but eyebrow-raising—neutrality: "Otway did not prosper in his military character; for he soon left his commission behind him, whatever was the reason, and came back to London" (*Lives*, I, 244).

Impassive compression of this sort is typical of the way in which Johnson manipulates his source material in the biographical section of the *Life of Otway*. It is a particularly effective method, as used by Johnson, for conveying moral implication. Nowhere is this more clear than in his discussion of perhaps the central issue for Otway's biographers, his relationship to his society, and particularly to the aristocracy which so dominated it. Johnson retells the familiar story as follows:

> Want of morals or of decency did not in those days exclude any man from the company of the wealthy and the gay if he brought with him any powers of entertainment; and Otway is said to have been at this time a favourite companion of the dissolute wits. But, as he who desires no virtue in his companion has no virtue in himself, those whom Otway frequented had no purpose of doing more for him than to pay his reckoning. They desired only to drink and laugh; their fondness was without benevolence, and their familiarity without friendship. Men of wit, says one of Otway's biographers, received at that time no favour from the Great but to share their riots; "from which they were dismissed again to their own narrow circumstances. Thus they languished in poverty without the support of innocence."
>
> (*Lives*, I, 243)

Though Johnson takes no pains to quote accurately, he chooses carefully the point at which to curtail his narrative. His source here, the preface to the 1712 edition of Otway's *Works*, continues by adding that "We know indeed no guilty Part in Mr. *Otway's* Life, any other than those fashionable Faults which usually recommend to the Conversation of Men in Courts; but which serve for Excuses for their Patrons, when they have not a Mind to do for them."[9] Shiels, likewise, had lifted this passage from his predecessor's work but was not content to leave it at that. He added:

> From the example of Mr. Otway, succeeding poets should learn not to place any confidence in the promises of patrons; it discovers a higher spirit, and reflects more honour on a man to struggle nobly for independance, by means of industry, then servilely to wait at a great man's gate, or to sit at his table, meerly to afford him diversion. . . . But who can read Mr. Otway's story, without indignation at those idols of greatness, who demand worship from men of genius, and yet can suffer them to live miserably, and die neglected?[10]

Though these passages ring Johnsonian,[11] both in substance and attitude, Johnson himself remains silent on Otway's misfortunes. Nor does he pursue the contentions of Shiels and the earlier biographers that Otway was persecuted by "powerful enemies" intent on his ruin.[12] In fact, the only genuinely sympathetic statement Johnson allows to Otway the man is that "he appears, by some of his verses, to have been a zealous royalist, and had what was in those times the common reward of loyalty; he lived and died neglected" (*Lives*, I, 248). And even this is tacked on to the end of the *Life* without previous context, thus appearing to be more a comment on a favorite universal problem than an encouragement of generous thoughts about Otway.

The following statement might well have provided the topic sentence for the *Life of Otway*: "an irregular and dissipated Manner of Life had made him the Slave of every Passion . . . and that Slavery to Passions reciprocally produces a Life irregular and dissipated."[13] The subject, of course, is Richard Savage, and the difference between Johnson's representation of Savage and of Otway points to the problem of the *Life of Otway*. With an eye on the *Life of Savage*, Paul Alkon describes Johnson's analysis of moral character as follows: "Though he certainly holds the individual morally accountable for his conduct, Johnson's sympathetic awareness of the social pressures that are in many instances 'out of our power' ultimately prevents his moral essays from degenerating into doctrinaire prescriptions."[14] It is precisely this sense of sympathetic awareness (present in the accounts of Shiels and others) that is absent from the *Life of Otway*. Because Johnson conceives of Otway as a man fundamentally in "want of morals and of decency," he fails to temper his moral condemnation with more charitable reflections.

No early eighteenth-century man of letters was better liked than William Congreve. In literary circles alone his friends included Dryden, Southerne, Addison, Steele, Vanbrugh, Garth, Walsh, Swift, Pope, Gay, Tonson, Gildon, Dennis, Lady Mary Wortley Montagu— one could go on and on. Congreve's social skills must have been considerable to say the least. Yet, as Congreve's most recent and thorough biographer points out, "anyone who reads the many contemporary statements about Congreve's qualities as a man, and then, in chronological order, the scores of biographical sketches that appeared during the next two centuries, cannot help recognizing that, as time went on, Congreve the man—as distinguished from the dramatist— became progressively more distasteful to his biographers."[15] The most influential eighteenth-century biographer to find him distasteful was Samuel Johnson, who is perhaps second only to Macaulay in damaging Congreve's reputation with posterity. The method is the same as for Otway: Johnson constructs his character from available source material and then compresses that material to produce a coherent, unified portrait.

Again, as with Otway, it is the controversial aspect of Congreve's life that most damaged the prominent reputation he held with his contemporaries. They are: his place of birth, his reasons for quitting the stage, his attitude toward his profession, and his will. Congreve was born in Yorkshire and moved to Ireland with his family at age four. This is what he told Giles Jacob, and it has been confirmed in parish records by Malone and Hodges among others. Congreve's friend and fellow dramatist, Thomas Southerne, himself an Irishman, seems responsible for the rumor that Congreve in fact was born in Ireland. And while it is rejected by Charles Wilson, the pseudonymous author of the *Memoirs of the Life, Writings, and Amours of William Congreve Esq.*, by Shiels, and by the *Biographia Britannica*, as well as by Jacob, the source Johnson acknowledges, Johnson, notwithstanding, follows Southerne in accepting Ireland as Congreve's birthplace: "Neither the time nor place of his birth is certainly known: if the inscription upon his monument be true he was born in 1672. For the place, it was said by himself that he owed his nativity to England, and by every body else that he was born in Ireland. Southern mentioned him with sharp censure, as a man that meanly disowned his native country" (*Lives*, II, 212). The reason Johnson chose to follow Southerne becomes clear when he proceeds to the following generalization:

> To doubt whether a man of eminence has told the truth about his own birth is, in appearance, to be very deficient in candour; yet nobody can live long without knowing that falsehoods of convenience or vanity, falsehoods from which no evil immediately visible ensues, except the general degradation of human testimony, are very lightly uttered, and once uttered are sullenly supported. Boileau, who desired to be thought a rigorous and steady moralist, having told a petty lie to Lewis XIV. continued it afterwards by false dates; thinking himself obliged "in honour," says his admirer, to maintain what, when he said it, was so well received.
>
> (*Lives*, II, 213)

Johnson is more concerned with finding desired judgments in the facts than with the facts themselves—even if this necessitates turning to less reliable sources. His interest here, as indicated by the inclusion of the lengthy Boileau anecdote, is in establishing the nature of Congreve's weakness in the most universal terms possible. Thus, in the third paragraph of the *Life of Congreve* vanity emerges as the central motivating force in Congreve's life. And the *Life* itself becomes more an exemplification of human vanity than an inquiry into the known facts about William Congreve.

Johnson mentions in passing that "Congreve, a very young man, elated with success, and impatient of censure" (*Lives*, II, 222), in his defense against Collier, chides the parson for taking *The Old Batchelour* seriously, as it was the product of the convalescence of an adolescent boy. Johnson, like Collier, responds to Congreve's flippancy with hostility: "There seems to be a strange affectation in authors of appearing to have done every thing by chance. *The Old Batchelour* was written for amusement, in the languor of convalescence. Yet it is apparently composed with great elaborateness of dialogue, and incessant ambition of wit" (*Lives*, II, 214). The studied pose which a Congreve could adopt, another sign of his vanity, was intolerable to Johnson.

The Collier controversy was, of course, a central event in Congreve's career. For Shiels, for the *Biographia Britannica*, and for the *Biographia Dramatica*, it "had begun . . . that disgust to the theatre" which was completed by "the indifferent success" of *The Way of the World*.[16] Eighteenth-century critics assumed, partially from Dryden's report and partially from the defensiveness of Congreve's dedicatory preface and "Epilogue," that the play was a failure. It was, in fact, a modest success, but the mysterious Charles Wilson, for one, nevertheless helped perpetuate the tale of its failure: "The unkind Reception this excellent Comedy met with, was truly the Cause of Mr. *Congreve's* just Resentment; and upon which, I have often heard him declare, that he had form'd a strong Resolution never more to concern himself with Dramatical Writings."[17] It is Wilson's view that the audience rejection of *The Way of the World* precipitated Congreve's quitting the stage, and it is this view which Johnson accepts: "Congreve's last play was *The Way of the World*, which, though as he hints in his dedication it was written with great labour and much thought, was received with so little favour, that, being in a high degree offended and disgusted, he resolved to commit his quiet and his fame no more to the caprices of an audience" (*Lives*, II, 223–24). Although this claim had been challenged by Johnson's friend Thomas Davies and others, Johnson chooses audience rejection rather than the Collier controversy (or a combination of the two) as the principal cause for Congreve's early retirement again to emphasize Congreve's vanity.

What was perhaps the greatest single contribution to the legend of Congreve's vanity emerged from Voltaire's visit to Congreve during his exile in England. Voltaire was a great admirer of Congreve's comedies and praises them highly, but he also notes his disappointment in the man:

> He was old and almost dying when I knew him; he had one defect, that of insufficiently valuing his first profession of a writer, which made his reputation and his fortune. He spoke to me of his works as bagatelles beneath him, and asked me, in our first conversation, to view him only as a very ordinary gentleman. I replied that if he had the misfortune to

be only a gentleman, like all the others, I should never have come to see him, and I was shocked by this misplaced vanity.[18]

Hodges rightly describes this as an "ill-considered but influential snap-judgment," noting, however, that "this story has seldom been overlooked in even the shortest sketches of Congreve's life."[19] Despite overwhelming contemporary evidence, Voltaire made Congreve the textbook example of authorial vanity. Goldsmith retells the story, seconding Voltaire's sentiments, in his *Memoirs of M. de Voltaire.* Even the otherwise generous and sympathetic Shiels adds his condemnation of this "most absurd piece of vanity." It is hardly surprising then that Johnson would not be inclined to take Congreve's side here. In *The Rambler* 25 he had used Congreve's attitude toward authorship as an example of the "absurdity of pride," and he later cites the Rev. Mr. Temple's letter to Boswell, which accuses Gray of "that weakness which disgusted Voltaire so much in Mr. Congreve" (*Lives*, III, 430). This episode of "despicable foppery" (*Lives*, II, 226) is, of course, given prominent play in *The Life of Congreve.*[20]

Finally, there is the confusion surrounding Congreve's will, which was not cleared up until Hodges's 1941 biography. Hodges explains that Congreve carefully constructed his will to leave the bulk of his estate (about £10,000) to his daughter Mary, Lady Godolphin, the product of his long-term affair with the second duchess of Marlborough.[21] Congreve's eighteenth-century biographers, whatever they may have suspected about Congreve's relationship with the duchess, were unaware that Lady Mary was Congreve's child. Consequently, they found his choice of heirs questionable.

Shiels raises this issue after noting that Congreve was a "particular favourite of the ladies." He alludes specifically to the duchess and Anne Bracegirdle, adding that "some think, he had made a better figure in his Last Will, had he remembered his friendship he professed for Mrs. Bracegirdle, whose admirable performance added spirit to his dramatic pieces; but he forgot her, and gratified his vanity by chusing to make a rich duchess his sole legatee, and executrix."[22] Shiels does not quite have his facts right (few did), although Curll had taken the trouble to print Congreve's will. Mrs. Bracegirdle was left £200 and Francis Godolphin (the duchess's husband) was made executor. Yet even though Shiels, too, pursues the vanity theme, he is mild mannered and restrained compared to his former employer. Johnson mentions Congreve's will at the end of the biographical section of his *Life* in the context of the well-known monument to Congreve erected by Henrietta, "to whom, for reasons either not known or not mentioned, he bequeathed a legacy of about ten thousand pounds; the accumulation of attentive parsimony, which, though to her superfluous and useless, might have given great assistance to the ancient family from which he descended, at that time by the imprudence of his relation reduced to difficulties and distress" (*Lives*, II, 227). Again, it is worth noting that Congreve has been done an injustice: his family had recovered from its Commonwealth troubles by the time of the playwright's death.

Most recent commentators on the *Lives* agree with J. P. Hardy that in constructing his biographies, "Johnson sought to give prominence to such details as would clearly highlight the individual character."[23] To put it another way, Johnson formulates his view of the individual character and selects details to illustrate and support that view. His concern is with morality, not history, for, as he himself puts it, "there is more thought in the moralist than in the historian."[24] What results is Johnson, not Otway or Congreve, and, as Rader points out, this means judgment, not facts.

And since, in these cases, his judgment is untempered by what Robert Folkenflik calls (in a phrase from Johnson himself) "a Degree of Compassion" or what Lipking calls "the leap of sympathy which Johnson thought the basis of all good biography,"[25] the result is far short of Johnson at his best. Neither playwright is presented as sufficiently profane to outdo the "giddy libertine" or "drunken ravisher," but both are reduced to two-dimensional case studies in small-time immorality. Readers of the biographical sections of these *Lives* can hardly expect Johnson to be kinder to the plays of Otway and Congreve, the products of their "cool deliberation."

In his introductory study of Johnson, Donald Greene holds as fundamental the principle that for Johnson "literary criticism is in the end (like political criticism) a branch of general human morality." He amplifies parenthetically: "It may be pointed out that most other important critics, from Aristotle to Eliot and Leavis, would not disagree: the greatest critics have also been great moralists."[26] Yet while Eliot and Leavis themselves recognize Johnson as one of the greatest advocates of morality in literature, they do not agree about the way morality functions as a norm in Johnson's literary criticism.

According to Leavis, "For Johnson a thing is stated, or it isn't there." Johnson the critic "cannot appreciate the ways in which not only Shakespeare's drama but all works of art *act* their moral judgments." Though Leavis sees Johnson as the victim of the critical limitations of his age, his view of Johnson's use of morality in criticism is nevertheless severe:

Admirably preoccupied as he is with technical examinations and judgments of sensibility, he can't, when asked what this something more is, rise above—or go deeper than—an answer in terms of "please." Plea-

[232]

sure added to instruction: that, though his perception transcends it, is the analysis to which the critical idiom he inevitably uses is tied. When he has occasion to insist on the serious function of poetry, the vocabulary of "instruction" is his inevitable resort.[27]

Eliot sees Johnson's view of the relationship between pleasure and instruction as more complex and consequently more useful. He observes that in matters of practical criticism, Johnson "is never given to overrating a poem on the sole ground of its teaching a pure morality." Morality alone is not enough; pleasure, too, is necessary. And in formulating the relationship between the two Johnson is able to employ his perception of literary form to transcend the limitations of critical idiom. Pleasure and instruction are not "separable" elements in a poem; rather, both are "organically essential to it. We do not have *two* experiences, one of pleasure and one edification: it is one experience which we analyze into constituents."[28]

W. R. Keast presents still another version of Johnson on the relationship between pleasure and instruction. He agrees that for Johnson "literature is an activity or process directed to the pleasure and instruction of the common reader." But "works succeed or fail—are excellent or poor—to the extent that they satisfy the general conditions of pleasure, namely truth and novelty. . . . All the steps in the process are relative to the last—the satisfaction of the general conditions of pleasure."[29]

All three agree that for Johnson literature must please and instruct. But Leavis's Johnson subordinates the pleasure to the instruction while Keast's reverses the order of priority and Eliot's synthesizes the two into an inseparable, organic unit. An examination of Johnson's views of the plays of Otway and Congreve through comparison with his sources and contemporaries provides an unusually good forum for reconsidering the complex relationship between pleasure and instruction in his criticism while, at the same time, examining his moral position on Restoration drama.

Eighteenth-century criticism of Otway begins with Dryden, who was the first to identify Otway's special ability "to express the passions which are sealed in the heart by outward signs," a gift "not to be obtained by pains or study, if we are not born to it."[30] In fact, "Dryden touched every aspect of Otway's work that later critics were to elaborate—his following of Nature, his moving the passions, his faulty motivation and inelegant expression. . . . In penetrating and comprehensive appreciation of Otway's work later criticism never went beyond Dryden."[31]

But it was Addison, not Dryden, who was the direct source of these notions for most eighteenth-century readers and locus classicus for critics from Shiels and Goldsmith to Dick Minim, who provides an accurate summary of Addison: "In Otway he found uncommon powers of moving the passions, but was disgusted by his general negligence, and blamed him for making a conspirator his hero; and never concluded his disquisition, without remarking how happily the sound of the clock is made to alarm the audience."[32] And Dick Minim was not the only critic to formulate his opinions of Otway from Addison alone.

While Addison has indeed added little of substance to Dryden's view of Otway, he altered the critical idiom by seeing Otway through the new moral perspective of the post-Collier critics.[33] Later critics were not inclined to question Addison's moral qualms about Otway; in fact, Addison's doubts seem quite modest when compared, say, to those of the author of the "Remarks of the Tragedy of the Orphan" (claimed by Bertram Davis to be Sir John Hawkins)[34] which appeared in the 1748 *Gentleman's Magazine*. After an initial plot summary, Hawkins opens a full, frontal attack:

> If we proceed to examine the above *Fable*, it will be very difficult to find any *moral precept* that it tends to recommend or illustrate; tho' the Poet seems to have been aware, that somewhat of this kind was necessary, and accordingly has, in the close of the 5th Act, in the person of *Chamont*, made a reflexion, which seems to be at once very immoral, and no necessary consequence of his Fable. I say immoral, because it charges Providence as being the author of a series of misfortunes, which are altogether owing to the vicious and impudent conduct of the persons concerned.

In other words, Otway's lack of morality necessarily results in diminished artistry, a point Hawkins develops:

> It will be needless to say what must have been the consequence, had Otway's abilities been equal to his work; since, in that case, its effect on our minds must in many respects have been the reverse of what it now is; this at least must be allowed, that we should have neither been shocked with *impiety*, nor disgusted with *obscenity*, and that room would have been given for the exercise of a degree of compassion for the distress of the suffering characters, far greater than it is now possible to feel on their account.[35]

Hawkins's remarks were sufficiently effective to compel acknowledgment from Shiels, a great admirer and defender of Otway: "The tragedy of the Orphan is not without great blemishes, which the writer of a criticism on it, published in the Gentleman's Magazine, has very judiciously and candidly shewn."[36] But Shiels counters by reminding his readers of the dissolution of the times and Otway's ability to move the passions, thereby maintaining that Otway still deserves our attention. Shiels's tolerance, however, did not carry the day. Francis Gentleman, for one, pursues Hawkins's "Remarks" on *The Orphan* in *The Dramatic*

Censor. Gentleman, a true Collierite, undertakes a scene-by-scene analysis of the play in order to point out its immoral passages. He concludes that it should be permanently banished from the stage.[37] Nor will Gentleman allow Otway the excuse of contemporaneity. The man is condemned for embracing the immorality of his times, and his plays are damned as products of those times.

It is in this context of praise for Otway's adherence to nature and skillful manipulation of the passions qualified by a growing distrust of his morality that Johnson presents his assessment of the plays. He begins with *The Orphan*:

> This is one of the few plays that keep possession of the stage, and has pleased for almost a century through all the vicissitudes of dramatick fashion. Of this play nothing new can easily be said. It is a domestick tragedy drawn from middle life. Its whole power is upon the affections, for it is not written with much comprehension of thought or elegance of expression. But if the heart is interested, many other beauties may be wanting, yet not missed.
>
> (*Lives*, I, 245)

If R. K. Kaul is correct in considering this passage "one of the few exceptions to Johnson's general condemnation of Restoration and eighteenth-century tragedy,"[38] his statement nonetheless stands in need of qualification. For in doing no more than echoing Dick Minim, Johnson is surely damning with faint praise. A play without "much comprehension of thought or elegance of expression" is not likely to have been one of Johnson's favorites. But because the heart *was* interested, whatever its faults, *The Orphan* had passed the test of time. And this, for Johnson, is sufficient reason to warrant his critical attention.

Nor, however, does Johnson ignore the moral issues raised by Otway's plays, particularly *Venice Preserved*,

> his last and greatest dramatick work . . . which still continues to be one of the favourites of the publick, notwithstanding the want of morality in the original design, and the despicable scenes of vile comedy with which he has diversified his tragick action. . . . The striking passages are in every mouth; and the publick seems to judge rightly of the faults and excellencies of this play, that it is the work of a man not attentive to decency nor zealous for virtue; but of one who conceived forcibly and drew originally by consulting nature in his own breast.
>
> (*Lives*, I, 245–46)

Johnson here refuses to adopt any of the extreme positions of his contemporaries. He does not try either to apologize for Otway's moral shortcomings or, like Shiels, to excuse them. At the same time, he sees no need to protect the public from them by banishing them from the stage. (He is not, however, unhappy to note that Garrick's 1749 revival of Otway's *Friendship in Fashion* was "hissed off the stage for immorality and obscenity" [*Lives*, I, 243]. Otway's comedies had not retained their original popularity.) Finally, and characteristically, Johnson refuses to draw a direct connection between the man and his works.

Perhaps Johnson's most familiar statement of moral censure will help provide a context for understanding the significance of his position on Otway:

> His first defect is that to which may be imputed most of the evil in books or in men. He sacrifices virtue to convenience, and is so much more careful to please than to instruct that he seems to write without any moral purpose. . . . This fault the barbarity of his age cannot extenuate; for it is always a writer's duty to make the world better, and justice is a virtue independent of time or place.[39]

Johnson's critique of Shakespeare's morality seems strikingly similar to his critique of Otway's. Both are poets of nature who are expert at moving the passions; both neglect moral content and precept; and neither can be excused by the age in which he lived. But while Shakespeare because of his excellence in other areas can ultimately transcend his limitations, Otway cannot. Furthermore, while Shakespeare's sins are sins of omission, Otway's are of commission.

Yet Johnson's refusal to distinguish Otway from Shakespeare on moral grounds again puts him at odds with many of his contemporaries. Hawkins, for example, excludes Otway from the canon of great poets, since the truly great are "not content with barely holding up the *mirror to Nature* . . . but that they have constantly endeavoured to inculcate some *prudential maxim*, or *moral precept*." And while such a hard-line moralistic condemnation clearly follows from his discussion of *The Orphan*, Hawkins's example of moral rectitude is somewhat surprising: "In this particular, our admirable *Shakespear* seems to stand without an equal; in him we find the most instructive lessons."[40]

Both Hawkins and Johnson evaluate other writers by comparing them to Shakespeare. But while Hawkins, the more restrictive moralist, is content with an orthodoxy based on Shakespeare's perfection, Johnson is able to find fault with his model poet. On moral grounds and with great facility, Hawkins dismisses Otway, for most eighteenth-century critics Shakespeare's nearest rival at tragedy;[41] Johnson is content with a balanced, milder censure. That Johnson had no special admiration for Otway is clear. Boswell records (from Langton) that when asked his opinion of Dodsley's *Cleone*, Johnson replied, "Sir, if Otway had written this play, no other of his pieces would have been remembered." The startled Boswell adds "it must be remembered that Johnson always appeared not to be sufficiently sensible of the merit of Otway."[42] But Johnson, unlike Hawkins or Gentleman, and contrary to his own practice in the biographical section of the *Life of Otway*, does not rest his case on his own moral judgment. Judge he does, and in so doing he provides sufficient evidence to explain both Otway's moral *and* artistic failures. But since Otway has pleased many and pleased long, Johnson must at the same time explain the cause of that pleasure in order to fulfill his obligations as literary critic. And to do so openly qualifies his moral stance.

An examination of Johnson's criticism of Congreve's plays reveals a similar method and practice. Critical discussions of Congreve, like those of Otway, were predetermined somewhat through a general guilt-by-association verdict that was applied to any playwright of the late seventeenth century—especially any comic playwright. Consideration of the relationship of Restoration comedy to its time generally focused on three questions. Are these plays just representations of reality circa 1660–1700 (few seemed to consider Lamb's position at this time)? If so, should such reality be represented on the stage? Is such truth-to-nature sufficient reason to excuse the guilty author? What was in fact at stake in this debate was the very nature of comedy. The well-known exchange between Steele and Dennis on *The Man of Mode* presents the two basic positions. Briefly, for Dennis, comedy should mirror the age in order to correct it; for Steele, it must provide a model for the age while refusing to call attention to certain weaknesses, especially in its heroes and heroines.[43]

Even on the purely aesthetic issues raised by Dennis and Steele, Johnson could not take sides. As Stuart Tave points out, the author of *The Rambler*, who cried out with Steele against the dangers of raillery, wrote Juvenalian satire and remained throughout his life "a vigorous upholder of the natural dignity of wit."[44] But to believe in the natural dignity of wit is not necessarily to find all kinds of wit acceptable. Steele himself defended Congreve's wit in *The Tatler*, no. 193, but Pope's challenge—"Tell me if Congreve's Fools are Fools indeed"— made commonplace the notion that Congreve was witty to excess, a sentiment echoed by critics such as Gentleman, Goldsmith, Murphy, Shenstone, and, of course, Dick Minim. With time, Steele's demand for good nature rather than wit in comedy was so successfully met that Steele himself was accused, with the main body of Restoration dramatists, of excessive wit.

Johnson refuses to dismiss Congreve's comedy simply because it is a comedy of wit. Instead, he seeks to define the special quality of that wit: "his personages are a kind of intellectual gladiators; every sentence is to ward or strike; the contest of smartness is never intermitted; his wit is a meteor playing to and fro with alternate coruscations." James Gray finds a similarity between this passage and the criticism of the metaphysical poets in the *Life of Cowley* and concludes that Johnson rejects Congreve's wit on the same grounds. His argument is bolstered by Johnson's verdict on the language of *The Old Batchelour*, in which he sees "one constant reciprocation of conceits, or clash of wit, in which nothing flows necessarily from the occasion, or is dictated by nature"[45] (*Lives*, II, 228, 216).

Congreve indeed shares with the metaphysicals a lack of passion coupled with overabundant intellect and "very little of nature, and not much of life." But Johnson recognizes a significant difference between them. He criticizes the metaphysicals—but not Congreve—for harsh diction, pedantry, and "the most heterogeneous ideas . . . yoked by violence together." And in spite of their subtlety, the literary experience they produce raises, at best, occasional admiration—not pleasure. Moreover, when Johnson describes the dialogue of *The Old Batchelour* as "one constant reciprocation of conceits, or clash of wit, in which nothing flows necessarily from occasion, or is dictated by nature," he is not pointing to metaphysical wit but rather to a discrepancy between character and dialogue. The wit may be "quick and sparkling" (in fact, it is "so exhuberant that it 'o'er-informs its tenement'"), but it is too often put in the mouths of derivative, and even inappropriate characters. Johnson indeed has reservations about Congreve's wit, but they are not the same as his reservations about metaphysical wit, or satiric or Juvenalian wit.

Continuing his attempt to capture the essential in Congreve's wit, Johnson says of his comedies that they have "in some degree, the operation of tragedies: they surprise rather than divert and raise admiration oftener than merriment" (*Lives*, II, 228), a description which would perhaps seem more appropriately applied to *The Conscious Lovers*. Gray sees in this that Johnson is troubled by Congreve's confusion of genre. But in *The Rambler* 125 Johnson points out that "comedy has been particularly unpropitious to definers," since "the means by which the comic writers attain their end" are not "limited by nature." For support, he cites Horace's famous dictum (which also serves as Congreve's epigraph for *The Double-Dealer*) that "comedy sometimes raises her voice." And, when he encounters such a mixture in *1 Henry IV*, he remarks that "there is in these lines a very natural mixture of the serious and the ludicrous produced by the view of Percy and Falstaff."[46] Mixture of genre would, again, not seem to be Johnson's real objection to Congreve's wit.

In fact, what Johnson seems to be referring to as Congreve's "peculiar idea of comic excellence" is the witty courtship game so often prominent in Restoration comedy, epitomized by the proviso scene of *The Way of the World*. It should therefore not be surprising to find that Johnson, so eminently a man of sense, should join in his century's rejection of the highly artificial and stylized form of comedy characterized by the wit-game. And while I would emphatically agree with John Harrington Smith's well-known view that the lovers playing the wit-game nevertheless "take love seriously" and that this game is a "psychological aid in facing the seriousness of marriage,"[47] I cannot deny that its very success leaves it vulnerable to the kinds of charges Johnson makes—"fictitious and artificial" with "little humour, imagery or passion." No critic who subscribes to "the doctrine of literal probability" according to which "reality is a test of art" can fully admire Restoration comedy, and Johnson used "experienced reality"—his own experienced reality—as "an objective test of art."[48]

Johnson's answers to the central eighteenth-century critical problems about Restoration comedy, then, are, first, that it is not a just representation of human nature (and hence its relationship to its own time becomes irrelevant as a critical issue) and, second, it must nevertheless stand trial for gross moral turpitude. For Johnson, unlike Lamb, artificiality does not preclude immorality.

But in spite of his reservations, Johnson proclaims that "Congreve has merit of the highest kind: he is an original writer, who borrowed neither the models of his plot nor the manner of his dialogue" (*Lives*, II, 228). He thus joins the long line of critics dating back to Dryden who paid tribute to Congreve's artistic excellence. All of his plays met with great approval from critics of stature (if not always from audiences); the comedies were so highly admired that almost every eighteenth-century critic (Johnson is a singular exception here) felt it necessary to repeat Dennis's remark that when Congreve, "the living Ornament of the Comick Scene, . . . quitted the Stage, . . . Comedy left it with him."[49] Unlike his personal reputation, Congreve's critical reputation remained secure.

Instead, critical controversy about Congreve focused on moral issues, particularly whether or not his artistic virtues were sufficient to counterbalance his want of morality. The support of such critics as Addison and Steele made it an interesting debate. Addison develops a distinction "between being Merry and being Lewd" which allows Congreve, with his "Wit, Humour and good Sense," to comply "with the corrupt Taste of the most Vicious Part of [his] Audience" without damning himself morally. Similar plays attempted by "persons of a low Genius," however, result in what Addison calls "degenerate Compositions." Thus, Congreve's artistic virtues are able to overcome his moral lapses."[50] But critics of other persuasion "mentioned Addison's praise . . . as proof that even the best minds could be blinded to the immoral qualities of Congreve's plays,"[51] and consequently redoubled their efforts against them. William Popple, for example, a great sharer of Steele's reforming instincts, could not help applying Steele's principles to the plays of the latter's friend Congreve; *The Double-Dealer*, for example, though it "abounds in wit . . . beauty . . . [and] pro-priety," is intolerable "critically and morally."[52] Popple would banish such plays from the stage. So, "with reluctance," would Francis Gentle-man[53] and, with no reluctance whatsoever, Edmund Burke.[54]

Johnson, with his strong feelings about the moral responsibility of the writer, has sympathy with their view: "the general tenour and ten-dency of [Congreve's] plays must always be condemned. It is acknowl-edged with universal conviction that the perusal of his works will make no man better; and that their ultimate effect is to represent pleasure in alliance with vice, and to relax those obligations by which life ought to be regulated" (*Lives*, II, 222). But unlike Popple, Gentle-man, or Burke, Johnson can also sympathize with an author for cater-ing to the demands of his audience ("The drama's laws the drama's patrons give,/ For we that live to please, must please to live"). Con-greve, like Dryden, is an author of obvious merit who has passed the test of time; thus, he warrants a similar attempt from Johnson to re-solve the conflicts between good literature and good morality. Con-greve's case resembles the more familiar one of *The Beggar's Opera*, about which Johnson maintained, "I myself am of opinion, that more influence has been ascribed to 'The Beggar's Opera,' than it in reality ever had; for I do not believe that any man was ever made a rogue by being present at its representation. At the same time I do not deny that it may have some influence, by making the character of a rogue familiar, and in some degree pleasing."[55]

When dealing with significant literary works, works of the best au-thors which have pleased many and pleased long, Johnson makes careful judgments both artistic and moral. He has serious moral reser-vations about the works of both Otway and Congreve. And neither the tragedy of the "natural" Otway nor the comedy of the "artificial" Con-greve appeals to his sensibility. But in neither case is he content with his own judgment. In literary criticism, unlike biography, Johnson feels the need to contend with another authority, the judgment of the public. Thus, his practice is at odds with the principle expressed in my opening passage from *Rambler* 77. And fortunately so, for had he fol-lowed that principle his criticism would probably have earned the fate of Hawkins's, Popple's and Gentleman's. His refusal—or inability—to do so is characteristic of why Johnson is the great critic of the eigh-teenth century.

The dialectic between pleasure and instruction which so dominates critical discussion of Johnson is itself inherent in his criticism. Eliot's synthesis of them may well take place in Johnson's best of possible liter-ary works. But in the world of literature Johnson experienced, that synthesis is at best incomplete. The works of Otway and Congreve provide some pleasure and some instruction, and each constituent part is given careful consideration. But the languages and methods for dealing with each remain separate; no synthesis is to be found. Johnson's readers are left to add up the sum of the parts and draw their own conclusions. And without a synthetic judgment, the works of Otway and Congreve escape the final censure the men receive.

N O T E S

1. *Works*, IV, 43–44.

2. *Lives*, I, 398.

3. Lawrence Lipking, *The Ordering of the Arts in Eighteenth-Century England* (Princeton: Princeton Univ. Press, 1970), p. 445.

4. Ralph Rader, "Literary Form in Factual Narrative: The Example of Boswell's Johnson," in *Essays in Eighteenth-Century Biography*, ed. Philip B. Daghlian (Bloomington: Indiana Univ. Press, 1968), p. 13.

5. Among the sources available to him were Wood's *Athenae Oxoniensis*, Langbaine's *An Account of the English Dramatic Poets*, the preface to the 1712 edition of Otway's *Works* (called "Some Account of the Life and Writings of Mr. Thomas Otway"), Jacob's *Poetical Register*, the *Biographia Britannica*, a 1745 *Gentleman's Magazine* article and Theophilus Cibber's *Lives of the Poets*. Pat Rogers has discussed the general problem of source attribution in the *Lives* in "Johnson's *Lives of the Poets* and the Biographic Dictionaries," *Review of English Studies*, 31 (1980), 148–71. My account of the specific sources for *Otway* and *Congreve* differs from his, but since his preliminary study provides only brief attributions with minimal explanation, detailed response is impossible.

6. Theophilus Cibber, *The Lives of the Poets of Great Britain and Ireland* (London: R. Griffiths, 1753), II, 325.

7. "This kind of inability he shared with Shakespeare and Jonson, as he shared likewise some of their excellencies. It seems reasonable to expect that a great dramatick poet should without difficulty become a great actor; that he who can feel could express; that he who can excite passion should exhibit with great readiness its external modes: but since experience has fully proved that of those powers, whatever be their affinity, one may be possessed in a great degree by him who has very little of the other, it must be allowed that they depend upon different faculties or on different use of the same faculty; that the actor must have a pliancy of mien, a flexibility of countenance, and a variety of tones, which the poet may be easily supposed to want; or that the attention of the poet and the player have been differently employed—the one has been considering thought, and the other action; one has watched the heart, and the other contemplated the face" (*Lives*, I, 242).

8. Cibber, *Lives of the Poets*, II, 325–26.

9. *The Works of Mr. Thomas Otway* (London: J. Tonson, 1712), p. [6].

10. Cibber, *Lives of the Poets*, II, 334.

11. For a discussion of the relationship between Johnson and Shiels see William R. Keast, "Johnson and 'Cibber's' *Lives of the Poets*, 1753," in *Restoration and Eighteenth-Century Literature: Essays in Honor of Alan Dugald McKillop*, ed. Carroll Camden (Chicago: Univ. of Chicago Press, 1963), pp. 89–101. Keast notes that Johnson used Shiels as a source for a number of the *Lives*, though he does not mention the *Life of Otway*. He also notes that Shiels had drawn on Johnson for his own work. The implications of his suggestion that Johnson may "have been simply repossessing what he had given Shiels . . . a quarter of a century before" (p. 101), while fascinating, are beyond the scope of this essay.

12. Cibber, *Lives of the Poets*, II, 332.

13. *Life of Savage*, ed. Clarence Tracy (Oxford: Clarendon Press, 1971), p. 137.

14. Paul Alkon, *Samuel Johnson and Moral Discipline* (Evanston, Ill.: Northwestern Univ. Press, 1967), p. 112.

15. John C. Hodges, *William Congreve the Man* (New York: MLA, 1941), p. xv.

16. David Erskine Baker, *Biographia Dramatica* (London: Rivingtons, 1782), p. 96.

17. *Memoirs of the Life, Writings, and Amours of William Congreve Esq.* (London: E. Curll, 1730), p. 11. Pat Rogers argues convincingly (but, necessarily, inconclusively) that Wilson was Giles Jacob. See "Congreve's First Biographer," *Modern Language Quarterly*, 31 (1970), 330–44.

18. Voltaire, "Philosophical Letters," in *Candide and Other Writings*, ed. Haskell M. Block (New York: Modern Library, 1956), p. 352.

19. Hodges, *William Congreve*, p. xv.

20. An unusual, midcentury passage, in a note in the *Biographia Britannica*, provides an interesting counterpoint to Johnson: "It is somewhat strange to hear an author accused of vanity, for under-valuing his own works. We often meet with censures even upon great men, for talking continually of themselves and their writings; but it is a very singular censure that is passed upon Mr Congreve, that he was troubled with an unseasonable vanity, which hindered him from talking of them at all. The truth of the matter seems to have been, that instead of feeling an unseasonable vanity, he had out lived the season of vanity, if ever he had any, and having no longer any thing of the pride of an author about him, it is not at all wonderful that his conversation was not relished by Mr Voltaire, whose merit, as an author, is superior to every thing—but the sense he has of that merit" ([London: Innys, 1750], III, 1448). But Johnson, if he had noticed this passage, declines to comment on it. And, in spite of its effectiveness as a counter, Johnson carried the day. Congreve and vanity became inseparable. Robert Folkenflik (*Samuel Johnson, Biographer* [Ithaca, N.Y.: Cornell Univ. Press, 1978], p. 116) supports as conclusive Bergen Evans's claim (Diss., Harvard Univ., 1932) that the *Biographia Britannica* was Johnson's principal secondary source for the *Lives*.

21. Hodges, *William Congreve*, pp. 117–23.

22. Cibber, *Lives of the Poets*, IV, 93.

23. J. P. Hardy, *Samuel Johnson: A Critical Study* (London: Routledge & Kegan Paul, 1979), p. 183.

24. *Life*, II, 195.

25. Folkenflik, *Samuel Johnson*, p. 212; Lipking, *Ordering of the Arts*, p. 427.

26. Donald J. Greene, *Samuel Johnson* (New York: Twayne Publishers, 1970), p. 196.

27. F. R. Leavis, "Johnson as Critic," in *Samuel Johnson: A Collection of Critical Essays*, ed. Donald J. Greene (Englewood Cliffs, N.J.: Prentice-Hall, 1965), pp. 81–85.

28. T. S. Eliot, "Johnson as Critic and Poet," in *On Poetry and Poets* (London: Faber and Faber, 1957), pp. 182–83.

29. W. R. Keast, "The Theoretical Foundations of Johnson's Criticism," in *Critics and Criticism: Ancient and Modern*, ed. R. S. Crane (Chicago: Univ. of Chicago Press, 1952), p. 399.

30. *Of Dramatic Poesy and Other Critical Essays*, ed. George Watson, 2 vols. (London: Dent, 1962), II, 201.

31. Aline Mackenzie Taylor, *Next to Shakespeare: Otway's Venice Preserved and The Orphan and Their History on the London Stage* (Durham, N.C.: Duke Univ. Press, 1950), p. 249.

32. *Works*, II, 187. The relevant passages, from *The Spectator*, nos. 39 and 44 respectively, read as follows: "*Otway* has followed Nature in the Language of his Tragedy, and therefore shines in the Passionate Parts, more than any of our *English* Poets. As there is something Familiar and Domestick in the Fable of his Tragedy, more than in those of any other Poet, he has little Pomp, but great Force in his Expressions. For which Reason, tho' he has admirably succeeded in the tender and melting Part of his Tragedies, he

sometimes falls into too great a Familiarity of Phrase in those Parts, which, by Aristotle's Rule, ought to have been raised and supported by the Dignity of Expression.

It has been observed by others, that this Poet has founded his Tragedy of *Venice Preserved* on so wrong a Plot, that the greatest Characters in it are those of Rebels and Traitors. Had the Hero of his Play discovered the same good Qualities in the Defence of his Country, that he showed for its Ruin and Subversion, the Audience could not enough pity and admire him: But as he is now represented we can only say of him, what the *Roman* Historian says of *Catiline*, that his Fall would have been Glorious (*si pro Patriâ sic concidisset*) had he so fallen in the Service of his Country" and "the sounding of the Clock in Venice preserv'd, makes the Hearts of the whole Audience quake; and conveys a stronger Terrour to the Mind, than it is possible for Words to" (Ed. Donald F. Bond, 5 vols. [Oxford: Clarendon Press, 1965], I, 167–68, 186).

33. Dennis, who was able to resist the creeping Collierism of the early eighteenth century, was perhaps the last critic of importance to remain untroubled by moral issues in Otway's plays. For example, in the context of the *Cato* controversy, he was able to maintain of *The Orphan* that "the Moral, tho' not express'd at the End of the Play, yet most intelligibly implied, is a wholesome, but terrible Instruction to an Audience to beware of clandestine Marriages" (*The Critical Works of John Dennis*, ed. Edward Niles Hooker, 2 vols. [Baltimore: Johns Hopkins Univ. Press, 1939–43], II, 67).

34. Sir John Hawkins, *The Life of Samuel Johnson, LL.D.*, ed. and abr. Bertram Davis (New York: Macmillan, 1961), p. ix.

35. *Gentleman's Magazine*, 18 (1748), 503, 553.

36. Cibber, *Lives of the Poets*, II, 328–29.

37. Francis Gentleman, *The Dramatic Censor* (London: J. Bell, 1770), II, 40–60.

38. "Dr. Johnson on the Emotional Effect of Tragedy," in *Cairo Studies in English*, ed. Magdi Wahba (Cairo: Privately printed, 1966), p. 211.

39. *Works*, VII, 71.

40. *Gentleman's Magazine*, 18 (1748), 503.

41. While Charles Gildon is probably unique among eighteenth-century critics in preferring Otway to Shakespeare, serious comparisons between the two are commonplace. Pope, Gay, and Rowe are just a few of the reputable critics hard put to find a tragedian more deserving of at least second place in English tragedy. Dennis, in turn, presents the following balanced comparison, "*Shakespear* had a very good Genius for Tragedy, and a very good Talent for Comedy. And since him *Otway* had likewise a Talent for both" (Dennis, I, 403). Voltaire finds both Shakespeare and Otway guilty of the same violations of taste and decorum; the only difference is that Otway's "foolishness is modern, while Shakespeare's is ancient" (Voltaire, *Candide and Other Writings*, pp. 341–47). Otway's plays are merely a manifestation of the basic corruption of the English stage which resulted from Shakespeare's dominance. Goldsmith considered Otway "next to Shakespeare, the greatest genius England ever produced in tragedy" (*Collected Works*, ed. Arthur Friedman, 5 vols. [Oxford: Clarendon Press, 1966], I, 500). And even Hawkins acknowledges—as the provocation for his essay—that "of the dramatic poets this nation has produced, next to *Shakespear*, scarce any has been so much applauded as Otway" (*Gentleman's Magazine* 18 [1748], 502).

42. *Life*, IV, 20–21.

43. *The Spectator*, I, 278–80; Dennis, *Critical Works*, II, 241–50.

44. Stuart Tave, *The Amiable Humorist: A Study in the Comic Theory and Criticism of the Eighteenth and Early Nineteenth Centuries* (Chicago: Univ. of Chicago Press, 1960), pp. 23, 66.

45. "Dr. Johnson and the 'Intellectual Gladiators,'" *Dalhousie Review*, 40 (1960), 350–59.

46. *Works*, IV, 300–302; VII, 489.

47. *The Gay Couple in Restoration Comedy* (Cambridge, Mass.: Harvard Univ. Press, 1948), p. 76.

48. Jean H. Hagstrum, *Samuel Johnson's Literary Criticism* (Minneapolis: Univ. of Minnesota Press, 1952), pp. 7, 60. An attempt to cast Johnson and the widow Porter as Mirabell and Millamant should make this clear.

49. Dennis, *Critical Works*, II, 121–22.

50. *The Spectator*, IV, 66.

51. Emmett L. Avery, *Congreve's Plays on the Eighteenth-Century Stage* (New York: MLA, 1951), p. 4.

52. *The Prompter: A Theatrical Paper (1734–1736)*, ed. William W. Appleton and Kalman A. Burnim (New York: Blom, 1966), pp. 121–22.

53. "No man who ever wrote for the stage has shewn more capital, more correct, or more pleasing delineations of life; his characters are beautifully contrasted, his language pointed, his wit brilliant, his plots amazingly regular and pleasingly intricate, his scenes variegated, and his disposition of the whole masterly; two faults, one of a very heavy nature, countervail his extensive merit, his flashes of wit are too frequent, often too much for the person who utters them, his dialogue rather profuse, and a most abominable vein of licentiousness runs through the whole; virtue reluctantly peeps in while vice with brazen front bolts forward unblushing, unrestrained: Had this author written under the commendable restrictions of this age, his luxuriousness would have been brought within better bounds. His pieces must give pleasure either in action or perusal but are like the sweet scented rose, with prickles beneath, which while it gratifies one sense wounds another; it is with reluctance we pronounce the sentence of moral justice which condemns his four comedies to oblivion, as pernicious" (*The Dramatic Censor*, II, 467–68).

54. "But he who seems to have shared the Gifts of Nature as largely as he abused them, was the celebrated Mr *Congreve*, who, to the charms of a lively Wit, solid Judgment and rich Invention, has added such Obscenity, as none can, without the greatest Danger to Virtue, listen to; the very texture and ground work of some of his Plays is Lewdness, which poisons the surer, as it is set off with the Advantage of Wit. I know 'tis said in his Excuse, that he drew his Pictures after the times; but whoever examines his Plays will find, that he not only copies the ill Morals of the Age, but approved them." This passage, from *The Reformer*, no. 2, urges Garrick to earn the title of a genuine "Stage Reformer" by replacing the turn of the century comedies still "in vogue" with "good and moral Plays." (*The Early Life, Correspondence, and Writings of the Rt. Hon. Edmund Burke, LL.D.*, ed. Arthur P. I. Samuels [Cambridge: Cambridge Univ. Press, 1923], pp. 300–301.)

55. *Life*, II, 367. Nor is Johnson's view here uncontested; fifty years of debate did not remove *The Beggar's Opera* from the realm of controversy any more than it did Restoration comedy. Thus, Hill points out that when "on Sept. 15, 1773, on which day at the Old Bailey fifteen prisoners were sentenced to death, forty to whipping, 'Sir John Fielding informed the Bench of Justices that he had last year written to Mr. Garrick concerning the impropriety of performing *The Beggar's Opera*, which never was represented without creating an additional number of real thieves.' *Annual Register*, 1773, i.132." Sir John Hawkins agrees fully with Fielding, adding that "'Rapine and violence have been gradually increasing ever since its first representation.' *Hist. of Music*, v. 317" (*Lives*, II, 279).

CONTRIBUTORS

John L. Abbott is Professor of English at the University of Connecticut.

Frank Brady, who died in September 1986, was Professor of English at the Graduate Center, City University of New York.

Martine Watson Brownley is Professor of English at Emory University.

Brian Corman is Associate Professor of English at Erindale College, University of Toronto.

Thomas M. Curley is Professor of English at Bridgewater State College, Massachusetts.

Bertram H. Davis is Professor Emeritus of English at Florida State University, Tallahassee.

Robert DeMaria, Jr. is Associate Professor of English at Vassar College.

William H. Epstein is Associate Professor of English at Purdue University.

Robert Folkenflik is Professor of English at the University of California, Irvine.

James Gray is Professor of English at Dalhousie University.

Isobel Grundy is Reader in English at Queen Mary College, University of London.

Paul J. Korshin is Professor of English at the University of Pennsylvania.

Elizabeth R. Lambert is Assistant Professor of English at Gettysburg College.

Peter Seary is Professor of English at the University of Toronto.

INDEX